the great medieval heretics

the great medieval heretics

Five Centuries of Religious Dissent

MICHAEL FRASSETTO

BlueBridge

Jacket design by Stefan Killen Design

Cover art top by The Bridgeman Art Library International: Ms 722/1196 fol.372r St. Dominic and the test by fire of the heretic books and the orthodox book, from Le Miroir Historial, by Vincent de Beauvais, French School (15th century), Musee Conde, Chantilly, France

Cover art bottom by The Bridgeman Art Library International: The Last Judgement (detail of the entrance of the damned into hell), by Rogier van der Weyden (1399–1464), Hotel Dieu, Beaune, France

Copyright © 2007, 2008 by Michael Frassetto
Published in Great Britain under the title
Heretic Lives by Profile Books Ltd.

LIBRARY OF CONGRESS CATALOGING-IN-PUBLICATION DATA
Frassetto, Michael.
The great medieval heretics : five centuries of religious dissent / Michael Frassetto.
p. cm.
Includes bibliographical references and index.
ISBN 978-1-933346-12-0
1. Heresies, Christian—History—Middle Ages, 600–1500. 2. Heretics, Christian—Biography. I. Title.
BT1319.F73 2007
273'.6—dc22   2008005496

First published in North America in 2008 by
BlueBridge
An imprint of
United Tribes Media Inc.
240 West 35th Street, Suite 500
New York, NY 10001

www.bluebridgebooks.com

Printed in the United States of America

10 9 8 7 6 5 4 3 2 1

CONTENTS

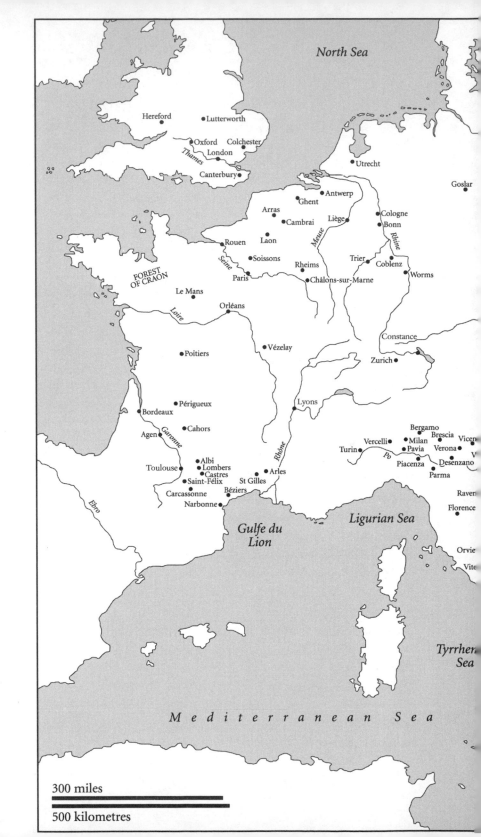

North Sea

Hereford • Lutterworth

Oxford • Colchester
London •
Canterbury •

Thames

Utrecht •

Goslar •

Antwerp •
Ghent •

Arras •
Cambrai •

Liège •

Cologne •
Bonn •

Rouen •
Laon •

Soissons •
Rheims •

Trier •

Coblenz •

Worms •

FOREST
OF CRAON

Seine

Paris •
Châlons-sur-Marne •

Meuse

Rhine

Le Mans •

Orléans •

Loire

Vézelay •

Constance

Poitiers •

Zurich •

Périgueux •
Bordeaux •

Cahors •

Lyons •

Agen •

Garonne

Bergamo •
Vercelli • Milan • Brescia • Vicen
Turin • Verona •
Pavia • Desenzano •
Piacenza •
Parma •

Albi •
Lombers •
Castres •
Saint-Félix •
Carcassonne •
Narbonne •

Toulouse •

St Gilles •
Béziers •

Arles •

Rhône

Po

V

Raven

Florence •

Ebro

Gulfe du
Lion

Ligurian Sea

Orvie •
Vite

Tyrrhen
Sea

M e d i t e r r a n e a n   S e a

300 miles

500 kilometres

Cities and Centres
🙠 *of Heresy in* 🙢
Medieval Europe

Baltic Sea

Vistula

Prague

BOHEMIA

MORAVIA

ec●

ube

Danube

●Nish

Adriatic Sea

Black
Sea

Philippopolis ●

Constantinople ●

Bari ●

Aegean
Sea

Ionian Sea

1. Northern French knights, with the support of the pope, force heretics from Carcassone, the great stronghold of Albigensian heretics during the Albigensian Crusade. The crusaders would not only weaken heresy in the south but would also damage southern French culture and help the kings of France extend their authority in the region. (HIP/Art Resource, NY.)

2. *One of the greatest of medieval popes, Innocent III was an aggressive opponent of the Cathars and all heretics. He launched the Albigensian Crusade against the Cathars of southern France and laid the foundation for the Inquisition. He also approved the order of St. Francis in order to bring one of the most powerful religious impulses under the control of the Church. (HIP/Art Resource, NY.)*

3. One of the great tools at the disposal of the Church for the suppression of heresy was the public display and execution of unrepentant heretics. This highly stylized image depicts St. Dominic, founder of the Dominican order, presiding over one such display. Heretics, including Pierre Autier, the last of the great Cathar leaders, would come to an unhappy end at a public execution, which, despite the presence of Dominic here, was carried out by the secular authority. (Scala/Art Resource, NY.)

4. Although not the all-powerful institution it is often said to be, the Inquisition was one of the most effective weapons the Church had in its war against heresy. The inquisitors, often members of the Dominican and Franciscan orders, were given the authority to root out heretics. One of the most successful of the inquisitors, Bernard Gui, left a valuable manual of the work of inquisitors and recorded the beliefs of many heretics, including Fra Dolcino. (Erich Lessing/Art Resource, NY.)

5. *Since the time of Constantine and the Council of Nicaea (325), ecumenical councils like this one held at Vienne (1311) were called to resolve the great issues facing the Church. Pope Clement V held this council to discuss a wide range of issues, including a new crusade, the dispute within the Franciscan order, and the fate of the Knights Templar. It was also at Vienne that the great mystic Marguerite Porete was condemned for heresy and then burned. (Scala/Art Resource, NY.)*

6. *The Oxford theologian John Wyclif, whose teachings inspired religious revolution in England and on the continent and prefigured the teachings of Martin Luther. (HIP/Art Resource, NY.)*

7. Despite assurances of safe conduct and other promises, Jan Hus was given little chance to defend his views at the Council of Constance and was burned for heresy. His charismatic leadership of the Bohemian Church attracted a great following, however, and his death at Constance inspired a revolt against church and state that led to recognition of a semi-independent church in Bohemia. (Snark/Art Resource, NY.)

HERIBERT'S WARNING

'*a* new heresy is born in this world and in our days.'
So declared the Monk Heribert at the turn of the first millennium. Addressing himself to 'all Christians in the Orient and in the Occident, North and South, who believe in Christ,' he warned that a new heresy was being spread throughout Périgord in France by 'men of iniquity' who claimed the authority of the Apostles.[1] Displaying a horror soon to be characteristic of the members of the established Church, the 'orthodox' throughout Europe, Heribert sought to secure their well-being from the, in his view, perilous doctrines advanced by these new preachers of iniquity.

The heretics Heribert had discovered were, as he saw them, pseudo-apostles bent on undermining the integrity of the faith and on converting people to their error. Though false apostles, they seemed to live chaste and pious lives, which was all the better for undermining the Church. Pretending to follow the apostolic life, they did not eat meat, did not drink wine except on the third day, and refused to accept money. They were often found in prayer, genuflecting a hundred times a day, and were active and successful missionaries and preachers. Heribert alleged that they had 'corrupted and brought to them numerous people, not only laypeople, who have given up their belongings, but also clerics, monks, and nuns.'[2] In their simple life of preaching and poverty, the heretics might seem to be following the core teachings of the Church, in a resumption of the apostolic life, but, he contended, the appearances were deceiving. The heretics might have adopted the apostolic life, but they followed it imperfectly because they had rejected the core teachings of the Church itself. They were 'perverse' and 'hidden and deceptive,' and entered churches only to corrupt others. They denied alms had any value and, rejecting all property, held all wealth in common. The heretics also rejected the mass, maintaining that the Eucharist was nothing more than a piece of blessed bread. They might attend mass, but only as a pretense and so that they might corrupt others and lead them to turn their backs on the altar. They took communion but threw the host behind the altar or placed it in the missal instead of eating it, like good Christians. They rejected the cross and accused those who honored it of being idol-worshipers, and they refused to pray like the 'orthodox' and proclaim: 'For yours is the Kingdom, and you rule all creatures for ever and ever, Amen.'[3]

Beyond their rejection of Catholic doctrine and adoption of unorthodox teachings, the heretics were able to 'perform many wondrous feats.'[4] Not only could they convert members of the laity and priests, monks, and nuns to their ways; once converted, the new heretics could not be turned back to the true faith. 'No one,' Heribert asserted, 'no matter how rustic, adheres to their sect who does not become, within eight days, wise in letters, writing and action, [so wise] that no one can overcome him in any way.'[5] Heribert then goes on to describe a spectacular miracle, which he claims to have witnessed himself. A group of heretics were bound in chains and placed in a wine barrel which was open at the bottom and shut at the top. The barrel was then turned over and guards were set over it. On the following morning, the heretics were gone, and, inside the barrel, a vase which had had but a little wine in it was found to be full.[6] The letter concludes with references to numerous other marvelous deeds and a final warning that the heretics were invading Périgeux and other areas.

Heribert does not identify the leader of the group of heretics in the region of Périgord. In this respect his account differs from the reports of many later writers on heresy, but it features numerous of the central themes in the development of heresy in the Middle Ages, as well as some of the challenges facing those who attempt today to find out about the lives of medieval heretics.

Some of the most serious challenges concern the documents themselves: Heribert's letter demonstrates, better than almost any other one from the Middle Ages, the difficulties of using these documents. On one level, like most of the available sources, the letter was clearly written by a good Catholic, a monk who clearly sought to warn his fellow Christians against 'heretics.' The letter was written by one of the victors in the great struggle between heresy and orthodoxy in the Middle Ages and bears the mark of the biases held by members of the established clergy. It was the clergy who possessed the truth; the doctrines and dogmas sanctioned by the Church were the only true teachings, and those perceived as offering something different, even if that was based on the Gospels, were deemed to be in error. Moreover, the heretics are not allowed to speak for themselves; their teachings, and the motivations they had for accepting and spreading those teachings, are based on the interpretations of Heribert; and these were in all likelihood based on a stock collection of beliefs drawn from St. Augustine of Hippo and other earlier writers, who had outlined what the heretics were supposed to believe. Although Heribert did not ask the leading questions that the inquisitors would raise in the thirteenth and fourteenth centuries, he was influenced in his account by literary traditions which described the beliefs of the heretics from the earlier history of the Church.

Ancient sources, especially those of Augustine, described a number of religious dissidents. Augustine spoke against the Manichaeans, condemning their dualism and rejection of the Hebrew Scriptures. He also denounced the Donatists, who believed that the validity of the sacraments depended on the priest's morality, and the Pelagians, who emphasized personal responsibility for obtaining salvation. Other early texts recorded the heresy of Priscillian, a Christian dualist who was executed in 385. Also of concern to ancient writers was Arianism, which maintained that the Son of God was created by the Father, and was not coequal with the Father. Denounced at the Council of Nicaea (325), Arianism was adopted, but later rejected, by many of the Germanic peoples who reigned after the fall of the Roman Empire.

Even though the sources themselves are often problematic, they can nevertheless offer important information about the emergence and nature of heresy, as does the letter of Heribert. The letter, known for some time from a twelfth-century copy but recently found in a manuscript of the eleventh century, provides evidence concerning the origins of medieval heresy. It has traditionally been taken to demonstrate the influence of Bogomil missionaries on the emergence of heresy in western Europe, and it has been suggested that the arguments which apply to the twelfth-century document hold just as well for the eleventh century. Arguments in favor of reading the letter as an authentic eleventh-century document remain controversial, but, if the letter of Heribert is accepted as a reliable account, it would provide evidence for the early arrival of the Bogomils and would reinforce the opinion of those who accept Bogomil's influence on the heresy of Stephen and Lisois. Even if these leaders of the heresy at Orléans were not influenced by the Bogomils, it is generally held that missionaries from Bulgaria, preaching a message first taught in the tenth century by the simple village priest Bogomil, helped to shape the teachings of the Cathars, whose popularity in southern France had a dramatic impact on the career of Count Raymond VI of Toulouse.

Heribert's letter is also suggestive about the nature of the heretics' beliefs in his day and throughout the later Middle Ages, and it indicates the possibly dualist nature of medieval heresy. Bogomil and generations of his followers taught a Christian dualism that emphasized the transcendent nature of God and the authority of the devil over the world. The rejection of meat and wine by Heribert's heretics may well reveal a Christian dualism which identified the material world as inherently evil. Their prayer recalls that of dualists of the eastern Mediterranean, and their rejection of images of Christ on the cross and of the Eucharist is also indicative of a rejection of the material world. These teachings gained increasing prominence among heretics in southern France, Italy, and other parts of Europe in the mid-twelfth century and were among the core beliefs of the Cathars, whose movement was perceived as the greatest threat to the Catholic Church in the Middle Ages. The Cathars' challenge was deemed to be so serious that it inspired the Church to launch a crusade and the Inquisition to destroy their movement. These efforts ultimately proved successful, even though it is sometimes said that the crusade did more to damage southern French culture and independence than it did to destroy heresy. The Cathar heresy, however, proved to be attractive to many Christians throughout the thirteenth and fourteenth centuries despite the extent of the persecutions it provoked, and one final flourishing of the heresy took place under the direction of Pierre Autier and his followers in the early fourteenth century.

Even if the heretics in Heribert's letter were not Christian dualists, they did seek to live the apostolic life and did base their teachings on the Gospels. Devotion to the scriptures and the life of Christ and the Apostles was promoted by all the leading heretics, whether dualist or not. The evangelical life was the most important model of Christian piety throughout the Middle Ages, and the heretics of Périgord adopted this model in their ascetic lifestyle, refusal to accept money, attention to prayer, and active missionary work. Indeed, the life of active preaching and poverty emerged as a core value for heretics from Bogomil to Pierre Autier. The great leaders of heresy of the twelfth century, most notably Henry the Monk, took up the life of missionary preaching, condemning the failures of the Church and seeking to promote a more pure and pristine version of the faith. Attracting a large, although short-lived, following, Henry sought to restore the Church to its original, apostolic purity, and the power of his preaching encouraged many to give away their worldly possessions. More successful and long-lasting was the movement initiated by Valdes of Lyons, whose heresy was firmly based on the Gospels and the apostolic life. The very essence of his heresy involved the life of preaching and poverty, and his and his followers' unwillingness to give up the practice of preaching led to their denunciation by the Church and ultimate condemnation as schismatics and heretics. Heribert's group at Périgord may be said to have also anticipated the radical and violent apostolic movement of Fra Dolcino, whose extreme devotion to the apostolic life led to the outbreak of attacks on the Church and its representatives. Despite their strict adherence to the apostolic life, Valdes, Henry, and the sectaries of Périgord were deemed heretics because of their rejection of Church authority and criticism of ecclesiastical materialism – being too good a Christian was at times as big a problem as not being Christian enough.

Heribert's letter, in reviewing the nature of the heresy at Périgord, thus traces the basic outlines of heresy, especially popular heresy, in the Middle Ages. It reveals the essential problems the documents pose, and it illustrates the basic character of heresy from the eleventh to the fourteenth centuries. It also hints at the emergence of a different kind of heresy in its report on the miracles and prodigies associated with the heretic movement of Périgord, which had an apocalyptic flavor.[7] Apocalyptic and prophetic sentiments were very important in the development of medieval religious beliefs, both orthodox and heterodox. Apocalypticism fueled the violent movement of Fra Dolcino and the Apostolici or Apostolic Brethren in the early fourteenth century. Their eschatological expectations drove them to renounce both material possessions and the authority of the Church and to open warfare between members of the movement and the Church itself. A rough contemporary of Dolcino, Marguerite Porete also cultivated a prophetic and mystical belief that undermined the traditional role of the Church in society and in the plan of salvation. Marguerite Porete was a member of the Beguine movement, which adopted an apostolic lifestyle, and her *Mirror of Simple Souls* was a handbook of the spiritual life and mystical path to God that offered a means to salvation independent of the Church. Her execution was a reminder of how sternly the Church was prepared to deal with those who questioned or undermined its authority.

The dedication to the apostolic life and the desire to return to the true Christian path revealed by the heretics at Périgord also found expression in learned circles. Indeed, leading heretics in the Middle Ages were found not only among the 'rustics' mentioned in Heribert's letter but also among the most educated members of society. Two of the greatest and most influential of the medieval heretics were the trained and learned theologians John Wyclif and Jan Hus. Their teachings examined some of the central doctrines of the Christian faith and came to conclusions that anticipated the teachings of Martin Luther. Motivated by many of the same concerns that inspired earlier heretical leaders, Wyclif and Hus applied their vast learning to questions of religious belief and practice and to the proper ordering of the Church in society. Their conclusions, like those of their many predecessors, rejected the teachings of the established Church and led to their eventual break with it or even, in Hus's case, to a fiery end.

The outlines of the history of heresy in the Middle Ages can be seen in the letter of Heribert. Driven by concerns of proper belief and practice, many Christians in the Middle Ages were condemned as heretics by an increasingly hierarchical and powerful Church. Responding to the call of the true faith, heretics sought to create a more pure Church and a religious experience that followed the teachings of Christ more faithfully. From Bogomil in the tenth century to Jan Hus in the late fourteenth and early fifteenth, religious leaders outside the boundaries of the Church provided an alternative to the normative Church and its teachings. They offered a challenge to its authority and, at times, faced the full fury of the religious and political leaders of their day. The heretics also contributed to the growth of the medieval Church and influenced the development of orthodox belief and practice. Although many of the heretics faded from the pages of history or suffered a dramatic end, they were a pivotal part of the history of the Church in the Middle Ages and important agents in the evolution of medieval religious belief and practice.

CHAPTER ONE

POP BOGOMIL AND COSMAS THE PRESBYTER: THE TENTH CENTURY

One of the earliest, most influential, and most elusive of all medieval heretics made his appearance first in tenth-century Bulgaria. This was the preacher Bogomil. The themes and tenets of his teaching mark a clear break from the great heresies of the ancient world and echo down throughout the whole of the Middle Ages. Living in an area heavily influenced by the Byzantine Empire and by the Orthodox Church so closely associated with it, Bogomil developed a large following throughout the eastern Mediterranean. The impact of his ideas was felt far beyond his homeland and the Byzantine Empire, and during the centuries following his death reached the countries of Germany, France, and Italy. Yet despite being the founder of a lasting legacy of religious dissent, and despite his prominence in the history of heresy in the Latin and Greek worlds, we know of his teachings only through the writings of orthodox ecclesiastics, whose evidence must be interpreted with care. The most important of these ecclesiastics was the priest Cosmas.

As with many other medieval heresies, the emergence of Bogomilism – as this one came to be known – was the result of a complex mix of religious and social developments, in this case in Bogomil's native Bulgaria. Although perhaps Bulgaria at the time of the emergence of the heresy was not a land of chaos, as it is sometimes depicted, it was a region that was undergoing a profound and important transformation.[1] Not the least of these changes, of course, was the

Christianization of the Bulgarians, which began under their great King Boris (ruled 852–89). The confusion that would affect Bulgarian religion in the tenth century was already manifest during the reign of Boris, who, for both political and religious reasons, sought to convert to Christianity. His retirement to a monastery in 889 reveals that he truly accepted the new faith, even if it is unclear how early this inner conversion occurred. In 864, when he was baptized, the Bulgarian ruler may well have believed in the Christian faith, but he was also concerned with the independence of his kingdom and his own authority. Under the new faith, Boris would be recognized as king by the grace of God and would stand in a more exalted position than the boyars (nobles) in his kingdom. He also sought to move out from under the shadow of the Byzantine Empire, and thus his conversion involved negotiations with the pope in Rome and western missionaries, who were powerful exponents of Latin Christianity. He turned to them because the pope and his allies would grant certain organizational concessions to the Church in Bulgaria without being in the position to impose any political authority over the king and his Church. The emperor in Constantinople and the Byzantine Church saw the threat of western interference in its neighbor, Bulgaria, and worked to ensure that Boris converted to Orthodox Christianity. Boris did, in fact, accept baptism at the hands of the patriarch of Constantinople, and his baptismal sponsor was the emperor Michael III. Despite this, later on Boris made overtures again to the pope and his representatives; the latter moved into Bulgaria and replaced the Greek priests and missionaries, who had begun the process of establishing the Church there. But when the pope refused to grant Boris's request for an archbishop, the Bulgarian ruler turned again to the Byzantine Empire and its Church. The competition and polemic that developed between Latin and Greek missionaries surely confused a newly converted and nominally Christian people and undermined the authority of the representatives of the Church, either Roman or Byzantine.

This complex and often ambivalent relationship with the Byzantine Empire and Orthodox Church continued into the tenth century, when Boris's successors, Symeon (ruled 893–927) and Peter (ruled 927–67), fought against, and then accepted, the Byzantines. Further complicating matters was the continued attraction of the traditional Bulgarian religion, to which a large part of the nobility and peasantry still adhered during Boris's lifetime and after. Boris faced a revolt of the nobles, inspired in part by their rejection of Christianity, and his immediate successor, Vladimir (889–93), repudiated and persecuted the new faith until his overthrow by Symeon, aided by Boris. The lingering attraction of paganism at all levels of Bulgarian society was complemented by animosity toward the Byzantines and their Church. During his reign, Symeon adopted an aggressive policy toward Constantinople and even sought to have himself crowned as Byzantine emperor. He promoted an independent Bulgarian Orthodox Church and cultivated hostility toward the Byzantine Empire, its culture, and its religion. His successor, Peter, at first also followed an anti-Byzantine policy, but his initial success against the Empire led to his receiving important concessions, including the hand in marriage of a member of the imperial family. This led to yet another dramatic influx of Greek clergy into Bulgaria and to the growing influence of Byzantium at the Bulgarian court and, possibly, on the whole Bulgarian culture and society. Greek clergy and Bulgarians influenced by them became increasingly important, and monasticism, which had first entered Bulgaria during the reign of Boris, grew substantially during the reign of Peter. Renewed Byzantine influence thus brought a new group of clerics and Byzantinized the leadership of the Bulgarian Church. It also renewed Byzantine influence on monastic life, which rested upon the establishment of large-scale plantations, worked by many peasants, and advocated a highly ascetic and world-renouncing lifestyle. For many, though, this new influence was not particularly welcome and, according to one scholar, contributed to the rise of a religious nationalism in Bulgaria that would lead to the emergence of heresy.[2]

The matter of religious nationalism remains, however, debatable. But the confused religious and socio-political environment of tenth-century Bulgaria opened the way for an alternative form of Christian belief and practice, which would be deemed heretical by the official Church. The first recorded mentioning of the heresy that would become known as Bogomilism is in a letter from the patriarch Theophylact Lecapenus, which has been dated between 940 and 950. The patriarch noted the appearance of this heresy during the reign of Tsar Peter.[3] Although he did not call it Bogomilism, he described it as 'a mixture of Manichaeanism and Paulianism'; in this way he identified its fundamental religious dualism and suggested that it originated in an ancient eastern Mediterranean dualist tradition.[4] He associated the new heresy with the Persian religious leader Mani (216–74?CE), who had developed a faith that drew on Christian teachings, gnosticism, and Persian religious traditions, posited the existence of two gods – a good and an evil one – and rejected the material world as the creation of the evil god.

Mani was seen in the Middle Ages as the originator in a long chain of heretics, which stretched to the Bogomils and even to the Cathars of western Europe. This view is now generally discredited, but it was upheld by serious scholars until well into the twentieth century.[5] The chain of dualist heresies comprised Theophylact's 'Paulians,' a designation which may refer to the followers of a heretic named Paul, or to those with a special devotion to the Apostle Paul. They are, however, generally identified as the Paulicians of Armenia, a group which was transferred to the Balkans by the Byzantine emperors; most likely they held dualist notions which contravened orthodox Church teaching.[6] As Peter of Sicily notes in his history, the Paulicians actively proselytised in Bulgaria, possibly already in 869–70.[7] This was a time when the religious situation there was most unsettled; hence their appearance would not have seemed out of place when Greek and Latin missionaries were also preaching in Bulgaria, but it complicated matters further, as the two Churches competed with each other for the devotion of the nominally Christian Bulgarians. The preaching of the Paulicians is often thought to have either introduced dualist teachings or reinforced dualist notions that already existed in the culture.

The new heretics in Bulgaria were most certainly not the heirs of the third-century prophet Mani and may not have been directly influenced by the rather militaristic Paulicians. They were, however, clearly dualist Christians, according to the anathemas Theophylact included in his letter.[8] He condemned, namely, those who believed in two ultimate principles and held the view that the devil created the world and ruled over it. Those who rejected the law of Moses, opposed lawful marriage, and denied that Mary was the mother of God were also declared anathema. Theophylact further condemned anyone who denied that the Son of God assumed the flesh, suffered physically, and died on the cross, together with all those who taught that the body and blood given by Christ to his disciples was the Gospel.

The various teachings denounced by Theophylact in his letter to Tsar Peter are those most generally associated with Christian dualism throughout the Middle Ages, and his letter may be little more than a catalogue of teachings of previous heretics, which he used to discredit the new movement. His identification of them as 'Paulians' and 'Manichaeans' has been questioned by scholars, but Theophylact's instincts were sound even if he had little direct knowledge of the heretics: he captured well and correctly the nature of the heresy emerging in tenth-century Bulgaria.

Theophylact's letter, which makes no mention of the movement's founder, contains the first reference to the emergence of what would be termed Bogomilism. The most important early source for the heresy, however, is the eyewitness account in the sermon of the Bulgarian presbyter Cosmas. The earliest extant manuscript of this work comes from the fifteenth century, and it has been argued that Cosmas wrote it in the thirteenth century. It is most likely, however, that the sermon was composed c.970, possibly in eastern Bulgaria, and, as suggested by certain of Cosmas's comments, certainly after the death of Tsar Peter. Such a dating would make the heresy several decades old by the time of the writing of the sermon. Thus Cosmas's work would reveal a more developed Bogomil heresy than the one which appears in Theophylact's letter.[9] Cosmas's account was also less dependent on earlier theological traditions than that of Theophylact. Rooted firmly in his personal experience of the new heresy, Cosmas's sermon against the Bogomils therefore provides a much more accurate depiction of the beliefs and practices of the early heretics and of the original teachings of the founder of Bogomilism. The sermon itself was very influential in later generations; it was adopted by members of other Slavonic Orthodox Churches and used by the Russian Orthodox clergy to denounce new heresies.

Little is known about Cosmas himself, except what can be discerned from his sermon on the Bogomils. There is little evidence concerning the dates of his birth and death, or when he entered priesthood. There is general agreement that Cosmas was a priest, as the accepted title of his work indicates, but exactly what kind of priest he was is uncertain. On the one hand, it has been said that, because he did not make reference in his sermon to the great ancient heresies, he was not a 'sophisticated theologian': such absence would suggest a more modest background.[10] On the other hand, it has also been conjectured that Cosmas was no simple village priest but rather held a position of some prominence in the Bulgarian Orthodox Church; and it has even been suggested that Cosmas was a bishop, on the grounds that his work was addressed to other bishops of Bulgaria.[11]

Although his exact rank remains uncertain, Cosmas was surely a devoted son of the Orthodox Church, leaving this first-hand account of a new heresy in Bulgaria. His work was written in Old Slavonic — a language promoted by King Boris, who patronized the missionaries introducing into Bulgaria a translation of the Bible in Old Slavonic — and it clearly supports the established eastern Orthodox Church. The sermon contained not only the warning about the Bogomil heresy and its condemnation, but also a defense of the 'orthodox' faith and a call for its reform. A substantial portion of the work addresses the failures of the Bulgarian Orthodox Church, which is blamed for allowing heresy to appear in the first place. Cosmas, in some ways, is not that far removed from his nemesis, Bogomil: the Orthodox presbyter was as critical of the Church as was his heretical opponent. He was most particularly critical of those who took up the monastic life without adequate preparation.

Monasticism had become increasingly popular during the reign of Peter, and many believed that the only way to gain salvation was to become a monk, living their life in celibacy. As Cosmas asserts, however, many of those who joined monasteries were hypocritical and failed to leave the world behind in the way monks should. Many monks lived unchaste and drunken lives, devoting themselves to their own bellies and wasting time in idle gossip. Others would break their vows by wandering from monastery to monastery, instead of staying in their original community in obedience to the rule and their abbot. For Cosmas, who may have indulged in rhetorical hyperbole on the theme of the corruption of the monks, this behavior was one of the key factors in the success of Bogomil's movement, and the priest drew strong links between the failures of the monks and the rise of heresy in Bulgaria. Like other ecclesiastics in the coming centuries, Cosmas urgently called for a reform of the Church, to stem the tide of heresy and to improve religious life overall.

The life of Bogomil is as shrouded in the mists of the past as is that of Cosmas, and what little we know of that life comes from the sermon written against him, and from his teachings. The founder of the heresy is mentioned only once in Cosmas's sermon and receives no direct reference in any other contemporary document. One indication of his status, however, is revealed in that lone mentioning by Cosmas, who identifies his rival as Pop Bogomil. The title 'pop' was used for ordinary village priests, and so it is likely that Bogomil was a simple priest, preaching at first to the small community in which he lived.

His name, which he may have adopted later in life, is a translation of the Greek name Theophilos, which was fairly common in Bulgaria at the start of the tenth century. The name probably means 'beloved of God,' or (depending on the placing of the accent) it can also be translated as 'worthy of God's mercy,' 'one who entreats God,' or, in the most recent translation, 'worthy of God's compassion.'[12] Cosmas offers a play on Bogomil's name by declaring that he is not Bogomil but 'Bogunemil, "unworthy of God's compassion".'[13] The descriptive nature of his name has led some modern commentators to argue that the name indicates that there was no individual founder of the movement and that only tradition dictates that he existed; but it is perhaps a case of excessive skepticism to deny Bogomil's existence, even if his personality and other elements of his biography are difficult to discern.

Beyond the name of the founder, Cosmas provides no other direct references for Bogomil's biography. He does, however, offer important insights into Bogomil's teachings and even hints concerning his life. The various criticisms he ascribes to Bogomil are suggestive of the way he lived. His rejection of marriage indicates that he led a celibate life, and it is probable that he lived simply, in accordance with the teachings of the Gospels, and adopted a life of poverty. Cosmas admits as much in his description of Bogomil's early disciples, which is most likely applicable to their mentor. The heretics, and most assuredly Bogomil himself, 'are gentle and humble and quiet. They seem pale from their hypocritical fasts, they do not utter vain words, they do not laugh out loud, they do not show curiosity, they take care not to be noticeable and to do everything externally so that they may not be told apart from orthodox Christians.'[14] Of course, Cosmas declares that they are ravening wolves inside, but he cannot fail to notice the simple piety of the Bogomils, which is much more similar to the behavior of true monks and Christians than that of the Orthodox monks whom Cosmas also condemns. This monastic lifestyle, inspired in part by true monastic practice and by the Gospels – which Bogomil himself very probably knew in an Old Slavonic translation – clearly reflects the behavior of the founder of the Bogomil movement.

Bogomil must also have been a charismatic and successful preacher, if we are to judge by the growth of the movement he founded. It is generally believed that he attracted a substantial following with his preaching – especially among the peasantry, as most would agree. The success of his preaching can be discerned from two passages in Cosmas's treatise against the heretics. The Orthodox presbyter notes in one section that people 'approach them [the heretics] and take their advice about their souls' salvation ... and when they see anyone simple and ignorant, there they sow the tares of their doctrines.'[15] And later in the work he explains that the 'heretics cloak their poison under hypocritical humility and fasts, and again they take the Gospel in their hands, and, giving it an impious interpretation, they try to catch men this way and lead them to perdition.'[16]

Bogomil's disciples, following his example, spread throughout Bulgaria and the Byzantine Empire within a generation of the founding of the heresy. His teachings found a receptive audience among his country-men, many of whom believed, like the Orthodox Cosmas, that the clergy of the established Church were not fulfilling their obligations of living holy lives and preaching the Gospel. Indeed Bogomil, by the probity of his life, stood in stark contrast to the corrupt and worldly monks, the Byzantinized clergy, and the distant and powerful hierarchy that lived in Bulgaria at the time. Although there is almost no direct evidence concerning his life, what little there is suggests, therefore, that he was a zealous preacher who lived simply and piously. His very mode of life stood as an indictment of the established Church, which failed the newly Christianized people of Bulgaria. Understandably, the Orthodox Church was filled with a growing concern about his teachings.

Along with such suggestions concerning Bogomil's life, Cosmas also provides the earliest commentary on the teachings both of the founder and of the early practitioners of the heresy. His treatise clearly reveals that, from its very inception, Bogomilism was a dualist faith. This fundamental feature was to affect the teachings and practices of the Bogomils for centuries to come. In religion, dualism is a type of doctrine which involves belief in two gods, one good and one evil. At its heart, Bogomil's dualism was one that rejected the material world, identifying it as a place of evil. Hence Bogomil and his followers refused the physical pleasures and the material aspects of cult in the Orthodox Church, notably the water in baptism and the bread and wine of the Eucharist. As Bogomilism evolved and spread into the Byzantine Empire and even into western Europe, this dualism of matter and spirit would remain the sect's essential feature, even if the theology behind it became more sophisticated and the Bogomils became divided over the exact understanding of what their dualism entailed.

Although Cosmas argues that the Bogomils were not consistent in their terminology concerning the devil, he plainly asserts that 'they claim the devil as creator of mankind and all the divine creation.'[17] Indeed, Cosmas expands on this central tenet of Bogomil's teaching later on in the treatise: Bogomil and his followers say that 'it is by the devil's will that all exists; the sky, the sun, the stars, the air, mankind, the churches, the cross; all that belongs to God they ascribe to the devil; in short everything that moves on the earth, whether it has a soul or not, they ascribe it to the devil.'[18] Moreover, the devil was given the name Mammon, by which they refer to the 'creator and architect of things terrestrial.'[19] It is Mammon who ordered 'men to take wives and eat meat and drink wine,' and those who live in the world and marry are servants of Mammon.[20] This is clearly an echo of the biblical passage stating that one cannot serve God and Mammon, and in this way Bogomil identified himself and his followers as the true believers in God and his revelation.

The Bogomils, according to Cosmas, corroborated this belief by references to the scriptures. They found support, for instance, in the Gospel according to Matthew, where the devil says to Jesus, 'All these things I will give you, if you will fall down to worship me' (4: 9). They believed that the devil offered Jesus things in the world that he, the devil, had created, and therefore the devil was master of the world. The heretics cited John's Gospel as well, including the verse in which Jesus declares, 'Now the ruler of the world is coming, and has no power over me' (14: 30), which they took to mean that the devil was the lord and creator of the world. Cosmas may dispute the Bogomils' biblical exegesis, but it is important that they turned to scripture to support their beliefs – Bogomil and his followers always claimed to be true Christians – and it is equally important that they believed the scriptures taught that God did not create the world but the devil did.

The belief that the devil was the world's creator had important consequences for Bogomil belief and practice, but his own teachings about the devil were shaped by a further passage from the scriptures. According to Cosmas, Bogomil and his followers believed that the parable of the prodigal son (Luke 15: 11–32) was about the devil. On this reading, the younger son, who deceived his father, was the devil, and the older son was Jesus. This made God the father both of Jesus and of the devil, who were then brothers. Thus Bogomil taught what is called 'mitigated dualism,' rather than 'absolute dualism.' In mitigated dualism the devil or creator of the world is himself a created being, or at least subordinate to the one true God, whereas in absolute dualism the good and evil deities are equal powers existing in all eternity.

Later on in the history of the sect, some Bogomils would adopt absolute dualism. The founder of the heresy, however, seems to have taught a mitigated dualism, which reveals another possible influence on the emergence of the heresy as well as his own creative powers.

Although the Paulicians are often seen as an influence on Bogomil, his dualism was distinctly different from theirs. According to one recent scholar, the trinity of God and his two sons Jesus and the devil, which featured in the teachings of the early Bogomils, is reminiscent of the Zurvan Zoroastrian trinity of Zurvan, Ahriman, and Ohrmazd, and there is some evidence to suggest contacts between the Bulgars and the Iranian Zurvanites (third to seventh centuries CE).[21] This link is, however, rather tenuous; Bogomil's mitigated dualism and understanding of the relationship between God and the devil reveal the independence of his thought, thus testifying to the originality of his teachings. Whatever his sources, Bogomil promoted the belief that the devil was both the son of God and the creator of the world with everything in it. This view of our world had a profound influence on all the other beliefs and practices of the Bogomils.

Bogomil's teachings on God and the devil had a direct impact on his understanding of Christ and of his presence on earth. Later accounts state unambiguously that Bogomil heretics had a Docetist Christology, namely that they upheld the belief in a non-human, celestial Christ, who only seemed to assume the flesh and suffer on the cross in his humanity. Docetist beliefs would fit in well with the dualist cosmology taught by Bogomil, but Cosmas, in this discourse on the heresy, offers only one suggestion that the founder might have held such beliefs and that his Christology was Docetist, yet that testimonial is not conclusive. This happens in a passage where Cosmas claims that the Bogomils deny that Christ performed any miracles because they believe that the devil was the creator of all things. The founder and his disciples, Cosmas explains, say: 'Christ did not restore any blind person's sight, he cured no cripple, he did not raise the dead; these are only parables.'[22] Indeed, to do so would be to accept the goodness of creation and the power of Christ in an evil material world. Rather, the Bogomils would contend that the Evangelists presented the sins as diseases; they would explain that the five loaves of bread Christ used to feed the masses were really the four Gospels and the Acts of the Apostles. This allegorical interpretation of Christ's miracles could support a Docetist Christology, as it could be predicated on the belief that the material world is the kingdom of the devil.

Bogomil's teachings on the person of Christ, or at least those of his disciples as recorded by Cosmas, are indeed a bit confused. The rejection of Christ's miracles is in line with a Docetist view, but Cosmas's discussion of the heretics' refusal to venerate the cross suggests that Bogomil may not have fully worked out his Christology. Denial of the cross was a feature of early Bogomilism; Cosmas notes that the heretics 'chop up crosses and make tools of them,'[23] but this seems to be in line with their general rejection of material objects rather than emerging from some Christological viewpoint. Moreover, the Bogomils refused to adore the cross because the son of God was crucified on it and therefore 'the cross is even more the enemy of God.' They argued further, 'If anyone killed the king's son with a cross of wood, would the wood be dear to the king? The same is true of the cross of God.'[24] This argument against the veneration of the cross suggests that they viewed it as the place of Christ's actual suffering and death; but such a view, in turn, presupposes that Christ assumed the flesh, because Christ in his divinity cannot suffer and die. The Bogomils would eventually work out an elaborate Docetist Christology, in which Christ very clearly did not assume the flesh and was not born of the Virgin Mary – they taught that he entered her body through her ear and only appeared to have been born of the Virgin – but the earliest Bogomils and the founder himself appear to have preached a somewhat mitigated and confused Christology. Or at least they failed to work out the full implications of their Docetism, as it applied to various aspects of their teaching.

One doctrine which seems, however, to have emerged as a consequence of a Docetist Christology is – quite apart from the Bogomils' essential dualism – their attitude toward the Virgin Mary. In his letter, Theophylact makes the rejection of the Virgin one of the main features of the heresy, but Cosmas pays only passing attention to it. He notes that 'they do not honor the most glorious and pure mother of Our Lord and God Jesus Christ, and utter madness against her.'[25] He qualifies this statement, however, by remarking that this error is greater than all their other evils, and he notes that he cannot 'record in this book their words and their insults with regard to her whom the prophets foretold.'[26] In this way, perhaps, he indicates the extent to which Bogomil offended

Orthodox sensibilities concerning the Blessed Virgin, and in a later section of the treatise he accuses his followers of claiming that 'the most holy mother of God sinned.'[27] It is possible, moreover, that Bogomil's 'insults' included the rejection of the virgin birth of Christ as it was taught by the established Church, or the denial of that veneration which the Orthodox bestowed on Mary as the mother of God. In any case, Cosmas seems clearly disturbed by Bogomil's attitude – so disturbed, in fact, that he cannot discuss it at any length. And Bogomil's refusal to honor Mary reinforces the belief that he taught a form of Docetism in which Christ would not have been born of the flesh. The rejection of Mary is also part of a broader repudiation of the prophets and saints venerated by the Orthodox Church.

Consistent with their dualist cosmology, Bogomil and his sectaries, like all dualists since Mani and others from the earlier history of Christianity, rejected the prophets of the Hebrew scriptures. In later generations of Bogomils, the devil would be associated with the God of the Old Testament, which offered them justification for rejecting the Hebrew scriptures. Cosmas, however, does not make that connection in his treatise, even though he denounces Bogomil and his followers for refusing to accept the law of Moses and the teachings of the prophets and blames their rejection of the law on the devil. They 'spurn the law God gave to Moses' and 'reject what the holy prophets prophesied about Him [Christ].'[28] Cosmas notes, specifically, that Abraham, Azarias, and David were rejected, and that Bogomil and his sect called John the Baptist 'the precursor of antichrist.'[29] In casting aside the Hebrew prophets, John the Baptist, and the Hebrew scriptures, Bogomil asserted his exclusive preference for the books of the New Testament and for the teachings of Christ. According to Cosmas, the heresy was based solely on the false interpretation of the Gospels and Acts of the Apostles. False or not, Bogomil's understanding of the scriptures discarded both the importance of the Old Testament and the scriptural exegesis of the Orthodox Church.

In fact Bogomil imparted to his followers a much broader rejection of the teachings and institutions of the Orthodox Church; as Cosmas noted, 'they insult every law which is part of the tradition of God's Holy Church.'[30] This attitude toward the Church and its teachings most plausibly derived from Bogomil's repudiation of the material world, but also from a general dissatisfaction with the Church, which is shared by Cosmas and revealed in his critique of it and of its clergy. The Bogomils refused to honor the saints recognized by the Church. They did not respect their relics and denied that miracles were performed by them through the power of the Holy Spirit. In accordance with the belief that the devil rules over the world and everything in it, they argued that '[t]he miracles did not take place according to the will of God, but it was the devil who did them to trick mankind.'[31] Not only did they repudiate saints and relics held sacred by the Orthodox, but they also refused the veneration of icons, one of the central expressions of religious devotion in the Orthodox Church. Just as they derided the practice of honoring the cross, the Bogomils mocked those who honored holy icons and denounced the latter as idols; and this, according to Cosmas, made these heretics worse than the demons, who feared icons. The Bogomils denounced the practice of honoring religious images by declaring that 'those who venerate icons are like the pagan Greeks,' who worshiped false idols.[32] Cosmas offered a spirited defense of both practices in his treatise, which demonstrates the importance of the matter both to the orthodox and to the heterodox.

Bogomil most probably rejected the entire sacerdotal and sacramental structure of the Church. In his discourse, Cosmas notes that the heretics attacked the priests, 'yapping at them like dogs following a mounted man.'[33] They criticized not only those who deserved to be condemned on the grounds of their immorality, but also those who deserved respect for the quality and purity of their lives. They did not honor the clergy as God intended, concluded Cosmas; and he also observed that the heretics could not be Christians because they did not have any priests. Along with their rejection of the clergy, Bogomil and his disciples denied the validity of the sacraments offered by the Church. For them, the Eucharist was 'a simple food like all others,' and the sacrament of communion, or the mass itself, were not instituted by divine command but rather by the teachings of men.[34] Moreover, Bogomil understood the scriptural passages concerning Christ's sharing of the bread and wine at the Last Supper in an allegorical sense, which was markedly different from the teaching of the Church. Cosmas wrote: 'You tell that they [the words of the Gospels] refer to the four Gospels and the Acts of the Apostles, not to holy communion; by "body," you understand the four gospels and by "blood," the Acts of the Apostles.'[35]

The rejection of the sacrament of the bread and wine may have stemmed from their dualism and abhorrence of the material world, an attitude clearly revealed by their rejection of the Orthodox practice of baptism with water. The belief that the world, with all the things in it, was created by the devil led all Bogomils to reject the use of any material substance like water in any of their rituals; they would replace the baptism with water by a spiritual baptism, even though Cosmas does not specifically mention this in his discourse. From the very beginnings of the movement, however, Bogomil and his adherents found baptism with water so distasteful that they loathed baptized children. Indeed, so profoundly did they oppose this form of baptism, that if 'they see a young child,' wrote Cosmas, 'they shrink from it, as if from some evil smell; they spit and cover their faces, when they themselves are filth to men and to angels.'[36] The Bogomils denied that baptism was instituted by God; the rejection of John the Baptist was rooted, in part, in John's practice of baptism with water.

Along with a cosmological dualism and rejection of the Orthodox Church, Bogomil most likely taught a number of positive doctrines, which Cosmas only grudgingly recorded. His followers were taught to live simple and pious lives. Cosmas describes them as 'gentle and humble and quiet,'[37] and he notes that they fast frequently. Bogomil and his followers rejected the practice of marriage; he encouraged celibacy – the hostile reaction to children may have been the result of the belief that they were the devil's own and that procreation contributed to the extension of the devil's realm. Bogomil may also have taught his disciples to pray the Lord's Prayer four times a day and four times a night, and he may have instructed them not to make the sign of the cross when they prayed.

It is also likely that the basic organizational structure of the sect was established during Bogomil's lifetime, or at least by the time when Cosmas was writing. Cosmas condemns members of the sect who 'go about in idleness and are unwilling to employ their hands with any task; they go from house to house and eat the goods of others, those of the men they have deceived.'[38] The fundamental division of the Bogomils was between the 'perfected' and the ordinary believers, those who were sympathetic to the sect without having joined the heresy. In later generations a more complex organization emerged involving bishops, but it is likely that a two-fold division was established right from the outset — between those who preached the message of the sect and those who heard it and offered support to the preachers in the form of food and shelter. Although this simple structure was established very early on, the followers of Bogomil, citing the letter of James (5: 16), were taught to confess their sins to each other. Indignant over this violation of orthodox practice, Cosmas was all the more exercised because it was 'not just the men who do this, but the women as well.'[39] And it is a commonplace in the history of heresy, and of religion, that women often played a crucial role in a new development.

Finally, Cosmas notes that the Bogomils were instructed to deny their beliefs, a practice to be repeated by heretics over the next several centuries in both eastern and western Christendom. In the opening passages of the treatise, Cosmas declares that the heretics appear to be as gentle as sheep, but in fact are ravening wolves; in other words, they hide their true nature behind a false appearance, in order to capture otherwise unsuspecting souls. He notes in a later passage that, when someone confronts their actual beliefs, they deny them 'so forcefully that you would think that there was no harm in them.'[40] They defend this practice by citing the passage from the Gospel according to Matthew, where Jesus tells his followers not to pray like the hypocrites. It was a means of protecting themselves from the persecution of the secular and religious authorities and of ensuring the continued success of Bogomil's teachings.

Although a shadowy presence to the extent that some historians question his actual existence, Bogomil was the founder of the first great heresy of the Middle Ages. Preaching his version of the Christian faith early in the reign of Tsar Peter, Bogomil attracted a substantial following in Bulgaria at a time when most Bulgars were only nominally Christian and exposed to a wide range of religious influences – Paulician and Roman and Byzantine Christian – and buffeted by cultural and socio-political turmoil. Within a generation or two, the teachings of Bogomil had spread to a sufficiently large number of people, so that the Orthodox Cosmas recorded them in his treatise. He revealed a Christian heresy rooted in cosmological dualism and in the rejection of the established Church. It was this combination that proved to have great impact on the development of the Church in Bulgaria, the Byzantine Empire, and, most importantly, western Europe.

CHAPTER TWO

STEPHEN AND LISOIS: HERETICS
IN THE ELEVENTH CENTURY

*t*he emergence of the Bogomils signaled the revival of heresy throughout the Mediterranean and heralded its reappearance in Latin Europe
for the first time since late antiquity. Religious dissent was breaking
out in several places in western Europe at the turn of the millennium. The most
important and most dramatic of all the occurrences of heresy in the early eleventh century took place in Orléans. Its improbable leaders were two pious and
respectable canons. Their names were Stephen and Lisois.

The heretical developments at Orléans in 1022 were, in some ways, foreshadowed in Aquitaine and other regions. In the year 1018, 'Manichaeans
appeared throughout Aquitaine seducing the people. They denied baptism and
the Cross and every sound doctrine. They abstained from food and seemed
like monks; they pretended to be chaste, but among themselves practiced
every sort of vice. They were messengers of Antichrist and caused many to
turn away from the faith.'[1] In this way Ademar of Chabannes (c.989–1034),
a monk of southwestern France, announced the rebirth of heresy in western
Europe in the Middle Ages, after more than five centuries when it had lain
dormant.

Although, as we have seen, heresy had already emerged in Bulgaria and
in the Byzantine world in the tenth century and had subsisted there almost
continuously, in some form or other, since late antiquity, this was a relatively

new phenomenon so far in the medieval West. Ademar's announcement of the sudden resurgence of heresy – or religious dissent, as it is sometimes called – heralded important changes for western Christendom. It also raised the possibility that the phenomenon was due to contact with Bogomil missionaries and was broad enough to spread, beyond Ademar's native Aquitaine, across all of western Europe.

Ademar described the heretics who appeared in his homeland as Manichaeans because he believed that they advocated a dualist religious heresy. The heretics' beliefs and practices, as recorded by Ademar, recall those adopted by Bogomil and his followers. Indeed, Ademar's description of the heretics as simple, pious folk who secretly indulged in debauchery offers a further echo of the behavior of the Bogomils as Cosmas explained it, and forms part of a long tradition of demonizing heretics and others outside the bounds of society. Consequently, some scholars have argued that the influence of Bogomil missionaries on the origin and growth of heresy in western Europe was felt already in the early eleventh century.[2] The Bogomils from Bulgaria were active missionaries, as the founder encouraged them to be, and some have suggested that it was their appearance in the early decades of the eleventh century that focused the inchoate opposition to Church teachings and to the clergy which could be registered throughout society at that time. On this traditional view, the Bogomil missionaries, who lived ascetic and devout lives, may well have been seen by those in France and other parts of western Europe as the true representatives of Christianity, as many Bulgarians had seen them, and they were thought to offer an attractive alternative to the religious life dictated by the established Church. The eleventh-century arrival of the Bogomils in the West remains, however, a controversial point which most, though by no means all, recent historians do not accept. But the issue is not whether the Bogomils helped to shape heresy in France and other parts of western Europe; it is, rather, when this happened. The importance of the Bogomils in the development of heresy in Latin Europe should not be understated even if the exact moment of their arrival may never come to be known.

On the now generally accepted view, the Bogomils only arrived in western Europe in the twelfth century, but the first expressions of heresy in Latin Europe took place in the years around the turn of the millennium, as Ademar reveals. And the phenomenon was manifest not only in Aquitaine but also in Italy, in the

German Empire, and in several other places in France, from the last decades of the tenth century until the middle of the eleventh, with a cluster of outbreaks from the late 1010s to the early 1030s. For Ademar of Chabannes and other 'orthodox' ecclesiastics throughout western Christendom, these heretics were part of a united front that swept across the continent. Indeed, a corridor of heresy has been identified, which began in Italy and worked its way north, into France and into the Low Countries. The heretics were believed to have been inspired by the devil and intent on destroying the Church and on perverting all good Christians. Nevertheless, just as we have seen in the case of the emergence of the Bogomil heresy, there were several more 'mundane' and less 'diabolical' causes of the birth of medieval heresy after the year 1000.

Like the Balkans in the tenth century, at the turn of the millenium western Europe was in a state of great economic and social turmoil: historians have identified the period from 950 to 1050 as the age of the feudal transformation.[3] Many places in Latin Europe, especially in what would become France, were racked by a violence which both contributed to, and was part of, the breakdown of the old socio-economic and political order. Since the ninth century, much of Europe suffered from foreign invasions, most notably those of the Vikings. During the tenth century Viking assaults increased in ferocity and duration, as many of the invaders from the north began to settle in parts of France and England. The traditional military machine, led by the king himself, Robert the Pious of France, often proved ineffective against these raiders from Scandinavia, and the authority of the king partly diminished as a result of his failure to protect his subjects. Local representatives of power such as the counts and dukes claimed the traditional rights of the king in his place and built up semi-private armies to defend their lands. But these great regional powers were not always up to the task, and an even greater decentralization of authority ensued. By the late tenth and early eleventh century – the very time when heresy reappeared in western Europe – a new form of power, that of the castellan, began to take shape in France and other parts of Europe. Emerging as a result of the failures of the great powers to protect the countryside, but also at a moment when foreign invasions were about to end, this new type of leader appeared to impose his will on local society simply because of his possession of a castle. Not only did the castellans exploit the local peasants by demanding payment in return for protection, but they were also involved in private warfare which destabilized society and terrorized the peasants.

In the face of the breakdown of political order, the people of western Europe had recourse to the other pillar of society, the Church. But, although it traditionally offered solace to the powerless and support to the powerful, the Church had suffered at the hands of invaders and castellans alike and had only modest success in limiting violence in society. Moreover, the Church itself was undergoing a profound transformation: this period laid the foundation for the so-called Gregorian Reform of the later eleventh century.[4] Around the year 1000, the old order of the Church was fading away, as new institutions and a new understanding of the Church and its place in the world was taking shape. The traditional understanding of the saints as local spiritual protectors was giving way, being replaced by a notion of the universal saints, such as Peter and Mary. At the same time, the very figure of Christ was being transformed: the focus came to be, increasingly, on the human Jesus. Locally prominent saints faced 'competition' from Jesus and the Apostles; nevertheless, the cult of the saints, local and universal, remained at the center of everyday devotion, and the number of pilgrims to their shrines increased. As a result of this mounting devotion numerous churches were built throughout Europe, to accommodate the throngs of pilgrims. So widespread was this construction that one contemporary writer declared that the world was clothing itself in 'a white mantle of churches.'[5]

While the central teachings of the faith were undergoing transformation and religious fervor was growing among the people of Europe, Church institutions were themselves being reformed and restructured. One of the main points of emphasis in this process of reformation was the improvement of the life and behavior of the clergy. Already in the early tenth century, monastic life had undergone a reform associated with the French monastery of Cluny. The leaders of that movement sought to restore monastic lifestyle to its original purity, stressing separation from the world and increasing the religious obligations of the monks. The latter were to spend their time praying, singing Psalms and doing the works of God. While the liturgical routine of the monks became increasingly complex and elaborate, their personal life was restored to apostolic simplicity; they lived chastely, ate simply, and owned nothing.

Gradually, this emphasis on apostolic simplicity and purity came to shape

the lives of priests and higher secular clergy as well. Although this was technically against Church law, in the tenth century local priests often had wives
or mistresses; some bishops even fathered children. But now, in the spirit of
reform, the clergy were increasingly expected to live celibate lives, in imitation
of Jesus and the Apostles. This demand for sexual purity arose, in part, from
a growing attention paid to the sacraments, especially the Eucharist; and these
were administered by the priests. The mass, at which the Eucharist was offered,
became a more elaborate affair and was increasingly focused on the priest rather
than on the congregation. The Church also enlarged the number of sacraments,
exercising increasing claims to authority over marriage.

The changes that took place around the year 1000 laid the foundation for
a real revolution in the life and structure of the Church, but their immediate effects were not always positive. The increasingly elaborate sacramental
structure of the Church and the expansion of its claims to authority alienated
many faithful at all levels of society. Others were further disenchanted with the
Church because of its growing economic wealth; although they advocated personal poverty, even the most reform-minded members of the Church benefited
from gifts of land and other wealth from pious nobles. This was presumably
regarded as a failure of the Church to live up to its own ideals, as it would be
deemed in later generations. Moreover, the increasing focus on the priest as
the central figure in Church life only heightened attention to the failures of
many priests. Indeed, priests were often appointed by local counts and dukes,
who built churches on their land as acts of religious devotion. The priests they
appointed were frequently simple peasants subject to ducal authority, and they
were generally unqualified for the priestly office. They were ignorant of the
scriptures and the rites of the mass; they were also usually married, and often
acquired a particular fondness for the sacramental wine used at the eucharistic
rite. Their failure to live up to the newly emerging standards of priestly behavior only highlighted the religious values of chastity and poverty.

It should not be surprising that devout Christians at the time, dissatisfied
with the failures of the local clergy but inspired by the ideals of apostolic
purity and simplicity, and in the face of broader social transformations, sought
an alternative religious life. The conditions they faced led to the outbreak of
heresy in a number of places in western Europe during the closing years of
the tenth century and the opening decades of the eleventh. In the generations

to come, the number of heretics and centers of heresy would increase expo-
nentially. But that should in no way diminish these relatively few episodes
of heresy around the turn of the millennium, especially since there had been
almost no outbreaks over the previous five centuries. Nor should this number
of episodes, which is smaller than the figures for the twelfth century, mini-
mize the seriousness of the matter for eleventh-century churchmen. In fact,
the response of the Church leaders was dramatic: it included the first officially sanctioned execution for heresy since antiquity. Indeed, according to
one account written in the mid-eleventh century, heretics who appeared across
Italy and Sardinia were hunted down and killed by the Catholics, and another
account records that the local populace gave them a choice between forsaking
heresy and being killed.

The harsh response from Church and state leaders, and even from the
average layperson, to the appearance of heresy was the result of their belief that
this was a widespread movement, inspired by the devil to destroy the Church.
The breadth of the movement is open to much modern debate, but at the close
of the tenth and opening of the eleventh century heretics emerged at various
points of western Europe, and at times their connections to other epicenters
of heresy were clear. The earliest of such outbreaks, which took place in 970,
is that of Vilgard of Ravenna, who was overly devoted to the great Roman
poet Virgil and other classical writers and taught many things contrary to the
faith, according to one contemporary author. It was said that many others in
Italy, Sardinia, and Spain were infected by his heresy and were exterminated by
orthodox Christians. Vilgard was followed by the peasant Leutard of Vertus, in
northeastern France, who spoke out against the Church in the year 1000. After
a swarm of bees had entered his body and instructed him on various matters,
Leutard returned home, put away his wife, and then destroyed the crucifix
at the local church and urged the people not to pay the church tithe. He was
denounced by the local bishop, and, overwhelmed by the learning and authority
of the bishop, he committed suicide by throwing himself into a well (an anti-
social act which parallels the false accusations against Jews of poisoning wells
later in the Middle Ages).

As Ademar of Chabannes noted, heretics who denied the teachings of the
Church appeared in Aquitaine in 1018, and most likely continued to operate
in that area throughout the 1020s, and possibly into the 1030s. The powerful

bishop of Arras-Cambrai in northern France, Gérard, discovered such a sect in his diocese in 1025 – a sect which, among other things, denied baptism and legitimate marriage and accepted only the books of the New Testament. The heretics of Arras returned to the fold upon receiving the benefit of an extremely long sermon by Gérard, in which he denounced their errors and defended the orthodox faith. They may well have been persuaded to re-convert also as a result of their three-day prison stay, in which they were quite possibly tortured, combined with the stately magnificence in which the bishop gave his sermon. Whatever the reason, the heretics signed a confession of the faith with a simple X, accepting the teachings of Gérard.

The episode at Arras is important, among other things, because it revealed connections between heretics in northern Europe and elsewhere. Gérard himself wrote a letter chastising a fellow bishop in Chalons for allowing heresy to fester, and the group Gérard discovered claimed to be followers of a certain Gundolfo, a missionary heretic from Italy. In some ways the likelihood that heresy percolated from Italy is confirmed by the discovery of heresy in Monforte, near Turin, in 1028 and by the increasing number of trade contacts between northern and southern Europe. Heresy also appeared at Périgord in the 1020s, at Toulouse in 1022, and at Goslar in Germany in 1051. At Monforte the heretics were killed in a popular rising and at Goslar, having identified themselves by refusing to kill a chicken, they were hanged at the order of Emperor Henry III (ruled 1039–56). The emergence of heresy was clearly seen as a serious threat by the orthodox Church and its supporters.

The number of outbreaks of such episodes and the degree to which the various sects rejected the teachings of the Church indicate the extent of people's dissatisfaction with the state of the Church in western Europe; on the other hand, the attention paid to these heretics throughout western Europe reveals that Church leaders of the time regarded heresy with utmost seriousness.

In 1022 a sect of heretics was discovered at Orléans, which sent a tremor through the ecclesiastical establishment. The group itself, according to a contemporary account, may have been in existence for several years before it was exposed. This outbreak of heresy, which involved, according to the various chroniclers of the event, from ten to fourteen of the most pious and holy men and women of the region, was such a profound shock to 'orthodox' Christians that the authorities condemned its leaders, Stephen and Lisois, and their followers to death. Unlike most of the other occurrences of religious dissent in the first half of the eleventh century, which had only one commentator or at most two, the heresy of Stephen and Lisois at Orléans was recorded by no fewer than five independent contemporary and near-contemporary witnesses. The heresy at Orléans attracted the attention of contemporaries for several reasons, including the high rank and status of its members and their tragic end at the stake. Moreover, Stephen and Lisois taught doctrines which, as some modern commentators have suggested, echoed the teachings of Bogomil, and one contemporary described them as Manichaeans, suggesting that they were dualist Christians like the Bogomils. These heretical leaders also advocated many of the important themes that would characterize the popular heresies of the future, but at the same time their group comprised a clerical elite which in some ways foreshadowed the academic heresies of the later Middle Ages. Their heresy also involved the highest level of ecclesiastical politics, and their condemnation for erroneous belief was, in part, the result of their being on the losing side in this struggle. In this way Stephen and Lisois anticipated later religious innovators who found themselves on the wrong side in matters of ecclesiastical politics and organization and, like Valdès and John Wyclif, were declared heretics.

The heresy, according to Ademar, emerged as the result of the preaching of a rustic from Périgord, who carried with him a powder made from the ashes of children; anyone who ingested this powder was irrevocably turned into a Manichaean, rejected Jesus Christ, and 'practiced abominations and crimes of which it is shameful even to speak.'[6] Ademar's accusation foreshadows those brought against 'witches' in the early modern period. These were supposed to perform black masses and to worship the devil; but the partaking of the powder is clearly an inversion of the rite of the Eucharist, and it is similar to the alleged rituals of those 'witches.' Ademar not only accused the sect of indulging in the perversion of the eucharistic rite; he also claimed that they adored the devil in the form of an Ethiopian, or angel of light.

Although Ademar posited a diabolical origin for the sect at Orléans, the heresy originated in a circle of elite clerics, who had connections to powerful Church leaders and were in touch with some of the most important cultural trends of the day. The heretics at Orléans were men and women in the religious orders, esteemed for the piety of their lives, and they were led by the canons Stephen and Lisois. These two were especially well connected at the highest levels of religious and political society, even to the extent that they ministered spiritually to the queen of France. Despite the apparent respectability of the group and its leaders, the heretics raised enough suspicion to make themselves 'infiltrated' by the knight Arefast. It was this knight who exposed the group and helped to bring about their fiery demise.

The tale of Arefast and Stephen and Lisois was told by Paul of St. Pere de Chartres, a monk of the community who celebrated the memory of the former knight and benefactor of his monastery. This account was recorded some sixty years after the event but is regarded as reliable by many, who believe it was based on an oral history handed down over the years, possibly from Arefast himself.[7] According to Paul, the heresy was discovered by Arefast, a vassal of Duke Richard II of Normandy (ruled 996–1026/27), after his own chaplain, Heribert, returned from Orléans having been instructed by Stephen and Lisois and converted to their beliefs. Upon learning of the heresy, Arefast turned to his lord, Richard, and informed him of the group at Orléans. The duke, in turn, reported the matter to the king of France, Robert the Pious (c.970–1031), who ordered Arefast to go to Orléans, so that the error would be driven from the kingdom. Accepting this command from the king, Arefast first traveled to Chartres, where he hoped to get advice from the famed Bishop Fulbert (c.960–1028); but Fulbert had gone to Rome to pray. In place of Fulbert, Arefast found assistance from one of the clerics of Chartres, Everard, and was advised to prepare himself to do battle against the heretics by going to mass every morning, praying, and taking the Eucharist. Everard also told Arefast to protect himself with the sign of the cross; thus fortified he should go to the heretics, assume the role of a willing disciple, and learn all he could about their teachings.

Prepared in this way, Arefast approached the group led by Stephen and Lisois on the pretense that he wished to learn things from them about the faith. At first he was taught stories from the holy scriptures, and, when he seemed to submit to their teachings, he was told that he would be introduced to the higher teachings of the sect. They said that they would treat him like

a tree of the forest, which, when transplanted into a garden, is amply supplied with water until it is well rooted in the soil. It is then pruned of thorns and superfluous branches so that, after it is cut off near the ground with a hoe, it may be grafted with better cutting, which later will bear sweet fruit.

So you, in like manner, being transferred from the evil world into our holy companionship, will be well supplied with the water of wisdom until you are instructed and are strong enough to be shorn of thorns of evil by the sword of the Word of God, and when we have driven absurd teachings from the shelter of your heart, you can receive with purity of mind our teaching bestowed by the Holy Spirit.[8]

The heretics thus promised to bring Arefast gradually to the truth as they understood it, and to reveal the wisdom of the Holy Spirit to him. Revelation was central to the sect of Stephen and Lisois. Their followers were to receive a special gnosis: truth granted by the Holy Spirit itself. In other words, the heretics offered Arefast a special connection with God, and also the true understanding of God's word instead of the errors and rituals of the official Church.

Having been introduced to the basic elements of their belief, Arefast was taken further and led to higher teachings. The new faith rejected many basic doctrines of the 'orthodox' Church, several of which had also been repudiated by the Bogomils. The heretics of Orléans proposed a Docetist Christology. Christ, they told Arefast, was not born of the Virgin Mary; he did not suffer and die on the cross and did not rise from the dead in the flesh. Baptism did not cleanse the soul of sin and the sacrament of the Eucharist was worthless. Stephen and Lisois rejected the martyrs and confessors and denied the validity of all the teachings of the Church.

This denial prompted Arefast to ask how anyone could obtain salvation. The heretics responded that his eyes had been opened to the true faith by their instruction, and he would be granted further insights by the imposition of the hands. This rite would fill him with the Holy Spirit, who would teach him 'the profundity of divine excellence of all the Scriptures.'[9] Once this had happened, he would receive heavenly visions and be at one with God. The practice of the laying on of the hands, it should be noted, was reminiscent of the Bogomils' initiation and foreshadowed a similar ritual performed by the Cathars in the twelfth century. This was a rite in which the perfect literally placed his hands on the initiate, by way of conferring the powers of the Holy Spirit on to him. But it also recalled a rite of the Apostles, who were identified as the source and inspiration of all Christian belief and practice, be it orthodox or heterodox, throughout the Middle Ages.

Imposition of the hands and the secret initiation were at the center of the teachings of Stephen and Lisois, and Paul describes yet another new element in the process of initiation. The group would come together at night in a designated place, each member carrying a candle and chanting the names of demons. Upon the arrival of a demon, they would extinguish the candles, and each of them would grab the nearest woman and lie with her, even if she were a relative or a nun. Children born of these illicit unions would be burned, and the ashes were saved and venerated by the members of the sect. Anyone who ingested such ashes would become a permanent member.[10] Although it is most unlikely that the heretics indulged in the rites described by Paul (especially when it is recalled that the pagan Romans made the same allegations about the early Christians), the author of the account felt it necessary to include an incrimination of this kind, just as Ademar had done in regard to the same heretics, and just as the inquisitors and the chroniclers of later heresy would demonize the heretics they faced. In this way he managed to demonstrate the evil nature of the heretics led by Stephen and Lisois and to show that their true father was the devil. Their 'secret' sinful ways were thereby made to appear in sharper contrast to their apparent religious piety and chaste lifestyle – merely a front designed to capture simple souls and enroll them to serve the devil.

Despite the unlikelihood of the existence of such peculiar nocturnal rites, the heretics at Orléans clearly revealed a unique understanding of the faith, which ran counter to much of the orthodox teaching. Arefast had uncovered their false doctrine as he intended, and only awaited the opportune moment to expose them for the heretics they were. This opportunity arose at Christmas in 1022, when King Robert and Queen Constance arrived in Orléans, at Arefast's request, with several leading bishops, to join in uncovering the heresy. Upon their arrival, Arefast had arranged matters so that he and the heretics would be brought before the royal couple and the bishops in their attendance. Dragged before the council in chains, Arefast revealed his true identity and explained his secret mission to those in assembly. He then described his experience with the heretics and revealed their doctrines, including their Docetist Christology, repudiation of the Church's teachings, and denial of the sacraments.

Demurring at first, Stephen and Lisois eventually stepped forward as leaders of the group, to confirm that Arefast had explained their teachings correctly.

Their announcement, no doubt, shocked the royal couple and the bishops, since Lisois was a canon of the cathedral of the Holy Cross of Orléans, deeply loved by the king, and Stephen another respected canon, confessor to the queen herself. Their learning and piety, which may have tapped into the monastic spirituality that was becoming popular at the time, surely contributed to their heterodox understanding of the faith, and their status allowed them to develop their teachings without fear of persecution by other clerics.

Stephen and Lisois were further interrogated by the bishops in attendance. Having admitted that they did, in fact, teach the doctrines that Arefast attributed to them, they discussed their beliefs under further questioning from the royal couple's bishops. In this way, along with the more spiritual or Gnostic teachings they had already revealed to Arefast, they provided what some have considered to be a rationalist approach to the faith. When asked about the virgin birth, death, and resurrection of Christ, they declared: 'We were not there and we cannot believe that to be true.'[11] Although not providing an explanation for the Docetist Christology imparted to Arefast, Stephen and Lisois offered a defense of their rejection of official Church teachings and declared that they would not accept matters of faith on the authority of the Church, preferring their own inspired interpretation. When asked why they did not believe that Jesus Christ was born of the Virgin Mary by the power of the Holy Spirit, they responded: 'What nature denies is always out of harmony with the Creator.' In this way Stephen and Lisois asserted their unorthodox approach to matters of faith and provided a more rationalistic and individualistic approach to the scriptures and religious belief in general.

The most dramatic moment of the interrogation came when the two were asked whether they believed that God the Father created everything through the Son. Their reply provides great insight into the nature not only of the teachings of Stephen and Lisois, but also of heresy in the early eleventh century in general:

> You may spin stories in that way to those who have earthly wisdom and believe the fictions of carnal men, scribbled on animal skins. To us, however, who have the law written upon our heart by the Holy Spirit (and we recognize nothing but what we have learned from God, Creator of all), in vain you spin your superfluities and things inconsistent with the Divinity.[12]

This pronouncement made before a royal and episcopal gathering – a pronouncement which may have led one contemporary chronicler to suggest that the heretics believed in the eternity of the universe – confirmed the illuminationist or Gnostic nature of the sect, which Paul had revealed earlier in his account. Stephen and Lisois defiantly rejected the traditional teachings of the Church and its understanding of scripture. Although scorning the 'fictions … scribbled on animal skins,' they most likely did not repudiate the Bible itself, but rather what they saw as the flawed understanding of it by the official Church. Theirs was a more spiritual or mystical reading of the scripture; it was, as the Austrian historian Heinrich Fichtenau explained, a Pentecostal reading, which placed emphasis on the action of the Holy Spirit.[13] The true understanding of the faith came to those who received it from the Holy Spirit through the imposition of the hands, and not from the teachings or materialistic sacraments of the Church. Stephen and Lisois stood at the head of a spiritual elite which, they believed, had established a special connection with God.

Having revealed themselves and their beliefs fully to the council, Stephen and Lisois insisted that the meeting be brought to an end. They called on the king and bishops to do with them as they wished, declaring: 'For we shall see our King, reigning in heaven, Who will raise us in heavenly joys to everlasting triumphs at His right hand.'[14] Openly expressing their unorthodox teachings, Stephen and Lisois and their followers were recognized as heretics and were condemned by the king and his council. They were then clothed in the dress of their orders and deposed from their clerical offices. They were driven out of the assembly hall, care having been taken to ensure that the enraged multitude would not harm them, and Queen Constance struck out the eye of Stephen, her former confessor, with her staff, to display her displeasure and to disassociate herself from him. The entire group, with the exception of one cleric and one nun, who recanted their errors, were burned at the stake: this was the first recorded execution for heresy since ancient times. According to Ademar, the heretics 'showed no fear of the fire, predicted that they would emerge unscathed from the flames, and laughed as they were bound to the pyre.'[15] To complete the destruction of the sect at Orléans, the body of the cantor Theodatus, who had died three years earlier, was exhumed and left exposed. Although he appeared to be most pious during his lifetime, it was discovered that he, too, had been a heretic and should have been punished for his religious dissent.

Despite the very real and deeply religious convictions of Stephen and Lisois, the violent suppression of the heresy at Orléans by the king and queen of France has led R. H. Bautier to argue that religion had very little to do with the affair.[16] Stephen and Lisois appear to him not so much as the leaders of a new and dangerous religious sect but as the losers in a battle over ecclesiastical and royal politics which involved the royal couple and various nobles and bishops in northern France. It was this political struggle that formed the backdrop to the events involving Stephen and Lisois in 1022.

The city of Orléans itself was a great intellectual center and the focus of a power struggle between the king and the count of Blois, Eudes II. Competition for control over Orléans involved an appointment to the office of bishop, and candidates on the side of both Count Eudes and King Robert stood to ascend to the episcopal throne. Robert asserted his authority in order to make the appointment; this act was met by opposition from Fulbert of Chartres, who refused to consecrate Robert's candidate, Thierry. In 1022, Thierry was forced from office and eventually went to Rome. The council was held and the heresy, which had developed under Thierry's watch, was revealed in Thierry's absence, after Arefast had turned for help to Duke Richard and Fulbert, allies of Count Eudes and of his episcopal candidate. The leaders of the heresy, Stephen and Lisois, were closely associated with the king and queen and, indirectly, to the king's now departed candidate to the bishopric. And it was this close connection with the perpetrators of heresy that undermined the king's authority in Orléans. His condemnation of Stephen, Lisois, and their followers may well have resulted from the determination to emphasize his own religious orthodoxy and rightful claim to the throne. Bautier's analysis is a useful reminder of the importance of ecclesiastical politics in the history of heresy – that is, in deciding what counts as such. In the future, many, including members of the Franciscan order and Jan Hus, would be declared heretics for reasons that had to do with ecclesiastical politics as much as they had to do with genuine issues of belief.

Yet, even if Stephen and Lisois were indeed victims of power politics, their denunciation as heretics would have carried little weight, had there not been a real fear of religious dissent in the early eleventh century and had they themselves not held suspect beliefs. Their refusal to accept correction at the council of Orléans clearly put them outside the bounds of the faithful and marked them as heretics, just as the refusal to accept Church authority would mark later religious leaders as heretical. As Arefast revealed in his dramatic speech before the king and queen, Stephen and Lisois led a group that rejected Church doctrine on nearly every topic and, in many ways, foreshadowed the teachings of twelfth-century heretics. Their devotion to the scriptures in the way they understood them, as well as their Docetism, heralded the beliefs of Valdes on the one hand, of the Cathars on the other. Often described as an elitist sect, Stephen and Lisois surely accepted the call to spread their beliefs as all Christians should. Their acceptance of Arefast, and of Heribert before him, as disciples demonstrates the missionary zeal of the group, which had already begun to spread its beliefs from a clerical elite to the laity by the time of its destruction at royal order.

Despite being condemned as heretics by King Robert and the bishops, Stephen and Lisois and their followers very clearly represented an important development of the Church in the early eleventh century. Their understanding of the scriptures may have cast them beyond the pale of what was considered 'orthodox' at the time, but the importance they placed on the written word, and on the text itself, reflects the growing importance of literacy.[17] Indeed, the written word had begun to acquire a more exalted position in society as medieval civilization began to evolve away from a more strictly oral culture, and religious leaders, both orthodox and heterodox, adopted a new approach to the text of the scriptures. Even though many people were still unable to read Latin, they placed greater emphasis on the written word, and many were attracted to charismatic interpreters of it, like Stephen and Lisois. The group of those who could interpret scripture (or some other text) and the group of those who could not read Latin have been identified as 'textual communities' by the historian Brian Stock.[18] These 'communities' were bound together by a shared understanding of the text as interpreted by someone like Stephen and Lisois, or the Italian heresiarch Gundolfo in Arras, or orthodox figures such as Bernard of Clairvaux or Julian of Norwich. The gradual introduction of Arefast to the teachings of the group at Orléans and the unique interpretation of the scriptures adopted by this group provide insight into the ways such textual communities developed and functioned. The central role of the text is demonstrated not only by the evangelization of Arefast, but also by the declaration of Stephen and Lisois, before the king and his bishops, that the Holy Spirit had written the law on their hearts. Rejecting the Church's understanding of the scriptures, they believed they had received illumination from the Holy Spirit itself; that illumination allowed them to discover the true meaning of the scriptures, which subsequently they taught to the textual community that formed around them.

Brought to a fiery end, Stephen and Lisois nonetheless made an important mark on the history of medieval heresy; theirs was perhaps the most dramatic expression of religious dissent in the early eleventh century. Although distinct through their spiritual elitism, the teachings and organization of the sect reflected the religious and cultural developments of their times and contained the elements of many later heresies. Docetism and the practice of the imposition of the hands reflected beliefs and practices both of earlier and of later heretics. The intermingling of ecclesiastical politics and religious beliefs also prefigured later developments, and the emphasis on personal religious choice was echoed by religious dissidents from the twelfth century to the sixteenth.

The importance of Stephen and Lisois's sect lies not so much in its immediate impact, which was admittedly limited, but in its manifestation of religious beliefs and practices that would gradually be adopted, at least in part, by the mainstream Church. In the generations that followed, 'orthodox' reformers would adopt some of the tenets of Stephen and Lisois and of other heretics from the early eleventh century and incorporate them into the mainstream teachings of the Church. And the failure to implement these reforms, or the conviction that the established Church did not go far enough in reforming itself, set the stage for the next great wave of heresy. This would emerge in the early twelfth century, to make a more dramatic and more lasting impact on medieval religion and society.

CHAPTER THREE

HENRY THE MONK AND THE EARLIER TWELFTH CENTURY

*t*he next great heresiarch is Henry the Monk, who not only inherited the mantle of earlier heretics but also adopted a more radical program of religious reform than that of the Gregorians. Also known as Henry of Lausanne or Henry of Le Mans, Henry had a profound impact on his time and was perhaps the most important of the leaders of heresy before the rise of the Cathars and the Waldensians at the end of the century.

When heresy had appeared around the turn of the first millennium, it elicited a dramatic response from the Church, as the tragic fate of the community at Orléans indicates. And it was not only the heretics at Orléans who faced the sword of persecution, but also those in Italy and those at Goslar where, as mentioned, in 1051 a number of heretics were executed. The views of these people – as we have seen in the case of Stephen and Lisois – offered a profound rejection of the teachings of the Church and introduced an alternative program of Christian belief and practice. Although the origins and extent of heresy at this time remain disputed, it is quite clear that its emergence after the year 1000 was a great blow to Church leaders. The appearance of heresy also revealed the increasing Christianization of the people of the Middle Ages and the seriousness with which they approached their faith. Heretical leaders like Stephen and Lisois provided for many a truer Christian faith, which rejected the inadequacies and excesses of contemporary belief and practice.

Even though the emergence of heresy marked a dramatic moment in the life of the Church and heretical leaders captured the attention and support of many among the laity throughout western Europe, heresy itself left the stage quietly by the middle of the eleventh century. While episodes had broken out repeatedly during its first decades, they ceased just as suddenly after the execution of the heretics at Goslar. Explanations for this abrupt disappearance vary. It could be that the foreign missionaries who, according to some scholars, were instrumental in the emergence of heresy, had ended their evangelical work in western Europe. Or the heretics may simply have gone underground for their own safety, as the Waldensians would in later times. Indeed, the very suppression of heresy by the Church, with its powerful allies among kings and nobles, may have put an end to the movement before it could blossom and last. At the same time, the institutional Church may have absorbed that movement by adopting many reforms the heretics had proposed – especially their focus on apostolic life and their emphasis on ritual and sexual purity.

Church leaders may not have consciously adopted the program of the heretics, but many ideas of the latter would be found in the Gregorian Reform movement, which took shape just as heretics reappeared in Latin Christendom. Itself part of a broader movement that stretched back to the tenth century and ultimately transformed much of medieval society – the heresies after the year 1000 could be regarded as the 'far left wing' of the broader reform movement – Gregorian Reform was an effort to restructure the religious life and the ecclesiastical organization of Christian Europe; it is most clearly identified with its most vigorous advocate, Pope Gregory VII (1073–85). Reformist ideas were first adopted by Pope Leo IX (1048–54) and promoted by each of his successors into the early twelfth century. The popes not only emphasized the necessity for improved moral and ethical behavior on the part of the clergy, they also redefined the nature of moral behavior, especially in regard to the matter of simony (the buying and selling of Church offices). The long tradition of exchanging money or gifts and swearing oaths of loyalty to secular overlords who often appointed the clergy to their positions came to a close as a result of the efforts of the Gregorians. Although this would create great difficulties between the clergy and the rulers of Europe, the new definition of simony would remain in place throughout the Middle Ages. Moreover, the Church hierarchy was reorganized so that the ultimate authority belonged to the pope, who claimed it as successor to the Apostle Peter, the first bishop of Rome; all the bishops, priests, abbots, and monks, together with all the Christians, were henceforth subordinate to the authority of the pope as the leader of Christendom.

The Gregorians' reforms also focused on the personal morality of the clergy. Clearly borrowing from the reforms of the early eleventh century and from the ideals of the heretics, the papal reformers stressed apostolic poverty for all the clergy. Indeed, one of the leading reformers, Peter Damian (c.1007–1072), embodied the ideals of apostolic poverty and was, in some ways, a forerunner of the wandering saints of the twelfth century. Of equal importance for moral reform was the emphasis on sexual purity, which was a means to distinguish the clergy from the laity and, especially, to establish a ritually pure clerical class.[1] Although rules existed against clerical marriage since antiquity, clergy of all ranks continued to marry and to sire. As late as the tenth century, there were examples of bishops fathering children, and lower-level priests appointed to the local church, themselves often simple peasants, had wives well into the eleventh century. One of the central goals of the Gregorians was to abolish this practice. Clerics could no longer marry or take mistresses; they were to live a life of celibacy and sexual purity. They would thus be able to approach the altar in a ritually clean state, the altar, that is, wherefrom they would preach and offer the sacrament of the Eucharist – the body and blood of Jesus Christ. Indeed, the awesome responsibility of handling the body of the Lord was an important justification for making clerical celibacy mandatory. The moral character of the priest at the altar became an important concern for the Gregorian reformers, as it had been for the reformers and heretics of the early eleventh century. Some of the advocates of papal reform even went so far as to declare that, if the priest was in a state of moral impurity, the sacraments he performed were not valid. This extreme position, which recalled the teachings of the Donatist heretics of late antiquity, was never adopted; but the movement as a whole focused on clerical morality and demanded improvement in the lives of all priests. The new code of purity, along with the new definition of simony, was confirmed by papal decree and by the decisions of the First Lateran Council in 1123.

Despite the profound and lasting impact of the Gregorian Reform on the history of Church and society in western Europe, its immediate effect in the early twelfth century was, at best, mixed, because of its successes and failures. The movement altered the internal structure of the Church and dramatically reshaped its relationship with secular power, but there were those who felt that reform failed to go far enough in purifying the Church and correcting the morals of its priests. The reform's focus on sacraments and clergy raised questions about the role of both in religious belief and practice, and the failure of clerics throughout Europe to adhere to the new regulations reinforced criticism of the Church. Among the critics were saintly figures like Robert of Arbrissel (c.1047–1116) whose personal example of piety and outspoken critiques of Church practices were equaled only by those of a new wave of heretics who challenged the teachings and authority of the established Church.

The new century opened in fact with numerous reports of religious dissent, heralding the beginning of an almost continuous stream of heresy, which lasted until the end of the Middle Ages. The earliest account, in the first decades, is that of Guibert of Nogent, who reported an outbreak in Soissons in which some have recognized evidence of Bogomil influence.[2] Not long after the appearance of that heresy, Tanchelm preached in Antwerp, denouncing the clergy and rejecting the sacraments. He married a statue of the Virgin Mary and his followers are reported to have venerated him as God; they are even said to have drunk his bathwater, just before his death at the hands of a priest in 1115. Toward the middle of the century, Eon d'Etoile preached heresy in Brittany, claiming that he was the Son of God, and attracted a number of followers from the peasantry before being imprisoned by the bishop. More representative of the heretics of the period, however, is Peter of Bruis in Provence, whose career lasted for some twenty years; he, too, has been seen as influenced by the Bogomils. He rejected baptism, church buildings, crucifixes, the Eucharist, and various good works. His protest was violent and his death, in 1139 or 1140, occurred when his enemies pushed him into a bonfire of crucifixes he had started.

Even within their brief periods of activity, the heretics of the first half of the twelfth century demonstrated significant dissatisfaction with the Church of the time. These heretics also reveal the influence that charismatic individuals such as these wandering preachers had on their contemporaries. Peter of Bruis in particular is noteworthy for his spell over those around him, and has been recognized as the ally and perhaps teacher of Henry the Monk. At the very least, in the words of the great abbot of Cluny, Peter the Venerable (c.1092–1156), Henry was the heir of Peter's wickedness. And it was Henry, more than Peter, who was seen as the great threat to the Church and attracted the attention of the greatest religious figure of the age, Bernard of Clairvaux (1090–1153).[3]

Henry's career, the longest among medieval heretics, can be broken down into three phases. The first started around 1116, when he first appeared as preacher of penitence and reform in the town of Le Mans and in the course of that year challenged the established social and religious order. The second phase started in 1135, when he reappeared in southern France, in the diocese of Arles, after an absence of some twenty years. Preaching heretical doctrines again, Henry was brought before the Council of Pisa in 1135; probably not long before that, he had engaged in debate with a monk named William, who left the most detailed record of Henry's teaching. The final phase began in 1139 and lasted until Henry's capture in 1145, when he was pursued by Bernard of Clairvaux. By that time he had spread his teachings in Languedoc, a region that would later become one of the great centers of heresy.

Henry first preached in the town of Le Mans, possibly having come from Lausanne in modern Switzerland; the probability is high that he was born in France or a French-speaking territory of the Empire. Little else is known of his origins or background, and there is much uncertainty about his status in life. He may have been a priest; most likely he became a monk in the mid-1130s or earlier, to judge by the comments of his rivals. Bernard of Clairvaux, the great Cistercian abbot, declared that Henry was learned and literate, but he may have acquired what learning he had later in life. Whatever his exact social status, Henry was a force to be reckoned with. He was one of many wandering preachers, who, like Robert of Arbrissel, marched 'barefoot through the crowds, having cast off the habit of a regular (e.g. a monk), his flesh covered by a hair shirt, wearing a thin and torn cloak, bare-legged, beard tangled … only a club was missing from the outfit of a lunatic.'[4] Like Robert, Henry was a charismatic figure and a wandering holy man possessed of great rhetorical skills. Indeed, even Henry's rivals remarked on his apparent holiness, which was allegedly a false front, and on his preaching ability, of which one contemporary noted that by 'his speech even a heart of stone could be moved to repentance.'[5]

It was his appearance and reputation as a reform-minded and inspirational preacher that recommended Henry to Hildebert of Lavardin, bishop of Le Mans

(1109–25) and later archbishop of Tours (1125–33), when the future heretic first appeared in his diocese in 1116. Hildebert himself was a most pious shepherd of his flock and a devoted advocate of the ideals of the Gregorian Reform movement, as well as the founder of a number of new religious houses and patron of Robert of Arbrissel. The bishop was also one of the early medieval humanists and a talented poet, and thus represented the best of twelfth-century religious and intellectual life. At the time of Henry's arrival, Bishop Hildebert was preparing to make a trip to Rome and expected little more than penitential preaching from Henry, whom he welcomed with courtesy and friendliness. Before departing for Rome, Hildebert instructed the clergy to allow Henry free entry into the city and granted him the license to preach.

According to the chronicler of Le Mans, the good intentions of the bishop were betrayed by 'the deceits of a Trojan horse,' because Henry hid 'the madness of a ravening wolf under sheep's clothing.'[6] Indeed, the chronicler depicts Henry as a false prophet and a 'pseudohermit.' He notes that Henry appeared 'hair cropped, beard untrimmed, tall of stature, quick of pace ... barefoot as the winter raged; easy of address, awe-inspiring voice, young in years, scornful of ornate dress.' Henry had a reputation for holiness and wisdom according to the chronicler, and seemed to set an example for all by his pious and celibate lifestyle. He seemed like one of the prophets and was able to 'declare the sins of mortal men which they hid from others.'[7] But all this was a clever ruse perpetrated by the wandering preacher, of whom the chronicler asserts that he enjoyed the pleasures of women and adolescent boys: they attended him and 'caressed his feet, his buttocks, his groin, with tender hands.'[8] But the very same allegations were made even against orthodox wandering preachers, and, where heretics are concerned, they were among the most commonplace accusations throughout the Middle Ages.

For all these allegations, it is most likely that Henry patterned his life after Jesus and the Apostles, if his entry into Le Mans and his pious behavior, which even the chronicler was forced to recognize, are anything to go by. Arriving on Ash Wednesday, Henry, just as Jesus had done on his entry to Jerusalem, sent two disciples ahead of him, to meet the bishop. Henry's followers appeared as penitents; each one bore a staff upon which a cross was fastened. Coming after them, and in the wake of the bishop's departure for Rome, Henry began preaching and attracted large and enthusiastic crowds. He spoke out against the abuses and excesses of the clergy, especially the more privileged and wealthy. His sermons were welcomed by the people of Le Mans, who had, at best, uneasy relations with the higher clergy of the town. Even some members of the clergy, mainly those in lower orders or those without land and wealth, supported Henry and looked up to him, as if he were an oracle. Although the chronicler of Le Mans left no account of Henry's exact preaching, it is clear that he spread a harshly anticlerical message, which provoked the people of Le Mans to violence against the ministers of the Church. At the very least, Henry most probably denounced their corruption; he may also have attacked the sacraments and the increasingly elaborate buildings of the Church. His sermons, which sounded as if 'a legion of demons were all making their noise in one blast through his mouth,'[9] exposed the hypocrisy of the clergy of Le Mans. His own example of moral purity and apostolic piety stood as an example which put the churchmen to shame. Henry's assault on the failings of Church and clergy alike was no doubt rooted in his own understanding of the Gospels and of the life of Jesus.

Despite the message of peace that Jesus himself taught, Henry's own preaching led to attacks on the clergy: they would surely have been killed or seriously harmed, had not the local count protected them from violence. In turn, some of the clergy sought to debate with Henry. Led by William Drink-No-Water – a name suggestive of less than ideal behavior – the clergy tried to approach Henry, but they were assaulted and pushed down into the mud and filth of the streets. Escaping with their lives thanks to the count, members of the clergy then wrote a letter to Henry, calling on him to stop his preaching. The letter, which was read out to Henry upon his refusal to accept it, declared that he had been welcomed to the city in a spirit of brotherly love, in the hope that he would spread the word of God. But instead of peace, the letter continued, Henry sowed discord, called the clergy heretics, and preached false words that denied the truth of the Catholic faith. Listening to the message, Henry shook his head and responded to each sentence by saying: 'You lie.'[10]

Rather than obey the demands of the clergy of Le Mans, Henry continued to preach and instituted his most dramatic reform so far. He proclaimed, as the chronicler noted, that 'women who had lived unchastely should, all unclothed, burn their garments, together with their hair, in the sight of everyone; that no one in the future should receive gold or silver, property, or betrothal gifts with his wife, nor should she bring him a dowry, but the naked should marry the nude, the ailing the sick, the pauper the destitute.'[11] As with much else that he said, Henry's teaching on marriage struck a chord and inspired the people of Le Mans to follow his lead. At this point, the chronicler once again denigrates his efforts, asserting that Henry admired the features of the women who appeared before him and collected large sums of gold and silver. Despite these allegations, it remains true that Henry was seeking to improve his followers' lot; at his request, the young men of Le Mans took in marriage those of the city's prostitutes who had given up their trade. Henry, to help the former women of the streets, gave each of them some money to buy new clothes – although not enough to make up for what they had lost, according to the chronicler.

Even if, as the chronicler joyfully points out, Henry's efforts failed, in that many prostitutes returned to their former profession and their husbands found new wives or mistresses, thereby committing adultery, attempts such as his, to rescue fallen women from a life of misery just as Robert of Arbrissel had done, would be deemed later on by Pope Innocent III (1198–1216) to be a most praiseworthy kind of work. Henry's new doctrine, however, was designed not only as pious good work but also as a challenge to new Church teachings on marriage. In many ways carrying on Gregorian ideals of piety and religious life, Henry repudiated the Church's recent encroachment on the rite of marriage; the Church had come to claim the authority to consecrate this bond, and designated marriage as one of its sacraments. The Church had also implemented new rules of consanguinity which could be particularly burdensome, and society as a whole had come to accept the tradition of dowry. In his call for young men to marry prostitutes and to abandon various social conventions, Henry rejected both the claims of the Church and the practice of dowry. For him, marriage was not a sacrament to be controlled by the Church; it was the simple exchange of a promise of love and faithfulness between two willing partners. Marriage was a matter of consent, not the result of priestly consecration.

Henry implemented a program in Le Mans which mixed penitence and moral reform and was rooted in the Gospels, also drawing on some of the ideals of the Gregorian movement. But in spite of his own personal example and rhetorical skill, Henry's dominant place in the city would not last long. Bishop Hildebert would soon return from Rome and confront the preacher he had held in such esteem before going to the papal city. The 'welcome' which greeted the bishop upon his return only increased his desire to confront Henry: the people of the city rejected his blessing, declaring: 'We want no knowledge of your ways! We don't want your blessing! Bless filth! Consecrate filth! We have a father, we have a pontiff, we have an advocate who surpasses your authority; he exceeds you in probity and knowledge.'[12] And they went on to denounce the clergy and to exalt Henry and his preaching in front of the bishop.

Hildebert, the chronicler tells us, bore all this patiently, expecting to debate matters with Henry. His position was strengthened when part of the city burned in a fire, which many of the people of Le Mans interpreted as God's judgment against them for following a heretic. In a public debate, Hildebert rapidly undermined Henry's support by unveiling the ignorance and lack of training of a popular preacher. So the bishop asked Henry by what special right he had come to take up his vocation; but Henry did not know the meaning of the word 'vocation.' He then asked the heretic what office he possessed, to which Henry responded that he was a deacon. The bishop went on to ask if Henry had attended mass, and, when Henry responded that he had not, he proposed that they should sing the morning hymns together. Henry was forced to admit that he did not know the order of the mass. Then, to demonstrate his rival's inadequacy even further, the bishop sang the hymns to the Mother of God. Thus Henry was exposed by the bishop, who consequently banished the heretic from the city of Le Mans. But, although much of his support had disappeared, Henry's pious example, his critique of the clergy, and his repudiation of the new definition of marriage continued to influence the people of Le Mans. He himself would emerge once again to indict the failures of the Church.

Little was heard from Henry for some twenty years to follow, until he was brought before Pope Innocent II (1130–43) and the Council of Pisa (1135); but it is likely that he was not completely inactive during this intervening period. Leaving Le Mans probably with a small band of followers, including two priests, Henry moved south and was found preaching in the towns of Bordeaux and Poitiers. Along the way, the simple anticlericalism he taught at Le Mans developed into a more intense rejection of the Church, its clergy, and its teachings. According to the chronicler of Le Mans, Henry, the 'pseudohermit,' began to spread his poison in nearby regions and 'propounded a perverted dogma which a faithful Christian ought neither recapitulate nor hear.'[13] As a result of his activity in the diocese, Henry attracted the attention of Bernard Guarin, archbishop of Arles from 1129 to 1138, who seized the wandering preacher and brought him to Pisa. Henry was condemned as a heretic at the Council, where he most likely met Bernard of Clairvaux and Peter the Venerable, his staunchest opponents, leaders, respectively, of the Cistercian and Cluniac monastic orders and great defenders of the Church against heresy. Overawed by the Council and its dignitaries, Henry abjured all the heretical doctrines he preached and was handed over to Bernard. The abbot of Clairvaux then gave Henry letters of introduction to the Cistercian monastery there, so that he could become a monk at Clairvaux. It is unlikely, however, that Henry ever reached Clairvaux; the chronicler of Le Mans explains that Henry left the province, began to preach heresy again, and made such a great impact that Christians hardly attended mass any longer and refused 'offerings to the priests, first fruits, tithes, visitation of the sick, and the usual reverences.'[14]

The chronicler of Le Mans gives a general sense of the nature of Henry's teachings, but the full extent of his dissent from the established Church became known only with the discovery, in the middle of the twentieth century, of a tract detailing a debate between Henry and a certain Monk William. The debate occurred most probably when Henry was coming to the attention of the archbishop of Arles; it is generally thought to have been held between 1133 and 1135. Although the name of the Catholic monk involved is not known with any certainty, he may have been William of Saint-Thierry (1085–1148), companion of Bernard of Clairvaux, and author of numerous works of theology and of polemical writings against the theologians Peter Abelard (1079–1142) and Gilbert de la Porrée (1076–1154). For all the uncertainty of its attribution, the treatise remains an important source for understanding Henry's teachings and the Catholic reaction to this wandering preacher.

The treatise was clearly composed as a warning about the danger Henry posed to the established Church. In his introduction, William addresses an unnamed ecclesiastical dignitary, stating that 'by many arguments and proofs he [Henry] has been shown to be a heretic,' and advises that Henry be kept 'away from the limits of your church.'[15] William's concern to raise the alarm against Henry is reinforced in his account of the debate at a point where he refers to his opponent as a leper and insists that he, William, 'must shout unceasingly that you are a leper, a heretic and unclean, and must live outside the camp, that is to say outside the church.'[16] Along with his warning, William included extensive discussions of the Catholic faith. He felt it necessary not only to present Henry's ideas but also to provide a thorough defense of Catholic doctrine that would further demonstrate the error of Henry's ways. Aware of his anticlericalism and rejection of certain key points concerning the intermediary role of the Church and its ministers, William took great pains to defend both the clergy and the Catholic understanding of the sacraments. It should be noted, however, that at no point does William impute to Henry the rejection of Christian belief on the core matters of the person of Jesus, the godhead, or the Virgin Mary. This distinguishes Henry from Bogomils and Cathars, bringing him closer to reformers like Robert of Arbrissel. No matter how Henry's teachings are to be characterized, William's account of the debate demonstrates what a serious threat Church leaders took Henry to be. It also reveals the maturation of Henry's own ideas.

Henry's dissent was no doubt regarded as being all the more troubling in view of his source of inspiration. William opened discussion with a few questions. To whom does Henry owe obedience? Who commissioned him to preach? What scriptures does he follow? Henry's answers to these questions are indicative of the direction taken by his thought during the years which followed his appearance at Le Mans. He declared, namely, that he obeyed God and not man because all obedience is owed to God; that he was sent by Jesus Christ; and that he honored his scriptural command 'Go, teach ye all nations' (Matthew 28: 19). Furthermore, he indicated that it was Jesus's proclamation 'Thou shalt love thy neighbour as thyself' (Matthew 19: 19) that was a source of inspiration for him. Indeed, in answer to the question about the scriptures, Henry asserted his devotion to the Gospels: 'I accept the Scriptures of the New Testament, by which I verify and corroborate the aforesaid statements.'[17] Despite the vehemence of his repudiation of the Church, he was not willing to reject all tradition out of hand; he recognized the value of the writings of St. Augustine of Hippo and other Church Fathers even though he claimed that their ideas were not essential to salvation. In this way he clearly rooted himself in the evangelical tradition which the Church itself had claimed as its own, and he attempted to usurp the latter's right of interpreting the New Testament and Gospel of Christ. It may be suggested that Henry desired not so much the destruction of the established Church as the restoration of its pristine purity as originally intended.

His understanding of the Gospels, however, led him both to deny certain of the medieval Church's claims to an intermediary role between God and the believer and to reject much of what Church leaders thought to be essential to the faith. At the core of his teachings was a rejection of Catholic doctrine on the sacraments, even though he did not necessarily reject the sacraments themselves. His position on these matters, he claimed, was rooted in the truth of the scriptures; but the sacraments should not be administered without evangelical support. For this reason Henry challenged official doctrine on the sacrament of baptism. He rejected the practice of baptizing children with chrism and oil because, as William informs us, the renegade monk declared that there was no command in the Gospel to do so. Moreover, he appeared to be most skeptical of the practice of infant baptism, and he seemed to challenge Catholic doctrine on the matter of original sin. Quoting scripture again in support of his beliefs, Henry declared: 'It is a wicked thing to condemn a man for another person's sin, in accordance with the text, "The soul that sinneth, the same shall die"' (Ezekiel 18: 20). And again, 'The son shall not bear the iniquity of the father. Everyone shall bear his own burden' (see Ezekiel 18: 20 and Galatians 6: 5).[18] William accuses Henry of falling into the Pelagian heresy; and yet for Henry this is not a matter of following in the footsteps of this or that earlier heretic, but rather of following the scriptures themselves. Infant baptism is not justified in his eyes because the child has not yet reached the age of understanding and cannot freely accept the faith nor be held responsible for any sins that he or she has committed. In fact, according to some versions of the treatise, Henry argued not only that Christian children who died before the age of understanding would attain salvation but also that the children of Jews and Muslims who died before reaching the age of reason would be saved as well. Although somewhat radical in its particulars, especially in regard to Jewish and Muslim children, Henry's teachings on baptism were firmly rooted in the scriptures and reserved the practice of baptism for those able to understand the faith.

Henry's assault on the teachings of the Church concerning the sacraments extended beyond his critique of baptism, to include the rejection of Catholic doctrine on marriage. This developing doctrine had come to define the sacramental nature of marriage. Henry had already demonstrated his opposition to Catholicism on the subject when he preached in Le Mans. In his debate with William he offered further arguments against the Catholic views. For Henry, marriage needs no Church ceremony or religious rite; it does not have to be consecrated by a priest to be valid. Although rejecting the intermediary role of priest and Church, Henry recognized that marriage was a ceremony that bound two people together and stated that the agreement of the persons involved constituted legitimacy. Moreover, drawing from the scriptures, Henry argued that only fornication, or adultery in one version of the text, could dissolve a marriage. Thus Henry accepted the indissolubility of marriage as Jesus and the Church had taught it, but he denied that the Church had any place in establishing its validity.

William and Henry also debated the matter of penance and confession. Henry rejected the Catholic practice of the sacrament. William claimed in turn that it was necessary to have a mediator in order to achieve reconciliation and that, because Christ was a mediator and the priest stood in his place, confession to a priest was necessary. But Henry, drawing again from the Gospels, denied that confession to a priest was required. He argued that there is 'no Gospel command to go to a priest for penance, for the apostle James says, "Confess your sins to one another"' (James 5: 16).[19] Nonetheless, William's reply with an argument about the dangers of offering confession to peasants and to the illiterate suggests that Henry did not reject the practice of confession and penance completely; rather, he sought to return to what he was taking to be the practice of the primitive Church, as revealed in the passage from the letter of James. Indeed, rather than denying the value of confession and penance, Henry intended to restore the practice of the Apostles and to eliminate the intermediary role of the priest.

This elimination of the priest from the sacraments of baptism, marriage, and penance is also to be found in Henry's position on the sacrament of the Eucharist. As with confession, here too Henry maintained that 'Mass may be sung and Christ's body consecrated, provided anyone can be found worthy to do so.'[20] William denounces this position in most vehement terms, implying that Henry's view would make administration of the Eucharist impossible and therefore amounts to a rejection of the sacrament. But this was clearly not Henry's intent. He possessed none of the abhorrence of the material form of the eucharistic elements which the Cathars and other dualist heretics would exhibit, nor was he fundamentally opposed to the institution itself. His knowledge of the Gospels was too good for him to repudiate a practice which Christ himself had instituted – to reject it outright. Indeed, as William conceded, Henry advocated the administration of the sacrament by anyone worthy of doing so. Henry's criticism formed part of his larger critique of the clergy: it was not the sacrament itself, but those who administered it that were the problem. Henry, according to William, argued that the body of Christ 'cannot be consecrated by an unworthy minister.'[21] Although William accuses Henry of resembling the Arians – heretics in the early history of the Church – Henry was more akin to the Donatists, who deemed the sinful priests to be unworthy of the office – a position also advocated by some members of the Gregorian Reform movement. Far from rejecting the Eucharist, Henry intended to eliminate any form of corruption from the administration of the body and blood of Christ.

Writing off the role of the clergy in the sacrament of the Eucharist was part of Henry's broader criticism of priesthood. This constituted one of the centerpieces of his dissent against the Church already at Le Mans, but he seems to have elaborated on it by the time of the meeting with William. Indeed, in an assertion that reinforced his belief that the priesthood could no longer assume its intercessory role, Henry declared that 'Priests of today ... have not the power to bind or loose, for they are stripped of this power by having criminally sinned.'[22] Henry was no doubt disgusted with the behavior of the clergy of his day, which acquired wealth and power and extended the claims of the Church into ever new areas of jurisdiction. Not only did they make more and more exorbitant claims for themselves, but they were often corrupt and unworthy to stand in the place of Christ. Consequently, Henry pressed for the moral reformation of the clergy, intending them to live more truly apostolic lives, as he himself did. Although William does not quote Henry directly, he undertakes an extended defense of the various appurtenances of the bishop's office. It is most likely that Henry opposed the bishop's use of the ring, mitre, and pastoral staff as unnecessary displays of wealth and power, especially since there was no evangelical support for these things. This criticism was probably an extension of Henry's opposition to the growing worldliness and economic wealth of the priesthood. Indeed, Henry struck directly at the heart of the institutional Church as it had developed in the eleventh and twelfth centuries, by declaring that 'bishops and priests ought not to have benefices or wealth.'[23] There was none of this in the Gospels, and surely neither Jesus nor the Apostles pursued such worldly glories; in seeking them, the Church and its representatives had moved away from their call to live like Christ and to serve the poor and the weak. The pursuit of worldly wealth and power was not the proper 'obligation' of the Church and would lead to its corruption.

This rejection of clerical worldliness, which Henry saw as the root of corruption, also contributed to his denial of the need for church buildings. He declared that there was no need to build churches of stone or wood – a stunning assertion at a time when the first stirrings of the Gothic style in church-building were felt and magnificent Romanesque churches were still being built. It must be noted, however, that even Bernard of Clairvaux expressed horror at the grand style in which churches were being built, even though he did not go as far as Henry. Henry's rejection of churches of stone and wood emerged not only from his disdain for the excessive wealth and luxury of the clergy, but also from his reading of the Gospels. Jesus had declared, after all, that he would be among them whenever two or three gathered in his name; he did not stipulate that they had to be in a church or before an altar, but merely that they gathered together, in the purity of their hearts, to honor him. Henry felt it was not necessary to go to a church in order to pray; God would hear his children when they called on him wherever they were. Churches were just another external sign that had little to do with the faith as revealed in the scriptures and ran counter to Henry's understanding of the internalization of matters of faith.

Finally, William revealed one component of Henry's teaching which denied both the value of church-building – often viewed as a pious good work – and the intercessory role of the Church and its clergy. Henry asserted, namely, that 'No good work helps the dead, for as soon as men die they either are utterly damned or are saved.'[24] Henry seemed to be rejecting the doctrine of purgatory that was taking shape in the twelfth century and all the beliefs and practices associated with it. Indeed, William argued that 'certain sins are cancelled out in the next world by the gifts of friends and the prayers of the faithful,'[25] but Henry would have none of that. Contributing to the construction of a church, for Henry, would offer little to save a soul that failed to live according to the Gospels. Offering gifts to monks like William so that they might recite prayers for the living or dead would have little impact on the destiny of their souls. In this way, Henry once again undermined claims of the Church and clergy to act as mediators between God and humans.

In the debate with William, therefore, Henry's teachings, which first took shape during his appearance at Le Mans, emerged in their mature form. The simple and dramatic challenge, enunciated at Le Mans, to the behavior and authority of the clergy and to the Church's understanding of marriage evolved into a more elaborate rejection of the Church and its sacraments. Henry denied much of its traditional intercessory role, refused to accept Catholic teaching on the sacraments, and rejected the authority of the clergy, criticizing their integrity. But his program was not simply a destructive one; for he sought to create a new understanding of the faith, rooted firmly in the Gospels and the teachings of Jesus. He saw much of contemporary Church practice as an unnecessary elaboration of the original intention of its founder and envisioned instead a community of the faithful which was bound together in the faith by mutual confession and by the shared reception of baptism and of the Eucharist. Henry preached a faith which in his view was more fully in line with the Gospels – a faith based on the ideals of apostolic simplicity and individual moral responsibility, in imitation of Jesus and the Apostles.

Thus, by the time of the Council of Pisa in 1135, Henry's thought had achieved its mature form and made a profound impact on those who heard him. Hence his career was not at an end, although he was condemned as a heretic by the Council and confined to a monastery at its order. Once again, Henry would disappear from view only to resurface some years later in the Languedoc – a region to become notorious as a hotbed of heresy in the later twelfth and thirteenth centuries. Matters had become so serious at this point that a special commission was sent to Toulouse; this event foreshadowed a similar legation, involving Diego of Osma and St. Dominic, which would be sent to suppress the Cathars later in the century. This first commission included Henry's abbot, Bernard of Clairvaux, and the papal legate, Alberic of Ostia. It was sent to Languedoc in the summer of 1145, with the intention of finally putting an end to the long career of Henry the Monk.

By the time of Bernard's arrival, Henry had been preaching his fiery denunciations of the Church and its ministers and advocating his own understanding of an evangelical Christianity for some time since his condemnation in 1135. After leaving the Council at Pisa, Henry evidently refused to enter the monastery at Clairvaux and moved south, passing through Cahors and Périgeux before eventually arriving in the important town of Toulouse in the Languedoc, where he would find a receptive audience. His impact on the region was so profound that Abbot Bernard, writing to Count Alphonse of Toulouse to announce his imminent arrival in the Languedoc, declared that 'churches are without congregations, congregations are without priests, priests are without proper reverence, and finally, Christians are without Christ.'[26] Bernard denounces Henry as an apostate and a dog returned to his vomit; he condemns him further for his heretical teachings. Bernard's biographer and secretary, Geoffrey of Auxerre (died after 1188), confirms the abbot's account of Henry's teachings. Henry once again emerged as an opponent of the Church, 'irreverently disparaging the sacraments as well as the ministers of the Church.'[27] And both Bernard and Geoffrey agreed that Henry opposed Catholic baptism, prayers for the dead, pilgrimages, the invocation of the saints, the building of churches. As Geoffrey puts it, 'in a word, all the institutions of the Church were scorned' by Henry.[28]

Despite his apparent support in the region, Henry took flight upon hearing the news of Bernard's arrival. The great abbot was enthusiastically welcomed by the people of Toulouse. Bernard of Clairvaux preached in the areas where Henry's support had been strongest, in order to turn the people of the city back to the Catholic faith, so that heresy would no longer plague the region. Having reduced support for Henry in the Languedoc, Bernard returned to his monastery before his rival was captured, which happened sometime after his departure. Indeed, Henry's support melted away in the face of Bernard's preaching, combined with the effect of the heretic's own decision to flee. According to Geoffrey of Auxerre, even though Henry went into hiding, 'his ways were so obstructed and his paths so hedged that he was hardly safe anywhere afterward.'[29] Henry was finally captured, probably sometime in the autumn of 1145, by the bishop and his men and was placed in the bishop's prison, where he most probably died not long after.

Although Henry died in obscurity and only a lingering residue of his ideas may have survived, his long and dramatic career reveals a strong undercurrent of dissatisfaction with the Church and its representatives. The failures and successes of the Gregorian Reform movement were played out fully in Henry's career, and his indictment of the Church would echo in the coming generations. Even in his own time, Henry's repudiation of the Church resonated with those around him, as the episodes in Le Mans, Arles, and Toulouse indicate. Rejecting the various accretions that the Catholic Church had added to the basic practice of the faith over the centuries and especially in a few previous generations, Henry proposed a more pristine and pure expression of Christian belief and practice. Denying the way the sacraments were defined and administered, rejecting the establishment of marriage as a sacrament, and challenging the intermediary claims of the priesthood, Henry offered a viable Christian alternative to the doctrines of the established Church. In their most developed form, Henry's teachings further rejected the emerging doctrine of purgatory, the cult of the saints, and prayers for the dead. Throughout all of this, Henry remained a preacher of penitence, calling the laity and the clergy to lives of moral purity and condemning severely the corruption and worldliness of the churchmen. Henry's direct influence may not have survived his disappearance from the stage of history for long, but his call to moral reform, his denunciation of the excesses of the Church, and his rejection of central Catholic teaching would be echoed by the end of the century by new heretics responding to new social, cultural, and political conditions.

CHAPTER FOUR

VALDES OF LYONS
AND THE WALDENSES

lthough outbreaks of religious dissent of varying intensity had plagued the western Church periodically since the year 1000, the greatest and most sustained heretic movements occurred only in the second half of the twelfth century. The somewhat individual wandering heresiarchs of the earlier half gave way to founders of movements which outlasted their progenitors. Heresy became a more integral part of the social order and spread throughout all levels of society, including the peasantry, nobility, and the newly forming bourgeoisie. The rapid growth of heresy at the end of the twelfth century elicited an equally dramatic response from the Church. Just as the earliest heretics of the medieval West suffered persecution and death, so too did the heretics who emerged after 1150; but these religious dissidents would face a more organized and violent opposition. Two distinct strains of heresy took shape in the late twelfth century and somehow endured in the face of this intense persecution. While one of them, Catharism, would fade away by the fourteenth century, the other, Waldensianism, would survive the Middle Ages, remaining a living 'church' to this very day.

The origins of the Waldensian church, unlike those of the Cathar heresy, can be traced to a specific time and place: they are associated with the conversion of the merchant Valdes of Lyons, the variants of whose name include Waldes, Valdesius, Vaudès, and Peter Waldo (this last one remained popular until the late twentieth century). Pious legends among the Waldenses of the later Middle Ages traced the origins of the movement back to the apostolic age, which guaranteed the authenticity and integrity of their tradition. It was during the later Middle Ages, probably in the fourteenth century, that the addition of 'Peter' to the founder's name was made: this was surely intended to identify him with St. Peter the Apostle, to relate him to the primitive period of the Church, and to confirm the apostolic origins of the Waldenses. Other Waldenses maintained, however, that their church emerged later than the apostolic period, but still at an early moment in the history of the Church. Like other medieval heretics, also like the Protestant reformers of the sixteenth century and the modern critics of the Catholic Church in the twenty-first century, they identified the conversion of the Roman Emperor Constantine (ruled 305–37) as the pivotal moment in the history of the Church. The moral purity and spiritual purpose of the Church were lost when Pope Sylvester I (314–35) accepted from him the donation of authority over the western Roman Empire: Constantine had been cured of leprosy by Sylvester, then converted to Christianity, and he transformed the Church into a temporal power. This group of Waldenses claimed that Sylvester abandoned the long-standing poverty of the Church for worldly power and that only a small group retained the tradition of poverty; the Waldenses themselves were the heirs to the opponents of Sylvester's transformed Church. This account of the movement was recognized not only by the Waldenses but also by orthodox ecclesiastics, who wrote polemics attacking this story of Waldensian origins.

Despite the appeal of the Waldenses' version of their own origins, the birth of the heresy must be placed in the context of the profound social and religious transformations of the twelfth century. Indeed, Valdes's experience of conversion and the great attraction he felt for his new life – features of which in many ways prefigure the life of St. Francis of Assisi and his founding of the Franciscan order in the early thirteenth century – can be little understood without considering the broader changes in the Church and society of his day. Valdes not only tapped into the changing nature of spirituality but also reflected the new social and economic reality to which the Church had to respond.

The birth of the Waldensian movement was, in part, a reaction to these new conditions of the later twelfth century. In the earlier Middle Ages, both

Church and state had evolved in the rural-agrarian context which prevailed since the collapse of the urban world of the Roman Empire. Already in the eleventh century, however, and with greater force in the twelfth, European society changed: it became more urbanized and more commercial. As centers of trade and industry, towns and cities across Europe became hubs of growing economic vitality. Since they were the focal points of long-distance trade, a new class of international merchants assumed prominence in society, even though the established religious and social order had yet to find a place for them. The newly flourishing towns also attracted displaced peasants, or those fleeing from the burdens of rural life. They contributed to the general population growth and assumed positions in the expanding cloth industry and in other commercial ventures of the towns. They participated in the building boom which attended upon the growth of urban areas; they saw to the construction of numerous churches and cathedrals in the new, magnificent Gothic style. The new urban society also contributed to the growth of literacy, as the merchant class developed proficiency in Latin and an even greater command of the vernacular. And the merchants fostered the emergence of the money economy together with the development of banking and money-lending institutions, which ran afoul of Church doctrine on the practice of usury.

Although the Church was in many ways slow to respond to the dramatic transformation of the social and economic order, it too underwent significant change in the twelfth century. The roots of this change can be found in the previous century and more dramatically in the early twelfth century, as is already evident in the life of Henry the Monk and the other wandering preachers of his time, orthodox and heretical. Religious life and spirituality became increasingly shaped by the growing ideal of the apostolic life. This ideal was manifest in almost contradictory ways; it was identified both with the cloistered lifestyle of the Cistercian monks and with the very different one of wandering preachers like Henry and Robert of Arbrissel. In whatever fashion it appeared, however, the desire to live a life in imitation of the Apostles greatly influenced religious belief and practice during the twelfth century. Pious Christians sought to live communally, as the monks did, in imitation of the apostolic community of Jerusalem, or to adopt lives of evangelism, spreading the Gospel as the Apostles had done; by the time of Valdes's conversion, the call to preach in imitation of the Apostles was becoming particularly urgent. At the heart of both these expressions of the apostolic life was a desire for poverty; not merely economic poverty, but, as the historian and theologian Pere Chenu notes, 'the social poverty of those who for one reason or other were living on the fringes of society – feudal society based on territorial stability – and who were consequently outlaws.'[1] Paradoxically, at the same time that apostolic poverty assumed an ever greater role in religious life, the Church itself had become increasingly wealthy and powerful. The pope, partially as a result of the legislation of the Gregorian Reform, was one of the most important and influential figures in Church and society. Not only were the popes involved in political disputes, they were also leading juridical figures in society, and the papal court was becoming a court of last appeal, exercising jurisdiction over an increasingly broad range of issues. The Roman curia had developed a reputation for avarice; in order to gain access to the papal court, petitioners necessarily had to pay increasing sums to various office-holders. Indeed, the *Gospel According to the Mark of Silver* was a popular parody of Roman practice at this time. And it is against this background of changing spirituality, of ecclesiastical worldliness, and of failure to address the profound social and economic changes that the birth of the Waldensian movement can best be understood.

The history of the Waldenses begins with the conversion of Valdes, a wealthy merchant of the commercial town of Lyons, which was situated on an important route for pilgrims, crusaders, and merchants and boasted some 10,000 to 15,000 citizens.[2] The town was noted as a commercial and industrial center which had built up its economic prosperity on manufacture and trade of cloth. From all the accounts, Valdes emerges as one of the success stories of the new urban and commercial economy; he was the owner of substantial properties in and around Lyons. Along with significant moveable wealth, Valdes most likely owned a number of properties and buildings in Lyons and a wide range of properties outside the city, including fields, pastures, vineyards, woods, and other holdings, which brought him substantial revenue in the form of rents.[3] According to contemporary accounts, Valdes made a fortune in business. He most certainly invested in the cloth industry of his town, as well as buying and selling cloth. Like most merchants of his time, he must have indulged in early banking practices, including lending money at interest. This opened him to the charge of usury, which was condemned by the Church. It has also been suggested that he may have served as a financial administrator for the local bishop, but it is generally held that he was a wealthy and successful businessman, part of the rising merchant class.

Success in the world seems, however, to have affected Valdes's conscience; more likely than not, he had some reservations about the way he made his money. At any rate, although the accounts are somewhat confused, he underwent a profound religious conversion. One Sunday in early 1173, according to the Laon Anonymous, a contemporary chronicle, Valdes was attracted to a crowd surrounding a jongleur who was reciting the story of St. Alexis.[4] The story of this fourth-century saint had particular resonance for Valdes. The version he would have heard – most likely compiled as a poem, in French, in the late eleventh century – described a wealthy noble of Rome who married a wealthy noble woman. On his wedding, Alexis left his wife and fortune behind, to live a life of mendicancy in Syria, where he gave away the possessions he had with him and started collecting and distributing alms. Years later, he returned home, was not recognized by his family, and ended his life collecting alms in his father's house. The jongleur's tale so moved Valdes that he invited him back home, to discuss things with him further.

Deeply moved by the story of Alexis, Valdes visited a local theologian on the morning after his meeting with the jongleur, to get advice for the care of his soul and to learn of the best way to attain God. After receiving instruction in matters of faith, Valdes asked the theologian how to best care for his soul, and the master replied in the words of Jesus himself: 'If you wish to be perfect, go and sell everything that you possess' (Matthew 19: 21). Unlike the young man in the Gospel, Valdes did not walk away saddened, but with a new purpose. He returned home and offered his wife a choice between his moveable wealth and his property, which, as the Laon Anonymous notes, included 'lands, waters, woods, meadows, houses, rents, vineyards, mills, and ovens.'[5] She chose, perhaps most wisely, the real estate. Valdes then made restitution to all from whom he had profited unjustly, that is, from those on whom he had charged interest. Finally, he set aside yet another substantial portion for his two small daughters and placed them under the Order of Fontevrault. Having taken care of his wife and family and of those he had wronged in business, Valdes donated a substantial part of his wealth to the poor and began a life of religious poverty which was to have a lasting influence on the world around him.

Shortly after Valdes adopted this new life, a terrible famine struck parts of France and Germany, and he provided relief to his fellow citizens from May 27 to August 1. Three days a week, according to the Laon Anonymous, Valdes 'gave bountifully of bread, vegetables, and meat to all who came to him.'[6] On the feast of the Assumption of the Blessed Virgin (August 15), he distributed a large sum of money to the poor in the streets, proclaiming: 'No man can serve two masters, God and mammon' (Matthew 6: 24). At this point he attracted a large crowd from the people of Lyons, many of whom believed that he had lost his senses. Climbing to a spot where all could hear him, Valdes declared:

> My friends and fellow townsmen! Indeed, I am not, as you think, insane, but I have taken vengeance on my enemies who held me in bondage to them, so that I was always more anxious about money than about God and served the creature more than the Creator. I know that a great many find fault with me for having done this publicly. But I did it for myself and also for you; for myself, so that they who may henceforth see me in possession of money may think I am mad; in part also for you, so that you may learn to fix your hope in God and to trust not in riches.[7]

Valdes made a clear break with his former life and demonstrated, to one and all, that he would no longer pursue success and fortune as he once had. On the day after his great distribution of wealth, he asked a former associate to give him some food. The friend obliged, declaring that he would always provide for him. Valdes's wife was greatly dismayed by this and complained to the local bishop, who commanded that Valdes might not take food with anyone in the city but his wife.

His public declaration, like that of St. Francis in the next generation, was intended to reveal his dedication to the life of evangelical poverty. It was further intended, perhaps, as the first step in a life of preaching; as he had stated, his public display was meant to instruct the people of Lyons on the subject of the false hope for worldly riches. Indeed, contemporary sources indicate that the life Valdes adopted involved poverty and preaching from its very beginning, and these two ideals were at the center of the movement he inspired. In order to spread the Gospel, Valdes commissioned two priests, not long after his conversion, to translate passages from the Bible and from certain Church Fathers into the vernacular. A local grammarian, Stephen de Ansa, translated the various texts – he dictated them to the scribe Bernardus Ydros, who wrote them down. According to a later account, these texts involved passages or, as the Waldenses called them, *sententiae* ('opinions,' 'sentences') from the books of the Old and New Testaments as well as from the works of Ambrose, Augustine, Jerome, and Gregory the Great. The texts in question were frequently read by Valdes and provided the foundation for the preaching and missionary work which he undertook and which had great appeal to the people of Lyons and beyond.

Indeed, it was the Gospels themselves that provided the inspiration for Valdes's conversion, and the apostolic life he adopted inspired others to follow him. By 1177 according to the Laon Anonymous, if not even earlier, Valdes began to attract a number of disciples, including laymen and laywomen as well as priests, all of whom assumed a life of voluntary poverty and began to preach. He and his followers – the Poor of Lyons, as they came to be known – began gradually to criticize their own sins and those of others in Lyons, publicly and privately. Valdes sent his followers to teach the Gospel; they spread out from Lyons to the surrounding villages and preached in public squares, private homes, even churches, and they appeared naked as the naked Christ. Valdes himself preached what he had learned by heart from the Gospel translations he had commissioned. His preaching, together with the popularity of the evangelical life he had adopted, quickly came to the attention of the local archbishop, who must surely have frowned on this unlicensed lay preaching – especially as it criticized the faults and excesses of the local clergy and was quite popular with the townspeople. And it is possible that the archbishop, whom contemporaries mistakenly identify as Jean Bellesmains (or, in English, John of Canterbury), put a ban on the preaching of Valdes and his followers at some point before 1179. Although Jean was appointed archbishop only in 1181, hence he clearly could not have issued a prohibition before that date, subsequent events suggest that some tension existed between the movement of lay preachers and the official hierarchy.

It is equally plausible that Valdes and his followers would not easily abandon their life of evangelical poverty, since both he and his followers believed themselves to be divinely inspired. God himself, they claimed, had called upon Valdes to take up the life of apostolic poverty and to preach the message of the Gospel.

One contemporary follower observed that, when God saw 'the works of the prelates set upon cupidity, simony, pride, avarice, vainglory, concupiscence, concubinage, and other disgraces ... the Son of the Highest Father commissioned you, Valdes, choosing for the apostolic calling, so that through you and your companions He might resist the errors, since those put in charge were not able to.'[8] Moreover, writing about the origins of the Waldenses in the early thirteenth century, Stephen of Bourbon (d. 1261) noted that they openly defied the archbishop when he prohibited their preaching, citing the example of the Apostles. Valdes reacted to the archbishop's prohibition by declaring, just like the Apostle Peter had done, '"We ought to obey God, rather than men" (Acts of the Apostles 5: 29) – the God who had commanded the apostles to "Preach the gospel to every living creature" (Mark 16: 15).'[9] Reflecting what must have been Valdes's understanding of his call for preaching, Stephen observed that Valdes said this 'as though the Lord had said to them what He said to the apostles.'[10] For Valdes, the call for preaching was a divinely inspired one; besides, preaching and poverty were essential to Valdes's intention of living the life of the Apostles. Nevertheless, in spite of its scriptural basis, his dedication to poverty and preaching became a source of tensions with the Church. Strictly orthodox in many ways in their earliest days and committed to combat the Cathar heresy, he and his followers would run afoul of the Church because of their disobedience and usurpation of the clerical right to preach. As Stephen noted, the archbishop declared Valdes and his followers excommunicated and expelled them from the city.[11]

But the final break between Valdes and the Church would come only later; and even before being finally cast out and declared a heretic and a schismatic, he would still seek official approval from the highest levels of Church hierarchy. In response to the prohibition and excommunication pronounced by the archbishop, a small group of the Poor of Lyons, and possibly Valdes himself, attended the Third Lateran Council in Rome in 1179, hoping to obtain papal sanction for their life of evangelical poverty. The course of events at the Council is somewhat confused in the various sources; one of them indicates that Valdes and his followers were summoned to appear before the Council and condemned as schismatics. A first-hand account of the meeting in Rome, however, and the Council canons themselves offer a different and more plausible description of the proceedings.

The main report of the Waldenses' appearance at the Lateran Council in 1179 comes from a work entitled *De nugis curialium* ('On the Courtiers' Trifles'), by the Englishman Walter Map (*c*.1140–1208/10). Map had served King Henry II as royal justice before becoming chancellor to the bishop of Lincoln, in which capacity he attended the Council. In a somewhat mocking and derogatory account, Map, who does not identify Valdes as one of the participants, describes the appearance of the Waldenses. A group of 'simple and illiterate men,' they appeared before the Council and presented the pope 'a book written in French which contained the text and a gloss of the Psalms and many of the books of both Testaments.'[12] In this way they hoped to demonstrate their devotion to the scriptures and to prove the orthodoxy and authenticity of the life they lived. They hoped, further, that the pope would authorize them to preach, so that they could fully answer the call of the scriptures and live the life of preaching and poverty God had intended them to lead. Map notes that the Waldenses had given up all their possessions, dressed simply and, like the Apostles, were naked and followed the naked Christ. But, despite his observation that they pursued a Christ-like existence, Map denounced the group as 'nothing more than dabblers' – not 'the experienced men' they declared themselves to be – and hence little prepared to preach the word of God.

After describing the petition of the Waldenses and indulging in his diatribe against them, Map informs us that the clerics assembled at the Council chose him to interrogate the Waldenses. In this passage Map reveals his keen and sarcastic wit, taking pains to prove the ignorance of Valdes's followers. Two members of the group were given the opportunity to present their beliefs – to their interrogator and to the bishops and other clergy at the Council; they spoke, according to Map, 'not for love of seeking the truth but hoping that when I had been refuted my mouth might be stopped like one speaking wicked things.'[13] Then he asked them 'very easy questions of which no one could be ignorant.' He began with three questions concerning the Trinity, asking if they believed in God the Father, the Son, and the Holy Spirit, to which they replied: 'We do.' He then asked if they believed in the Mother of Christ, and they responded in the affirmative again, which elicited 'derisive laughter from everyone present' and forced them to withdraw in confusion.[14] Their answer to the final question implied that they put the Virgin Mary on equality with the Trinity, which demonstrated either theological ignorance or heretical beliefs concerning the Virgin. After describing the humiliation of the Waldenses before the Council, Map concludes his account with a warning about the threat that they represented for the Church.

Although the followers of Valdes seem to have been humiliated at the Council, they do not appear to have been banned or condemned, even in Map's uncomplimentary account. Indeed, the contemporary Laon Anonymous suggests a very different outcome at the Council, and one that was much more favorable to the heretics' movement. In this account, the group was led by Valdes himself and, far from being mocked and scorned, it was openly welcomed. The Council did denounce heresy but the Waldenses were not among those condemned – who included the Cathars, the Publicans, and the Patarenes. In fact the pope, Alexander III (1159–81), 'embraced Valdes, approving his vow of voluntary poverty.'[15] The saintliness of the movement's founder and his devotion to the apostolic life certainly found resonance with some leaders of the Council, who may well have recognized its value for the well-being of the Church, just as Pope Innocent III would recognize and approve of the order of St. Francis in the early thirteenth century. Alexander, however, was not ready to go as far as Innocent; he forbade Valdes and his followers to preach without the consent of the local priests. In this way Alexander saw the merits of a life of religious poverty but hoped to limit the potential for error from members of the group who lacked proper theological knowledge. For all the pope's best intentions, however, the Waldenses only observed this restriction for a short while, and their disobedience and insistence on preaching would cause problems both for their movement and for the Church.

If the Laon Anonymous is correct, after their appearance at the Council, Valdes and his followers returned to Lyons, where they quickly resumed their life of poverty and preaching. This violation of the prohibition set at the Third Lateran Council, as well as the rising tide of the Cathar heresy, which was spreading throughout the Languedoc, led to the calling of a council in Lyons by its archbishop, Guichard (the predecessor of Jean Bellesmains), in March 1180 or 1181. It was presided over by the papal legate, the cardinal and Cistercian monk Henri de Marcy, who, later on, was to lead the Church in the struggle against the Cathars in the Midi. Valdes's appearance at the council marks an important phase in his life as well as in the development of the movement; there he demonstrated both the essential orthodoxy of his teachings and the importance of poverty and preaching for his way of life.

Called before the council because of the continued preaching of his follow-ers under the pretext of poverty, Valdes was made to issue a profession of faith. The profession put before him is noteworthy: it indicates the real concerns of the Church at that time. The fear was not so much about a band of itinerant preachers dedicated to poverty, but rather about the dualism associated with the contemporary Cathar heresy. The profession of faith issued by Valdes was based on a text that had been used repeatedly by the Church throughout its history, whenever it felt threatened by dualist heretics. It had been used for the first time in the early sixth century, having developed as a defense against the dualist Priscillianist heresy prominent then; the profession of faith was employed as part of the rite of ordination of Gallican bishops. It was also used by Gerbert of Aurillac, later Pope Sylvester II (999–1003), at his ordination as archbishop of Rheims in 991; then again by Gaucelin, archbishop of Bourges (d. 1029), at the time when heresy, under a form which some contemporaries believed to be Manichaeanism, resurfaced in the medieval West. The profes-sion, therefore, was intended to prevent Valdes and his followers from falling into the Cathar heresy and from advocating dualist doctrines. Valdes's opposi-tion to the Cathars made it easy for him to subscribe to the profession.

Although the profession was based on earlier models, it was adjusted so as to meet contemporary needs. It surely indicates the fundamental beliefs of Valdes and his followers, intended as it was to confirm their orthodoxy. At the heart of this text was the confirmation of Valdes's belief in the central teachings of the Catholic Church, together with his repudiation of the errors of the Cathars. Valdes declared that he believed in the Gospels and that the Father, Son, and Holy Spirit were 'coessential, consubstantial, coeternal' as is 'contained in the creeds, the Apostles' Creed, the Nicene Creed, and the Athanasian Creed.'[16] In direct opposition to the Cathar teaching, which maintained that the devil was responsible for creation, Valdes further confirmed that he believed that God is 'the creator, maker, governor, and in due time and place, disposer of all things visible and invisible, all things of the heavens, in the air, and in the waters, and upon the earth.'[17] Unlike the dualist Christians whom the Church feared and loathed so much, he accepted both the Old and New Testaments, as well as the teachings of Moses and John the Baptist. Further still, the founder of the Wal-denses had to testify that he believed that Jesus was 'born of the Virgin Mary by true birth of the flesh ... [and] that He ate, drank, slept, and rested when weary from travel.'[18] In this way he distanced himself from dualist errors and confirmed his essential orthodoxy on matters concerning the Trinity.

Valdes's profession of faith was not limited to Trinitarian issues but addressed a variety of concerns related to the teachings of the Church. It confirmed his acceptance of 'orthodox' Catholicism on sacramental and sacerdotal matters. Thus Valdes asserted his belief that all the sacraments were valid; he approved of infant baptism and expressed the belief that infants were saved if they died immediately afterward; and he recognized the validity of properly consecrated marriages. He also accepted Catholic doctrine concerning the Eucharist, affirming that 'the bread and wine after consecration is the body and blood of Jesus Christ.'[19] More importantly, he proclaimed that there is no salvation outside the one Catholic Church. He maintained that even sinful priests can legitimately confer the sacraments, as long as the Church accepts these priests; in this way Valdes confirmed his devotion to the Church by distinguishing himself from the Donatist views of other heretics, who denied that immoral priests were still valid.

Having affirmed the central teachings on matters of the faith, the priesthood and sacraments, Valdes then made profession of the life he and his followers would adopt. Although accepting that those who do not adopt poverty can be good Christians, Valdes renounced the world and its wealth, explaining that he and the other Poor of Lyons had given away all their wealth and possessions. He declared that 'we shall take no thought for the morrow, nor shall we accept gold or silver or anything of that sort from anyone beyond food and clothing sufficient for the day.'[20] Valdes showed resolution 'to follow the precepts of the Gospel as commands,' and concluded that anyone who claimed to belong to the Waldenses but did not adhere to his profession of faith should not be accepted among his followers.[21] This profession may be seen as an agreement between the Waldenses and the Church. By confirming the group's orthodoxy and acceptance of Church and priesthood, Valdes may have overcome the suspicions of churchmen and gained approval for his lifestyle of preaching and poverty; at the very least, there was no specific prohibition on preaching, and it can be assumed that, had Henri de Macy and Guichard opposed it, some official statement would have recorded that.

If some reconciliation was reached at the council in Lyons, it very quickly fell apart. The reasons for the collapse of that agreement are not altogether clear, but the death of Guichard and the appointment of Jean Bellesmains, who was apparently less receptive to the ambitions of Valdes and his sectaries, probably contributed to it. The breakdown may also have been due to the fact that Valdes or, more likely, his followers abused the privilege of preaching. Valdes himself seems to have gained approval, but other members of the Poor of Lyons may have started to preach without license from the local priests or from the archbishop; on the other hand, the priests themselves may have refused to grant such license to all of them, Valdes included. Although Valdes expressed devotion to the Church and respect for the clergy, disassociating himself from those who did not, his followers were perhaps less respectful; they may have begun to preach anticlerical sermons. Since the group lacked any formal organization or hierarchy beyond the personal leadership of Valdes, it was possible for them to adopt more radical positions than the founder – a development that would, in fact, happen soon enough. Whatever the cause, the archbishop revoked the agreement and withdrew the right of preaching from Valdes and his devotees. Yet they refused to listen and continued to preach. Indeed, rather than obey the archbishop, they declared that they should follow God rather than men. In response to their disobedience and continued preaching, Archbishop Jean took the further step of expelling Valdes and his Poor from the city of Lyons.

This was a crucial turning point for the Waldenses. Not only did they continue to preach without license, but they found popular support wherever they went, attracting even more adherents. Moving outside their traditional homeland, Valdes and his followers attacked heresy, especially that of the Cathars, and spread their message of evangelical poverty. Their movement grew in the face of opposition from the orthodox Church because Valdes and his followers personified the apostolic ideal: their simple lifestyle and poverty were a challenge even to other heretical preachers. But the movement started to take a more aggressive stance toward the opposition; some of Valdes's followers seemed to adopt heretical ideas, and these, ironically enough, were influenced by the Cathars, whom Valdes so strenuously opposed.

Continued disobedience, together with the dissemination of the Waldenses and their growth in numbers, led to a final and permanent break with the Catholic Church. At a meeting in Verona in 1184, Pope Lucius III (1181–85) issued the decree *Ad abolendam*, which signaled not only a change of relationship between the Church and Valdes and his Poor of Lyons, but also a new orientation toward heresy in general.[22] Up until that point, the prosecution of heresy was the responsibility of the local bishops; they could choose to be most forceful and aggressive in the suppression of religious dissent, but also quite restrained if they so wished. Pope Lucius's decree changed all that. It started a process of centralization in the suppression of heresy which was to culminate in the papal sponsorship of the Albigensian Crusade and in the emergence of the Inquisition. The decree sought to address the problem of heresy at a universal level. This aim was fostered through the support the *Ad abolendam* and the pope received from the emperor Frederick Barbarossa (ruled 1152–90), who had recently settled a long-standing dispute with Rome. Concerned with heresy in Lombardy, the decree was focused on that region, but also directed at other hotbeds of heresy throughout western Christendom. Although Lucius did not fully develop the apparatus necessary to put the decree into effect, he sought to enforce episcopal responsibility for the identification and suppression of religious dissent. The pope commanded in his new decree that all the bishops and archbishops, in person or through an appointed deputy, should visit, once or twice a year, every parish of their diocese where heretics were suspected to reside. In each one of these parishes three or more reliable people were to denounce, under oath, all those whom they knew or suspected to be heretics; anyone who refused to take the oath would bring himself under suspicion of heresy. All those identified as heretics were then to swear that they were not, under penalty of anathema. Lucius, however, went beyond commanding the active opposition to heresy by the episcopacy – for the suppression of heresy he recruited secular authorities. According to the *Ad abolendam*, secular office-holders – 'counts, barons, rectors, consuls of cities and other places' – were expected to take responsibility in punishing the heretics turned over to them by the Church; and any lay authority who failed in this duty would be excommunicated, deposed from office, and stripped of all legal rights.[23] Towns which sheltered heretics were to suffer commercial boycotts, and the lands of known heretics were declared forfeit. To guarantee obedience to the new decree even further, the bishops and archbishops were expected to publish it on every feast day, under penalty of suspension from office for three years if they failed to do so.

While displaying a new and more aggressive attitude toward heresy in general, the decree also denounced the order of Valdes as heretic. Lucius first condemned 'all heresy, howsoever it may be named,' and then proceeded to identify specific groups, thus: 'we lay under a perpetual anathema, the Cathari, Patarini, and those who falsely call themselves Humiliati, or Poor Men of Lyons, Passagini, Josepini, and Arnaldistae.'[24] Having listed the major heretical groups, Lucius continued with a condemnation which seems directed especially at Valdes and his followers. Turning now his attention to those who have 'assumed to themselves the office of preaching,' he pronounced perpetual anathema on 'all who shall have presumed to preach, either publicly or privately, either being forbidden, or not sent, or not having the authority of the Apostolic See, or of the bishop of the diocese.'[25] Although Lucius recognized that Valdes was not guilty of any doctrinal error, he excommunicated him and his followers on account of their disobedience: he declared their preaching to be in error because it was done without the authority of the mother Church. Without the formal sanction of the pope or archbishop, the poverty and humility of Valdes and the Waldenses could not be authentic either; it was not unlike the false piety which the earlier heretics had demonstrated.

The decree *Ad abolendam* repudiated the central tenets of Valdes's creed, denying the validity of his teaching and of his way of life. And thus Valdes was declared excommunicate and anathema: his refusal to follow man instead of God had led to his ejection from the Church he had hoped to restore and reform. From 1184 on, the evangelical movement founded by him would increasingly come to be seen as heretical.

Although the decree from Verona formally declared Valdes and his followers anathema, they all continued their lives of evangelical poverty. Expulsion from Lyons did little more than open the movement to broader horizons, and the pronouncements at Verona had little immediate effect on the local communities where Valdes and his followers preached the Gospel. In fact, in many places in the Languedoc, the Midi, and Lombardy, Valdes and his Poor were among the most active and successful opponents of the doctrinal heresy promoted by the dualist Cathars. As Walter Map indicated, the Waldenses went 'two by two, barefoot, clad in woolen garments, owning nothing, holding all things common like the apostles, naked, following the naked Christ.'[26] Their way of life in imitation of Jesus and the Apostles posed a stark challenge not only to the orthodox clergy but also to the preachers of the Cathar heresy, who prevailed in southern France and northern Italy. By virtue of pursuing the apostolic ideal and presenting a true model of Christian living, the Waldenses were even more of a threat to the Cathars than the official missions sent by the Church to combat heresy. Valdes's life of poverty and preaching found great favor among the populace in the areas influenced by heresy; even some members of the clergy welcomed him and the Poor of Lyons as allies in the fight against the Cathars. Indeed, the Waldenses were invited to participate in public debates, to defend their teachings, and to oppose the heretical ideas of the various enemies of the Church, especially the Cathars. Valdes's movement also attracted members of the clergy such as the learned Spanish priest Durand of Huesca, who wrote an important work, the *Liber antiheresis* (*Book Against the Heresy*, c.1191/2), a defense of Christian belief against the errors of the Cathars.

Thus, in the generation or so after his denunciation at Verona and in the closing decades of the twelfth century, Valdes witnessed a dramatic growth of his movement. While rejecting Church authority to prohibit their preaching, Valdes and his followers still taught Catholic doctrine. And there were many who ignored the declaration at Verona and saw the movement as a valid expression of Christian and Catholic life. This success demonstrates that Valdes was able to tap into the fundamental spiritual yearnings of his age and clearly reveals the importance of the apostolic life in the twelfth century. The rapid growth, however, did not come without a cost. Over the last two decades of his life, Valdes saw the movement that bore his name being plagued by schism and by the increasing adoption of clearly heretical teachings.

Until his death, probably in 1205, Valdes hoped to reconcile himself with the Church, and his own moderation in matters of doctrine and organization signals a desire to return to the fold. By all accounts, however, he continued to live in poverty and to preach, even though he and his followers had been strictly forbidden to do so by bishops, councils, and the pope. The primary focus of their preaching was the call to repentance, but they were also very much concerned with the doctrinal heresy of the Cathars. In groups of two, in sandals and simple clothing, possessing little else, they all entered the Languedoc and other regions where the Cathars flourished, with the intention of combating their errors. Nonetheless, it appears that heretical ideas crept into the teachings of the Waldenses once they were there. Adopting more extreme views than Valdes ever would, some of his Poor came to believe that swearing oaths was strictly forbidden. Some also maintained that all killing was wrong, even judicial executions, and that every lie constituted a mortal sin. Even more serious, and clearly at odds with the position of Valdes himself, was a view taken by at least one branch of the Waldenses in the Languedoc: they adopted a Donatist attitude toward the clergy and denied the validity of the baptism administered by Catholic priests. The Poor of Lyons alone were true disciples of Christ and thus they were the only ones who could legitimately bestow baptism. Denying the baptismal right not only to the Catholic priests but also to the Cathar heretics, this group performed baptisms as well as rebaptizing people, in violation of the Church. Moreover, they claimed, in contrast to the teachings of Valdes, that only those who died in a state of complete poverty would be worthy of gaining salvation. Valdes repudiated this group around 1200 and most likely distanced himself from a similar group in Metz, which adopted more extreme views than Valdes himself and expressed a more critical attitude toward the orthodox Church.

An even more dramatic schism occurred in Italy, where the Waldenses had begun their missionary work as early as 1184, under the name the Poor of Lombardy. Just as the Waldenses in the Languedoc and Metz had absorbed religious ideas and practices from the local heretical communities, so too did the Poor who preached in Lombardy. It is also possible that an apostolic or heretical movement already existed in the region and influenced the Poor. However this may be, distance from their leader and the lack of any formal organization allowed for an independent development of the Lombard Poor.

The Italian Waldenses diverged from the main group and their founder in several distinct ways. Like the group in the Languedoc, the Lombard Waldenses assumed a more aggressive stance toward the clergy, one which approached Donatism. In this matter, in particular, the influence of local conditions can be detected best, because of the long-standing anticlerical sentiment that existed in the region. The Poor of Lombardy rejected the established clergy and attacked the sacraments they performed, including marriage. What is more, they also took steps to replace the Catholic clergy with their own ministers. Unlike Valdes, who claimed the right to administer the sacraments in case of need and on an ad hoc basis, the Poor of Lombardy sought to establish a permanent ministry for the administration of the sacraments. But the creation of a permanent order to confer the Eucharist and other sacraments ran counter to Valdes's intentions and interfered with his hopes for a reconciliation with the Church. The Poor of Lombardy also recruited nuns from the local convents and proclaimed that salvation could only be found through them.

An even more serious breach between Valdes and his Italian followers involved the adoption of manual labor by the latter. Indeed, according to the *Rescriptum Heresiarcharum* (*Reply of the Leading Heretics*, written c.1218), Valdes himself is supposed to have said, just prior to his death, that the Lombard poor 'could have no peace with him unless they separated themselves from the "congregations of laborers" who were then in Italy.'[27] Under the influence of an Italian heretical group, the Humiliati, the Lombard brethren took up the practice of working for subsistence wages and did not follow the strict regimen of poverty. They also settled down in one place, abandoning the practice of itinerant preaching which was at the core of Valdes's teaching in favor of a communal life of religious devotion. Although identifying themselves as part of the movement inspired by Valdes, the Lombard Waldenses disavowed the two central features of the lifestyle established by him. Moving away from his original practices, they foreshadowed those of later Waldenses and revealed the fundamental adaptability of their doctrine. The founder himself, however, would have none of this; he insisted on strict devotion to the message of the Gospels, which included both poverty and preaching, and, as noted in the *Rescriptum*, he did not consider those who labored to be part of his order.

Valdes and the Lombards also differed on matters of organization. Valdes himself did little to provide any sort of administrative structure to the movement he founded beyond his own charismatic leadership. The Lombard Poor, however, introduced a rather elaborate organizational structure, which, like their other innovations, met with Valdes's disapproval. As part of their sedentary, almost monastic lifestyle, the Lombards divided themselves into what the *Rescriptum* termed 'brethren' and 'friends.' The brethren were members of a ministerial class of sorts, and they were fully committed to a life of preaching and poverty. The friends were lay supporters who listened to their preaching and teaching. This distinction was only one of the organizational developments opposed by Valdes. An even more serious difference emerged over the establishment of an institutionalized leadership. The Lombards elected Jean de Ronco, and after him Otto de Ramazello, as 'rector' or 'provost.' The rector's responsibility was to oversee and administer the group and to ordain ministers or brethren to preach to the lay supporters of the Waldenses. This step was unacceptable to Valdes for whom the one and only leader of the Waldenses was Jesus Christ. As already noted, the various innovations of the Lombard Poor prefigured many later developments of the Waldensian heresy, but conflicted with the original intent of Valdes, who emphasized his own vision of preaching and poverty. Valdes repudiated the Italian group shortly before his death.

By his death in 1205, Valdes of Lyons had seen his movement evolve, from a small group of preachers devoted to a life of evangelical poverty, into an international movement which had become increasingly unorthodox in its doctrinal and organizational structure. Embodying the ideal of an apostolic life, which was at the center of twelfth-century spirituality, and foreshadowing the thirteenth-century movement of St. Francis of Assisi, Valdes founded a movement which survived the Middle Ages and merged with the Protestant churches of the sixteenth century to form the modern Waldensian church. Devoted to a life of preaching and poverty, Valdes clearly hoped to reform the Church and restore it to its evangelical purity, recalling it from its worldliness and materialism to a more pristine form. Nevertheless, his refusal to abandon his life of preaching laid the ground for his own excommunication and for the increasing doctrinal heterodoxy of his followers. Although remaining true to orthodox Christian dogma and hoping for a reconciliation with the Church, Valdes witnessed the growing radicalism of his followers, many of whom he wrote off from his movement. Despite his excommunication, he remained committed to Christian teaching and to his ideal, and, together with his followers, struck out against a shared enemy, the Cathars. And it was that dualist heresy that provided the greatest challenge to the Church. The Cathars and their noble supporters would bear the greatest brunt of the Church's response to the growth of religious dissent in the late twelfth and thirteenth centuries.

CHAPTER FIVE

RAYMOND VI OF TOULOUSE: THE CATHARS AND THE ALBIGENSIAN CRUSADE

ccording to the Cistercian historian Caesarius of Heisterbach (c.1170–c.1240), when the papal legate in southern France, Arnaud Amaury, was asked by the crusaders about to sack the city of Béziers, in 1209, how to tell the good Christians from the heretics, he replied, 'Kill them all. God will know his own.' There is no proof, of course, if Arnaud Amaury actually made that statement, but his alleged words reflect the attitudes involved in the most violent official response to the spread of heresy in the Middle Ages. The Albigensian Crusade, called by Pope Innocent III (1198–1216) in 1209 to suppress the growth of the Cathar heresy in southern France, was the most concentrated and destructive effort by the Church to ensure religious orthodoxy. With the support of the northern French barons, who were concerned with territorial acquisition just as much as with the suppression of Catharism, the Crusade did serious damage to culture and society in the south and caused countless deaths. The main victims of this assault were the simple peasants and villagers who had been attracted in great numbers by the preaching and behavior of the Cathars. The one who lost perhaps the most was not, however, a Cathar but one of the greatest figures of the south: Count Raymond VI of Toulouse (1156–1222), whose toleration of the heretics and tepid support for the Church helped to inspire the Crusade – and it, in turn, seriously undermined his position.

Raymond suffered on account of the dramatic growth of the Cathar heresy in his country, coupled with his failure to stem the tide. Raymond had originally shown a toleration to the preaching of the Cathars which rendered him suspect in the eyes of the Church and ultimately a victim of its ferocious backlash against the heresy; for its rise and spread were deemed to be the most serious threat to the established Church at the time. Therefore, in order to understand the life and career of Raymond best, it is necessary to examine the origins and teachings of the Cathars.

Although it was once believed that the earliest manifestation of Catharism occurred in the early eleventh century, when the outbreaks of heresy at Orléans and elsewhere in western Europe took place, it is now generally held that the first Cathars emerged in the mid-twelfth century, when foreign missionaries appeared at various places in France and in the Holy Roman Empire. Indeed, Catharism is perhaps best understood as the combination of indigenous western religious dissent and Bogomil religious dualism, and thus it may be said to have begun when Bogomil missionaries arrived in Latin Europe and their teachings were adopted by Christians in the Empire, France, and Italy. According to the Premonstratensian provost Everwin of Steinfeld, the first of the heretics who came to be called Cathars appeared in the Rhineland city of Cologne, in 1143 or 1144.[1] In his correspondence with Bernard of Clairvaux, Everwin described a group of heretics who did not drink milk or eat any food produced in some way as the result of coition. They rejected marriage and baptism in water and practiced the laying on of the hands, which was also a rite of initiation into the sect. Unlike earlier heretics of the twelfth century, notably Henry the Monk, Tanchelm, Peter of Bruys, and others, these ones were anonymous; Everwin does not identify even a heresiarch leading the group. He notes, however, that they were divided into three ranks: the auditors, the believers, and the elect, which signified degrees of progress within the group. These heretics claimed that their beliefs were not new but went back to the time of the martyrs. They also claimed to have fellow believers in Greece, most likely a reference to the Byzantine Empire, where Bogomil missionaries had spread their heresy during the eleventh and twelfth centuries. The basic outline of their creed and their claim to have coreligionists in the Greek world signal the beginnings of the Cathar movement in Latin Europe.

Reports from slightly later sources in the mid-twelfth century confirm the birth and wide diffusion of a new movement of heresy which merged indigenous religious dissent with foreign, most likely Bogomil, influence. In 1163, Eckbert, the future Benedictine abbot of Schönau, described the beliefs of these heretics in his *Thirteen Sermons Against the Cathars*. He drew his information for the sermons from a recent encounter with them at Mainz and from debates he had had with them at Bonn and Cologne during the previous fifteen years. In his sermons, Eckbert argued that the heretics were to be found everywhere throughout western Christendom and were called 'Piphles' in Flanders, 'Texerant' in France, and 'Cathars' in Germany. The last name comes from the Greek word for 'pure' (*katharos*), but Eckbert derived it from 'cat' because the heretics allegedly worshiped the devil in the form of a cat; and it is this name that has been generally used to identify Eckbert's heretics. Like Everwin, Eckbert described their beliefs in a way which suggests Bogomil influence. According to the sermons, the heretics taught a Docetic Christology, maintaining that Jesus Christ only appeared to take the flesh but in fact did not. Eckbert noted, further, that the group believed in the transmigration of souls and in the creation of the world by an evil god. Like the group at Cologne in the 1140s, Eckbert's Cathars practiced the rite of the laying on of the hands to initiate believers into the sect.

Evidence for the emergence of the Cathar heresy (or its precursor) in the south, where it was to have its greatest impact, appears in the account of a meeting in 1165 at Lombers, a castle that lies between Albi and Castres. At this meeting, local heretics known as '*bons hommes*' or 'good men,' joined in debate with various bishops of the region in the presence of important secular leaders.[2] The 'good men,' like the Bogomils, did not openly proclaim their heresy or speak falsehood, refusing to discuss baptism, marriage, or their own beliefs. They also gave rather veiled and ambiguous responses to questions concerning the Eucharist and confession and refused to swear any kind of oath. Rejecting the Old Testament, they based their arguments only on the New Testament. They spoke freely, however, of the failures of the Church, were critical of the clergy, and even called the bishops at the meeting wicked men. They were in turn declared heretics in the name of Bishop William of Alby by Gaucelin, bishop of Lodeve, who also advised the knights to stop supporting the 'good men.' The fact that the knights needed his warning suggests one of the reasons for the eventual success of the Cathars in southern France; Raymond VI was not alone in granting tolerance to these heretics.

The accounts of Everwin and Eckbert and that of the meeting in Lombers provide highly suggestive hints of the emergence of the Cathar heresy and reveal the infiltration of missionaries from the Byzantine world into Latin Europe. These missionaries most probably established the first Cathar communities and brought with them Bogomil dualism from Bulgaria – possibly following trade routes that led into the Rhineland, Lombardy, and elsewhere.

But the most unambiguous evidence of the establishment of heretical dualism in western Europe comes from the account of the so-called Council of St. Félix-de-Caraman, which is traditionally dated to 1167 but more likely took place in 1174. Although the document reporting this meeting probably conflates several such meetings and was purportedly written in 1232, it offers clear evidence of the origins and nature of Catharism in the Languedoc and southern France. The Council was a meeting of Cathar bishops from northern France, Albi, and Lombardy along with representatives of Cathar churches in Carcassonne, Agen, and Toulouse, and it was presided over by an eastern missionary, Papa Niquinta or Nicetas of Constantinople.

Nicetas introduced important administrative reforms to the emerging Cathar churches of western Europe and a fundamental change in the beliefs of the heretics. He proclaimed that the teaching of earlier Bulgarian missionaries was flawed at its heart, whereas he taught the true doctrine. He introduced his eager western disciples to the teachings of the so-called Dragovitsan church, which maintained absolute dualism. Nicetas preached the doctrine of the two principles. He asserted, namely, the existence of two equal deities, the good and the evil; these were locked in an eternal struggle and the evil god created the material world. He also organized the Cathar churches in western Europe, founding dioceses patterned after the established Catholic ones, defining geographic boundaries, and confirming the autonomy of each bishop within his diocese. He also administered the basic sacrament of the Cathar church, the *consolamentum*, a ritual that prepared the believers to step into the ranks of church elite and established them as the church's priestly order. Having redefined the basic teachings and ecclesiastical organization of the Cathar churches, Nicetas returned to Constantinople. After him, Catharism in the Languedoc and elsewhere in western Europe developed into a major threat to the Catholic Church.

The success of Catharism lies in the basic teachings and practices of its church. The Cathars offered a fully developed theology, in opposition to that of the Catholic Church – one which could provide an alternate explanation of evil in the world. Cathar dualism proclaimed that the world had been created by Satan, the evil god associated with the Old Testament; therefore all material creation was evil. Satan was a fallen angel, who had rebelled against God; he made human bodies out of clay and imprisoned other fallen angels in them. The Cathar view of creation as intrinsically evil led to the rejection of the traditional doctrine concerning the incarnation of Christ. The Cathars believed instead that Christ only appeared to take the flesh, and only appeared to suffer on the cross. He was 'born' of the Virgin Mary, according to one Cathar source, by entering her ear.

Although important as a rival to Catholic teaching, Cathar doctrine was less central to the success of the heresy than the behavior of its members. Indeed, the simple lifestyle and the religious devotion of the Cathar leaders often stood in staunch opposition to the worldliness and power of the Catholic hierarchy, which added to the ignorance of many among the parish clergy. Moreover, the Cathars erected a rival organizational structure, which could provide support for its clergy and laity alike. At the head of the Cathar churches were the bishops, who administered the consolamentum – the ritual which elevated the ordinary believer to the rank of *perfectus* ('perfect'); and it is perhaps a key to the growth of Catharism that women could become perfects no less than the men. The perfects adopted a life of poverty, celibacy (avoiding even physical contact with the opposite sex), and regular prayer. As the clerical order of the heresy, the perfects were called on to travel about, preaching the faith and taking confession from the laity. They also performed the *apparellamentum*, a confession designed to purify them of minor infractions, and the ritual of blessing of the bread at meals. Their own message, their criticism of the official Catholic clergy and sacraments, and their personal piety attracted many people to the Cathar heresy, including those who, like Count Raymond VI and other southern nobles, supported it without fully joining it, or tolerated it through animosity toward the abuses of the Catholic Church and clergy. The Cathar laity was not expected to live as strictly as the perfects but it supported them with food, lodging, and protection; it also attended their sermons. It honored the perfects with the *melioramentum* – a form of confession and request that the perfects pray for them.

The early growth and survival of Catharism was also dependent on the support of the secular nobility. True, Count Raymond V of Toulouse sought help against the preachers of the two principles, both from the pope and from his secular overlords; but many southern nobles either turned a blind eye on the heretics or supported them actively, even joined their church. Efforts by the Catholics, including missions by Cistercian preachers and special missions sent by the pope himself, proved ineffective because of the tolerance of the nobility of the Languedoc. Although there was no pronouncement of support for the heretics, the nobility as a whole showed little inclination to suppress the Cathars or support the Church's early efforts against them. Moreover, this reluctance to act against the heretics filtered down into society, where Catholics and Cathars lived side by side, often in the same household. The ease with which heretic and Catholic coexisted and the toleration granted from above allowed Catharism to spread throughout the Languedoc and to emerge as a serious rival to the authority of the Church. The failure of the greatest power in the south, that of Count Raymond VI of Toulouse, to restrict this growth led to the outbreak of the Albigensian Crusade.

Raymond, born in 1156, was the son of Count Raymond V (1130–94), who had initiated action against the first Cathars and sought aid against them from both Church and state. As son to the count of Toulouse, Raymond was related to powerful figures of the day who included King Louis VII of France and King Richard I the Lionheart of England: the latter's sister, Jeanne, was Raymond's fourth wife. Very little is known of Raymond's early years, although upon becoming count of Toulouse he would be one of the leading figures of the south. He was, apparently, a most obedient and patient son – unlike others, most notably his future brother-in-law Richard I, who chafed at waiting for power or openly rebelled against their fathers. As contemporary accounts suggest, Raymond was sent on occasion to lead a siege or a raid by his father, but otherwise there is no record of his activities; all in all, he does not seem to have gained the experience needed for good rulership. He was appointed count of Mauguio by his father, but even then many of the official duties of the office were performed by Raymond V. And it was only in 1194 that Raymond VI, at the mature age of 38, appeared fully on the stage of history, becoming count of Toulouse upon the death of his father.

Assuming authority in 1194, Raymond lacked the kinds of experience that other nobles had, and he faced the fragmentation of the lands of his predecessors. By all accounts he was a charming and attractive ruler, even though he lacked the necessary assertiveness that his more successful contemporaries possessed. He seems to have had little taste for combat, his preparation for warfare not being much during his father's lifetime; he withdrew from the battlefield without even drawing his sword on two occasions during the Albigensian Crusade. He also had a weak will and used to vacillate, often losing his nerve at times of crisis, and he could be tactless in spite of his natural charms. And yet for all his flaws Raymond remained a popular and romantic figure. He was a great lover of luxury and cultivated an extravagant court, which attracted many nobles and troubadours of the south. Raymond was a great supporter of the troubadours and promoted their works; he found them particularly useful for the art of seduction, which, according to contemporary sources, he used to great success. Raymond was notorious for his licentiousness – apart from abandoning one wife for another, he even seduced his father's mistresses and committed incest with his sister.

Although not the most morally upright figure, Raymond was a man of conventional piety. After his death in 1222, his son, Raymond VII (1197–1249), compiled a list intended to demonstrate his father's loyalty to the Church in order to secure a Christian burial for him. The document listed numerous charitable benefactions. Raymond seems to have been particularly supportive of the Cistercian order, and many of his charters reveal donations to the Cistercians and other monasteries and churches. He expressed a desire in his will to die as a member of the Order of the Hospitallers and left the order a substantial benefaction after his death.

But, even though he demonstrated support for the Church, Raymond was not above hostility toward the political ambitions of the clergy. He was putting his own interests ahead of those of the Church when they came into conflict, and he may have even held anticlerical attitudes. Unlike his father, he also exercised a certain laxness in the prosecution of heresy, as did many southern nobles. And it was widely held that Raymond was not simply being tolerant of the heretics, but he secretly supported them and may even have desired to be one of them. At the very least, he allowed Cathar perfects to preach before him, leaving them unmolested; he may very well have allowed Cathars even to reside at court. It was alleged that the count himself repudiated the Old Testament and believed that the devil had created the world. He was reported to protect the perfects and to provide them with food and money; he generally indulged them, he even married one – his second wife Matilda, daughter of King Roger of Sicily, who was sent to a Cathar convent when he repudiated her in 1193.

Many of the accusations that Raymond was himself a Cathar were made by one of his bitterest enemies and hence are suspect. It is more plausible that Raymond was a tacit supporter of the heretics, if only because this attitude was so widespread in the south of France. In fact, the general support for religious dissidents and the hostility to the clergy were firmly rooted in the region, as the success of Henry the Monk may indicate. Raymond himself was in any case limited by the political situation of his day from acting more forcefully, had he wished to. Many leaders of the towns, as well as the most prominent nobles of the region, were sympathetic to the Cathars, if not more: the sister of the powerful and influential count of Foix was herself a perfect. Hence they were unlikely to join in any effort to suppress them. Furthermore, Raymond did not have the necessary military forces, nor could he call on a feudal levy to enforce his will, and even if he had tried to suppress the heretics by force he would most probably have failed, if not through his own incompetence, then because of some terrible civil war such an enterprise may well have generated. It is not surprising that, when asked to take action against the Cathars in 1205, Raymond declared that he was a good and obedient son of the Church and would see to it that heresy was suppressed, but in fact proceeded to do absolutely nothing. Ultimately, the spread of Catharism on Raymond's domains became a matter of some urgency to the papacy. In response to his obvious lack of action, the Church adopted ever more aggressive steps against him. In 1204 and 1205, Pope Innocent III petitioned King Philip Augustus of France (1165–1223), the barons of the north, and other princes to suppress the heresy, since Raymond was reluctant to do so. Philip, however, was little interested in getting himself into a war in the south, as he was then much too involved in a dispute with John, king of England.

Pope Innocent also responded to the spread of the Cathar heresy by sending delegations of missionaries to preach to the heretics with the goal of converting them. The missionaries he sent included leading Cistercian monks, whose austere and pious lives were thought to be an important counterweight to those of the Cathar perfects. Dominic de Guzman (c.1180–1221), founder of the Dominican order in 1215 and declared a saint after his death, also preached against the heretics throughout the region. In 1207 he participated in a great debate in Montréal, along with Cathar leaders and other Catholic ecclesiastics; but no verdict was given there, due to the sensitivities of the townspeople. A subsequent debate at Pamiers was more clearly successful for the Catholics, who welcomed numerous converts from heresy. And, in the period between the two debates, a large number of Cistercian monks arrived in the area, to reinforce the evangelical mission. Yet in spite of the exemplary lives and skilled preaching of Dominic and the Cistercian monks, their efforts failed to make any significant headway against the Cathars. In fact, the Cathars in Carcassonne managed to expel the bishop in 1207 and around the same time held a great council of their own at Mirepoix, in the lands of the count of Foix. Catharism had taken deep roots and remained a significant force in the Languedoc; many of the rival preachers left after their ephemeral successes.

The most important missionary, however, was the pope's personal legate, Peter of Castelnau, a Cistercian monk, canon lawyer, and theologian. He was born just north of Montpellier and therefore had the benefit of being a man of the south. He arrived in 1203 and began the arduous task of converting the Toulousains and of persuading the bishops of Languedoc that it was their responsibility to work against the spreading of the heresy. Possessing the full authority of a papal legate, Peter deposed bishops who seemed unable or unwilling to take steps against heresy and replaced them with others, more amenable to the pope's commands. What is more, Peter sought to exploit the unsettled political situation of the lands of Raymond, the count of Toulouse, by working with his vassals. By 1207, Peter came to realize that no victory over the Cathars was possible without the count's support. But Raymond had displayed little initiative in that regard. It was two years since he had promised to suppress the heretics without doing anything in the interim. Disappointed by the Count's failure, in late April 1207 Peter forged a truce among the warring nobles of the Languedoc and organized a league aiming to bring an end to heresy on the count's lands. Raymond himself was invited to join the league but refused, indignant at the idea of joining an organization so clearly designed against him. In response, Peter of Castelnau immediately excommunicated the count. He declared him guilty of violating the truce held on feast days, of pillaging monasteries, and of other crimes, but, most importantly, of protecting the heretics instead of expelling them from his lands.

The excommunication was made all the worse for Raymond when

Innocent confirmed it on May 29, 1207. In a harsh, uncompromising letter, Innocent declared:

> Do not forget that life and death themselves are in God's hands. God may suddenly strike you down, and his anger deliver you everlasting torment. Even if you are permitted to live, do not suppose that misfortune cannot reach you. You are not made of iron. You are weak and vulnerable, like other men. Fever, leprosy, paralysis, insanity, incurable disease may attack you like any of your kind … The hand of the Lord will no longer be stayed. It will stretch forth to crush you, for the anger which you have provoked will not lightly be evaded.[3]

The pope ordered the bishops of the region to publish the ban of excommunication in their churches until Raymond submitted. He laid an interdict over all of his lands, thereby prohibiting the holding of Church services or the administration of the Eucharist. He ordered that no one was to have any dealings with the count and released Raymond's vassals from their oaths of allegiance. In correspondence once again with King Philip Augustus, in the hope that he would take up leadership of the crusade, Innocent envisaged the possibility of the king deposing Raymond and inviting others to replace him.

Raymond's position was, clearly, most difficult, but there were certain rituals to go through that would have lifted the penalty; the king himself had been excommunicated before. But Raymond acted in a most arrogant fashion. The pope, on the other hand, had reached his limit and was little willing to compromise. As was customary, the papal legate, Peter of Castelnau, visited the count's court to inform him personally of the excommunication and to undertake any discussion that could bring an end to the impasse. The first meeting between the count and the papal legate, however, failed to resolve anything, in part because of Raymond's ill-mannered reception of the legate. The count claimed, or so it seems, that he could find numerous Cathar bishops to prove that their church was better than Peter's. The excommunication of the count and interdict over his lands remained in force, making way for an increasingly bad situation.

Following the failed meeting between Raymond and Peter, both the pope and his representative in Languedoc sought to resolve the situation. On November

12, 1207, Innocent wrote to Philip Augustus yet again, in an attempt to persuade him to invade the south in order to punish Raymond and suppress heresy. The king's response was noncommittal at best, but events would outpace both king and pope. In January 1208, Peter of Castelnau met with Count Raymond once more. Raymond himself had sent a letter to Peter in late December, indicating that he was willing to submit to his authority, provided that the excommunication and interdict were lifted. Peter and another papal legate, the bishop of Couserans, met the count at St. Gilles, where Raymond hoped to be able to outmaneuver the papal representatives and gain absolution at the cheapest possible price. An unpleasant argument ensued; at the end of the day nothing was resolved, and the excommunication and interdict remained in place. According to the pope himself, Raymond threatened the legates by declaring that he would keep a watchful eye on them. On the following day, Peter of Castelnau was assassinated by a representative of the count, who was immediately blamed for the murder. The question of his involvement is, however, open to debate; it should be said on behalf of the count that he was probably not enough of a fool to murder the pope's legate. Peter, who had created much ill will in the south, could simply have been the victim of a rash vengeful act by some angry noble.

The assassin was never identified and Raymond remained the primary suspect; his failure to express anything like sadness strengthened the belief that he was, in fact, guilty of ordering the crime. Rather than move decisively to prevent any worsening of the situation, Raymond delayed further, giving his enemies the opportunity to react first. And on March 10, 1208, Innocent III proclaimed a crusade against Raymond and his lands, addressing the king and nobles of France as follows:

> Since those who fight for liberty of the church ought to be fostered by the protection of the church, we, by our apostolic authority, have decided that our beloved, who in obedience to Christ are signed or are about to be signed against the provincial heretics, from the time that they, according to the ordinance of our legates, place on their breasts the sign of the quickening cross, to fight against the heretics, shall be under the protection of the apostolic seat and of ourselves, with their persons and lands, their possessions and men, and also all of their other property; and until full proof is obtained

of their return or death all the above shall remain as they were, free and undisturbed.[4]

Innocent thus offered a full indulgence – equal to that offered to crusaders to the Holy Land – to all those who took up arms against Raymond, a man whom the pope excommunicated for the crimes of heresy and complicity in the murder of a papal legate. The pope also promised the crusaders freedom to seize any, and all, lands belonging to Raymond; the ultimate right to those lands being of course reserved for Raymond's overlord, King Philip Augustus. The letter to the king and nobles of France was followed by similar letters to the legates in the south, who were called upon to preach for the Crusade.

Philip Augustus was, however, reluctant to involve himself in the campaign, being concerned with matters in the north and matters to do with the king of England; he even cautioned the pope against taking too precipitous an action against Raymond. Yet in the end Philip allowed a considerable number of his own vassals to participate in the Crusade.

The reaction to the pope's call for crusade was immediate and dramatic, as the French nobility enthusiastically signed up for the war in the south. According to the historian of the Crusade, William of Tudela, the response was overwhelming; an army larger than any he had ever seen came together in the spring of 1209. The response of the nobility was most understandable: what attracted them was the offer of the indulgence, which provided a much easier path to absolution than undertaking a crusade to the Holy Land. The struggle against heresy at home offered the French knights a just cause to fight against, and this was a much less difficult and expensive path to follow. But the available rewards were not only spiritual: the crusading knights could obtain material benefits, which included the acquisition of large and prosperous fiefs in the south.

The remaining papal legate in the south, the Cistercian Arnaud Amaury, recruited a number of powerful and important nobles to the cause of the Crusade, including Otto III, duke of Burgundy, and Hervé de Donzy, count of Nevers. His drive to recruit benefited from the fact that Philip granted his vassals the right to participate. Arnaud began preaching for the Crusade in the winter of 1208–9, and he encouraged his brother Cistercians to do the same.

It was the increasing success of his enemies that forced Raymond to act.

He hoped to find allies against the army of crusaders, which had been steadily growing after Innocent's proclamation of the Crusade, and he turned first to his suzerains. In the autumn of 1208, Raymond appealed to Philip for aid but found little affection there, as the king recalled a number of injuries Raymond had caused him. Whatever support Raymond could still have expected disappeared when he visited his other lord, Emperor Otto IV of Germany, one of Philip's great rivals. The emperor could only offer little help, as his own fortunes were at a low point. Finally, Raymond turned to Arnaud Amaury. He sought the legate's forgiveness and absolution, humbling himself before the Cistercian and kneeling at his feet, as a sign of contrition. Arnaud, however, did not give in; he informed the count that only the pope could lift the excommunication.

Returning home in late 1208, dismayed by the preaching of the Cistercians and the growing support they received for the Crusade, Raymond struggled to find allies against its rising tide. He forgave the citizens of Nîmes for siding with his enemies in the past and confirmed privileges for those under his authority. His most desperate gambit, however, was his effort to forge an alliance with his nephew, Raymond-Roger, viscount of Trencavel and lord of Albi and Carcassonne, who may well have been a supporter of the Cathars in the face of the common threat against them. Despite the family connection, the two nobles had been rivals for some time, and Raymond's attempt to persuade his nephew to join him against a common foe came to naught.

Practically alone, without friends or allies, by the end of the year 1208 Raymond came to realize that his only hope was to find a way of reconciling himself with the Church. At this point, Raymond made a serious and apparently sincere effort in that direction. At the same time, however, he sought to maneuver himself into a more favorable position and wrote to Innocent complaining that he could not reach any agreement with a legate as inflexible as Arnaud Amaury. He sent two ambassadors to Rome with the letter, instructing them to accept any terms Innocent would offer. He declared his devotion to the Church and admitted to his many faults, including protection of the Cathars and failure to honor the Church. Raymond also informed the pope that he was willing to surrender numerous castles and possessions as proof of good faith. The pope responded to this offer by appointing his secretary, Milo, and a canon from Genoa, Thedisius, as papal legates for the region – much to the count's pleasure. Milo was instructed, however, to obey Arnaud Amaury in all things; he was warned to treat the count with great caution and be aware of his duplicity.

As preparations for the Crusade continued apace, Raymond was restored to communion with the Church. On June 18, 1209, in front of the great abbey church in the town of St. Gilles, Raymond did penance. Stripped to the waist and before a great crowd of bishops, priests, and lay people, he agreed to obey the papal legates in all matters and admitted to a large number of offenses against God and the Church; these included favoring the heretics on his lands rather than expelling them, violating the Peace of God and the holy days of the Church, abusing the clergy and appropriating Church lands, promoting the Jews to positions of public power, employing mercenary troops, and levying unjust and excessive tolls. Curiously enough, he was not forced to confess participation in the murder of Peter of Castelnau, but only to admit that he was 'suspected' of some involvement in it. He was led into the church by Milo, who flogged him with a switch all the way to the altar, and there the papal legate pronounced his absolution.

On the following day, at Milo's request, Raymond issued a document confirming the agreement he had reached with the Church. The legates were not to be interfered with in the exercise of their duties. Seven castles, most of them in the Rhône Valley, were to be surrendered to the Church, and the garrisons of their fortresses were ordered to hold these castles at the legates' command. The various towns and nobles under Raymond's authority in the Rhône Valley were forced to promise cooperation with the legates. In this way the count demonstrated his acceptance of the terms of the agreement. The document was an act of good faith designed to prove his obedience to Pope Innocent and his legates.

After his humiliating act of submission, Raymond took one further step: he asked to be able to take the cross against the heretics. This request was granted, and he joined the crusaders at Valence on June 24. The count's reasons for joining the Crusade are not hard to discern – he was primarily motivated by a strong desire for self-preservation and for the destruction of his rivals in Occitania. The lax devotion to the Catholic faith and the relative tolerance of the Cathar heretics which he demonstrated in the past suggest that he was not moved by religious fervor; but he was very much aware that it was too late to prevent the Crusade from entering his lands. By taking the cross and undergoing the obligatory forty days of military service he would gain all the protections granted to crusaders, including the preservation of his own titles and his extensive land holdings throughout the region. Not only would he gain crusader immunity, he would also be able to assume a position of leadership in the Crusade and become privy to its plans and objectives. Moreover, he could redirect the Crusade itself, so as to make it suppress his rivals. Most importantly, he could turn it against his nephew, Viscount Raymond-Roger, who had caused him such trouble. Raymond may have hoped that the Crusade would invade his nephew's lands and defeat him, thus weakening him sufficiently for the count to be able to impose his will on this most difficult vassal. Other unruly nobles could also face the same fate and, once the Crusade had left the south, Raymond could reestablish himself as the most powerful lord of the land – indeed his position could even be stronger than ever before.

Joining the army at Valence in late June, the count took advantage of his new position and turned the Crusade's attention from his lands to focus on those of Raymond-Roger and of the Trencavel family in the area of Albi – notably the important towns of Béziers and Carcassonne. Once the army reached Montpellier, Raymond himself guided it, through the territory owned by his nephew, toward Béziers, which was well fortified and an important commercial center. The army reached the town on July 22. Its citizens had been busy preparing for the impending siege, which they felt confident they could withstand on account of the strength of the town walls and of their own determination to preserve the integrity of their home. Indeed, taking a strongly fortified town was a difficult task, and the people of Béziers believed they could outlast the forty days of service that the crusaders owed: a prolonged siege would discourage the attackers, sending the message that it could last beyond their term of service.

Expecting to face a siege of some duration, the crusaders sent the bishop of Béziers to negotiate with the townspeople. The bishop arrived with a list of names of 222 Cathar heretics resident in Béziers (a town with a population of some eight to ten thousand people) and declared that, if either the heretics were surrendered or the Catholics in town were to depart, the Crusade would spare them and their property. The people of Béziers refused; shortly after the siege began, and very quickly ended. Instead of a long, drawn-out process, the capture of Béziers took place in just a few hours. Some of the townspeople initiated hostilities, and in the confusion that followed the gates were breached and one of the worst massacres of the Middle Ages followed. According to contemporary accounts, thousands of people took refuge in the church of La Madelaine and died when the crusaders burned it to the ground. The mounted knights and foot soldiers indulged in a horrible slaughter, killing men, women, and children – Catholic and heretic alike. They plundered homes, invaded churches, burned large sections of the town, and indulged in wanton destruction and looting. Although contemporary reports of a massacre of tens of thousands are surely exaggerated, it was true that very many died, and the fall of Béziers sent shock waves throughout the region.

After Béziers, Raymond and the other crusaders moved on to the great town of Carcassonne, which they reached by August 1. Their morale was buoyed by the capture of Béziers and they hoped to repeat their success at Carcassonne. Raymond-Roger had taken command in the defense of the city, whose population swelled after the disaster at Béziers; the viscount faced the possibility of a prolonged siege during the hottest part of the summer and the prospect of food and water shortages. His overlord, Peter II, king of Aragon (1174–1213), arrived to mediate between the crusaders and his vassal. But Peter, a leader in the reconquest of Spain and a devout Catholic, had little sympathy for the Cathars and was very critical of his vassal's failure to expel them. He arrived with only a small military contingent; he could not have offered much support even if he had wanted to defend his vassal. The king tried to negotiate the surrender of the town for a guarantee of freedom of passage for Viscount Raymond-Roger and eleven companions, but the viscount rejected the offer. The siege itself lasted for about a fortnight before the viscount agreed to surrender, and on August 15 the town of Carcassonne fell to the crusaders. Its occupation took place with little of the destruction that had occurred in Béziers. The papal legate himself sought to ensure that none of that was repeated at Carcassonne, perhaps in the hope that more moderate treatment would help the crusaders to win people's hearts in the Occitan, helping to bring heresy there to an end. Raymond-Roger had agreed to surrender the town to the crusaders in exchange for his safety, but, in a clear violation of contemporary practice, he was captured and imprisoned upon leaving. He was to die of dysentery in a prison near Carcassonne, on November 10, 1209.

After the fall of Carcassonne, a successor to Raymond-Roger had to be found; the office of viscount was offered to a succession of crusade leaders ending with

Simon de Montfort, earl of Leicester, a noble of the Ile-de-France known for his personal bravery and Christian devotion. He had previously participated in the Fourth Crusade and was one of the few crusaders to have reached the Holy Land and refused to attack Zara when the rest turned on that Christian town. De Montfort used his new possessions as a base for conquering the Trencavel lands to start with, then for pursuing the Crusade against the heretics; he pursued it relentlessly until his death, even when the pope sought to limit it. Thus he came to be identified with the Crusade. He encountered great difficulties in maintaining a significant army in the field because of the limitation of service to forty days, compounded with the pope's temporary withdrawal of support; yet Simon was successful in the war and took control of much territory.

By the time this new leader of the Crusade assumed his position as viscount, Raymond VI had completed his term of service and retired from the Crusade, feeling that he had fulfilled his obligation. But both Simon de Montfort – who had continued the military campaigns in the Trencavel lands in spite of various setbacks and of the difficulty of maintaining his army – and the Church leaders, especially Arnaud Amaury, remained skeptical of the count's intentions. They complained that he had been less than zealous in his performance as a crusader and failed to discipline the heretics on his territories. In fact Arnaud Amaury and the other two papal legates, Milo and Thedisius, excommunicated the count for a second time in September 1209. In the face of this pressure from the Church and de Montfort, Count Raymond took steps to preserve his place and power. He appealed to his overlords, Philip Augustus of France and Otto IV of Germany, for aid and protection, but neither was interested in getting involved and lent him little help. Having to look elsewhere, Raymond sent an appeal to Innocent in Rome. Whatever he wrote in it, the petition seemed to have some effect on the pope; for he encouraged restraint on the part of his legates and asked them to allow Raymond an opportunity to prove his devotion to the Church.

In July 1210 Raymond met with the legates at St. Gilles. Although he arrived with the expectation that he would be reconciled with the Church and some of its members were willing to implement such reconciliation, the papal legate Thedisius declared that the count had not fulfilled the terms outlined in earlier papal bulls. Heretics still thrived on his lands, tolls were still imposed, and mercenaries still remained in his employ. Until these matters were resolved there could be no reconciliation. Raymond may have exploded in rage, but there was little he could do short of acceding to the demands of the legate.

For the remainder of the year, Raymond witnessed Simon de Montfort's campaigning in the Trencavel lands. Although de Montfort suffered some disappointments, by the end of 1210 he had secured several key towns and welcomed numerous reinforcements, including those brought by his wife, Alice of Montmorency. Raymond's military ill fortune was matched by further difficulties with the Church. The count met with the legates at a council in Montpellier in January and February of 1211. At the assembly, the legates presented him with a series of conditions which, if met, would lead to his reconciliation with the Church. The conditions themselves, however, demonstrated how little the legates desired to come to terms with the count. According to a contemporary, albeit not completely reliable, account, Raymond was to give up his tolls and mercenaries, as demanded previously, but he was also to destroy his castles and place restrictions on his vassals. He was to allow Simon de Montfort to travel without hindrance across his territories; he was to go on crusade to the Holy Land and join a military order. The count rejected these demands and left the meeting without a word to the legates. Peter II, king of Aragon, who was in attendance, was offended by the demands, a result with disastrous consequences for the future. But the count's refusal to accept the terms had the desired effect: the legates were able to renew the ban of excommunication against him and the pope subsequently confirmed their sentence.

Raymond faced increasing hostility both from the legates and from de Montfort. The latter had started a campaign to encircle the city of Toulouse, which was split between those who supported the count and those who did not. In May, de Montfort succeeded in taking the city of Lavaur. The fall of Lavaur was a turning point in the war and an example of the extreme brutality with which the Crusade was often pursued. For the first time, de Montfort approved of the execution of nobles and knights who had opposed him. The commander of the garrison and eighty of his knights were hanged, and Geralda, the lady of the castle, was thrown into a well and stoned to death. Along with them, four hundred heretics were burned – an example of terror that convinced other towns to accept de Montfort's authority. But during the summer de Montfort was unable to match this success, and his attempt to take Toulouse failed. Indeed Toulouse was a bit of a miscalculation on the part of de Montfort, whose reputation as a brilliant commander suffered accordingly. His saving grace, however, was in Raymond's being a terrible military commander and a poor strategist, who was unable to take advantage of his rival's setback.

Raymond sought to press his advantage and led a counterattack following de Montfort's failure outside the walls of Toulouse. The count organized a massive army, which included his own contingents and those of the count of Foix, of the viscount of Béarn, and of other southern nobles who had little sympathy for the invaders from the north. Simon de Montfort had taken refuge with a small force at Castelnaudary and made a stand there as Raymond began the siege. But it was a poorly designed and implemented siege. Despite significantly outnumbering his rival, Raymond failed to surround the town and refused to meet the besieged enemy in pitched battle. The camp he pitched to the north of the town faced repeated raids by de Montfort's soldiers, and it sometimes appeared that Raymond himself was under siege. As the siege dragged on, reinforcements moved southward, to support de Montfort. The count of Foix, Raymond-Roger, marched out to meet them and suffered a terrible defeat not far from Castelnaudary, at St.-Martin-la-Lande. His army, which received no help from the count of Toulouse, was driven from the field thanks to the timely arrival of Simon de Montfort with a small force of mounted knights. Raymond-Roger's men were forced into disarray; many claimed to be crusaders in the chaos and were killed by their comrades, while the crusaders themselves killed large numbers of them. This disaster was followed by the withdrawal of the siege. It was a stunning defeat for Raymond, salvaged only by the belief, spread by Raymond-Roger, that de Montfort had been defeated, which led to the defection of numerous towns loyal to him.

De Montfort responded vigorously to the defections and sought to limit the damage caused by Raymond-Roger's false rumor. He was aided by a renewed enthusiasm for crusading that burst throughout Christendom in 1212 – the Children's Crusade occurred, Christians fought successfully in Spain, and calls for aid in Constantinople were made. The Albigensian venture benefited from this; crusading against heresy was preached everywhere in Europe, and de Montfort welcomed crusaders from Germany, northern France, Normandy, and Italy during the winter and spring of 1212. This enabled him to take the offensive against Count Raymond and others who opposed his authority. De Montfort won back the important regions of the Tarn and Garonne, together with numerous towns and strongholds along the way. He took the Crusade north into the Agenais, where Raymond held lands from King John of England; it was a risky move, which might have alienated the king of England, but it ended in another success for de Montfort. He seized the territory of Raymond's supporter, the count of Comminges, and gained full control of Albi, Cahors, and much of the south. One of his most important victories, the conquest of Moissac, was also one of his most brutal. After roughly six weeks of siege, from August to early September, de Montfort agreed to a negotiated settlement that spared the city but forced the leaders of Moissac to surrender the town's defenders, who numbered more than three hundred, and also a contingent from Toulouse; the crusaders quickly killed them all. Following his military conquest of much of the south, de Montfort held a council at Pamiers in November 1212 which organized his subjugated territories around northern customs and imposed new regulations on the people of Occitania.

Although Raymond was in large measure responsible for the Crusade and failed to limit the damage caused by de Montfort, he was not without supporters, especially after the dramatic successes of the chief crusader in 1212. The pope himself began to question the intentions of de Montfort, worrying that he was more interested in acquiring territory and political power than in suppressing heresy and in protecting the interests of the Church. As early as the spring of 1212, Innocent had written to his legates, asking them to give Raymond yet another chance to clear his name and to prove his devotion to the Church. The pope also forbade his legates to seize Raymond's lands or to dispossess his heirs. Innocent's letter was prompted not only by his uncertainties about Raymond and de Montfort but also by concerns over alienating the king of France and by his desire to promote crusading in Spain against the Muslims.

Innocent took even more definite steps to restrict the actions of de Montfort in January 1213. In two separate letters, to the legates and to de Montfort, he revised his policies toward the Crusade in the lands of Raymond of Toulouse. In his letter to the legates, Innocent wrote:

> Foxes were destroying the vineyard of the Lord in Provence; they have been captured. Now we must guard against a greater danger. We hear the Saracens of Spain are preparing a new army to avenge their defeat [by Peter II of Aragon at the Battle of Las Navas de Tolosa] ... Moreover, the Holy Land needs assistance.[5]

Preaching was to be directed toward crusading to the Holy Land and against Islam, not toward the heresy in Languedoc. In the second letter, Innocent complained to Simon de Montfort that,

> not content with opposing heretics, you had led crusaders against Catholics ... you have shed the blood of innocent men and have wrongfully invaded the lands of [Peter II, king of Aragon] his vassals, the counts of Foix and Comminges, Gaston of Béarn, while the king [of Aragon] was making war on the Saracens and though the people of these lands were never suspected of heresy.[6]

Innocent demanded, further, that de Montfort restore the lands seized from nobles innocent of heresy or of supporting it. He also declared that indulgences were to be offered only to those fighting the Muslims in Spain or in the Holy Lands; there was no indulgence for fighting in the lands of the count of Toulouse.

Innocent's decisions were inspired, in part, by Peter of Aragon, who had sent an embassy to Rome to discuss matters with him. Although Peter had arranged a marriage alliance with de Montfort and had recognized him as his vassal, viscount of Béziers, he had become increasingly uncomfortable with de Montfort's military successes. Peter had greater affinity with southerners like Raymond, even if his tolerance for heretics was limited. And Peter had led a successful crusade against the Muslims of Spain in 1212; the crushing victory he won at the Battle of Las Navas de Tolosa enhanced his reputation as a Christian king and crusader. As a consequence, his defense of Raymond and his complaints against de Montfort had great influence on decisions in Rome – at least until de Montfort and his supporters could reach the pope's ear.

But, even as Peter's petition was made to the pope, the legates held a council at Lavaur. Peter himself attended it to present another petition – in favor of Raymond, his son Raymond VII, and the other nobles dispossessed by the Crusade. The legates rejected the king's requests and denounced Raymond and the other Occitan nobles as heretics and enemies of the Church and crusade. They, too, sent representatives to Rome, which caused Innocent to recant and chastize Peter for misinforming him about the situation in the Occitan.

As a result of Innocent's vacillations, battle-lines were drawn between Peter and de Montfort; Raymond had now the staunch defender he had sought since the outbreak of the war. He, together with the counts of Foix and Comminges, various nobles of Gascony, and the dispossessed nobles of the Trencavel lands joined forces with Peter and the large army he brought with him as he crossed the Pyrenees. Lacking the military skill to defeat de Montfort, Raymond had now acquired an ally whose reputation as a commander and crusader was greater than that of de Montfort. Not only did Raymond have an ally of superior skill; the army commanded by Peter was at least twice, if not three times, the size of de Montfort's army. The support of that honored son of the Church and successful crusader, Peter of Aragon, further strengthened Raymond's position because it undermined de Montfort's claims that he was working to rid the land of heresy. Peter, Raymond, and their great army were therefore extremely confident – perhaps too confident – as they prepared for the battle which could bring the Crusade to a close; but de Montfort's sense of his own invincibility and deep faith that God was on his side left him equally certain of his fate.

The battle of Muret, near Toulouse, began on the morning of September 12, 1213, and by the day's end was an unmitigated disaster for Raymond and his allies. The count of Toulouse, despite his poor reputation as a soldier, offered the most sensible plan: to fortify their camp strongly and wait for de Montfort's attack from a position of strength, or else starve their enemy into submission, should de Montfort not attack. This plan, however, was scorned by Peter and the other members of the southern coalition, who desired an immediate and decisive battle. King Peter was so confident of victory that, true to his reputation, he spent the night before the battle with one of his mistresses and was so tired on the next morning that he could barely stand up during mass. He would lead his forces into battle and, unlike most commanders, take his place in the front lines wearing the armor of a common knight. The king marched out with his army and ordered his men to await the assault from de Montfort and his army. When de Montfort attacked, the poor organization of the troops and the lack of coordination between the various members of the coalition proved fatal. De Montfort's well-organized and highly disciplined troops made short work of their enemy; the army of the count of Foix was swept aside first, and then the army of Aragon was routed by de Montfort's charge. Peter himself was killed in the battle and his army quickly dispersed upon hearing the news of the king's death. Fleeing in terror, the troops of the southern coalition were quickly cut down by the crusaders or drowned in the River Garonne. The militia of Toulouse, which had launched an attack on the western wall of the town, was unaware of the massacre in the field below. The return of Simon de Montfort caused a panic; the Toulousains fled and were also killed by crusaders or drowned in the river. Contemporary accounts place the number of the dead at twenty thousand, which is unlikely, but the slaughter was significant and included Raymond's most important and powerful supporter. The battle of Muret was a great and humbling defeat for Raymond; it eliminated the Aragonese as a force in the politics of Occitania and strengthened de Montfort's position in the region even further.

Although Raymond was once again humbled on the field of battle, at least he had the hope that the pope and the king of France would not confirm de Montfort in the offices of the south. For the next two years the situation around him remained fluid, and the count saw both successes and setbacks. On the military and political front, he benefited from de Montfort's failure to follow up his victory at Muret with a conquest of Toulouse – a logical step, but one not taken because of de Montfort's inadequate number of troops. He also scored a minor triumph in the capture of his younger brother Baldwin, who had joined the Crusade in the hope of becoming count of Toulouse himself, and had fought with de Montfort at Muret. Baldwin was hanged as a traitor. Moreover, Innocent appointed a new legate, Peter of Benevento, who was instructed not to make any permanent settlement in Occitania, to preserve the political boundaries as they had existed before Muret, and to put Toulouse under the protection of Rome. This effectively restricted de Montfort's attempts to complete his conquest of the count's lands and forced him to look elsewhere in the region for military success. In April 1214, the counts of Foix, Comminges, and Toulouse, along with the people of Toulouse, appeared before the new legate, to seek absolution and restoration to the Church. Along with his submission, Raymond promised to turn over his titles to his son, Raymond VII, and to cede his territories to the Church.

Despite these minor victories, Raymond still faced major challenges. De Montfort did not rest after his triumph at Muret. In 1214 he strengthened his hold on the south, raiding the counties of Foix and Comminges, extending his control over Provence, and reducing other strongholds throughout the region. His successes were rewarded by the papal legate Robert of Courçon, who assumed the duties of Peter of Benevento during his brief absence. Robert granted to de Montfort the lands of the heretics in the Albigeois, Agenais, Quercy, and Rouergue. De Montfort earned a further diplomatic success at the Council of Montpellier in January 1215, which met under the presidency of the legate Peter of Benevento, now returned to the Occitan. The assembled bishops and archbishops unanimously agreed that the lands, titles, and rights of Raymond VI should be granted to de Montfort, and they requested that Peter invest de Montfort immediately with these honors. Peter, however, was restricted by his commission; he could only defer the final decision to the Council in Rome later that year. Although a limited victory, de Montfort nonetheless emerged in a stronger position after Montpellier. Even the crusade of Prince Louis, son of Philip Augustus, ended by benefiting de Montfort. Much delayed, the intervention of Louis in the affairs of the Occitan reinforced de Montfort's position in several ways. Louis himself was deferential to de Montfort as the chief crusader and bestowed on him the castle of Foix; he also approved of the destruction of the walls of Narbonne and Toulouse.

Raymond's great hope lay with the decisions of the pope at the Fourth Lateran Council, which took place in November 1215 in Rome. One of the greatest of all church councils, the Fourth Lateran addressed a broad range of topics, including religious reform, the definition of the Eucharist, political matters relating to France and the Empire, relations with the Jews, as well as heresy and crusading. Innocent was conflicted about the ultimate decisions concerning Raymond and his lands, and Raymond had his defenders at the Council. His old antagonist, Arnaud Amaury, the former legate and now the archbishop of Narbonne, spoke on his behalf, partly out of his animosity toward de Montfort, who had destroyed the town's walls and claimed rights over the city. Indeed, de Montfort's own ambitions in some ways played against him, supporting Innocent's suspicions that de Montfort was concerned with conquest more than with the suppression of heresy. Besides, other bishops from the south defended Raymond, and Innocent was aware of the count's acts of contrition and submission to the Church. Even if the count himself were guilty of supporting heresy and other crimes, his son, Raymond VII, was not and should not suffer for the crimes of his father. The rights of the young Raymond, furthermore, were supported at the Council by representatives of King John of England. But Raymond VI had equally powerful enemies at the Council, including the bishop of Toulouse, who spoke forcefully against him and the other southern nobles.

Because Raymond had never suppressed, nor would he ever suppress, heresy on his lands, de Montfort had assumed the territories by right of conquest and seemed a more likely candidate for the job of putting an end to heresy in the south. Innocent and the Council therefore declared that the lands of the count conquered by the crusaders were forfeited to de Montfort. Raymond was to live in exile on his wife's lands and was granted, on good behavior, a pension of four hundred marks a year. Lands of the count not conquered by the crusaders were to be given to Raymond VII once he came of age.

The Lateran Council of 1215 marked the high point for Simon de Montfort and the nadir for Raymond VI, but the wheel of fortune would turn once again, and 1216 marked the beginning of the end for de Montfort's control of the south. Indeed, the counterattack against de Montfort began not long after the Council. In April 1216, Raymond and his son returned home through the town of Marseilles, a town with no particular duties toward them but which welcomed them with cheers and oaths of loyalty. From there they traveled to Avignon, where they were again acclaimed and promised aid, and it was made quite clear that the nobility of Provence had little love for de Montfort and was willing to support the Raymonds against him. From Avignon, Raymond VI rode to Aragon to raise an army for the struggle against de Montfort, and the young Raymond rode to Beaucaire, which was held by de Montfort but declared itself in support of the Raymonds. Raymond VII took the town, but de Montfort's garrison held the citadel. Raymond VI arrived and a double siege ensued, the count attacking the citadel, de Montfort besieging the town.

Employing all his usual skill, de Montfort could neither entice the young Raymond out into the field of battle nor take the town. The young Raymond held the town, while his father drove the garrison into submission and forced de Montfort to withdraw in defeat. The victory at Beaucaire led to the defection of many other southern towns between 1216 and 1217 and undermined de Montfort's aura of invincibility.

The most important town to reject de Montfort's authority was Toulouse. Already in 1216, the town rebelled against de Montfort and drove his soldiers away from the city, but de Montfort arrived and suppressed the revolt, agreeing to spare the town in return for the payment of a fine of 30,000 marks. This burdensome fine did not sit well with the people of Toulouse, and in the summer of 1217 they offered to surrender the town to Raymond VI if he could hold it against de Montfort. In an act completely out of character, Raymond marched quickly and decisively to Toulouse with a large army from Spain, and his arrival in September, in the company of the counts of Foix and Comminges and other nobles and mercenaries, was greeted with great joy and enthusiasm. Although de Montfort's garrison had managed to retain control of the castle, Raymond secured the town as a whole, which quickly became the center for the rebellion against de Montfort. Once back in Toulouse, Raymond put its people to work, erecting a new defensive network of trenches and other barricades around the town, in preparation for the siege. And when it came, Raymond and his people were ready.

The siege of Toulouse lasted for some nine months, from late September 1217 until late June 1218, and its conclusion brought the first phase of the Albigensian Crusade to an end. It began with de Montfort arriving with what forces he could muster in his ride from Carcassonne. He saw that his only option was to take the town quickly, and he launched an all-out assault on Toulouse, which was bloodily repulsed. Having failed to take the town back, de Montfort, facing the end of the campaigning season and being short on men and money, was forced to wait until the spring. In the meantime, he encouraged the new pope, Honorious III (1216–27), to issue a call for crusade. The forces of de Montfort and Raymond engaged in modest jousting, but little was gained on either side during the winter. As the spring campaigning season began, both sides were reinforced by new troops; Raymond welcomed the arrival of his son among others. As the siege dragged on, the morale of the defenders increased, while the besiegers complained of the prolonged, difficult, and unsuccessful assault. De Montfort mounted a few direct attacks on the city, but he was driven back each time, with heavy losses on both sides. To bring the siege to a close, de Montfort ordered the construction of a great siege tower, but efforts to get it close enough to the town were met with heavy opposition from the Toulousains. In one of these struggles, on June 25, de Montfort himself was killed. His skull was crushed by stones hurled, according to tradition, by a woman operating a mangonel – a type of catapult used to throw missiles.

The war continued for a short time after de Montfort's death, but there was no one to replace him. Raymond VI had survived, and many towns returned to at least nominal allegiance to him. Following the victory at Toulouse, Raymond's son continued the reconquest of the south. The only serious challenge for him was the return of Prince Louis: in 1219 the latter took the town of Marmande, which suffered the most brutal slaughter since Béziers. Louis attempted later on to take Toulouse itself, but the town was too strong and too confident now; Louis broke off the siege and returned home. The south was once again in the hands of Raymond and his son, even though it would not stay long that way – once king, Louis would return and bring the region under his authority, making a settlement with Raymond VII in 1229.

The old count, Raymond VI, restored to his lands after long years of war, died in 1222. He was again secure in his holding, having weathered the storm of Simon de Montfort and of the Crusade, but he was never reconciled with the Church. He died in the habit of the Hospitallers but still under the ban of excommunication, and, despite repeated efforts by Raymond VII, he would remain outside the Church and was refused burial in consecrated ground. Raymond's dynasty survived thanks to the efforts of his son. The heresy that launched the Crusade also endured, but only to face a Church even more determined to extirpate it.[7]

CHAPTER SIX

PIERRE AUTIER:
THE LAST CATHARS

Raymond VI of Toulouse faced a crusade and the wrath of the papacy on account of his lukewarm devotion to the Church and questionable ties with the Cathars on his lands. But the Church had rapidly lost control of the Crusade itself, and the war in the Occitan changed, from one of religion, into one of conquest. Although claiming his rights in the south as a result of his role as chief crusader, Simon de Montfort was seen by many not so much as a defender of the faith as a political opportunist attempting to acquire titles and territories for himself. Beyond that, the Crusade ultimately failed to destroy heresy in the Occitan, or elsewhere in Christendom for that matter. Despite the massacre of Cathars at Béziers and elsewhere, the Albigensian Crusade did not eradicate the heresy; even after the leadership of the Crusade was taken up by Louis VIII, king of France (1187–1226), the Cathars felt strong enough to hold a council at Pieusse in 1225 and established a new diocese at Razès. Throughout the remainder of the thirteenth century, the representatives of the Catholic Church and the Cathar believers and perfects, men and women, were involved in a prolonged struggle, which the latter would eventually lose. They disappeared in the fourteenth century, after enjoying one final success under the guidance of their last important missionary, the perfect or 'Good Man,' Pierre Autier, who was executed in 1310.

The transformation which led one of the most feared sects, potential rival to the established Catholic Church, to this end was the result of both internal and external developments. Although the contention, once popular, that the life-denying aspects of the faith led to its own demise should not be exaggerated, it can be said that the heresy itself was plagued by certain contradictions and dissensions, and some of its doctrine surely alienated both the potential converts and the committed believers. Perhaps the fundamental flaw of the Cathar movement was the division between absolute and moderate dualists, which was apparent as early as the Council of St. Félix-de-Caraman (traditionally dated 1167, but more likely 1174). The split over doctrine limited the possibility for unity and led to competition between the various Cathar churches. Adding further confusion and uncertainty was the stringent moral code of the sect, which held that any perfect who suffered moral lapses and violated the rigid code of conduct lost the *consolamentum*; moreover, all those consoled by such a perfect also lost the consolamentum as a consequence of the perfect's sins. This meant, in the words of the inquisitor and former Cathar Rainier Sacconi, that 'all Cathars labor under very great doubt and danger of the soul.'[1] Although members of the community could be reconsoled, they remained in a state of uncertainty about their own salvation because of doubts concerning the moral integrity of the perfects. Moreover, the harsh attitude toward sexuality and, especially, toward the bearing of children could have negative consequences. Pregnant women were mocked at by the Cathars and told that they were carrying a demon in their belly. Female perfects were known to pray with pregnant women, asking God to free the women of the demons in them, and at least one woman with child was told that, if she died while pregnant, she could not be saved.[2] This clearly alienated many women, who might have otherwise supported the movement, and it led some into outright opposition to the Cathars. The problem was particularly difficult for the Cathars, because women played an important role in their success and also in passing on the faith within the family.

Despite various organizational and doctrinal problems, the Cathar heresy, which continued to attract followers throughout the thirteenth century, might well have endured had it not been for the increasing weight of the persecution imposed upon it by the Catholic Church, itself an increasingly centralized and efficient institution. The attack on the Cathars took two forms. First, there was the continued political and military assault on the Cathars following after the Albigensian Crusade – which, as discussed, had evolved into something closer to a political military venture than to a religious campaign and had concluded with the complete absorption of the Occitan into the kingdom of France. Although it ended as a war of conquest, the Albigensian Crusade did bring about a change in the relationship between heretics and the leaders of the south. The treaty of Paris, which settled the war in 1229, undermined the support for the Cathars throughout Occitania and limited their places of refuge. Perhaps the most important consequence of the treaty and defeat of Raymond VI and his line was the transformation of Toulouse from one of the great centers of the Cathar heresy into a Catholic city. The town itself was deprived of its walls and of the great network of defenses erected against the Crusade near the end of Raymond VI's life. Control over the city was granted to representatives of the king of France and garrisoned by royal troops, and the authority of the Catholic bishop of Toulouse was extended to include the city and numerous of its dependencies. At the same time, many other towns throughout the region suffered a similar fate; they were deprived of their defenses and placed under royal control. Moreover, Raymond VII took up the opposition to heresy, although he was slow to start and eager to retain as much control over his lands as possible. Even if, until as late as the early 1240s, Raymond had resisted the efforts to suppress heresy and had even supported the Cathars and their noble allies in revolt, in 1243 he became an aggressive enemy of the heretics. He publicly proclaimed his disavowal and his willingness to pursue the Cathars; he even offered a bounty of two marks of silver to those who helped toward arresting them and finding them guilty. He also expelled those who had supported the Cathars and fought against the Crusade, and in 1249, in Agen, he burned eighty people suspected of heresy.

The demise of the nobility's support for the Cathars was central to the decline of the heresy in the south; but just as crucial, if not more so, was the work of the inquisitors, who flooded the region following the end of the war. It was their work that helped to break the back of the movement and forced it underground. Established by Pope Gregory IX in the 1230s, the Inquisition set up a regular judicial body to root out heresy, and this body replaced the traditional episcopal tribunal. The pope turned to the Dominican order for staffing the inquisitorial tribunals; later on, Franciscans and members of other orders were included. People accused of heresy were brought before the inquisitors, who often asked leading questions which forced the accused to prove their innocence. Torture was resorted to at times, but the inquisitors' goal was to discover the heretics and to recall them to the faith. Other inquiries followed, building on the precedents and procedures established at Toulouse, and in the great inquest of 1245–46 more than five thousand people were interrogated, many of whom were found guilty of heresy and thus subject to imprisonment, exile, or loss of property. Under pressure from the inquisitors, the accused would at times denounce others, in order to prove their own commitment to the faith or to turn attention to other guilty parties.

By mid-century the machinery of repression had been effectively established on the lands of Raymond VII, but the Cathar perfects still enjoyed the respect of many throughout the south, and there was continued resentment of the northern powers. Attack against the inquisitors took place; they were sometimes murdered, expelled from various towns, or cut off from food and water. Open revolts against the authority of secular powers and of the inquisitors also occurred, but with little success. The most notorious counterattack took place in 1242, when Raymond and a collection of southern nobles participated in the revolt and a group of Cathars and their supporters attacked and killed a group of inquisitors in Avignonet. The revolt failed and Raymond finally submitted to royal authority, but the raid in Avignonet brought the death of a number of inquisitors, including the Dominican William Arnold, who had enjoyed great success since his arrival in the region in 1241. The murderers, having smashed their victims with axes and swords, seized books and various records belonging to the inquisitors; but the primary motive for the attack was to put an end to inquests in the rebels' homeland. Indeed, as one of the attackers noted later, they hoped that the attack would make it so that 'the affair of the inquisition could be extinguished, and the whole land would be freed, and there would not be another inquisition.'[3]

But, far from ending the persecutions for heresy, the murders led to the destruction of Montségur in the Pyrenees, the greatest Cathar stronghold.[4] It was in the fortress at the hilltop, which had attracted large numbers of Cathar perfects and believers, that the attack on the inquisitors had been planned. In response, the king's representative, with forces from the archbishop of Toulouse and the bishop of Carcassonne, laid siege to the fortress from the summer of 1243 to March 1244. Despite the staunch resistance of the garrison, the strength of the fortress itself, and the hope that Raymond VII would intervene, Montségur was taken. Although the defenders were spared, the heretics were not. Following the fall of the fortress, some 200 Cathar perfects, including important Cathar bishops, were burned in a great fire, which clearly signaled the beginning of the end for the heresy. Indeed, it was impossible for the Cathars to recover from the loss of so many of its leaders, and any hope of recovery was further limited by the continued vigor of the inquisitors and the final loss of support from Raymond VII and other secular leaders.

Nevertheless, it was in this environment of severe persecution from the Church and after the progressive decline of the Cathar churches in the later thirteenth century that a revival of the heresy, led by Pierre Autier, took place. The revival, lasting roughly from 1299 to 1310 under him, and, albeit greatly weakened, for nearly twenty years after his fiery death in 1310 – for the last trial of one of his followers occurred in 1329 – reveals the lingering attraction of Catharism despite its own inherent flaws and the persecution of the Church. Catharism managed to endure, and established networks between communities and their way of life set the foundation for its own resurgence under Autier. This revival extended throughout the Lauragais and as far as Toulouse and the Lower Quercy. Indeed the phenomenon was serious enough to attract the attention of three of the greatest inquisitors: Geoffrey d'Ablis, Bernard Gui, and Jacques Fournier (the future Pope Benedict XII).

Pierre Autier and his followers benefited from the developments within Catharism which had occurred in the second half of the thirteenth century, and also from certain developments involving the Church and local nobility. Despite the general collapse of the support of the nobility for the Cathars in the Occitan, a number of lesser nobles and the powerful count of Foix resumed their traditional tolerance of the heresy and hostility toward the Catholic Church. As a consequence, the leading inquisitors in the region were more concerned with the behavior of the nobility than with that of perfects like Pierre Autier. There was also lingering resentment of the northern French authority among both the secular and religious elite in the south, and this turned their attention further away from heresy. Moreover, although by Autier's time whatever organizational structure had once existed among the Cathars – bishoprics, local churches – had been destroyed for the most part, there remained a number of communities that maintained connections, if only tenuous ones. Most importantly, Cathar communities and perfects survived longer in northern Italy than they did in southern France, and were also in a better condition. The Italian Cathars would disappear during the fourteenth century, but by Autier's time they continued to be a source of instruction and encouragement to other Cathars. Indeed, this connection was exploited by the Autiers; in 1296 Pierre and his brother Guillaume went to Cuneo and other towns in Lombardy to receive the consolamentum and further initiation into the teachings of the Cathars. In southern France as well, Cathar perfects, believers, and sympathizers developed a way of life that preserved the traditional beliefs and practices despite the overwhelming burden of Catholic persecution. The perfects and their followers established safe houses throughout the countryside and secret underground networks through which messages and food were conveyed. It was in these safe houses that the perfects preached and ministered, rather than in the public square as they once had done, and they were guided from place to place by *ductores*, Cathar supporters who knew the land and its roadways well enough to lead them safely on their way in the dead of night. Believers and sympathizers not only protected and housed the perfects but also provided them with money, clothes, and a wide range of foodstuffs including fish, bread, oil, wine, apples, figs, and nuts.[5] Finally, and as an indication of the desperate situation the Cathars faced, the shedding of blood was approved in order to protect the perfects and their followers – in other words, murders and physical assaults on informers and enemies were sanctioned.

Developments within Catharism and in the broader world made conditions ripe for a committed and zealous missionary; and Pierre Autier would be that missionary. A member of a Cathar family of Ax-les-Thermes, near Foix, whose adherence to the heresy stretched back into the early thirteenth century and which included two perfects, Pierre Autier came to conversion at some point in his fifties, relatively late in life, and after a very successful professional career. Along with Guillaume, his brother and fellow 'Good Man' of the Cathar faith, Pierre was a prominent and well-to-do notary as well as a member of the nobility of the robe, with connections to the powerful. So well placed was the last great Cathar missionary that he was invited to prepare documents for an agreement between the count of Foix and the king of Aragon. He also prepared a contract between the people of Andorra and the count of Foix and an agreement between the same count and other nobles over a disputed territory. A capable businessman, Autier amassed considerable wealth, which benefited him when he took up the life of a Cathar missionary. His wealth allowed him to buy books, deposit a substantial sum with money changers in Toulouse, and cover the expenses of his wide-ranging travels as a perfect. These included the purchase of a set of fine Parma knives, which he could use to disguise himself as a wandering merchant.

Autier built not only a successful career but also a large family. His wife, Aladaycis, bore him four daughters and three sons; one of these was Jacques, who would become a perfect himself. He also had a mistress, Moneta, the sister of another notary from Autier's home town, who bore him two children: a boy, Bon Guilhem, who accompanied him on his trip to Lombardy, and a girl. His daughters seem to have married well into families at Ax and nearby towns. Raimond, another brother of Pierre, married the sister of a notary, and Guillaume married into an important family of Montaillou. Pierre's own large family and the extensive contacts between them, maintained through the brothers and their spouses, would come to play a very important role in Autier's success as a Cathar 'Good Man,' or perfect, and missionary. They secured lodging, food, and protection against informers and other threats to his mission. The extended family network also provided a ready audience to the missionary work of Pierre, Guillaume, and the other 'Good Men' associated with the Autiers.

According to one of the most important sources for the Autier revival and heresy in the early fourteenth century, namely the register of Jacques Fournier, inquisitor and bishop of Pamiers, Pierre and Guillaume took up the new life of Cathar missionaries in 1295–96. One day Pierre was reading a book, possibly a gospel or doctrinal text of the heresy, in the presence of his brother. He handed Guillaume the book and asked him to read it. After allowing his brother to read for a while, Pierre asked him what he thought about the text. Guillaume answered, 'It seems to me that we have lost our souls.' And in his turn Pierre declared, 'Let us go, my brother, let us go to find our salvation.'[6] And so the two brothers embarked on the long and arduous task of becoming 'Good Men.'

At some point in the year 1296, Pierre, Guillaume, and Bon Guilhem left for Italy to study with the Cathar perfects of Lombardy. The trip which had taken other Cathars from Languedoc to Italy took them through Provence into Nice, and from there into Italy, to the trade city of Cuneo. Disguised as merchants, the three Autiers could blend in easily with the other traders while seeking out instruction from the learned Cathars of Italy. Bon Guilhem returned home in the summer of 1297, to make sure that the place was safe for his father's eventual return. Pierre and Guillaume remained in Lombardy and made contact with senior members of the Cathar church in Italy as well as with the elder of the church of the Occitan, Bernard Audouy, who had contacts in the Lauragais. While in Italy, the two brothers obtained further instruction in the beliefs and practices of the Cathars. They also received the consolamentum, became perfects of the Cathar church, and were thus ready to preach the faith. Before their return to Ax-les-Thermes, the brothers also received training in the ways of the consoled. They learned about the proper diet of the perfects, being slowly weaned from the custom of eating meat and animal fat and introduced to the practice of eating fish, vegetables, and foods which were not produced through coition. The Autiers were also initiated into the cycle of fasting to be followed, and were taught the routine of reciting the Lord's Prayer.[7]

By late 1298 or, more likely, 1299, the two brothers had returned to the land of their birth, accompanied by a small group of perfects they had met in Lombardy, which included Pierre Raymond of Saint-Papoul, Prades Tavernier, and Amiel de Perles, formerly known as Amiel d'Auterive. Leaving the relative safety of Lombardy for Autier's homeland, this small missionary unit began preaching to the network of kin and other close connections in the Lauragais area. Once home, they took shelter in safe houses, to protect themselves from the local religious and secular authorities. They stayed for a time with Raimond Autier, who had not joined them on the trip to Italy and may not even have been informed about the purpose of the journey, but who welcomed them all the same when Bon Guilhem asked his uncle if Pierre could stay with him. They stayed at the homes of other relatives too, both shortly after their arrival and throughout their ten-year mission. Guillaume de Rodes, a nephew of the Autiers, provided shelter for them; Pierre's daughter and husband also offered advice and shelter, and other family members continued to feed the missionaries, bringing them water, wine, bread, cheese, fish, and other things. Not only did the extended Autier family provide items necessary for the missionaries' survival, but some also joined the mission: around the year 1300, Pierre's son Jacques was granted the consolamentum and adopted the life of a fugitive missionary, like his father. Connections with the local lesser nobility also proved fruitful, as the missionaries gained from them as well protection and lodging.

Although Pierre and his fellow missionaries would spread far and wide throughout the Languedoc and preach the Cathar faith to many, the need for security was most necessary because of the constant threat to their existence from the authorities and their various informers. Indeed, within a year of their return, Pierre, Guillaume, and the others faced a grave danger when the beguin (associated with the Spiritual Franciscans) Guillaume Dejean approached the Dominicans at Toulouse and offered to act as a spy for the inquisitors and to deliver the Autiers into their hands. He claimed to know the Autiers and produced more information about heresy in the region, including the allegation that Guillaume de Rodes had housed heretics. De Rodes's brother, the Dominican friar Raimond de Rodes, got wind of these accusations and sent word to his brother about the conspiracy against their uncles, the Autiers. Raimond was known to other Dominicans as a spy who acted for the heretics and protected them by sending warnings such as this one. He asked his brother Guillaume if he had housed the heretics and informed him of Guillaume Dejean's plans. Guillaume denied the allegation, declaring that Dejean was a liar. He then sent word to Raimond Autier about the conspiracy and the news spread quickly among the Cathars of Ax-les-Thermes. Shortly afterward, a Cathar sympathizer, Guillaume Delaire, met Dejean in the town square in Ax-les-Thermes and asked if Dejean wished to meet the Autiers. When he received a positive reply, Delaire offered to lead the spy to Larnat, where both Pierre and Guillaume Autier were residing. On the way there, the spy and his guide were met by other Cathar sympathizers, and possibly by Pierre Autier. Dejean was then savagely beaten and questioned about his intentions. When he finally admitted that he hoped to have the Autiers arrested, he was thrown off a cliff into a ravine, and his body was never found.

This incident demonstrates not only the importance of secrecy and the constant threat faced by Pierre Autier and his fellow missionaries, but also the importance of the network of family and sympathizers who contributed to the success of the mission. Indeed, this is not the only example of the (sometimes violent) lengths to which the missionaries and their supporters went to protect the cause. In 1304, Arnaud Lizier was found murdered in front of the castle gate in the town of Montaillou, where the Autiers enjoyed solid support and the Cathars were quite numerous. The murder followed upon a remark made by Guillaume Autier to the effect that, if it were not for Arnaud Lizier, he could preach publicly in the town square of Montaillou. Lizier's death was no doubt caused by one of the supporters of the heretics in Montaillou, who wanted to ensure that the Cathar 'Good Men' could show themselves in town without fear. The murder was clearly intended as a message of threat to those who opposed the Cathars. In fact, Pierre Autier had boasted to a fellow Cathar that the Autiers and their allies had arranged the murder because Lizier did not like their sect.[8]

Despite the constant threat to their survival, the Autiers found a ready welcome and cultivated a devoted following throughout the region. A hotbed of Catharism for a long time, the Lauragais and beyond offered a broad base of support for its mission. Even though that mission remained mostly underground and preaching took place secretly, in safe houses, beyond the watchful eye of the Catholic Church and its Inquisition, Pierre Autier and his fellows were extremely active and permanently called upon by people in the region to minister to them and to offer them the consolamentum – which some Cathars would only accept near the end of their lives. The welcome received in the region necessitated the creation of more perfects. Traditionally, the procedure was performed by a member of the hierarchy, for instance a bishop or a deacon; but Pierre, who held neither of these ranks, was intent on supplying the necessary leadership for the movement, and in about 1300 he ordained several new perfects. At a ceremony in a supporter's house Pierre consoled his son, Jacques, and Pons Baille, son of a notary of Tarascon. The two young men knelt before the older perfect and asked to be received into the church. Then they heard a sermon on the Lord's Prayer by Pierre Autier and agreed to follow a life of purity, to adhere to the dietary rules of the Cathar 'Good Men,' and never to lie or swear an oath. Pierre Autier then forgave them for their sins, put his hands on them and placed the Gospels over their heads, bestowing the Holy Spirit on them, and declared:

> Bless and forgive us. Amen. May it be done unto us, O Lord, according to Your word. May the Father and the Son and the Holy Ghost pardon and forgive you your sins. Let us pray the Father and the Son and the Holy Ghost. Let us pray the Father and the Son and the Holy Ghost! Holy Father, receive Your servant into Your justice and infuse him with Your Grace and Your Holy Spirit.[9]

The benediction was followed by a recital of the Lord's Prayer and readings from the Gospel of John. The ritual was concluded with another recitation of the Lord's Prayer, and then Pierre kissed the two new perfects.[10] The rite of ordination was repeated later when Pierre consoled two men who took the names of Peter and Paul, and Pierre also sent Philippe d'Alayrac to Sicily to be consoled. In this way, Pierre took steps to extend his influence, spread the faith to a broader area, and respond to the needs of his flock throughout the Languedoc.

The ordination ceremony performed by Autier demonstrates not only the extent of the support they enjoyed in the region but also the importance of texts to the Cathars. Indeed, the possession of books, especially Gospels, was recognized as a sign of heresy in the south. Pierre had his own personal library, which included a book used in the consolamentum, bound in a special leather case, and the important Cathar text *The Vision of Isaiah*. Like all Cathar perfects, Autier traveled with the Gospels, often hiding them in his tunic to avoid suspicion. He used the books to minister to his followers and would read from the Gospels and other Cathar books during his services. The books themselves were often in the vernacular – Occitan – or, as with Gospel books, included facing Latin and Occitan versions of the text. Not only did Pierre Autier use the books when preaching the Word; he also used some of his more elaborate ones to impress and help convert followers. At one meeting he showed off to one of his followers, Pierre de Luzenac, a lavishly illuminated manuscript of the Gospels and letters of St. Paul in Occitan. On another occasion Jacques Autier invited the same Pierre de Luzenac to purchase a complete Bible for the Autiers the next time he was in the city of Toulouse, and Luzenac delivered an Occitan version of the letters of St. Peter and St. Paul.[11] The texts were central to the Autier mission and contributed to their own understanding of the Cathar faith.

Traveling under cover of darkness, through back roads, and observing other precautions, Autier preached a radical dualist form of Catharism which was not uniformly followed by his fellow missionaries: they introduced variations to their leader's teachings. Although historians once maintained that Autier's Catharism was a decadent and corrupt version of the faith that emerged in the late twelfth and early thirteenth centuries, it is now believed that he preached a pure and traditional form of the heresy, shaped by his personal vision. Central to Autier's beliefs was a radical dualism that posited two co-eternal principles of good and evil. He taught that God had created all the spirits and souls in heaven and that the works of Satan brought about the fall of humankind. Standing at the gates of heaven for a thousand years, Satan entered the kingdom of heaven by trickery and seduced God's angels, who were made of body, soul, and spirit. He promised them a variety of riches, power over other creatures, knowledge of good and evil, and wives, all on condition of following him, and for nine days the angels fell from heaven to earth, where they were enclosed in earthly bodies. Finally, God noticed what was happening and put his foot on the hole in heaven through which the angels had departed. He warned the remaining ones of the consequences of following Satan and informed those who had left that they could stay out for the time being, implying that one day they might be allowed to return. [12]

Once the angels left heaven, according to Autier's cosmology, they were forced further under the devil's control. Satan ordered the fallen angels to sing, but they were unable to do so, noting that they now lived in a foreign land. They asked why Satan had tricked them, and one of them told Satan that he would never win and they would return to heaven. Satan informed them they would not, and proceeded to stuff the angels into the earthly bodies he had created, attempting to infuse them with life. But unable to give these bodies the power to move, Satan turned to God for help. The heavenly father answered that he would animate the bodies only if Satan agreed that the souls would belong to God and the bodies to Satan. The devil accepted this bargain and ruled over the bodies. Now, although the souls belonged to God and had come from heaven, once Satan had forced them into bodies of his own creation, they had no memory of having been in heaven. For Autier, bodies were thus essentially evil and the creation of the devil.

The angels would eventually obtain salvation and return to heaven, in Autier's understanding of the Cathar faith, but only after as many as seven to nine transmigrations. According to long-standing Cathar belief, which underpinned Autier's own teaching, a soul imprisoned by Satan in a human body was transferred from one body to the next until it finally reached the body of a consoled Cathar. [13] At that point the soul would be ready to return to heaven. For Autier, the bodies of the Catholic clergy contained the imprisoned souls of the leaders of the angels who followed Satan and, as such, these souls would suffer longer and go through the greatest number of transmigrations before obtaining salvation. Resurrection would be spiritual only, not bodily, because human bodies were the creation of Satan and thus evil.

Autier's dualism shaped his teachings in other ways as well, not the least of which was his belief that the present world was not only the creation of the devil but hell itself. His radical dualism naturally affected his attitude toward the Catholic Church. He rejected Catholic baptism on the grounds that it involved immersion in water, which was part of the evil creation of Satan, and that infants could not assent to the sacrament. He also rejected the Catholic practice of the Eucharist, the mass, and marriage, which was repudiated because it was the means to produce children and bring more people into an evil world. Autier also taught a unique Christology which mixed traditional Cathar teachings and his own interpretation of the nature of Jesus and Mary. As all the Christian dualists, Autier taught a Docetist Christology which denied that Christ had assumed human form or was born of the Virgin Mary, either in reality or in appearance. Christ was pure spirit who only appeared to take human form, and he had no human needs. Christ did not eat or drink, he felt no thirst or hunger, no heat or cold, and he could not die. He obtained the power to bind and set loose from God in heaven, and he bestowed it on his Apostles, who formed the true Church. Autier and the Cathars were the successors of the Apostles, and the consolamentum was the rite they had inherited from the original disciples of Christ. Beyond the traditional Docetic Christology, Autier held that Mary was not a woman at all but rather the will to do good – a teaching that diverged from earlier Cathar beliefs and was not accepted by all of Pierre Autier's fellow missionaries.

With his well-defined faith and necessary texts and assistants, Autier was most concerned to convert the people of the region and to prepare them for death. He was anxious to persuade potential converts to perform the *melioramentum* or the *melhorier*, as it was called in the local language, the ritual greeting owed to Cathar perfects. This procedure, which the inquisitors termed *adoratio*, consisted of the Cathar believers kneeling before the perfect, placing their hands on the ground, and turning their head toward their hands. The believer then asked the perfect three times for their blessing (prior to Autier's revival of Catharism there were both male and female perfects, but females faded away as a result of persecutions). The specific formula of the first two requests opened with the Latin imperative *Benedicite* and was followed by 'Lord,' 'Good Christian,' 'give us God's blessing and yours,' or 'pray to God for us.' The third time round the believer declared, 'Lord, pray to God for this sinner, that He will deliver him from an evil death and lead him to a good end.' The perfect responded to the first two requests by saying, 'Have it from God and from us,' and to the third one he said, 'May God take your prayer, may God make you a good Christian and lead you to a good end.'[14] The ritual concluded with the exchange of a kiss. There was also an abbreviated version of it, which included more limited gestures, such as the tilting of the head, and the request 'Bless us,' which was acknowledged silently by the perfect. The melioramentum was thus a means through which the believer could offer a prayer to God, since he or she was still subject to Satan and could not appeal to God in heaven except through the intermediary actions of the perfects. Performing the melioramentum was also a way for the believer to demonstrate his adherence to the Cathar faith and his acceptance of the spiritual authority of the perfect.

For Pierre Autier and earlier perfects, performance of the ritual was no mere sign of respect, as some would claim when called before the inquisitors, but an indication of commitment on the part of the believers; hence, persuading potential converts to perform the melioramentum was one of the primary goals of Autier's mission. Attempts to gain converts sometimes involved evangelism with a particular individual. One especially important conversion was that of Pierre de Luzenac, a student and future notary. Pierre and his fellow missionaries worked especially hard to convince de Luzenac to perform the melioramentum. They met with him frequently, provided loans, gifts, and money for him, and even showed him the beautiful illuminated Gospel book that Pierre Autier owned. Despite repeated attempts to get him to perform the rite, de Luzenac refused to do so, out of fear for his own safety. Ultimately, however, Pierre and his son Jacques managed to convince him to accept the Cathar faith, and de Luzenac performed the initiation rite while taking shelter from a storm in a mill, in the middle of the night. On another occasion, Pierre Autier used all his powers of persuasion to convince Pierre Maury, a shepherd of the village of Montaillou. Greeting the shepherd by the hand, the Cathar perfect offered to make him a good Christian and to put him on the path to salvation. He discussed at length the virtues of the Cathar perfects, stressing their moral superiority to the Catholic clergy, and assured Pierre Maury that the Cathar way was the true path to follow. The shepherd accepted Autier's arguments, agreed to become a

Cathar, and, after privately practicing genuflecting with Autier, performed the melioramentum.[15]

Preaching to an individual was one means that Pierre Autier used to spread the Cathar faith and convince potential followers to perform the melioramentum, but a more common means was to preach to small groups. On one occasion, such a group traveled from Arques to see Pierre Autier and met him in the house of a follower in Limoux. They all enjoyed a communal meal, which included some fish brought by the group as a gift for Autier, and afterward Autier preached a sermon. The lesson consisted primarily of various moral precepts and probably contained little instruction in the higher matters of Cathar theology. As Guillaume Escaunier, one of those in attendance, reported on his appearance before the inquisitor Geoffrey d'Ablis, Pierre explained that 'in no way should they touch the naked flesh of a woman, and that they should not return evil for evil, since God had forbidden it, and that they should not lie or kill anything except that which drags itself along on its belly across the ground, and if they were going along the road and found a purse or a money-bag, they should not touch it unless they knew it belonged to one of their believers and then they should take it and return it to them.'[16] Autier clearly had an impact on the group: before retiring for the evening, he taught Escaunier how to perform the melioramentum, which indicates that he had won a new convert.

As significant as the melioramentum was to Pierre Autier and his fellow missionaries, perhaps the most important duty of the perfects was to administer the consolamentum. Even though their followers were sometimes reluctant to perform the melioramentum or to accept the dangerous and austere life of the 'perfected' Cathar, they were most anxious to obtain final consolation before death. The consolamentum was the rite that perfected a Cathar believer and imposed upon them the life of asceticism, prayer, and preaching, which most adherents of the faith were unable to adopt. It was increasingly also administered to Cathar believers on the point of dying, because it was believed that the consolamentum would cleanse them of their sins and prepare them for entry into heaven. Indeed, belief in the power of this ritual is revealed by one of Autier's followers, who reported the occurrence of a miracle during its performance, noting that 'a great light descended from the sky upon the house and reached to the sick woman who lay upon the bed.'[17] Moreover, by the time of the Autier brothers, it had become common to perform the rite on the believer's deathbed; sometimes the Cathar perfect arrived too late.

The demand for the consolamentum by Cathar believers and sympathizers in the Lauragais area and in other parts of the Languedoc required the frequent intervention of Pierre Autier and his fellow missionaries. On one occasion, Pierre was called on to console Count Roger-Bernard III at his chateau in Tarascon. One of Pierre's fellow perfects consoled even an infant girl at her parents' request, because they feared she would die. The girl survived, and Pierre criticized the action because she was too young to understand the rite, noting that one of the errors of the Catholic Church was precisely the baptizing of infants who had not reached the age of understanding. But it was, of course, more common to console the aged or the sick unto death, and the Cathar perfects of the Autier revival were often called upon to perform the rite at a moment's notice. Although once a public process, administration of the consolamentum in the later stages of the history of the Cathars was done privately. Pierre's brother Guillaume, for example, was called to console the dying mother of Pierre de Gaillac. Guillaume, however, could not do it because of the large number of people keeping vigil by the deathbed, and so Pierre's wife, Esclarmonde, asked them to leave on the pretext that the excessive heat of the day caused undue suffering for Pierre's mother. Once the crowd had left, Guillaume secretly entered the room and performed the consolamentum.[18]

The need for secrecy and the difficulty of consoling believers yet again who had recovered from illness and taken up their former life led Pierre Autier to accept the practice of the *endura*. In this rite, a consoled believer was forbidden any food or drink other than water; in this way he or she would die without falling back into sin, and so would not need to be consoled again. Although not a new practice and not a sign of the decadence of Autier's revival, as is sometimes said, the endura came into much more widespread use in the late thirteenth and early fourteenth centuries as a result of the Cathars' persecution as well as of Pierre's desire to bring as many people to salvation as possible. Fasting to death was sometimes an easy prospect for the believer who truly was close to dying; to ease the passage, the believer was allowed to drink cold water, but was required to say Our Father after the drink. Even those near death, however, sometimes faced a prolonged endura, which could last for days. One committed believer maintained her fast for twelve weeks before dying, and another one, whose endura lasted for thirteen days, bled herself and planned even more dramatic actions to prevent herself from abandoning the fast. For some, however, the fast proved too much and they demanded food and drink, thus undoing the consolamentum and requiring consolation a second time. On other occasions, family members keeping vigil by the sick would give them food or drink, for instance some chicken soup, to ease the process. Pierre Autier himself imposed the endura on a sick woman whom he left in the care of her daughter; and after three days the daughter gave her mother some food, and she subsequently recovered.

Despite the sometimes prolonged suffering of those on fast, or their lapses into eating again, many times during his career Pierre Autier ordered his followers to undergo the endura and commanded those in charge of the dying not to give them food or drink. On at least one occasion, he even kept vigil over a dying 'consoled' — a practice once as common among the Cathars as among the Catholic clergy; but it had decreased in popularity as the practice of fasting to death became more widespread. He and his brother Guillaume consoled Huguette, the wife of Philippe de Larnat, and stayed with her until she died. At times Pierre spoke to her, encouraging her in her fast and praising her commitment. He offered kind words of praise to her family, emphasizing that she was on her way to paradise and, if she survived, she would honor her obligations as a perfected Cathar.

Even though Pierre Autier and the other perfects exercised great caution and found wide support, the Cathar revival was under constant threat, and the combination of internal betrayal and arrival of skilled and determined inquisitors such as Geoffrey d'Ablis, who was appointed inquisitor for Carcassonne in 1301, and Bernard Gui, who became inquisitor of Toulouse in 1307, would bring it to a fiery finale by the close of the first decade of the fourteenth century. Already in 1301, not long after Autier's return from Lombardy, the revival was threatened by the Dominican spy Guillaume Dejean, and threats to the safety of the Cathars continued as long as Autier and the other perfects preached.

Perhaps the first lethal blow came in 1305, when the inquisitors arrested Guillaume Peyre, a committed Cathar closely associated with the Autiers. For all his zeal, Peyre felt abandoned by Autier and the other Cathars during his time in prison. Peyre had fallen into debt paying prison guards for his food, and the Autiers refused to lend him the money to pay his debt. As a result, he betrayed them to the Inquisition and helped to set a trap for Jacques Autier.

On September 8, Jacques and his companion Prades Tavernier were arrested in Peyre's hometown of Limoux, where they had gone under the pretext that a sick woman wished to be consoled. The arrest came as a shock and would have had a disastrous effect on the movement but for the successful escape of the two Cathars while en route to the inquisitors' prison in Carcassonne. Profound damage was done, however, by Guillaume Peyre, who not only betrayed Autier but also provided substantial information to the inquisitors concerning the extent of Catharism in the region.

Pressure on the Autiers increased with the arrival of Bernard Gui, one of the greatest and most successful Inquisitors. Gui's arrival coincided with the reconciliation of the count of Foix with the Church, as well as the continued efforts of Geoffrey d'Ablis. The activities of the two inquisitors forced Pierre Autier and the others to go further underground for their safety, and the perfects still able to perform the consolamentum had to move from one hiding place to another during their final year. Already in early 1309, Jacques Autier and two other perfects, Guillaume Belibaste and Philippe of Alairac, were captured, but the latter two escaped. In the late spring or early summer of 1309, Guillaume Autier and Prades Tavernier were nearly captured in the town of Montaillou, barely managing to escape in the guise of woodcutters, and in August of that year Bernard Gui issued a call for the arrest of Pierre Autier and other leaders of the Cathar revival. Over the next several months, Autier and nearly all the perfects were captured and brought before the Inquisition, and everyone above the age of fourteen in the town of Montaillou, one of the revival's strongholds, was arrested and interrogated by the inquisitors. By the end of the year nearly all the leaders of Autier's revival with the exception of Pierre were burned at the stake for heresy. The arrests clearly had a devastating effect on the movement, and a number of Autier's followers confessed to the inquisitors after he had been taken into custody.

For a variety of reasons and mainly in order to ensure that more information on heresy in the region would be discovered, Pierre Autier himself was allowed to survive for several months after his capture. Perhaps because he felt secure in the belief that his work would long survive him despite his opponents' efforts, or, more likely, because Cathar perfects were forbidden to lie, Pierre told his interrogators a great deal about his teachings and the church he had resurrected. He offered an extensive discourse on Cathar beliefs and even performed the melioramentum on a fellow believer, before the inquisitors. He provided extensive information on his followers and may even have induced one of them to confess. But, although he may have faced torture, he did not implicate any of the Cathars in the town of Montaillou. Finally, on April 9, 1310, Bernard Gui and Geoffrey d'Ablis condemned him as a heretic and handed him over to the secular arm for execution. In the presence of a great crowd of nobles and of the inquisitors themselves, Pierre Autier was burned at the stake in Toulouse. Before he died, though, he proclaimed that, were he given the chance to preach to the crowd, he would have converted them all to his faith.

Although the last of Autier's followers would survive until 1329, the Cathar revival was essentially brought to a close with the burning of the last great missionary; Catharism itself would not survive his death for long.

CHAPTER SEVEN

FRA DOLCINO
AND THE APOSTOLICI

Tell Fra Dolcino, you who may see the sun,
If he wants not to follow soon to the same
Punishment, he had better store up grain
Against a winter siege and the snow's duress,
Or the Novarese will easily bring him down.[1]

In canto twenty-eight of the *Inferno*, the prophet Muhammad delivers this ominous warning to Dante just as the Tuscan poet makes his way through the ninth circle of hell, being led by his guide, the Roman poet Virgil, and describes the torments that awaited upon Dolcino and other medieval heretics who refused to accept the teachings of the Church. Dolcino, however, would not have heeded the prophet's warning; he proceeded along a path of sometimes violent opposition to the Church of Rome, the clergy, and members of the various religious orders.

A slightly earlier contemporary to Pierre Autier and the leaders of the last Cathar revival, Dolcino assumed the leadership of the movement known as the Apostolici, or the Apostolic Brethren, after the execution of its first leader, Gerard Segarelli, and taught a very different heresy from that of the last great Cathars. Dolcino's was a millenarian heresy, which vigorously challenged the Catholic Church and its ministers and advocated a life of evangelism and absolute poverty, even more stridently so than Valdes and other advocates of the apostolic life had done. His teachings were based on a variety of sources which included the works of the mystic Joachim of Fiore (1130/35–1201/2), the doctrines of Segarelli, the books of the Bible, and Dolcino's own prophecies – which, he believed, came straight from God above. In particular, Fra Dolcino developed a new theology of history and foretold the destruction of the established ecclesiastical order and the establishment of a new kingdom of peace under his own direction and that of his followers. His teachings and charismatic personality attracted a substantial following in Italy. The Italian movement survived its leader's death in 1307 and ultimately brought the full weight of crusade and Inquisition against Dolcino and his Apostolic Brethren.

Although perhaps the best-known member of the Apostolici, Fra Dolcino was not the founder of this movement, or its first leader. The group's founder, Gerard Segarelli, was an illiterate and humble man who turned up in Parma in 1260. This was an important year in the development of the concepts of Joachim of Fiore. According to contemporary accounts, Segarelli had sought admission to the Franciscan order but was refused. Inspired by images of the Apostles in the Franciscan church in Parma, Segarelli adopted a life of apostolic poverty and preaching which was even more rigorous than that of the Franciscans.[2] Dressed in a white robe and barefoot, in imitation of the Apostles, he wandered through the streets of Parma shouting: *'Penitenʒ agite!'* ('Do penance!'). The force of his personal example attracted a substantial number of followers out of whom he set apart two select groups, in imitation of Jesus: twelve were designated 'Apostles' and another seventy were the 'disciples.' His followers declared their conversion publicly. Initiates were first instructed in the teachings of the Apostolic Brethren and in their way of life. This was followed, according to the report of the inquisitor Bernard Gui, by a ritual – performed at a church or altar or some other public place – in which the new member removed his clothes, renounced all wealth and possessions and made a vow to God, in his heart, to follow the apostolic life. Having undergone initiation, the new brother could no longer accept money, as he was to have no possessions and to live by alms alone. After taking the vow of absolute poverty, members of the Apostolic Brethren could no longer swear oaths of obedience to any mortal; they were now subject to God alone.[3] They were so devoted to the life of absolute poverty and they despised wealth and possessions to such an extent that they called themselves not *minores* ('lesser'), as the Franciscans did, but *minimi* ('the least').[4]

Although it seems that Segarelli did not proclaim any doctrines other than the need to do penance and live a life of poverty, a collection of teachings of extreme hostility to the Roman Church sprang up among his followers by 1299 – granted, without the violence that would develop under Segarelli's successor, Fra Dolcino. The Church of Rome, they said, was the whore of Babylon from John's Book of the Apocalypse; it had turned away from the faith of Christ. The Church and its ministers had lost the power and authority bestowed on them by Jesus Christ. All that had now been transferred to the sect of the Apostles of Christ founded by Gerard Segarelli. Theirs was the only true order; all the orders associated with the Church since the time of Pope St. Sylvester I (314–35), and all their members with the exception of Pope Celestine V (July 5–December 13, 1294), were liars and seducers. The pope himself had no power to offer absolution unless he was as holy as St. Peter and lived in complete humility and piety. The laity, claimed the Brethren, should not pay the tithe to any prelate of the Roman Church whose life was not conducted in imitation of the poverty and perfection of the Apostles. The Brethren were the ones who most truly followed that teaching, and it was only to those who were called Apostles that the tithe should be given. The Brethren were not to swear oaths under any circumstances and not to reveal any of their beliefs to the inquisitors. Hence they were allowed to deny their beliefs, hide the truth, or even lie to the inquisitors; but they had to confess their beliefs openly when death was inevitable.

Segarelli's life of extreme apostolic poverty and preaching challenged the wealth and power of the Church just as his teachings rejected its worldliness. The Church, in its turn, would reject Segarelli, his teachings, and the order he founded. In 1274 the Second Council of Lyons reiterated the ban on new religious orders, first decreed by Pope Innocent III at the Fourth Lateran Council in 1215. Although Segarelli may have had no intention to found an order, he had certainly developed a sizeable following, and the ban in 1274 was aimed at groups like his. Of course, having already repudiated the Church, the Brethren and their leader paid little attention to its decree. In 1285 Pope Honorius IV (1285–87) ordered them to accept an established rule, and when they refused he condemned them outright. They were now subject to persecution and imprisonment, and in 1291, in response to their continued growth, Pope Nicholas IV (1288–92) renewed the condemnation of Honorius. Persecution of the Brethren increased thereafter, and in 1294 four members – two men and two women – were burned for heresy. Eventually Segarelli himself was arrested; he was kept in prison for a while, before being burned at the stake in 1300. Having rid itself of Segarelli, the Church now faced an even more radical and aggressive opponent, Fra Dolcino.

The illegitimate son of a priest from Novara, Dolcino was most likely raised in Vercelli in the Piemont region and had acquired a degree of learning which, along with his forceful personality, made him a most formidable opponent. He had joined the Apostolic Brethren in 1291 and was captured by the Inquisition as many as three times, recanting on each occasion. Dolcino may well have been behind the increasingly heterodox ideas that infiltrated the movement; at any rate, the Apostles became openly heretical when he assumed the leadership of the movement after the death of Segarelli. Clearly the letter he wrote in 1300, which, he claimed, was inspired by the Holy Spirit, reveals the more radical and heretical direction the movement was to take.

A gifted and original thinker, Dolcino, as his manifesto of 1300 clearly shows, was also the heir to a long tradition of unorthodox teaching and of devotion, sometimes excessive, to apostolic poverty. Like his predecessor Segarelli, Dolcino was inspired by the ideal embodied in the lives of the strict adherents to the Franciscan rule. Indeed, his movement was, in some ways, an extremist version of the Spiritual Franciscans. These rigorist advocates of the original idea of poverty, as expressed by St. Francis himself, had become increasingly uncomfortable with the direction the order had taken, especially as it had become institutionalized and had found a niche in the universities of the day. Emerging in the mid-thirteenth century, the Spiritual Franciscans rejected the various privileges the Franciscan order had received from the papacy; they were critical of the order's acceptance of property and of the establishment of Franciscan houses for the brothers. Not only did they seek to restore the original dedication to the apostolic life established by the order's founder, but they also identified Francis as the herald – the angel of the sixth seal – of a new age of radical spirituality and devotion to absolute poverty. They were inspired by the writings of Peter John Olivi (c.1248–98), who worked out a doctrine of absolute poverty and an eschatology which predicted an apocalyptic struggle and the replacement of the corrupt Church by the true spiritual church. The Spirituals adopted these ideas; they regarded themselves, together with Francis, as heroes of the new age that would follow the destruction of the established Church and its institutions. Their uncompromising devotion to poverty, however, drove a wedge between them and the main body of the order, the Conventuals. Efforts at a compromise brokered by the order's leader and one of its greatest theologians, St. Bonaventure (1221–74), failed, and the Spiritual Franciscans found themselves increasingly ostracized. They suffered outright persecution under Pope John XXII (1316–34), who ordered four of them to be burned in 1318 and declared apostolic poverty heretical in 1323.

Dolcino, like the Spiritual Franciscans and their intellectual leader Peter John Olivi, was also influenced by Joachim of Fiore, the twelfth-century Calabrian monk, theologian, and prophet whose vision of history shaped the prophetic and eschatological views of the Apostolic Brethren and others in the thirteenth century and beyond.[5] Joachim developed an eschatological philosophy of history which identified a pattern of human and sacred history associated with the persons of the Trinity. According to him, there were three ages (*status*) in history. The first age was that of the Father, initiated by Adam and associated with the Old Testament. It was the age of marriage. The second age was that of the Son, associated with the New Testament and the order of the clergy. The third age was that of the Holy Spirit; it was the age of the monks and a time of peace and spiritual perfection. The third age was to be prefigured by the appearance of a new order of monks; it would be a time of tribulations, when Antichrist would appear. Encouraged by three popes to write, Joachim, or some of his writings at least, would face censure as heretical at the Fourth Lateran Council in 1215 and at other councils in the thirteenth century. His works nonetheless remained very influential, but those influenced by them fell under the same suspicion as the works themselves.

Building on the lessons of Joachim and the Spiritual Franciscans as well as on the model of Gerard Segarelli, Fra Dolcino published his first prophetic letter in August 1300, soon after succeeding Segarelli as the leader of the movement – which by then numbered as many as three or four thousand men and women spread throughout Lombardy, Tuscany, and the surrounding regions. According to the inquisitor Bernard Gui, who included a version of the letter in his register in 1316, Dolcino taught an evil doctrine and offered his many followers not prophecy but fanaticism and insanity. In his letter, however, the new leader was offering a different perspective and demonstrating to his followers that his teachings were those of the true church. In the opening lines, Dolcino confirmed that his congregation was a spiritual one, namely the true church which accepted poverty and the apostolic life, recalling the ideas of the Spiritual Franciscans.[6] The obedience of the Brethren was an internal one, owed only to God and to no exterior power. Dolcino assured his congregation that this obedience was sent in the last days by God for the salvation of the souls of the good. He also claimed a special understanding of the Old and New Testaments; he, Dolcino himself, was sent by God with a special revelation about the future, which he would share with his devoted followers.

After declaring that he and his followers constituted the true church of God, Dolcino reinforced this idea by identifying the Church and the leaders of the social orders as enemies to the true church. For Dolcino, the members of the secular clergy were ministers of the devil. The secular clergy, the lay people and their leaders, and all the members of religious orders, especially the Dominican and Franciscan, stood in opposition to God's true church. Moreover, these groups actively persecuted the Brethren, the one true spiritual and apostolic church, and this made them even worse, according to Dolcino. Although he approved of going into hiding on account of the persecution which he, his predecessor, and his followers faced, Dolcino consoled the last by predicting that all the persecutors and prelates of the Church would be killed; the ones spared would convert, join the Apostolic Brethren, and be subject to the sect's leaders.

Having declared that he and his movement were divinely instituted and inspired, Dolcino outlined a view of history in his letter and issued prophecies concerning events to come. Drawing from Joachim of Fiore but adding his own unique interpretation, Dolcino explained that there were four ages of the world. The first age was that of the fathers of the Old Testament, the patriarchs, prophets, and just men who lived up until the time of Jesus. In that first age, marriage was a praiseworthy institution, established for the multiplication of humanity.[7] Eventually, however, the people of the world declined from the pure and honest spiritual state of their ancestors, and so Christ arrived with his Apostles, disciples, and other followers, to heal human weakness. The arrival of Christ, according to Dolcino, initiated the second age, which lasted until the age of Pope Sylvester I and Emperor Constantine. During this second age – an age of the saints – a new mode of life emerged which provided the medicine necessary to cure the ills of the first age. The saints who lived during this age displayed true faith, performed miracles, and lived humbly and patiently. They lived chastely and offered the example of the good life, in contrast to the impure life of those who lived at the end of the first age.

In the second age, the best life was that of virginity and chastity rather than of marriage, and those following the true path adopted poverty rather than wealth, having no earthly possessions.[8] The second age, too, experienced decline, and the third age began in the time of Sylvester and Constantine, when the gentiles and many others converted to the true faith. During this age, Pope Sylvester and his successors began to acquire territorial possessions and wealth for the Church.[9] At times, Dolcino continued, the love of God grew cold during this age and new orders emerged, to revive spiritual passions and restore the proper devotion to God. St. Benedict of Nursia was the first to implement a new and better way of life when he instituted his rule for the monks. The devotions of the monks and the love of God, however, grew cold again, and then St. Francis and St. Dominic revived religious life and restored the strict acceptance of poverty and Christ-like life that Benedict and his monks had once demonstrated. But, just as it happened after Benedict, religious zeal again declined following the arrival of Francis and Dominic. The friars were not the heralds of the last days, and so, according to Dolcino, God sent his last witnesses. Although they did not create a new order but only established the last of the old ones, Gerard Segarelli, the Brethren, and Dolcino himself would restore the proper mode of life. Sent by God to take up the apostolic life, the Brethren would survive and bear fruit until Judgment Day. The fourth age would then commence, and in the time following the decline of the life of St. Francis and St. Dominic, Dolcino and his followers would provide the world with the necessary medicine to cure its ills.[10]

Having outlined his theology of history, Dolcino explained further that the history of the Church itself, from the time of Christ to the end of the world, was divided into four periods. In the first period the Church suffered persecution but was good, chaste, and poor. During the second phase, beginning in the time of Sylvester and Constantine, the Church acquired wealth and prosperity but still remained good and chaste. The clergy, monks, and members of all the religious orders followed the example of the saints: Sylvester, Benedict, Francis, and Dominic. The third age, however, was one of debasement and decline, when the Church no longer sought the pure spiritual life but was eager to acquire wealth, property, and power. Dolcino insisted that this was the current state of the Church, and it would remain in that perverse condition until all the clergy were cruelly killed. This, added Dolcino, would occur in three years, after which the Church would be restored to its pure state. In fact, Dolcino claimed that the fourth age had already begun: it was initiated by Gerard Segarelli and would last until the end of the world. Although persecuted, the true church was established among the Apostolic Brethren, who lived in true poverty and goodness, and offered reform of the religious life and return to pure apostolicism.[11]

Drawing from his understanding of the writings of the prophets of the Old and New Testaments, Dolcino then announced a series of prophecies that would occur over the next three years, the period of the predicted destruction of the corrupt Church and clergy. And, indeed, his first prophecy concerns the very destruction of the Church. According to Dolcino, all the prelates and clergy, from the highest to the lowest, who belonged to the decadent Church of the third age would be destroyed by the sword of God, wielded by a new emperor and his kings. Dolcino asserted that this great destruction would include all monks and nuns, all members of the Franciscan and Dominican orders, and members of the orders of hermits. Not even the reigning pope, Boniface VIII (1294–1303), would escape destruction, and all the corrupt orders would disappear forever from the face of the earth. He continued by explaining that the agent of this destruction, which he corroborated through further reference to the scriptures, would be Frederick II (ruled 1296–1337), the king of Sicily and the son of Peter, king of Aragon (d. 1285). Frederick would be elevated to the position of emperor and would create a number of new kings, to assist him in the work of God. Having ascended to imperial power, Frederick would lead the fight against the corrupt clergy and Church and would ultimately kill Pope Boniface.

Following the death of Boniface and destruction of the clergy, Dolcino predicted that all the Christians would enjoy a period of peace in a millenarian kingdom, in anticipation of the Second Coming. During that time a new pope would miraculously take the throne; he would be sent by God from above rather than being elected by the cardinals, all of whom would have been killed in the great struggle against the false Church. The new pope and the new emperor, Frederick of Sicily, would rule together until the time of Antichrist, who would then establish his authority and rule during the last days. Under the new holy pope, the members of the order of Apostles, Dolcino and his followers, as well as the monks and clergy who had not been destroyed by the divine sword, would receive the gifts of the Holy Spirit, just as the original Apostles had. This new order of Apostles, explained Dolcino, by reference to the Holy Scriptures, had already begun to take shape, as it was founded by Gerard Segarelli and further enlarged by Fra Dolcino himself when Segarelli was killed by the corrupt Church. The order of the Apostles and the age of peace would endure and bear its fruits until the end of the world.[12]

The letter of 1300 closed with Dolcino's commentary on the seven angels and the seven churches of John's Book of the Apocalypse. The scheme he posited was intended to support his model of history and to demonstrate once again that he and his order were sent by God to minister during the last days. Just as he had associated monastic leaders and reformers in the history of the Church with its various ages and mutations, now he identified these same leaders with the churches of John's Apocalypse. St. Benedict was the angel of Ephesus, and his church was the congregation of monks. The angel of Pergamum was Pope Sylvester I, and his church was the clergy. St. Francis was the angel of Sardis and St. Dominic was the angel of Laodiciea, and their churches were the Friars Minor and the Order of Preachers respectively. These angels, in Dolcino's view, were those of the past; their existence led the way to the emergence of the final three churches, which would arise during the last days. The first of the three angels of these churches was Gerard Segarelli – the angel of Smirna. Fra Dolcino himself was the angel of Thyatira, and the pope to succeed Boniface was the angel of Philadelphia. The churches of all three of them formed the new apostolic congregation founded by Segarelli.[13]

Despite Fra Dolcino's assurances to his followers, in the letter of 1300, that his prophecies were divinely inspired, the events he foretold did not come to pass by the end of 1303. Although Boniface died, he was not killed by Frederick, as Dolcino had anticipated, and Frederick did not become emperor, nor were the clergy slaughtered by the sword of divine vengeance. In fact the death of Boniface VIII in October of that year, as a result of the rough treatment he received at the hands of the minions of the French king, Philip IV, inspired a second manifesto from Dolcino.

Although he had not seen the fulfilment of his prophecies, Dolcino remained undaunted and continued to have a devoted following. To preserve the faith of his followers and prepare them for the coming tribulations and triumph, he issued this second letter in late 1303 or 1304, offering another series of prophecies. The letter of 1303/04, which further alienated his movement from the Franciscans and other elements in the Church, reasserted that his prophecies were divinely inspired and that he and his followers played a central role in the divine plan.[14]

This new set of prophecies focused on the lives and reigns of four popes, two good ones and two bad ones. The first pair (one good, one bad) identified the popes, but the other two were unnamed. From this prophetic scheme, the opponents of the Apostolic Brethren argued that Dolcino had identified himself as the second good pope. This allegation was made in an anonymous contemporary chronicle as well as by the inquisitor Bernard Gui, who asserted that Dolcino had announced that, if he were still living at the time, he would reign as the last holy pope.[15] Although the Italian prophet had made no such claim, he had outlined events involving the popes who were to reign, as he believed, at the end of time. He had also noted in his letter that he would remain in hiding at God's command and would appear at the proper moment, which may have led to the contention that Dolcino believed himself to become the final pope.[16]

According to the letter of 1303/04, Pope Celestine V, as revealed in the scriptures, was the first of the popes whose reigns signaled the coming of the millennial kingdom. Celestine was the good pope; he was then followed by Boniface VIII, the first bad pope, who had been captured by Philip IV's men and died in late 1303. The next pope, whom Dolcino did not name, was evil too, and destined to face divine wrath at the hands of an earthly ruler. Dolcino prophesied in his second letter that Frederick, king of Sicily, would march against the perfidious newly elected pope and against his cardinals, destroying the corrupt leaders of the Church utterly and completely, as was foretold in the scriptures. Frederick would then reign as emperor and God's elect, and would be joined by the fourth and last pope. This would be a holy pope, chosen by God and not by the cardinals (all captured and destroyed by Frederick). The fourth pope would fulfill not only Dolcino's prophecies but those of Ezekiel and other biblical figures too, who had foretold the coming of the last days. Indeed, Dolcino proclaimed that the holy pope was to be the angel of Philadelphia spoken of in John's Book of the Apocalypse.[17]

Dolcino also described the role of his followers in the events of the last days. Upon the destruction of the evil pope together with his cardinals and clergy, the Apostolici would be joined by the spirituals of all the orders; they would receive the grace of the Holy Spirit and renew the Church, dedicating it to the life of apostolic poverty.[18] They would preach the imminent coming of the Antichrist and the final tribulations. When Elijah and Enoch descended to do battle with Antichrist, the Apostolici would be safely removed to paradise. Returning after the defeat of Antichrist, they would join Frederick, the last emperor on earth, and convert all the nations of the world. They would usher in an age of the Spirit and of millennial peace, and they would flourish until the end of time.[19]

Dolcino concluded the prophecy with a schedule of the events that would unfurl over the course of the next three years. In 1303, he declared, ruin would come to the king of the south (Charles II, king of Naples, ruled 1285–1309) and to Pope Boniface VIII. The next year was to bring the destruction of the cardinals and of Boniface's successor. In 1305 the desolation of the clergy would take place: priests, monks, nuns, Dominicans, Franciscans, and hermits, and all the religious prelates who had contributed to the corruption of the Church, would be destroyed. The general destruction of pope and clergy over 1304 and 1305 would be accomplished, as Dolcino saw it, by Frederick, emperor of the Romans.[20]

Having issued this second manifesto, Dolcino led his followers into hiding in the mountains between Vercelli and Novara. There he most likely produced a third manifesto, which has been lost. He intended to remain there until God revealed that it was time for him to reappear publicly. Joined by some four thousand followers, both men and women, including Margherita di Franck and his four lieutenants (Longinus of Bergamo, Frederick of Novara, Albert of Tarento, and Valderic of Brescia), Dolcino proclaimed a millennial kingdom in which all goods were to be held in common and, according to at least one contemporary account, women were regarded as 'common property and could be used without sin.'[21] Some of his followers believed that Dolcino himself would be the pope of the new age prophesied in the letter of 1303, and he continued his preaching to the effect that the pope and other leaders of the Church were not worthy of their positions. Dolcino's preaching inspired not only his own followers, who remained undaunted when Frederick did not rise up to destroy the evil pope and his cardinals, but also members of the antipapal Ghibelline party as well as the local peasants, who resented the wealth and power of the established Church.

The vehemence of his teaching and the hostility toward the Church displayed by his followers and supporters, together with the presence of the Inquisition and the increasing opposition from the Church, produced the savage violence associated with the movement. According to a contemporary anonymous chronicler from the mountains where Dolcino and the Apostolic Brethren resided, the group hanged many Christians, including a boy of ten.[22] Refusing ransoms, they hanged men in front of their wives, or starved them to death in their prisons. They cut off the lips and noses of some women, the breasts or feet of others, and even the arm of a pregnant one, whose child died shortly after birth. The brutal violence of the rebellion was not limited to individuals but extended to villages and to the Church itself. Dolcino's followers burned and destroyed a number of villages in the lower Alps in Italy, including Mosso, Trivero, Còggiola, and Fléccia.[23] They also destroyed numerous cantons in the Crevacuore and many private homes in other regions. The Church, too, suffered severe damage at the hands of the religious rebels. In the village of Trivero, the church itself was burned, and the Apostolic Brethren disfigured the sacred paintings and sculptures, stole the altar tables, ripped off the arm of a statue of the Virgin Mary, tore down the bell tower of Trivero and smashed its bells. In their raids they stole 'books, chalices, and ornaments' as well as the property of the priests and the plate of the religious confraternity serving the Church.[24] From this almost unprecedented violence against the Church and local communities, Dolcino's followers accumulated a significant quantity of goods, which they stored in their mountain hideout.

The physical violence as well as the violence of Dolcino's rhetoric inspired an equally strong response from the Church. As the inquisitor Bernard Gui recorded in his register, Dolcino was guilty of a wide range of religious offenses.[25] He was guilty of preaching numerous errors, especially that the Church of Rome was not the true church and that the true church consisted of himself and his followers. Proclaiming that he was filled with the spirit of prophesy, he declared that Frederick would become emperor, establish ten kings in Italy, and kill the pope and all the cardinals. He erred further by asserting that he himself would then assume the throne of St. Peter and rule the Church with his followers. Dolcino, Gui continued, erroneously taught that the Church had four ages that were characterized by general decline of morality. According to him, the period from the time of Pope Sylvester I to that of Pope Celestine V was one in which the representatives of the Church were liars and fornicators and made themselves guilty of the sins of pride and avarice. In sum, so Gui, Dolcino's teachings were virulently antisacerdotal, rejecting the priesthood and the sacraments of the Church and declaring that religious orders themselves were unnecessary.[26] And, finally, his teachings were a source of inspiration for the violence of his followers. For all these reasons, at the complaints of the local bishop, in 1306 Pope Clement V (1305–14) issued a bull announcing a crusade against Dolcino and the Apostolic Brethren, complete with full indulgences for the participants.

As they had struggled against the local authorities and plundered the surrounding villages, Dolcino and his followers resisted the crusaders to the death. In the face of repeated attacks directed by the bishop of Vercelli, Dolcino and some of his Apostles, including Margherita, withdrew to a mountain in Novara. They were pursued by the forces of the Church, and Dolcino and some forty followers were captured in a last stand on Holy Thursday, March 23, 1307. Both Margherita and Dolcino were held captive for some months and tortured. Finally, they were both executed in a most gruesome fashion. Margherita went first; she was dismembered alive in front of Dolcino. In his turn, Fra Dolcino had his limbs ripped from his body with red hot pincers, and then his dismembered body and that of his devoted follower, Margherita, were burned.[27]

But not even the brutal execution of Fra Dolcino and his closest adherents, or the failure of his prophecies to come true, brought the sect to an end. Although many of Dolcino's followers, men and women alike, reconverted and sought restoration to the Catholic Church, many others refused and were discovered in Tuscany and other parts of Italy. Bernard Gui warned that many of Dolcino's followers escaped the clutches of ecclesiastical and secular authorities and, under the false appearance of piety and sanctity, were secretly disseminating their teachings to the simple.[28] Gui even felt compelled to send a letter to the bishops of Spain, where the Apostolic Brethren appeared in 1315, as he was fearful of the continuation and expansion of the sect.[29] And there are numerous other records of the appearance of Dolcino's Apostles, apart from that of the great inquisitor. They were believed to have infiltrated the Order of the Franciscans. Two members of the sect were convicted in Bologna in 1311. Suspected heretics brought before the Inquisition at Toulouse claimed that Dolcino was the founder of their sect, which was known to exist in southern France in 1321 and 1322. Pope John XXII (1316–34) sent the bishop of Cracow a warning about the Apostolic Brethren.[30] And the movement apparently survived well into the fourteenth century, as adherents to the sect were found at Trentino in the early 1330s, at Padua in 1350, in Sicily in 1372, and in Narbonne in 1374 – and, even as late as 1402, in Lübeck.[31]

The sect of the Apostolic Brethren would never again achieve the size it had reached under Dolcino, nor would it be seen as the serious threat it had been during his lifetime; it would finally disappear in the fifteenth century. The dramatic rise of the movement and the impact it had on contemporaries were clearly due to its leader, Fra Dolcino. He combined an extreme apostolic poverty with a highly millenarian eschatology, in a volatile mixture which inspired large numbers of followers and was deemed a serious threat by the established Church. His teachings, which envisioned a central role for his sect in the large scheme of events at the end of time, inspired numerous followers and gave them the courage to fight against what they saw as the forces of Antichrist. A visionary and a prophet, Dolcino offered a radical path for his disciples to follow: the ideal Christian life lived at the end of time. But Fra Dolcino was not the only visionary of his day to provide an alternative to the institutional structure of the established Church. Another departure from orthodox traditions would bring about the demise of the mystic Marguerite Porete.

CHAPTER EIGHT

MARGUERITE PORETE: MYSTICISM AND THE BEGUINES

O n the first of June 1310 at the Place de Grève in Paris, Marguerite Porete was burned at the stake, enduring what the great nineteenth-century historian of the Inquisition, H. C. Lea, called the first formal auto-da-fé in Paris.[1] Condemned as a relapsed heretic, Marguerite accepted her fate calmly and without fear, and she was regarded with great admiration by those who witnessed her death, many of whom burst into tears during the execution.[2] Her condemnation came as the result of her unwillingness to discuss or denounce the teachings found in her great mystical work, the *Mirror of Simple Souls*, which she wrote in Old French. Although judged heretical, the *Mirror* was a work of great popularity and influence during the fourteenth and fifteenth centuries and beyond; it was published in the twentieth century as an orthodox text. Indeed, both the reception and the contents of Marguerite's great work raise the question of the orthodoxy of her own beliefs. Was she, like her contemporary Fra Dolcino, a heretic clearly opposed to the Church and its teachings? Or was she a devout mystic and a victim of circumstances? Her life and death, in fact, intersected with several broader historical movements of her day, so that both her fate and the extent of her heresy can be truly understood only in the context of the religious and political developments of the late thirteenth and early fourteenth centuries.

Little is known about Marguerite's life until in the mid-1290s, when she first ran afoul of the ecclesiastical authorities, and what is known comes from her writings and from the inquisitorial documents compiled at her trial. Her date of birth is not known with any certainty, nor is the exact place of her birth, although she was most likely from Hainaut, a county in the Low Countries that was under the jurisdiction of the archbishop of Cambrai, and it has been suggested that she was from the town of Valenciennes.[3] Passages from her *Mirror*, however, provide some background on her social class. Echoes of the tradition of courtly literature are found throughout her work, which suggests that she may have come from the aristocracy.[4] Other passages of the text demonstrate the author's knowledge of important mystical texts of the twelfth century and of the Bible, which indicates that Marguerite was well educated.[5] Indeed, the extent of her learning is revealed by a chronicler's claim that she even translated the Bible into the vernacular; no evidence of this, however, can be found in the trial records, and there is no surviving copy of any such Bible. Condemned and burned as a *pseudomulier* ('false woman'), Marguerite identified herself as a Beguine, as did most contemporary texts that described her. One contemporary chronicle in particular, however, noted that she wrote a book which taught that 'a soul annihilated in the love of the Creator could, and should, grant to nature all that it desires,' which raises the possibility that she was connected to another movement.[6] The antinomian and pantheistic, even autotheistic, qualities of her teachings, as described by the contemporary chronicler, led H. C. Lea to proclaim her as the first member of the German heresy of the Free Spirit to appear in France, and Robert Lerner has identified her as one of the representatives of that heresy.[7] The nature of both movements, of the Beguines and of the Free Spirit, provides important insights into the life and death of Marguerite Porete; therefore a brief survey of both is necessary in order to gain a proper understanding of Marguerite, her teachings, and her horrible fate.

The Beguines are perhaps the more important and more influential of the two groups associated with Marguerite Porete, and the movement with which she readily identified herself. This self-identification, however, is complicated by the very nature of the Beguine movement, as well as by Marguerite's understanding of it. Indeed, the lifestyle she chose to follow as a Beguine in some ways helps to explain why she was executed and reveals the difficulties that the Beguines as a whole experienced at the end of the thirteenth century and beginning of the next – a period when increasing restrictions were placed on them, and the term *beguine* came to be synonymous with 'heretic.'

Despite the difficulties the Beguines faced during Marguerite's lifetime and for much of the rest of the Middle Ages, they first emerged in Liège in the late twelfth century, and by the middle of the next they were a popular and well-received religious movement (or movements). The designation *beguine* appeared in the 1230s.[8] Although at first suspected of heresy because of their lifestyle, the Beguines were welcomed by the Church hierarchy already by the early thirteenth century; they clearly addressed the need of the Church to respond to the spiritual demands of women, notably of urban ones. The Beguines were pious religious women, who lived alone or in small communities in cities which had grown larger and more populous in the course of the twelfth century. The emergence of these religious communities was, in fact, a reaction to social changes associated with the new towns and cities as well as to the changes in spirituality generated by these social changes. Beguine communities and their way of life became necessary because the traditional outlets for women's piety no longer proved suitable in the new urban environment: these communities offered a means for pious living to the economically less well-to-do. The established monastic communities of women did not fully adapt to the changing spirituality of the twelfth century, which, among other things, emphasized the apostolic life and a more internalized form of religious piety. Moreover, those traditional communities required of their novices to bring a dowry with them. Although the size of the dowry was less demanding than in the case of arranging a good marriage, it was still large enough to bar many women. Traditionally, the established monastic communities had been the preserve of aristocratic and even royal women, and thus social status also limited that accessibility of the convents to many women. At the same time, the new orders that emerged in the twelfth century, particularly the Cistercian monastic order, were reluctant to welcome women into their ranks. Although Robert of Arbrissel and other, more progressive, thinkers implemented reforms which encouraged the involvement of women, the newly forming orders of the twelfth and thirteenth centuries tended to limit their participation.

The first of the Beguine communities appeared in the urban centers of northern Europe, spreading throughout Flanders, France, and the Rhineland. These devout women who were unable to join traditional communities because of a lack of wealth or social status first formed associations around local churches. By the early thirteenth century they had started to occupy houses where they could live according to their own lifestyle. The earliest of these houses were established by prosperous bourgeois women who also welcomed those less well off, and they were all bound by religious piety. They lived simply, supporting themselves by sewing, weaving, embroidery, and the copying of books, and they regularly attended mass and the canonical hours of the day at the local church. Beguine women seemed intent on living in voluntary poverty and chastity, and thus their movement tapped into the growing interest in the life of apostolic poverty. The Beguines were unique, however, in that they took no vows and had no formal institutional structure, local conditions often shaping the individual community or beguinage. It was this lack of formal organization and the absence of a religious vow that contributed to the great popularity and success of the movement, but also laid the foundation for its downfall.[9]

Although the Beguines would eventually face increasing suspicion from Church leaders, they found widespread support for a period during the early and mid-thirteenth century. One of their earliest and most influential advocates was the bishop Jacques de Vitry (c.1160/70–1240), confessor to one of the important early Beguines, Marie d'Oignies (c.1177–1213), and the man who convinced Pope Honorius III (1216–27) to approve the way of life of Beguines. Many other bishops came to support the communities of Beguines, as did some members of the Franciscan order, with whom the Beguines shared a certain affinity. Most notably, the great English bishop and scholar Robert Grosseteste (c.1170–1253) staunchly supported them, declaring that the life of the Beguines was superior to that of the mendicants. And in France, the Beguines found support from the king himself. By the late thirteenth and early fourteenth centuries, however, this situation had changed; various questions about the life of the Beguines and rumors of their sexual immorality had surfaced. The very lack of a rule, or vow, now reflected badly on them since no formal restraints could be imposed on the behavior of these women. Beguines could live in community or independently; and the itinerant Beguine, who often followed her own understanding of the scriptures, was deemed a particular threat to society and to the Church. As a result of this growing distrust, in 1312 the Council of Vienne issued two decrees against the women who called themselves Beguines, declaring that there was 'an abominable sect of malignant men known as beghards and faithless women known as beguines.'[10]

Marguerite clearly identified herself with the Beguines and hence suffered by this association, but she was also associated with another heresy that the Church deemed particularly widespread and threatening. During Marguerite's lifetime, the Church had become increasingly aware of, and concerned with, a mystical and antinomian sect known as the heresy of the Free Spirit. The Council of Vienna, which had condemned the Beguines, associated them and their male counterparts, the Beghards, with the Free Spirit heretics, asserting that the Beguines believed that they could become perfect in this life and, once they had achieved perfection, they were incapable of sin and thus no longer subject to the laws of Church or state.[11]

In some ways, as will be seen below, Marguerite's own work, or at least a misreading of select passages taken out of context, implied antinomian and libertine teachings. But, although the condemnation of the heresy at the Council of Vienne – where the label Free Spirit was not used – provided the 'birth certificate' for the heresy, it seems, as Robert Lerner has demonstrated in his book on the subject, that there was no such movement.[12] There were, indeed, mystics like Marguerite who expressed an autotheism, but few, if any, who taught that their union with God allowed them to pursue a life of immorality and sexual excess. The willingness of the Church to create such an image, however, reveals the concerns with heresy that existed at the time as well as the readiness of Church leaders to resort to such procedures.

It is in this context of concerns over the Beguines and fear of a widespread antinomian heresy that the life and death of Marguerite Porete can best be understood, and a partial explanation as to why Marguerite suffered the fate she did can be attempted. She first came to the attention of ecclesiastical authorities at some point during the last decade of the thirteenth century and the first decade of the fourteenth. It was sometime between 1296 and January 1306 that Marguerite wrote the *Mirror of Simple Souls* – and it must be stressed that she wrote it herself rather than having it copied by a scribe – in the everyday language of Old French. She may well have already begun disseminating her book and its teachings and she was living the life of an itinerant Beguine, when she came to the attention of Guy II, the bishop of Cambrai. At a meeting at Valenciennes, the bishop publicly condemned her teachings and cast her book into the flames, burning it in front of Marguerite. The bishop also ordered her to stop spreading her teachings and writings and threatened to turn her over to the secular authority for punishment if she failed to heed his warning.

As subsequent events proved, it is clear that she did not obey the bishop's command and continued to spread her ideas. She even sent a copy of her book – thus indicating that Guy II did not destroy all its copies – to John, bishop of Châlons-sur-Marne, for his consideration of her ideas. For this reason, and because she was accused of continuing to spread her beliefs to the simple folk of the region and to the Beghards, sometime between 1306 and 1308 she was called to appear before the new bishop of Cambrai, Philip of Marigny, who was also the inquisitor of Lorraine. Even though he had the authority of an inquisitor, Philip chose not to interrogate Marguerite, who was sent to Paris instead. There she was taken into custody, in late 1308, by William of Paris, the Dominican inquisitor and former confessor of King Philip IV the Fair, who would play a critical role in determining Marguerite's fate.

From her arrival in Paris in late 1308 until her death in June 1310, Marguerite and her confidant and self-proclaimed defender, Guiard de Cressonessart, remained subject to the authority of the inquisitor and endured confinement in William's prison. Despite his repeated entreaties, Marguerite refused to appear before the tribunal to answer questions concerning her writings and teachings. Moreover, she would not even take the oath required of those who were called before the Inquisition. William offered Marguerite absolution as an inducement to appear before the Inquisition, but she refused even this effort and remained under a ban of excommunication. Faced with similar threats and inducements, Guiard eventually yielded but Marguerite did not, and William was forced to find another method of dealing with the silent Beguine.

Failing to come to a resolution by the usual means at the inquisitor's disposal, William turned to various learned men associated with the University of Paris. In March 1310, he sought advice from several professors of law and theologians at the university concerning Marguerite and her book, as well as certain matters of jurisdiction. These scholars took a dim view of Marguerite's book and recommended that the canon lawyers be given authority over the case. Following this meeting, however, William called together a commission of twenty-one theologians, who met on April 11, 1310. The commissioners were given some fifteen excerpts from Marguerite's book, so that they could determine the orthodoxy of her teachings. One of these passages contained the damning assertion that the liberated soul should give to nature all that it ask, which, when taken out of context, was understood to show that Marguerite taught an antinomian theology which promoted libertinism and the rejection of traditional morality and virtue. The canons may have understood the passage to indicate, further, that Marguerite also rejected the established Church and denied that the soul who had received God's love needed the Church to fulfill its traditional intermediary role between God and the individual Christian.[13] She had, in fact, maintained that the liberated soul had no need for the usual good works promoted by the Church, such as fasting, attending mass, and saying prayers. The commission, having reviewed such passages, deemed Marguerite's work heretical.

Marguerite, however, offered at least some defense of her work. She declared that three other scholars had reviewed it and did not find it heretical. She had sent a copy of the *Mirror* to three authorities, including the Franciscan John of Quaregnon (Hainaut) and the Cistercian Dom Franco of the abbey of Villers, which had long supported the Beguines, and both of them approved of the work. According to John, the 'book was truly made by the Holy Spirit and ... if all the clergy of the world heard only what they understood [of it], they would not know how to contradict it in any way.'[14] And Dom Franco asserted that he had proved from scripture all that appears in the *Mirror*. Little more is known of these authorities, but the third figure, Godfrey of Fontaines, a highly respected master at the University of Paris, is much better known. He, too, approved of the work, even though he was a bit more cautious in his appraisal, noting that it was a book meant only for the strong of spirit. The support of these learned men provided little help to Marguerite, who would face a further tribunal, but it suggests that her work may not have been as unorthodox as others had claimed.

Although she had garnered endorsements of the *Mirror*, on May 19, 1310, Marguerite was called before a second commission, which was composed of canon lawyers given charge to decide her fate. The commission determined that:

> From the time Marguerite called Porete was suspected of heresy, in rebellion and insubordination, she would not respond nor swear before the inquisitor to those things pertaining to the office of inquisitor. The inquisitor set up a

case against her nevertheless, and by the deposition of many witnesses he found that the said Marguerite had composed a certain book containing heresies and errors, which had been publicly condemned and solemnly burned as such on the order of the Reverend Father Lord Guy, formerly bishop of Cambrai. The above-said bishop had ordered in a letter that if she attempted again to propagate by word or writing such things as were contained in this book, he would condemn her and give her over to the judgment of the secular court. The inquisitor learned next that she had acknowledged, once before the inquisitor of Lorraine, and once before Reverend Father Lord Philip, the next bishop of Cambrai, that she still had in her possession, even after the condemnation mentioned above, the said book and others. The inquisitor learned also that the said Marguerite, after the condemnation of the book, had sent the said book containing the same errors to the Reverend Father Lord John, by the grace of God bishop of Châlons-sur-Marne. And she had not only sent this book to this Lord, but also to many other simple persons, beghards and others, as if it were good.[15]

In sum, she was condemned on several counts, notably because she was declared a relapsed heretic having resumed her teaching of the errors she had abjured before the bishop of Cambrai at Valenciennes. She was also found guilty of obstinately holding her erroneous belief and of being contumacious in her refusal to answer the inquisitor's questions. Consequently, William of Paris announced her condemnation on May 31, 1310. She was handed to the provost of Paris and burned at the stake on the first of June, going to her death with such dignity and piety that many who witnessed the execution were in tears.

At the center of the controversy concerning Marguerite was, of course, her mystical treatise, the *Mirror of Simple Souls*. The *Mirror* caused concern for two reasons. On the one hand, the work itself seems to have been quite popular, both in Marguerite's day and after her death; it is extant in numerous editions and translations. There are three surviving copies in Marguerite's Old French, the earliest of which may date to the fourteenth century; the other two are from the fifteenth and seventeenth centuries.[16] The *Mirror* was translated from the Old French into Latin already in the fourteenth century, and four Latin versions are still in existence. The Latin translations were the source of two independent Italian translations made in the course of the same century. By the fifteenth century, some thirty-six copies of the work circulated throughout Italy. The influence of her book was not restricted to the continent; it extended also to England, where a copy of the *Mirror* may have arrived as early as 1327. That copy was probably brought to the English court by someone in Philippa of Hainaut's entourage, when she arrived to marry King Edward III.[17] If the text got in that early it left little mark, but in the fifteenth century several translations of the *Mirror* were made from Old French into Middle English. The translations were most likely made by Cistercian monks, and in 1491 the Carthusian monk Richard Methely (1451–1528) translated the text from Middle English to Latin. Popularity alone cannot explain, however, why Marguerite was executed, nor serve as a demonstration of heresy, and, as Robert Lerner has noted, the number of copies, especially those made by the monks, demonstrates that there was nothing overtly heretical about the text, even though her influence must surely have unnerved Church leaders suspicious of the existence of the heresy of the Free Spirit.[18]

The *Mirror of Simple Souls*, a book of roughly 60,000 words in some 100 folios, is both a handbook offering spiritual guidance to individual believers and a mystical treatise which explores the relationship of human and divine love and its capacity to bring the soul in union with God.[19] The *Mirror* includes an opening poem that sets the tone for the rest of the work and is divided into 140 chapters, including the prologue. Although organized as a dialogue between *Amour* ('Love') and *Raison* ('Reason') concerning the soul, the work is not uniform in structure and can be repetitive. The *Mirror* consists of extensive passages in prose, which contain dialogues and passages of great drama, but it also includes poetry and *exempla*. The prose passages themselves are often rhythmic and glide from time to time into more free-flowing and lyrical passages and then into full poetry.[20] As Peter Dronke noted, Marguerite seemed best suited to write lyrically and at times used two particular poetic forms, the canzone and the rondeau.[21] Guided by the main characters, Love and Reason, other characters burst on to the scene unannounced, to offer advice on various matters, before disappearing from the text. Marguerite incorporates chivalric and courtly ideals and refers to an aristocracy of love as well as to well-known courtly tales. Although she did not make explicit mention of earlier mystical texts, she was clearly aware of these works, including those by William of St. Thierry and St. Bernard of Clairvaux, and the text itself contains 'an extensive mystical vocabulary.'[22] There are no direct or explicit references to the scriptures in the *Mirror* but there are echoes of the Bible throughout, suggesting that she knew the good book.

In the poem which opens the *Mirror of Simple Souls*, Marguerite introduces some of the important themes to follow, including one which was a potential cause of alarm for the Church. In a verse that could perhaps be read as being anticlerical, Marguerite asserts that theologians and the clergy will not be able to understand her work unless they proceed humbly. Humility is one of the essential virtues promoted in the opening poem and the key to understanding the text to follow. It is necessary to humble the reason and to accept love and faith as a way to rise above reason in order to come to understand both the work and the will of God. Marguerite declares that it is necessary to place all faith 'in those things which are given by Love, illuminated through Faith. And thus you will understand this book which makes the Soul live by love.'[23] She thus confirms the importance of love and the acceptance of God's will as the key to spiritual fulfillment, revealing the character of the book as both a mystical treatise and a handbook for guiding other souls.

The purpose of the work is more clearly enunciated in the opening passage of the prologue or first chapter, where Marguerite declares:

> Soul, touched by God and removed from sin at the first stage of grace, is carried by divine graces to the seventh stage of grace, in which state the Soul possesses the fullness of her perfection through divine fruition in the land of life.[24]

The treatise provides a description of the soul's mystical ascent to God through seven distinct stages, 'each one of higher intellect than the former and without comparison to each other.'[25] The difference between these stages, as Marguerite wrote, is as great as that between a drop of water and the ocean.[26] And, throughout the *Mirror of Simple Souls*, Marguerite identifies the differences between the seven stages and describes the state of the soul in each one of them. The spiritual ascent through these stages or states of grace leads to ultimate union with God, annihilation of the soul in God, and total identification with God.[27]

The first four states, which are very much in line with traditional orthodox mysticism, mark the growth of the soul toward God while it remains encumbered by 'some great servitude.'[28] In the first state, the soul is touched by God's grace; in fact, only divine grace can lead the soul to perfection. Once touched by it the soul is stripped of sin and becomes intent on keeping the commandments of God for the rest of its life. The soul has been commanded by God to love God, itself and its neighbor, and so guided by grace and the desire to love it will keep adhering to the law of God 'even if she lived a thousand years.'[29]

In the second state, the soul moves beyond what God has commanded and strives to accomplish all it can to please its beloved, God. The soul abandons all self and worldly things, despising riches, honors, and earthly delights. Having no fear of losing possessions, of the words of other people, or of the weakness of the body, the soul seeks to accomplish evangelical perfection and to follow the example of Jesus Christ.[30]

In the third state, the soul moves to break the will of the spirit. Immersed in doing the good works and asceticism of the second state, the soul has come to love these works but begins now to realize that it must sacrifice them for love. In this way the soul undergoes martyrdom by giving up what it loves, and in the process it comes to destroy the will. For, as Marguerite explains, 'it is more difficult to conquer the works of the will of the spirit than it is to conquer the will of the body.'[31] Accomplishing this, the soul then enters its fourth state and is drawn by love on to the level of meditation and 'relinquishes all exterior labors.' The soul reaches a state of joy and exhilaration; it is filled with love and can only feel the touch of love. In fact at this point it is so inebriated with love that it cannot believe that God can offer it any greater gift; but, as Marguerite cautions, the soul is deceived, for there are two other stages of greater nobility beyond love.[32]

In Marguerite's plan, the soul is now about to enter the fifth and sixth states, and it is this part of the Beguine's teaching that is the most daring and original, departing from more traditional forms of mysticism in describing the movement of the soul into a mystical state on earth.

The soul takes a step toward the supernatural in its fifth state, when it is thrown, from the dizzying heights of joy experienced in the fourth, right into the abyss of nothingness — and from a feeling of youth and pride into old age and loss of desire. The soul is left to consider that God is the source of all things, whereas that the soul is nothing if not of God. God bestows free will on the soul and pours into the will the awareness that it is not of God and that it is nothing; the soul comes to realize that it must dissolve its will in order to make its will the will of God.

In the sixth state the soul is completely liberated and purified, and it sees only God. Marguerite warns that the soul is not yet glorified, for this can only come in the seventh state, when it has left the body for eternal glory in paradise. But even so, the soul 'sees neither God nor herself, but God sees Himself of Himself in her, for her, without her. God shows to her that there is nothing except Him, and so loves nothing except Him, praises nothing except Him, for there is nothing except Him.'[33] The soul is therefore united with God and there is God wherever it looks; it has reached the highest level it can in this world.

The final state in Marguerite's *Mirror*, the seventh, describes the experience of the soul after death, which consists in the Beatific Vision and the soul's eternal happiness in the sight of God. Her picture of events here is very much in line with traditional Church teaching and its understanding by other mystics.

The annihilated or liberated soul of the sixth state is no longer bound by the rules of religion and society, having transcended them through union with God. The soul, as Love declares in one of the dialogues, has six wings, like the seraphim, the highest in rank among the angels. Two wings cover the soul's face; this reveals the soul has reached understanding of divine goodness. With two other wings, the soul covers its feet, because it has understanding of why Jesus Christ suffered for us all. With the other two, the soul flies up, to dwell in being and thus in the sight of God and in the divine will. Like the seraphim, the soul has no need for intermediaries, for there is 'no mediary between their [the souls'] love and the divine love.'[34] Hence it is freed from the traditional means of approaching God, as it has already become one with Him; it no longer seeks Him through penitence, sacraments, works, or other accepted religious practices.[35] The soul is without desires, except those of God; hence it neither desires nor rejects poverty, tribulations, masses, sermons, fasting, or prayer. It gives to 'Nature all that is necessary without remorse of conscience. But such nature is so well ordered through the transformation of Love ... that nature demands nothing which is prohibited.'[36] Moreover, the annihilated soul has 'entered into the abundances and flowings of divine Love' and is 'adorned with the adornments of absolute peace in which she lives.'[37] Thus in Marguerite's understanding the annihilated soul enjoyed in this world the mystical state which most other mystics reserved for the next.[38]

For Marguerite, the annihilated soul's move beyond the need for intermediaries encompasses the Church itself, or, as she styles it, Holy-Church-Below-This-Church or Holy Church the Little. This 'Church-Below' emerges at one point so as to participate in the dialogue and to learn about the liberated souls, which have moved on and are now part of the Holy Church the Great – the real Holy Church. The lesser Church is guided by reason rather than love, which dwells in Holy Church the Great; yet it praises love and teaches love according to the holy scriptures.[39] Marguerite also notes that many members of the Church – Beguines, priests, clerics, Dominicans, Augustinians, Carmelites, and Friars Minor – claim that she has erred because of her writing about 'the one purified by Love.'[40]

Without rejecting the Holy Church the Little, the worldly Church, or what it has to offer, Marguerite does describe a higher Church: it is the annihilated or liberated souls who form the true Church. In this way, she posits a religious elite or spiritual aristocracy above and beyond the encumbered souls of the world. But, although at points Marguerite Porete pushed the boundaries of orthodoxy and was perhaps too daring for her own good, her heresy, as the historian of heresy Malcolm Lambert noted, 'if it existed at all, was of a specialized character, concerned solely with the condition of mystical adepts at an advanced stage of perfection; there was no advocacy of libertinism and disregard for the moral law for anyone; and the accusations against Porete gave an unfair picture of her views.'[41] The numerous translations and editions of her work in the fourteenth century suggest that many regarded the *Mirror* as being above suspicion, and Gordon Leff observed that her path was 'not dissimilar from that of the orthodox mystics.'[42] Robert Lerner concedes that she 'was probably a heretic,' but continues by noting that, had she entered a traditional religious community, she would have attracted little attention. Her teachings and her mysticism are in fact similar to those of important and 'orthodox' figures such as Hildegard of Bingen and Mechthild of Madgeburg. And so the question remains: why was Marguerite Porete executed as a heretic?

To answer that question, one has to consider both the broader political and religious context and Marguerite's actions and beliefs. Her personal behavior surely stood against her. Her refusals to answer the inquisitor's questions and to

defend her teaching, indeed, her unwillingness even to take the necessary vow
to appear before the inquisitor, revealed her as a recalcitrant, uncooperative
character. In the eyes of William of Paris and other Church officials, this was
surely a sign of harboring heretical thoughts. Her disobedience to the orders
of the bishop of Cambrai and her own insistence on continuing to teach and
disseminate her *Mirror of Simple Souls* meant to them that she was indeed a
relapsed heretic. On the other hand, the great popularity and wide dissemination of the *Mirror* was also a factor against her. Then again, as a Beguine, especially an itinerant one, who did not live an acceptable cloistered life, Marguerite
was even more likely to stir suspicions of heresy at a time when the Beguine
lifestyle – settled or itinerant – was facing increasing disfavor. And her own
writings, which admittedly were presented in brief, out of context, and in the
worst possible light, seemed to implicate her in the heresy of the Free Spirit,
which the Church believed to be a vast movement of immoral and antinomian
heretics that could shake its own foundations. These fears of widespread heresy,
along with Marguerite's own silence in front of the inquisitors and the fact that
her work had gained popularity through its content, created a cluster of factors
which played the decisive role in determining her fate.

Marguerite's condemnation may also have been prompted by the growing
concern with heresy in France and by the willingness of secular and ecclesiastical authorities to use such fears for their own ends.[43] In the years just before and
after Marguerite's condemnation, the French court of King Philip IV (ruled
1285–1314) and its ecclesiastical allies struck at two important enemies, Pope
Boniface VIII and the great crusading Order of the Templars.[44] Philip and his
lawyers frequently used allegations of moral turpitude against various enemies
of the French crown, including the pope, French bishops, and Beguines.[45] Philip
accused Boniface of a wide range of crimes, such as blasphemy, the consultation
of demons, sexual immorality, and murder; indeed Philip was not above using
even physical violence against the octogenarian pope. And even more dramatic
perhaps was his assault on the Templars. The king's motivations remain unclear;
he may have truly believed that the military order was filled with blasphemous
heretics and therefore persecuted them ruthlessly. He and his allies alleged that
new initiates of the order underwent a ritual in which a Templar knight kissed
the new member on the base of the spine, the navel, and the mouth. The initiation ritual allegedly also involved urinating on the crucifix, and the members of

the order were accused of blasphemy, heresy, and homosexuality. Such charges formed the basis on which Philip ordered the arrest of the Templars in France in 1307. Perhaps not coincidentally, these charges were also considered at the Council of Vienne, which denounced the Beguines and, possibly, some of Marguerite's teachings. Eventually, the allegations against the Templars were used to bring about the suppression of the order in 1312 and the burning of the last Grand Master Templar in 1314.

It is here that the most important connections between Marguerite and the broader persecutions can be made. William of Paris, the Dominican inquisitor who oversaw her trial, was also closely connected to Philip IV. Not only was he Philip's confessor, he had also directed Philip's campaign against the Templars in 1307.[46] William, it appears, had a central role in Philip's efforts to present himself as a most Christian king, whose realm was unquestionably orthodox. Philip may have created what James Given calls 'fantastic enemies,' whom he was able to defeat, and in so doing 'reaffirmed the kingdom's solidarity and restored the sacred moral order.'[47] Marguerite's unfortunate end is not directly connected to the fate of the Templars or Boniface VIII, but her trial emerged at a time when the religious and political authorities in France strengthened the apparatus of persecution and closed ranks against heretics, real or otherwise, who were portrayed as rejecting the teachings of the Church and indulging immoral and decadent leanings. The institutionalized Church had increasingly repudiated diversity of opinion.

Marguerite Porete followed a unique spiritual path, which led to her ultimate demise. She offered a mystical way of reaching God in her *Mirror of Simple Souls*; she may well have felt that she herself had traveled the six stages that take place in this life toward the annihilation of the soul and union with Him. Her doctrines may have been unorthodox if not truly heretical, but, unlike Fra Dolcino, she was not overtly hostile to the established Church, nor did she seek to develop an alternative one, as had the Cathars and even the Waldenses. She may also be distinguished from earlier heretics, with the possible exception of Stephen and Lisois, by her aristocratic status and her belief in the Holy Church the Great. Her heresy, such as it was, involved the promotion of a spiritual elite who were able to follow her demanding mystical path. At the same time, however, her work seems to have been disseminated widely and developed a substantial following throughout France and beyond. In this way, Marguerite is similar to the last great heretics of the Middle Ages, John Wyclif and Jan Hus, brilliant scholars whose academic teachings and sophisticated theologies were declared heretical but had the power to inspire broad popular followings.

CHAPTER NINE

JOHN WYCLIF:
ENGLAND AND THE LOLLARDS

ccording to an English chronicler writing about the year 1382, 'In those days flourished master John Wyclif, rector of the church of Lutterworth, in the county of Leicester, the most eminent doctor of theology of those times. In philosophy he was reckoned second to none, and in scholastic learning without rival. This man strove to surpass the skill of other men by subtlety of knowledge to traverse their opinions.'[1] Indeed, it was as a teacher of philosophy and theology at Oxford that Wyclif made his name and developed a loyal following among other university masters and students. He also attracted support, as a result of his teaching and theological work, from the nobility, peasantry, and parish clergy. He was a profoundly influential scholar, whose teachings had an impact on religious life and thought in England and on the continent, most notably in Bohemia and on the work of Jan Hus. A daring thinker, Wyclif came to challenge much of the traditional theology and ecclesiology of the Church, undermining Catholic doctrine on the sacraments, on the institutional Church, and on priesthood. Although he remained in communion with the Church and died hearing the mass, Wyclif faced increasing animosity from those around him even before his death; nothing reflects the changing attitudes toward Wyclif better than the case of a contemporary who changed his description of the Oxford theologian from 'venerable doctor' to 'detestable seducer.'[2] Wyclif emerged not only as England's most important heretic but also as one of its first, since the kingdom had registered very few examples of heresy before the fourteenth century. A man of deep learning, unlike any previous medieval heretical leader in this respect, Wyclif nonetheless contributed to the emergence of a popular movement in England: the Lollards. This movement lasted into the sixteenth century, when it merged with the Protestant Reformation. Indeed, in his biblical fundamentalism, in his attitudes toward the priesthood and in related matters Wyclif has sometimes been described as a forerunner of Martin Luther and the Protestant reformers of the sixteenth century; this holds especially of his doctrine of the Eucharist, which emphasized the spiritual over the physical.[3] Although this topic remains a matter for some debate, Wyclif surely offered a dramatic alternative to the doctrines of the Catholic Church and a radical reworking of Christian teaching, which inspired a large national and even international following.

The exact date of Wyclif's birth remains uncertain, but his later scholarly career offers some suggestions for a possible date.[4] The future Oxford don was probably born at some point in the 1330s, possibly as early as 1330 and most likely not later than 1335/38. Little is known of his early years and of his family, and there is little agreement over the exact place of his birth. It is likely that he came from Yorkshire, but attempts to identify him with a Wycliffe family from a village of that name near Richmond have proved inconclusive. But, even though the exact date and place of his birth remain elusive, it is certain that the intellectual, religious, and political developments in England in the mid-fourteenth century shaped Wyclif's mature outlook and influenced the personal development of his later years, which are much better known.

The record of Wyclif's life becomes much better documented after he entered the schools of Oxford, where he was to spend nearly the whole of his adult life and which shaped many of his ideas. His entry to university indicates that he had already received the basic grammar school education. He was most likely ordained a priest in 1351, then joined the Augustinian order. From here on the events of his life come into clearer focus. He was first noted at Merton College in 1356, where he was a fellow. He appeared later at Balliol College, where, in 1360, he assumed the position of master of arts. His stay at Balliol, however, was relatively short; he seems to have abandoned his post after only a year or so, to take up a curateship in Lincolnshire in 1361. This was the first in a series of ecclesiastical benefices Wyclif held, and, although he most likely took up residence in Lincolnshire after his appointment, he seems not to have lived there very much. Indeed, as with most of his pastoral appointments, he exercised the office *in absentia*, leaving his routine ministerial duties with another cleric.

Throughout the 1360s Wyclif continued his academic career while acquiring canonries and other Church offices. In 1361 he received the license to study theology at Oxford for two years, an honor he renewed for another two years in 1368, and in 1372 he became a doctor of theology. For part of that period he had lived in rented rooms at Queen's College. In late 1365 he was appointed warden at Canterbury College by Simon Islip, the archbishop of Canterbury, who had reformed the college to accept secular clergy and not just regular clergy (that is, monks). Wyclif held this position until 1367, when Islip's successor, Simon Langham, ordered him to leave. The new archbishop decided that membership of the college should be limited to Benedictine monks, as it once had been, and so Wyclif and other secular clergy were no longer welcome. His efforts to fight the ouster, which reached Rome in 1370, proved unsuccessful, and he was ultimately forced to leave the college. This development might explain the vehemence of Wyclif's later criticisms of the monks, since it caused him both personal frustration and financial loss.[5] Indeed, he would thenceforth be identified as the advocate of those in secular orders and the first university opponent of those in monastic orders.[6] Despite this setback, Wyclif had already begun to acquire a number of ecclesiastical benefices that would provide him with the resources necessary to survive and continue his studies. In 1362, the university, as it was wont to do for its more promising students, had sent a petition for a canonry and prebend in York for the young Wyclif. The request was granted only partially, and Wyclif was given a prebendary at Aust in Gloucestershire, and a canonry in the church of Westbury-on-Trym near Bristol, which he seems to have held until the end of his life, even if he was not there to fulfill his pastoral duties.[7] In 1368 he was granted a rectory in Buckinghamshire and in 1371 was promised a canonry in Lincolnshire; he held the post in Buckinghamshire until his death but seems never to have actually received the other position. In 1374 Wyclif was granted the rectory of Lutterworth in Leicestershire by the king, in recognition of his services to the crown. Wyclif retired there in 1381 but turned over the parish duties to a curate named John Horn.[8] And, even though he had accumulated a number of ecclesiastical benefices, Wyclif seems to have spent most of his time at Oxford, from 1356 to his retirement in 1381.

It was during those years that Wyclif established his reputation as the leading scholar at Oxford, and even in all of England. At Oxford he came into contact for the first time with the nominalism of William of Ockham, which he adopted in his early years, before joining in the general reaction against it. Because philosophy at Oxford was in decline and there were no real philosophers of note either at the university or in the colleges, Wyclif was particularly influenced by scholars of an earlier generation, including Richard Fitzralph and Thomas Bradwardine and the even earlier eminence, Robert Grosseteste. Along with his introduction to higher studies and to the writings of earlier scholars, Wyclif himself began to teach. He gained prominence as a philosophy teacher in the 1360s, identifying himself as a 'real philosopher' rather than a 'doctor of signs.'[9] As he came to abandon nominalism and establish himself as a philosopher, Wyclif attracted a growing following at the university, in part because his philosophy came to offer certainty. His supporters were also attracted by the depth of his learning; one of Wyclif's rivals, Thomas Netter, admitted that he was 'astounded by his [Wyclif's] sweeping assertions, by the authorities cited, and by the vehemence of his reasoning.'[10] Not content with philosophy, Wyclif began teaching theology in 1371, one year before becoming a doctor in that subject. His philosophical positions, of course, influenced the direction of his theology, and he came to examine a broad range of matters, including the institutions of the Church, the clergy, and the Eucharist.

As a scholar of growing renown, Wyclif also wrote some 132 treatises on philosophical, theological, and even legal matters, less than half of which survive in English manuscripts; only sixteen of them survive in more than one English copy. His output was significant in all areas. A sufficient number of copies of treatises apparently survived in the generation after his death, before his official condemnation, and his writings also survived outside of England. His works on theological and ecclesiastical matters are perhaps the most numerous; most of his treatises on philosophy were written before 1371, when he turned to theology. Among his works of philosophy are *De actibus animae* ('On the Actions of the Soul'), 1368–69; *De ente praedicamentali* ('On Categorical Being'), 1368–69; *Tractatus de logica* ('Treatise on Logic'), 1371–73; *De ente* ('On Being'), 1371–74; *Summa de ente libri primi tractatus primus et secundus* ('Summa on Being, Book

One, Tracts One and Two'), 1372/73; *Tractatus de universalibus* ('Treatise on Universals'), 1374. In these and other works Wyclif set out his essential philosophical positions, which influenced both his own theology and the work of contemporaries at Oxford and beyond. In terms of metaphysics, Wyclif maintained two basic principles. He believed that 'Nothing is and is not at the same time,' a position holding pure negation, and that being exists and was the first unquestionable truth.[11] For Wyclif, being is transcendent and all things participate in it, and from this he reasoned that there was a chain of being that led from God to the individual. In this way Wyclif believed that God was irrevocably connected to the world he had created and to all the creatures in it. He also maintained that all being is eternal and that all beings, at all times, are apparent to God. Along with his teachings on being, of importance to Wyclif's later thought was his understanding of universals, which were discussed in his works on being and universals. He derived his ideas on universals from Augustine and believed that all universal concepts have their own subsistence. For Wyclif, universals were a means to understand the world; for all things participate in the universal concept and share a common nature although they are distinct from the universal, and they are made intelligible through that participation.

Perhaps of greater importance than his philosophical writings were Wyclif's many theological and ecclesiastical works, which were shaped by his philosophical assumptions as well as by his own moral values and perception of the institutional Church. These works began to appear in the 1370s, and he continued to produce theological and doctrinal treatises until his death, a number of them during the last few years of his life. But one of his earliest works was a commentary on the entire Bible. At some point between 1370/71 and 1375/76, Wyclif compiled his *Postilla super totam bibliam* ('Afterthought on the Whole Bible'), the only commentary on the whole Bible from the second half of the fourteenth century.[12] The *Postilla* not only considered every book of the Bible; it also emphasized the poverty and humility of the early Church, by way of criticizing the Church of the fourteenth century.[13] The *Postilla* also illustrated Wyclif's growing focus on the Bible and his recognition of the importance of putting the Holy Scriptures at the center of Christian life. His concerns with the Bible were expressed again in 1378, in his *De veritate sacre scripture* ('On the Truth of Sacred Scripture'). In that same year he wrote *De ecclesia* ('On the Church'), which outlined Wyclif's ideas on the visible and invisible Church and criticized Pope Gregory XI (1370–78). He continued and sharpened his critique of the pope and of the institution of papacy in 1379, in *De potestate pape* ('On the Power of the Pope'). These were among several treatises he wrote in the 1370s, in which he considered civil society, the Church, and the relationship between the two. He first explored these matters in *De dominio divino* ('On Divine Dominion') and *De statu innocenciae* ('On the State of Innocence') in 1373/74, then more fully in *De civili dominio* ('On Civil Dominion') in 1375–77, and then again in *De officio regis* ('On the Office of the King') in 1379. In the last work, Wyclif stressed the authority of the king over the clergy, recognized his duty to reform the Church – one of Wyclif's greatest concerns – and repudiated some of the opinions voiced in the work on civil dominion.[14] Along with his ecclesiological works of 1379, Wyclif wrote one of his most important and controversial theological works, *De eucharistia* ('On the Eucharist'), which offered his explanation of the nature of the change taking place in the substance of the host – an explanation that was ultimately condemned as heretical. Thus these works defined his position on a wide range of topics and revealed a daring thinker, who offered sometimes radical propositions about the nature of the Church, civil society, priesthood, and the sacraments.

Along with his numerous academic treatises, Wyclif composed many sermons, but only a small number of those he delivered survive. These sermons have been collected in the *Sermones Quadraginta* ('Forty Sermons') and used to disseminate his ideas to an audience beyond that of his scholarly works, one which included simple priests. He also produced numerous sermons he did not deliver, written on behalf of other preachers. This body of sermons was designed for use throughout the Church calendar year and pointed out the scriptural readings for various Sundays. Others of his literary sermons were written for various saints' days throughout the calendar and contained comments on the scriptural passages to be used for those services.

Wyclif's activities, however, were not limited to the intellectual field but extended to the political arena, a preoccupation he would also explore in several of his treatises. As early as 1370 or 1371, in his university lectures, Wyclif may have formulated for the first time an opinion on matters of lordship and dominion.[15] In 1371, when he probably first made acquaintance with John of Gaunt, duke of Lancaster (1340–99), uncle to the future King Richard II, Wyclif was ready to involve himself in England's political life. His political activities may well have been determined by his growing reputation as a philosopher and theologian; political powers may have seen in him an effective force against the more traditional university scholars of the day.[16] Whatever the reason for his involvement in political matters, Wyclif seems to have taken his first steps in that direction when he participated in the parliament of 1371. At issue was the wealth of the clergy and the rights of the secular authority over ecclesiastical wealth. At the parliament, two Augustinian friars argued that, in times of emergency, the secular power has the right to seize ecclesiastical property and to impose taxes on the clergy. Wyclif, possibly at the suggestion of John of Gaunt, took up the controversy, arguing on the side of the Augustinian friars and against the claims of Rome to be exempt from royal taxation at all times.

His position on clerical wealth earned Wyclif the growing hostility of Church leaders but greater support from lay powers, and he would be further involved in political affairs in the coming years. In July 1374 Wyclif was sent to Bruges on a diplomatic mission, as a representative of the king, to join in negotiations with papal legates over the matter of financial payments from the English clergy to the pope. The discussions were a dismal failure for the crown and an almost complete triumph for the papacy. Wyclif was paid the handsome sum of £60 for his services but was no longer present when the negotiations were completed, and his exact role in them remains unclear.[17] It is certain, however, that he continued to develop his ideas about the relationship of Church and state, which subordinated the clergy to the king and further enhanced his reputation with the secular leaders of England.

He took part in political affairs on several other occasions in the 1370s, each time advancing the interests of the English government. In 1376, Wyclif promoted the interests of his protector, John of Gaunt, and the claims of the English monarchy against the Good Parliament and William of Wykeham, bishop of Winchester, who had emerged as an important leader during the meeting and had taken the lead in criticizing the king's advisers for corruption and incompetence. Wyclif preached against William, whom he denounced for his worldliness, wealth, excessive devotion to politics, and neglect of spiritual duties; he also spoke out against clerical abuses and the wealth of the Church and its ministers. His preaching helped to undo the efforts of the Good Parliament and of William of Wykeham, much to the pleasure of Wyclif's patron, and inspired a move toward reforming the Church and the faith. But his outspoken opposition to the

Church's claims to secular power and wealth brought Wyclif his first taste of trouble. This was from William Courtenay, the bishop of London, who had spoken in defense of Wykeham. Courtenay summoned the theologian to the episcopal court at St. Paul's. John of Gaunt's power and influence served to undermine Bishop William's efforts against Wyclif. The duke of Lancaster's appearance at the proceedings with his ally, Lord Percy, marshal of England, led them to break up in disorder; the people of London rioted in support of their bishop following a bitter exchange between Gaunt and him.[18]

Wyclif's political activities took place while he was developing his ideas on civil dominion and reflected the positions he took on behalf of the royal government and his patron. As he had done in earlier years, Wyclif spoke on behalf of the secular authority in 1377 and again in 1378. In 1377 he defended the interests of the government in a dispute over the delivery of gold bullion to the papal court at Avignon, partly as taxes and tithes owed to the papal administration and partly as revenues from benefices which a number of cardinals held in England. As all medieval rulers believed, control over gold was necessary for the strength of the government and of the economy, and so Wyclif was asked whether England

> might lawfully for its own defense in case of need, detain the wealth of the kingdom, so that it be not carried away in foreign parts, even though the pope himself demands it under pain of censure and by virtue of the obedience owing to him.[19]

As expected, Wyclif's response was fully in the government's favor, and as he had only previously expressed in a short pamphlet. He argued that the papal tax collector, who traditionally took an oath to do nothing to harm the kingdom, had in fact violated his oath. Exporting large quantities of gold, Wyclif reasoned, was so detrimental to the health of the kingdom that the tax collector was guilty of perjury. Citing natural law, the Gospels, and individual conscience, Wyclif explained that the government's position was the correct one.[20]

In October 1378, Wyclif provided support for the state in a highly controversial matter concerning the rights of the Church. He was again called upon by his patron, John of Gaunt. The duke had ordered his soldiers to enter Westminster Abbey to apprehend two prisoners who had escaped from the Tower of London and sought sanctuary at the abbey. The soldiers, violating the Church's ancient right of sanctuary, caught one of the squires and killed the other one, who was allegedly guilty of treason; they also murdered one of the abbey's servants, who attempted to prevent the arrest. The bishop excommunicated all those involved in the violation of the sanctuary, and the matter was then brought before the parliament. Wyclif defended the actions of the soldiers, asserting that the prisoner who was killed died while resisting a legal arrest. Wyclif further set out the rights of the civil authority in pursuing a suspect and entering the sanctuary, and also limited the rights of those who claimed asylum in churches. His defense of the duke and of his men before parliament also formed the basis of his treatise *De ecclesia*. Wyclif's political activities served two important ends: they allowed him to develop his own ideas on secular and religious authority and they secured for him powerful lay patrons, who were to protect him when he faced the threat of excommunication and other ecclesiastical penalties.

Lay protection would be especially important and necessary for Wyclif by the late 1370s, when his teachings had become increasingly radical and critical of the Church. Not only had Wyclif's arguments on civil dominion over the Church and clergy earned him the enmity of the Church hierarchy, but his denunciations of Church power and wealth also raised the ire of the bishops. The first attempts to censure Wyclif came in 1377, a momentous year for the Oxford theologian. His ever more strident criticisms of the papacy did fall on deaf ears, and Gregory XI, perhaps as the result of the complaints of English Benedictines or of some other enemy who sent passages from *De civili dominio*, sent a letter, denouncing Wyclif, which arrived only late in the year 1377, to the masters and chancellor of Oxford, the bishops of England and the king, Edward III. The letter included a list of some eighteen of Wyclif's teachings which were deemed offensive. According to the pope, Wyclif 'has fallen into such a detestable madness that he does not hesitate to dogmatize and publicly preach, or rather vomit forth from the recesses of his breast certain propositions and conclusions which are erroneous and false.'[21] Gregory also accused Wyclif of 'preaching heretical dogmas which strive to subvert and weaken the state of the whole Church and even secular polity.'[22] Wyclif, according to the pope, was guilty of holding opinions similar to those of such condemned thinkers as Marsilius of Padua and John of Jandun and asserted that only a righteous man may hold authority. The pope alleged further that Wyclif had led the faithful away from the true path of righteousness with his false doctrines, including the belief that only God could absolve a penitent sinner, the belief that the Church was made up of those predestined to salvation or foreknown to be damned, and his teaching that the Church, with its claims to power and wealth, had become corrupted. Therefore, reasoned the pope, Wyclif should be punished. He ordered that the university should no longer allow such opinions as those of Wyclif to be taught at Oxford, under penalty of loss of the privileges received from the Holy See. The chancellor and masters were further commanded to arrest Wyclif or have him arrested in the pope's name and delivered to the archbishop of Canterbury or to the bishop of London, where a confession could be extracted from the theologian.

Wyclif himself sent a spirited reply to this letter of condemnation to Gregory's successor, Pope Urban VI (1378–89), asserting his devotion to the faith and especially to the Gospels. He also apologized to the pope, whom he greeted as a welcome successor to Gregory, for not being able to appear in person in Rome to defend himself, and it seems most likely that Wyclif intended to remain on good terms with the new pope. An important declaration – but Wyclif was saved not so much by his personal statement to the pope as by several external developments. The force of the papal declaration was weakened significantly by the death of Gregory in March 1378 and, even more so, by the beginning of the Great Schism, which lasted from 1378 until 1417. Following Gregory's death, two claimants to the papal throne – Urban VI in Rome, Clement VII in Avignon – asserted their legitimacy at each other's expense. The Schism divided Europe and caused great difficulty for the established Church, not the least of which was the failure of the papal denunciation of John Wyclif: the attention of the popes was drawn now to matters of state and away from the teachings of an Oxford theologian. Beyond that, however, it is likely that the papal condemnation of Wyclif in 1377 would have failed even without the advent of the Schism. The authorities at Oxford, notably the master and future chancellor, Robert Rigg, a great admirer of Wyclif who would remain one of his most ardent supporters, seemed little interested in punishing their most shining star. It may be argued that, even if Wyclif had not been the leading English scholar of his day, the chancellor and masters at Oxford would have been reluctant to punish him because they resented papal interference in their affairs. Ultimately, Wyclif and the authorities at Oxford agreed that the don would be held at Black Hall until his teachings were reviewed; he was subsequently absolved by the university and his teachings were deemed to be true.

But the most important reason why Wyclif was not censured may well have been the support he received from the leading secular authorities in England. Support from figures in high places helped him to avoid an appearance at the episcopal court. When he finally did appear at the archbishop of Canterbury's chapel at Lambeth Palace to defend himself, he suffered no punishment other than a warning not to spread false doctrines. Not only had the bishops seemed reluctant to pursue the pope's case, but Wyclif's safety was guaranteed by the queen mother, Joan, widow of Edward (the Black Prince) and mother of King Richard II (1367–1400), who had sent one of her knights with the express order that no judgment should be pronounced in the case.[23] His service to the crown and its allies, as a theorist and propagandist, was, and continued to be, of vital importance; hence the members of the royal family supported him against ecclesiastical authorities. (Indeed, rather than punish him, the crown sought his advice on the matter of the export of gold.) Moreover, the temporal authority surely welcomed Wyclif's increasingly vehement critiques of the Church and of its representatives; the vigorous reforms he promoted would limit the wealth and power of the Church, to the benefit of the crown. Wyclif maintained that it was the crown that was best situated to implement the reformation of the Church, an argument that enhanced his value to his royal and aristocratic patrons. As a result of protection from the queen mother, as well as strong support from his university colleagues and the chancellor, the efforts to condemn Wyclif and his teachings failed in England in 1378, and he continued to teach and participate in the political affairs of the country.

Wyclif's troubles, however, were not at an end. Although the efforts in 1377/78 to condemn him or limit his influence failed, a new process in 1380 was more successful, in part because his own, ever more radical, views increased opposition to him and provided his enemies with more ammunition. Disappointed over the failings of Pope Urban VI and over the Schism, Wyclif took a harder line on the papacy in his writings of the late 1370s, repudiating the Church hierarchy in its entirety, and laid the foundation for even more extreme statements in his writings of the 1380s. He also produced his massive work on the Bible, which asserted the fundamental truth of the text and maintained that it should be available to all Christians, lay and religious.[24] His work on the

Eucharist, however, in which he rejected the Catholic doctrine of transubstan-tiation, proved to be most problematic and marked the beginning of Wyclif's transformation, from radical critic and reformer into a heretic, or, as the con-temporary scholar wrote, from 'venerable doctor' into 'detestable seducer.'

In 1380, William Barton, chancellor of Oxford and fellow at Merton College, established a commission to examine Wyclif's eucharistic teachings. Barton, a doctor of divinity, had long opposed Wyclif's teachings in his own lectures and writings. Now he felt the time was right to take steps against his rival, who had begun to lose support among one of his most important con-stituencies – the scholars at Oxford in the mendicant orders. Barton appointed twelve doctors to the commission: six mendicant friars, four members of the secular orders, and two monks, and it appears from the composition of the commission that Barton, despite his personal opposition to Wyclif's teachings, intended to give Wyclif a fair hearing. One member of the commission was Robert Rigg, who would succeed Barton as chancellor in 1382; being a staunch supporter of Wyclif he would suffer for it in the mid-1380s.[25] The commission ultimately condemned two of Wyclif's propositions on the Eucharist, but only by the slight majority of seven to five, which reinforces the view that Barton intended a fair hearing. Wyclif's teachings that the substance of the bread and wine of the eucharistic offerings remains after consecration and that the body of Christ is figuratively and not physically present in the bread and wine were condemned as erroneous and a danger to the Church.[26] Responding to the commission's report, Barton declared that anyone holding, teaching, or defending these views would be imprisoned, stripped of any university func-tion, and excommunicated.

Wyclif, however, remained undaunted by the report, asserting 'that neither the chancellor nor any of his accomplices could weaken his opinion.'[27] Surprised and disappointed by the decision, he made up his mind to appeal against it rather than accept it. But he would not pursue his appeal in any ecclesiastical court, as both the law of England and the Church required. Instead, Wyclif turned once again to the king, seeking from the crown protection from his ecclesiastical rivals. The king seems to have ignored Wyclif's petition, but John of Gaunt may have become involved. The duke reportedly traveled to Oxford to discuss the matter with his former client and to convince him to obey the chancellor's instructions. The duke's wishes, and the king's unwillingness to entertain the petition, reveal the growing disquiet among Wyclif's former patrons about the increasingly unorthodox tenor of his teachings. It was one thing to advocate the supremacy of the temporal power over the spiritual in political matters and to condemn the corruption and abuse of the clergy, but quite another to advocate doctrines condemned by the Church as erroneous. As Wyclif's own teachings became ever more extreme, support from his allies in the government and Church began to wane.

Wyclif, despite John of Gaunt's wishes to the contrary, undertook his own defense, publishing his *Confessions* on May 10, 1381. In this tract he defended and reasserted the positions repudiated by the commission, attempting to restore his good name after the condemnation. He railed against the opinions of the commission members and fully stated his positions on the Eucharist against what he considered to be errors of the established Church. He asserted the need for doctrinal change in order to correct the flawed teachings of the Church on the sacrament. But his vehement defense of his own ideas on the Eucharist and demand for their institution alienated the aristocratic and royal patrons who had been essential to his success and whose support would be necessary to implement any of the reforms, doctrinal and institutional, that he advocated.

Wyclif suffered even further erosion of support from his former patrons and other sympathizers as a result of the outbreak of the Peasants' Revolt in June 1381. Although it is unlikely that he backed the revolt or that his teachings were directly responsible for it, his enemies surely blamed him and his ideas for it. They were aided by the confession of one of the revolt's leaders, the priest John Ball, who reportedly declared, just before his execution after the brutal suppression of the revolt, that 'for two years he had been a disciple of Wyclif, and had learned from him the heresies he had taught.'[28] Wyclif's reaction to the revolt also undermined any support he may still have expected and added more fuel to the fire for his enemies – he condemned the murder of the archbishop of Canterbury by the rebels while admitting that the archbishop had been guilty of excessive worldliness; and he denounced the revolt in general, but he argued that the rebels' biggest error was their failure to get support from parliament. He also expressed some sympathy for the rebels, even arguing that they had a legitimate complaint about excessive taxation, for which Wyclif blamed the clergy.[29]

Following the condemnation of his teachings and the Peasants' Revolt,

Wyclif left Oxford, retiring to his rectory at Lutterworth. There he continued to write at a feverish pace, completing treatises he had begun at Oxford and preparing numerous pamphlets and sermons in attack of the friars, whom he blamed for his exile from Oxford. In his last years, Wyclif completed three volumes on different kinds of heresy: *De simonia* ('On Simony'), *De apostasia* ('On Apostasy'), and *De blasphemia* ('On Blasphemy'). In these works, composed in 1381 and 1382, Wyclif offered some words of moderation, in a half-hearted attempt to regain support from his former allies, but mainly criticized the clergy forcefully and endorsed his position on the Eucharist. In his work on simony — the sin of the buying and selling of Church offices or spiritual preferment — Wyclif denounced as simony any form of clerical worldliness and corruption. And apostasy, for him, included the failure of members of the clergy to live up to the demands of their vocation and the support of the Church's teaching on the Eucharist. In *De apostasia*, Wyclif offered an impassioned defense of his own teachings on the Eucharist as well as denouncing the errors of others. *De blasphemia* is a long and somewhat disorganized catalogue of the sins and abuses of the clergy at all levels, with particular bile reserved for the cardinals and the friars. These works were followed by the *Trialogus* ('Trialogue') in 1382 — a discussion between Truth, Falsehood, and Wisdom, which offers a summation and restatement of many positions Wyclif took in earlier works, including a commentary on the Eucharist and further attacks on the friars. Of all his works, this was one of the most popular; it was printed at Basel in 1525, offering a possible link with the Reformers of the sixteenth century.[30] At the time of his death, in 1384, Wyclif was working on the *Opus evangelicum* ('Opus on the Gospel'), which revealed its author's respect for the Bible and for Augustine. In the first volume of the *Opus*, Wyclif provided a commentary on the Sermon on the Mount, and in the second volume, subtitled *De antichristi* ('On Antichrist'), he discussed the Gospel of Matthew.

Although free to write during his last years, Wyclif was troubled by two major events in his life: further persecution from his enemies and ill health. The hand of his critics was strengthened by the murder of the archbishop of Canterbury during the Peasants' Revolt, because the new archbishop, William Courtenay, had long led the opposition to Wyclif. As the leading primate in England, he took the initiative to stamp out heresies taking root in the kingdom.

He was motivated not only by Wyclif himself but also by Wyclif's support-ers at Oxford. Ironically, the atmosphere at Oxford had improved following Wyclif's departure. The new chancellor, Robert Rigg, had supported Wyclif at the commission that condemned the theologian and would as chancellor support Wyclifite scholars. In particular, Rigg was an advocate of Nicholas of Hereford and Philip Repton when both took clear Wyclifite positions. When Hereford preached a sermon arguing that clergy in orders, meaning monks and friars, should not be allowed to take a degree at Oxford, Rigg invited him to deliver the second sermon on Ascension Day, at which point Hereford defended Wyclif's teachings.[31] Similarly, Repton received the enthusiastic approbation of the chancellor when he defended Wyclif's teachings on the Eucharist and the clergy in a sermon he delivered.

Courtenay, shortly after assuming the see at Canterbury, called a council to condemn the teachings of Wyclif and his followers on May 17, 1382. Known as the Earthquake Council because an earthquake shook London during the meeting – an event seen as an omen both by Wyclif and by his opponents – the meeting was held at the house of the Black Friars in London and would formally condemn a number of Wyclif's teachings. The new archbishop called together nine bishops, thirty-six theologians and canon lawyers, and a number of lesser clergy to debate twenty-four propositions from Wyclif's writings. After four days of discussion and debate, the members of the council declared ten of Wyclif's teachings heretical; the other fourteen were deemed erroneous. Wyclif's views on the Eucharist, the sacramental powers of the clergy, clerical wealth, and papal power were among those declared heretical. Although Wyclif himself was not excommunicated, his followers were to be punished, and the archbishop submitted a petition to the government, subsequently approved, which called for the arrest and imprisonment of unlicensed preachers. Courte-nay also sent a friar to Oxford, to implement the decrees and enforce the will of the council and of the archbishop at the university. Despite their efforts on Wyclif's behalf and vocal support of his ideas, the chancellor and Wyclif's allies buckled under the pressure from the archbishop. Rigg accepted the con-demnation of Wyclif's teachings and published it at Oxford, thus forbidding the dissemination of Wyclifite doctrines there. He also forbade Wyclif and his supporters to teach at Oxford, and both Hereford and Repton were excommu-nicated for their views.

Along with the condemnation of the Earthquake Council, Wyclif was plagued by strokes, which makes his substantial literary production all the more remarkable. In November 1382 Wyclif suffered his first stroke, a debilitating attack that left him partially paralyzed. Despite continued poor health, Wyclif did not stop writing his sermons and treatises. His pastoral duties, however, were undertaken by his curate John Horn, as they had been since his return to Lutterworth. And it is Horn who offers moving testimony on Wyclif's last days and death following a massive stroke on December 28, 1384:

> On Holy Innocents' Day, as Wyclif was hearing mass in his church at Lutterworth, just as the Host was elevated, he fell smitten by an acute paralysis, especially in the tongue so that neither then nor afterwards could he speak.[32]

He lingered for three days after that and then died on December 31, 1384. Despite the condemnation of several of his propositions, Wyclif had remained in communion with the Church and was therefore buried in consecrated ground, in the graveyard at the church of Lutterworth.

Wyclif's story, however, does not end on the last day of 1384, but continues into the fifteenth century, in England and on the continent. The Lollards and various continental theologians and churchmen were influenced by Wyclif's teachings on different matters, and these opinions form Wyclif's greatest legacy. Disseminated by his direct and indirect followers, Wyclif's views on civil dominion, the Bible, the Church and its priesthood, and the Eucharist constitute a powerful body of ideas which in some ways foreshadowed the doctrines of Martin Luther and other Protestant reformers. The Reformation did not arrive in Wyclif's day, of course, but his ideas must be considered in order to understand his importance in the history of the late medieval church.

Among Wyclif's important teachings – although it is not given now the weight it was once believed to have in his thought, and it should not be considered to be part of his broader theological program – was his opinion on civil dominion.[33] His theoretical preoccupation with matters concerning the state may have attracted his attention to contemporary politics and drawn to him figures such as John of Gaunt. After his publication of the work on civil dominion in 1375–77, Gaunt called Wyclif to London to preach against the bishops, who came to a very critical opinion of the work, different from the stand taken by the duke of Lancaster.[34] Whatever the immediate impact, Wyclif himself would ultimately leave this work behind as he developed his ideas about the Church, but it remains of note nonetheless, and it helped in bringing him to the attention of the great powers of his day.

Underlying his conception of civil dominion was the belief that all earthly power derives from God's grace. His understanding of dominion drew from such earlier thinkers as Richard Fitzralph, Giles of Rome (through Fitzralph), and Marsilius of Padua.[35] He argued that the secular power represented by kings and lords was empowered by God himself and that, as proved by scripture, they had the authority to rule over the Church. Kings and lords must, however, follow the dictates of the pope so long as they adhere to the teachings of the Gospels, which are the central source of authority for Wyclif in both spiritual and secular matters. On the other hand, Wyclif rejects the authority of the pope to excommunicate anyone, claiming that only the individual can excommunicate himself through sin. Driving Wyclif's thought on dominion was not only his recognition that the power exercised by kings was scripturally sanctioned, but also his thought that true lordship was characterized by justice, so that, without it, there was no lordship. He did accept that tyrants could rule and were sent to punish sin and establish civil dominion, but a tyrant would not exercise true dominion. Civil law, Wyclif held, was established for the benefit of the community and in order to ensure the safety and necessities of life, but true dominion was exercised only by the righteous; the true lord followed the teachings of the Gospel and had received God's grace.

More important and developed than his expressed views on civil dominion was his understanding of the Church, which had a more lasting and profound impact on his thought than his understanding of grace and dominion had. Worked out in several treatises, including those on the Church, on the king's office, and on the powers of the pope, his conception of the Church drew from Augustine's *De civitate Dei* ('On the City of God'), but pushed to the extreme Augustine's identification of two cities – the earthly one and the heavenly one.[36] Although Wyclif recognized three distinct meanings of the term 'church,' he stressed that the true meaning, or the true Church, was that which is made up of the elect. Only those who were predestined to salvation are part of it, and the Church itself is comprised of three parts: 'one triumphing in heaven, one sleeping in purgatory, and one battling on earth.'[37] The saved are bound together by God's grace and constitute the true Church under Christ, just as those not among the elect are bound together for all eternity under the authority of Antichrist.[38] The two groups are strictly divided and no one, in Wyclif's view, knows to which group he or she belongs, nor can anyone claim to know or assert that they belong to the true Church, or claim to be its head.[39]

Wyclif's understanding of the 'true Church' had clear implications for his attitude toward the Church militant and its representatives, the pope and the clergy. As he declared in *De potestate papae*:

> The Catholic truth which I have often repeated consists of this: that no pope, bishop, abbot, or any spiritual prelate is to be believed or obeyed except in so far as he says or commands the law of Christ.[40]

For Wyclif, it was not necessary to follow the dictates of the pope or other cleric unless that dictate itself followed the law of the Gospel. Many of the institutions and sacraments of the Church were called into question by Wyclif's view on the visible Church; the intercessory role of the clergy was also denied, even though he never explicitly said so. Because it is uncertain whether any member of the clergy, including the pope himself, can be identified as belonging to the true Church, then, reasoned Wyclif, it was not necessary for the hierarchy to exist – which he often denounced for its avarice, worldliness, and corruption. The pope and other members of the hierarchy, because of their failure to live according to the Gospels, had demonstrated their very uselessness and, even worse, their identification with Antichrist. The Church and its leaders had become more concerned with worldly power and possessions than with the care of souls, and, like many of his contemporaries, Wyclif identified the moment of fall of the visible Church with the endowment of this institution by the Roman Emperor Constantine, in the fourth century. Wyclif believed that it was better to return to a time before the establishment of the imperial Church by Constantine and to disendow the Church, so as to make it possible for it to return to its apostolic purity.

Wyclif's repudiation of the visible Church on account of its failure to live according to the teachings of the Gospels demonstrates the fundamental importance of the Bible to him. Known as *Doctor Evangelicus* ('the Evangelical Doctor'), Wyclif placed an emphasis on the scriptures which links him not only to earlier medieval heretics like Valdes but also to the Protestants of the sixteenth century like Martin Luther. Yet Wyclif did not adopt the notion of *sola Scriptura*, as did Luther and the Protestant Reformers, but he recognized the value of the writings of Augustine and other exegetes and theologians on the Bible. Moreover, his emphasis on the scripture itself was nothing new, but part of a long tradition going back for centuries; his own commentary on the Bible borrowed from the Franciscan scholar Nicholas of Lyra, among others. But in spite of his debt to other exegetes and acceptance of the work of earlier theologians, Wyclif asserted the absolute truth of the scripture and the absolute centrality of the Bible to Christian life. So important was the Bible to Wyclif that he declared that 'all Christians, and lay lords in particular, ought to know holy writ and defend it,' and, again, 'no man is so rude a scholar but that he may learn the words of the Gospel according to his simplicity.'[41] Indeed, his rejection of the visible Church was the result of his belief that the Church and its ministers were not necessary intermediaries for understanding the Holy Writ. Although it is perhaps anachronistic to speak of the 'priesthood of all believers', it is certain that Wyclif hoped that all could read the Bible, and his sentiments concerning its importance inspired the first English translation of the text. Wyclif himself was most probably not involved in any such enterprise, even though an attribution to him was made as early as 1390; but he can certainly be seen as the guiding light behind the translation.[42]

Wyclif's stress on the importance of the Bible for all Christians stems from his understanding of it as the absolute and unchanging word of God. For him, those who raised questions about the scriptures or pointed out inconsistencies in the text were the real heretics, because the Bible was the truth – it was God's word. As he declared in his work on the sacred scripture:

> For since the whole of sacred scripture is the word of God, there could not be a superior, safer, or more effective testimony than this: if God who cannot lie says this in his scripture, which is the mirror of his will, then it is true.[43]

As the word of God, then, the Bible is the absolute and ultimate authority in all matters. But it must be noted that Wyclif was not a biblical literalist; rather, it was the underlying sense of the words of the Bible that was true. As he argued in *De veritate sacrae scripturae*, the Bible is the combination of the written word in the book and the meaning derived from the symbol in the text. Moreover, Wyclif asserted that there were five levels of truth in the Bible: the truth of life, the truths of life in their ideal being, the truths in their existence, the truths written on man's soul, and the truth of sounds or books. The Bible was, therefore, the source of all truth for Wyclif. It was the mirror of God's will and the mirror of right conduct for all Christians. It was also the voice of the Son of God and, as such, it was the law of the Church and the source of all true doctrines.[44] The Bible was, therefore, the final authority and the absolute truth, and the failure of the visible Church to adhere fully to its teachings rendered it unworthy of any authority it might claim.

Although Wyclif's political philosophy, which rejected the established Church and asserted temporal authority over it as well as biblical extremism, brought him to the limits of orthodoxy, it was his position on the Eucharist that was clearly heterodox and caused the greatest difficulties both during his lifetime and after. Wyclif did not come easily or early to his controversial understanding of the nature of the Eucharist; as late as 1378 he still accepted the Church's teaching on transubstantiation, before his own study and application of philosophical realism to the question led him to reject Catholic doctrine as in error.[45] And even then, he did not reject the sacrament as instituted by Jesus, but only denied a teaching of the Church which, as he explained, had been formalized during the reign of Pope Innocent III (1198–1216) and no earlier. It should be noted that Wyclif's concern was also motivated by his understanding of the Church and its clergy; eucharistic doctrine as taught in his day maintained the sacerdotal authority of these institutions, about which Wyclif had serious doubts.

But Wyclif came to reject the Catholic teaching on the sacrament for philosophical and theological reasons. He could not accept the standard explanations for the transformation of the Eucharist into the body and blood of Christ that were given in his day. These held that the bread and wine were completely replaced by the body and blood of Christ after consecration; only the appearance of bread and wine remained, while the substance was that of the flesh and blood of Christ. For Wyclif, this could not stand from a philosophical perspective because the bread and wine had to preserve their substance even if they were – in philosophical terms – only accidents. Moreover, Wyclif could find no scriptural justification for the doctrine of transubstantiation, a potentially more troubling problem than the philosophical difficulties of accepting Church teaching. He was, however, convinced that the rite was a sacrament instituted by Jesus at the Last Supper, when he said to the Apostles: 'This is my body' (Matthew 26: 26). This passage led Wyclif to the belief that, at the moment of that declaration, the body and bread existed together, and thus when the bread and wine are consecrated on the altar they exist with the body and blood of Christ, although not the literal body born of the Virgin Mary. Wyclif's teachings on the Eucharist, therefore, approached the Lutheran doctrine of consubstantiality. For him, the so-called miracle of the mass was not that the bread and wine were transformed into the body and blood of Christ, but that the two substances coexisted. The eucharistic offerings underwent a spiritual transformation whereby they were 'naturally bread and wine and sacramentally Christ's body.'[46]

These teachings laid the foundation for the continued growth and development of movements in England and on the continent into the fifteenth century, despite the condemnations faced by Wyclif before his death. As is evident from the activities of Robert Rigg, Nicholas of Hereford, and Philip Repton, Wyclif found support at Oxford even after he had been condemned by Church authorities in 1380, and even, for a brief moment, after the Earthquake Council. It was among Wyclif's Oxford supporters that the movement which came to be known as Lollardy first emerged. These university Lollards – a term of derision meaning 'mumblers,' first applied to one of Wyclif's followers in 1382 – adopted the Oxford don's teaching on the Eucharist, his ardent antisacerdotalism and criticism of ecclesiastical corruption, his views on the subordination of spiritual to temporal authority, as well as his belief in the necessity of moral reform.[47] They had supported him throughout the 1370s, attracted by his daring and radical solutions to various philosophical and theological questions, and preached on his behalf after the condemnations of 1380 and 1382. They were unable, however, to withstand Archbishop Courtenay's onslaught and were excommunicated and suspended from teaching. Some of them recanted their support for Wyclif and were brought back into the Church and university, but in 1382 a major step was taken in the suppression of Lollardy.

Wyclif's supporters were not completely eradicated by Courtenay, and over the next few decades they provided leadership and composed key works for the Lollard movement. During the late fourteenth century a Wyclifite English Bible was produced, numerous sermons were written, a gloss of the Gospels and a separate commentary on the Book of the Apocalypse were composed, and a theological dictionary of some 509 entries drawing, in part, from Wyclif's pastoral work was compiled at Oxford between 1384 and 1396, for the use of preachers without access to a good library.[48] Among those who continued to preach Wyclifite doctrines was Richard Wyche, a priest of Hereford who was active from the late fourteenth century until his burning in 1440. Another figure was William James, an Oxford scholar who was finally captured near Oxford in 1395. Along with those associated with Oxford, there was a number of lesser clergy and parish priests who promoted Wyclif's teachings. That group included, among others, William, a priest in Thaxted, John Brettenham of Colchester, William Sawtry, a chaplain of Norfolk who was the first Lollard to be burned (February 23, 1401, or shortly thereafter), and William Ramsbury of the diocese of Salisbury.[49] Perhaps the most important of the lesser clergy was William Swinderby, an orthodox preacher before his conversion to Lollardy and a speaker of great skill who attracted a significant number of followers to the movement, including John Oldcastle, a Lollard leader of the early fifteenth century. Swinderby naturally attracted the attention of the authorities, who pursued and condemned him, but he disappeared into Wales in 1391 before he could be captured and most likely continued to preach for some time to come.[50]

Wyclif's impact was felt well beyond his original Oxford circle and the lesser clergy that taught variations of his propositions and reached all levels of the laity. His strident denunciations of the clergy and of their worldliness and wealth certainly resonated with the laity responsible for paying tithes and taxes to support the Church. The Lollards included artisans and skilled craftsmen, townsfolk in Leicester, London, Northampton, and elsewhere, and even some gentry. Those attracted to the group included the poor, but also the more prosperous; some may have come from the highest levels of society. Perhaps the most important sub-group was that of the so-called Lollard knights, ten of whom were identified by name in the pages of contemporary chronicles. The knights – and it seems that there were well more than ten – played a key role in the growth and development of the movement, and their status and sympathetic attitude offered to the Lollard preachers and scholars a degree of protection which allowed them to continue their work of developing and disseminating Wyclifite ideas. The most prominent of the Lollard knights was Sir John Old-castle, a secular leader of the movement who raised rebellion in 1414 after his conviction for heresy. Intended to prevent his own punishment and institute a Lollard reform of the Church, Oldcastle's revolt failed and demonstrated the dangers of Wyclifite teachings. In consequence, the king ordered the suppression of Lollardy, and many of the leaders were hunted down and massacred. Lollardy, however, somehow survived and remained a viable, albeit underground, movement throughout the fifteenth century.

The final chapter of Wyclif's story involves his official denunciation and completes his change, from theologian and radical critic of the Church, into a heretic. This chapter opens just prior to Oldcastle's defeat and the persecution of the Lollards, and it reveals the hardening of attitudes toward heresy and heretics in England. In 1407, William Courtenay's successor as archbishop of Canterbury, Thomas Arundel, ordered the heads of the Oxford colleges to hold regular examinations of the college members, to ensure that Wyclif's teachings were not being taught and that all members were strictly orthodox. The archbishop also established yet another commission to examine the works of Wyclif. Four years later, the commission condemned some 267 propositions of Wyclif as heretical or unsound, and then sent the list to Rome for further consideration and condemnation by the pope. At the Lateran Council of 1413, a number of Wyclif's works, but not all of them, were burned. A moment of perhaps even greater consequence for Wyclif's teachings occurred at the Council of Constance in 1415, which also condemned Wyclif's Bohemian disciple, Jan Hus, and resolved the Great Schism. At this meeting, one of the most important in Church history, forty-five of Wyclif's doctrines, which had previously been condemned at Prague in 1403, were condemned again, including his teachings on the Eucharist, the clergy, the papacy, the tithes, and others.[51] This condemnation by one of the highest authorities of the Church confirmed that Wyclif had been a heretic unworthy to remain buried in consecrated ground. The order was given that his body was to be exhumed; but the local bishop at that time was the old Wyclifite sympathizer, Philip Repton, who did nothing. Wyclif's body was, however, exhumed by Repton's successor, Richard Fleming.[52] In the spring of 1428, the body was dug up and burned, and the ashes were thrown into a stream running through Lutterworth. Despite this ignominious end, Wyclif's legacy had a marked impact on further developments – in England and especially in Bohemia.

CHAPTER TEN

JAN HUS:
REFORM AND HERESY IN BOHEMIA

*a*lthough Wyclif made an important impact on the Church and (especially) on the Lollards in England, he may have left his deepest mark on developments on the continent, where his teachings found ardent supporters in Bohemia. Adopted by a number of reform-minded ecclesiastics there, Wyclif's teachings helped shape the direction of Church reform – a process which itself formed part of broader social, political, and religious developments in the later fourteenth and early fifteenth centuries. The complicated interconnection between political and religious trends further shaped the nature of Church reform in Bohemia and contributed to the transformation of reform ideals into heresy. The increasingly hostile relationship between German scholars and theologians on the one hand and Czech reformers and nationalists on the other, as well as the negative consequences of the Great Schism that had broken out in 1378, also affected events in Bohemia. Wyclif's teachings found increasing resonance with many Czech leaders and seemed to offer a solution to the many problems facing the Church in Bohemia; the most important of these reformers was Jan Hus, a leading scholar and theologian whose writings and, especially, whose execution at the Council of Constance in 1415 contributed to reform and revolution in his native land. And, beyond that, according to a modern biographer, Hus's ideas 'may be regarded as a transitional stage from the earlier medieval period to the Reformation.'[1]

Although Jan Hus gave his name to the reform movement in Bohemia, emerging as its most outstanding figure, and his tragic end at Constance inspired the Hussite Revolution and the birth of the Czech national Church, he was not the only reform leader in his country's Church. The movement for reform reached deep into the fourteenth century. It was initiated by the Holy Roman emperor and king of Bohemia Charles IV (1316–78) and determined by a number of factors, both religious and non-religious. Its roots can be found in the very nature of the Bohemian kingdom and of its larger overlord, the Holy Roman Empire. The region had become part of the Empire and was colonized by Germans, who were at first welcomed and respected but eventually came to be regarded less favorably by the native Czech population. Not only had the immigrants carved out a prominent socio-economic position, but they had also acquired the leading ecclesiastical offices and educational positions. German domination of the Church and of the University of Prague (founded in 1348) alienated the Czechs, who had become increasingly self-aware as their culture blossomed during the fourteenth century. Rising Czech nationalism easily merged with a growing desire for reform stimulated by the relationship between the hierarchy and the Germans. The Church in Bohemia, as in other parts of Europe, faced problems of corruption and clerical abuse. The Church was regarded as worldly and too concerned with land and wealth, a problem exacerbated in Bohemia by the fact that the Church was the greatest landowner in the kingdom – greater than the king himself.[2] The clergy were scorned for their immorality and lack of religious devotion. Hus himself would later denounce 'priests who shamefully squander pay for requiem masses in fornication, in adorning their concubines, priestesses, or prostitutes more sumptuously than the church altars and pictures, purchasing for them skirts, capes, and fur coats from their tithes and offerings of the poor.'[3] The wealthy Church and the corrupt clergy stood in stark contrast to the simple, poor Czech clergy – which only reinforced demands for reform and for the rejection of the German clergy.

In the last quarter of the fourteenth century, the situation in Bohemia and much of Europe worsened. One challenge that the universal Church faced was the Great Schism, which divided the Christian nations of Europe between those who supported the pope in Rome and those who supported the pope in Avignon. This division, and the excommunications each pope laid on the other, reinforced the need for a far-reaching reform of the Church. The Schism also weakened the power of the two popes, who were less able to impose order and discipline on the Church. At the same time when the Great Schism broke out, Bohemia's golden age came to an end with the death of Charles IV in 1378. He was succeeded by his son Wenceslas IV (1361–1419), a relatively ineffective ruler who never secured imperial coronation and found himself constantly at odds with members of the ruling family as well as with the nobility. His difficulties were not limited to opposition from the secular hierarchy, and in 1393 a conflict erupted between Wenceslas and the archbishop of Prague, which was ultimately resolved in favor of the king and forced the archbishop's resignation. Wenceslas also sought to play one side of the Schism against the other, and his involvement in papal politics left him little time or opportunity to monitor religious affairs in his kingdom.[4]

It was against this background that the first steps at reform had been taken by Charles IV. Owner of one of the great relic collections which contributed to Prague becoming an important center of the cult of the saints, he was a devout and religious ruler, whose piety in many ways was very traditional. He issued harsh legislation against heresy and the Beguines, but also sought to limit worldliness and excessive materialism both at his court and in the Church. Moreover, he was sincerely concerned about the well-being of the Church; he was among the leaders of Europe who encouraged the popes at Avignon to return the papacy to Rome. He was equally committed to the reformation of religious life and practice in his kingdom and forged an agreement with the pope in Avignon concerning the appointment of bishops in Bohemia. In other hands this might have led to corruption and abuse, but Charles's appointments were generally good and wise. The king also founded the University of Prague, which he hoped to make a leading intellectual center. To further guarantee both the health of the university and reformation of the clergy in his realm, Charles invited reform-minded Augustinian canons to the university, most notably Conrad of Waldhauser (also spelled Waldhausen).

The arrival of Conrad of Waldhauser (d. 1369) in Prague in 1360 set the stage for more dramatic reform efforts and initiated a line of reformist preachers who advocated the ideas of John Wyclif and paved the way for Jan Hus. Conrad began to preach against clerical abuses and corruption and was particularly critical of the monks and mendicant friars. He preached against false prophets and denounced simony and the cult of relics. His denunciations of moral laxity attracted the support of both clergy and laity, including women who abandoned their finery, usurers who paid back excessive interest, and the youth who gave up affected manners.[5] But his harsh critique of the Church and clergy endowed his enemies with the tools necessary to force him to answer before the pope. He was acquitted, but died in December 1369, on his way back to Prague from the papal court. He nonetheless attracted a sizeable following, including a number of prominent reformers who were active throughout the rest of the century. Among these reformers was Jan Milič of Kroměříž (c.1325–74), the father of Czech reform. Milič, an imperial notary from Bohemia, underwent a religious conversion after witnessing clerical corruption and hearing Waldhauser preach. He was ordained a priest, then granted a canonry by Charles IV in 1363, only to give up his offices and take up a life of poverty and preaching in Latin, German, and, most importantly, Czech. He preached penitence and Church reform, denouncing the sins of the clergy, and even, for a time, identified Charles IV as Antichrist – of whom Milič predicted that he would come in 1368. He founded a hospice, which he called Jerusalem, for reformed prostitutes, which was viewed critically by his enemies. Along with his harsh condemnations of the clergy, he advocated frequent communion and reform of the clergy and Church. Despite being called to the papal court, Milič inspired a number of followers who furthered the cause of reform.

Milič had numerous disciples, most notable Matthew, or Matthias, of Janov (c.1355–93), the great theorist of Czech reform who studied at the University of Paris and brought scholarly weight to the effort at reformation in Bohemia. Returning from Paris after the university's decision to accept the pope at Avignon – Janov was a supporter of the Roman pope – he became a canon at the cathedral in Prague in 1379. He later acquired further ecclesiastical benefices, but nothing that would lift him far beyond poverty, which he came to accept as the true Christian lifestyle. Devoted to the study of the scriptures, Janov carried the Bible with him at all times and found the answer to all his questions in its pages. Central to his own beliefs and one of the reasons why he took up Milič's reform, the Bible was so important to Janov that he advocated its translation, so as to make it accessible to those unlettered in Latin; he was also involved in the first translation of the Bible into Czech. Janov was deeply concerned about the imminence of Antichrist, whom he saw operating in his day. Antichrist stood for all that was contrary to the true faith and to Christ, and, as such, the pope at Avignon, a false pope, embodied Antichrist according to Janov. He also criticized, as did his mentor, the corruption of the Church. He opposed too much devotion to images, ritualism, and ceremonialism, and excessive concern with pilgrimage, indulgences, and the miraculous.[6] He demanded the return to the simple purity of the Bible and of the apostolic Church, which he praised over the elaborate and worldly Church of his day. To cure the ills of the latter, Janov prescribed frequent, even daily participation in the Eucharist. His calls for reform and frequent communion were met with stern opposition by the Church, which forced him to recant and forbade him to preach or hear confessions for some eighteen months. He put this time to good use, however, writing the great treatise of Czech reform, *Regulae veteris et novi testamenti* (1392; 'Rules of the Old and New Testaments').

Although Janov died in the year following the completion of his great work, the Czech reformation movement continued to grow and was further shaped by the influence of the teachings of John Wyclif. His works arrived in Bohemia because of the close connection between Oxford and the University of Prague, brought about by the marriage of Anne of Bohemia and King Richard II of England. Even as Wyclif's works were being condemned in England, Czech scholars were copying them and returning to Bohemia with them.[7] Wyclif's philosophy had a profound effect on thinkers in Bohemia, but perhaps even more influential were his attacks on the corruption of the Church and his ecclesiology and theology; they resonated within Czech reformation circles, which had begun to make similar criticisms. His virulent denunciations of the papacy as of 1378, together with the Great Schism, and his increasing disdain for the visible Church, to which he had denied any connection with the true Church, influenced the way Czech reformers regarded both Church and papacy. Czech reformers like Waldhauser and Janov shared with Wyclif an understanding of the centrality of the Bible and of its character as the truth because it was the word of God.[8] Wyclif also found greater support among the Czech masters and students at the University of Prague than among the German contingent, which on the whole opposed his ideas. This response to Wyclif drove a further wedge, reinforcing the social and political tension that already existed between Czechs and Germans.[9] Although an official attempt was made to suppress Wyclif's teachings in Bohemia, it failed, and his writings continued to shape the Czech reformation movement into the fifteenth century.

It was in this environment of failed political leadership, a growing religious reform movement, nationalistic animosities, Czech nationalism, and the arrival of the writings of John Wyclif that the great Czech reformer, Jan Hus, emerged. Of peasant origin, Hus was born in 1372 or 1373, or perhaps earlier (1369) – the date is uncertain – in the small village of Husinec on the River Blanice in southern Bohemia; little is known of his early life or family. He seems to have had a brother who predeceased him, as Hus asked a friend to look after his nephews shortly before his own death. All that is known of Hus's father is his name, Michael, and he seems to have had little influence on the direction of his son's life. Although the father may have receded from Jan's memory, his mother seems to have had lasting influence on him, as he revealed in one of his treatises. It was she, he recalled, who taught him to say: 'Amen, may God grant it.' It seems that she was behind his decision to become a priest, concerned as she was for her son to find a respectable profession, which would provide the financial security she apparently did not enjoy.[10] There is also a story from the late fifteenth century confirming the important role of Hus's mother in his life. According to this account, Hus was accompanied by her when he entered the grammar school in the nearby town of Prachatice in 1385. His mother brought a loaf of bread as a gift for the schoolmaster and, during the trip to the school, she knelt seven times to pray for her son.[11] Although the story may be apocryphal, it demonstrates the central role Hus's mother played in his first steps along the path to a clerical career. Beyond her lasting impact, though, little can be said of Hus's early life.

Events in the life of Jan Hus come into sharper focus once he began his education and entered the priesthood. His first step, of course, was taken when he entered the school at Prachatice, where he learned Latin, an essential skill for those wishing to become priests. During his years at Prachatice, Hus supported himself by singing in church choirs and participated in a blasphemous Christmas ritual, the 'Feast of the Ass,' in which a choir boy dressed as a bishop, rode a donkey, and led the other boys of the choir into a mock mass.[12] He also was introduced to the basic elements of medieval education: grammar, rhetoric, dialectic. He would study these subjects more fully at university, along with the other four liberal arts: arithmetic, astronomy, geometry, and music. In 1390, or

JAN HUS: REFORM AND HERESY IN BOHEMIA

perhaps as early as 1386, at the age of 18, Hus entered the University of Prague, enrolling under the name Jan of Husinec, which later on was shortened to Hus (the Czech word for 'goose'). He was most likely introduced to the city and university by a friend from his village, Christian of Prachatice.

Hus's university years were successful and enjoyable. He continued to support himself as a singer and developed a reputation for good humor, eloquence, and wit. He seems to have been intent upon pursuing a clerical career, hoping to ascend into the ranks of the ecclesiastical hierarchy. As he wrote later, 'When I was a young student, I confess to have entertained an evil desire, for I thought to become a priest quickly in order to secure a good livelihood and dress well and to be held in esteem of man.'[13] A university education was the best way for a poor young man like Hus to accomplish this end, and he undertook his studies most diligently. At the University of Prague he was introduced to Aristotle, who was known as 'the Philosopher' in the Middle Ages and whose system laid the foundation for all the higher disciplines, including philosophy and theology. He continued his study of Latin and he learned German, which he may have started at Prachatice; he worked toward becoming a bachelor of arts. Following the traditional three-year course of study, Hus was awarded his bachelor's degree in 1393, the first time that his name appears in an official document.

After receiving his degree, Hus immediately registered for study toward the master's degree, which would open numerous doors for him as a teacher and scholar. He spent the next three years studying at the university under its Czech, and not German, masters. His situation was eased somewhat by his appointment to a position in one of the colleges as servant; he was responsible for keeping the masters' rooms in order and for helping out in the kitchen, and he was given room and board for his labors. With less concern about financial matters, Hus was able to dedicate himself fully to his studies. Although it is uncertain whom he took as his primary master, Hus benefited from the possibility of studying at the university and living at its center. During his time there he was probably introduced to the works of Thomas Aquinas, whom he held in high regard, as well as to the philosophical and theological trends current at the time. He was exposed to Nominalism and came to know the works of St. Bonaventure, John Duns Scotus, William of Ockham, and others. It was also at this time that Hus was first introduced to the ideas of John Wyclif, which had become popular with Czech scholars at just about the time when Hus had arrived at the university.

His first contact was with Wyclif's philosophical works, which Hus found to be of great worth. Later on he came to know Wyclif's theological works and even copied four of his treatises for his own use.

Completing his course of study in 1396, Hus was awarded the master of arts degree and began his teaching career. From 1396 to 1398, he devoted his lectures to the works of Aristotle, offered tutorials and presided over student disputations, and after 1398 he lectured on the works of John Wyclif. He seems to have been a popular and successful teacher, attracting many students to his lectures, where his natural eloquence enabled him to give consistently interesting and informative lessons. His talents as a professor were recognized by his colleagues in the faculty of the university and by his former masters, who helped advance Hus's career. In 1398 he was given responsibility for the promotion of students to the rank of bachelor, and later he was granted the duty of promoting students to the level of master. His speeches at the promotion ceremonies reveal him as a man of good humor and kindliness and as a teacher able to establish close and warm relationships with his students.[14] In 1401, he was named dean of the Faculty of Arts and served in that position until the following year, when he became rector and preacher of Bethlehem Chapel, having been ordained a priest in June 1400. At that time, Hus also enrolled in the university's Faculty of Theology in pursuit of a doctorate in that field, which he never completed; yet he advanced toward his doctorate by earning lower degrees.

His ordination and interest in a theology degree signal a profound change in Hus's personal and professional life. It was at some point prior to ordination that he seems to have undergone a religious conversion which led to his committing fully to the religious life and turning away from the life of the careerist ecclesiastic, who sought ecclesiastical benefices and other privileges. Up to that point, as Hus himself freely admitted, he indulged in 'youthful follies,' playing chess and taking pride in his academic position and dress. He often wore elaborate university gowns, decorated with white fur. He willingly participated in the banquets of the university masters and generally enjoyed his life as a student and teacher, while ambitiously seeking advancement. All that ended sometime before 1400, but Hus provides no clear answer concerning the precise moment when this happened or the reason for such sudden and profound change. Near the end of his life, however, he noted that, when he was young, he had belonged to a 'foolish sect,' but God had shown him the way through the scriptures and thereafter he abandoned the life of frivolity. As with his predecessors in the Czech reformation movement, Hus seems to have come to personal reform and to the religious life through the serious study of the Bible.[15]

For twelve years following his appointment on March 14, 1402, Hus continued to hold his position as rector and as preacher of Bethlehem Chapel, which had been founded in 1391 by a wealthy Prague merchant. Thus he combined both popular and university reform traditions and made that chapel the center of the Czech reformation movement. During his tenure as rector, he delivered some three thousand sermons; many of them were originally composed or preserved in Latin.[16] His sermons attracted to the chapel large and enthusiastic crowds, including many noble women and even the queen. Unlike earlier rectors, Hus preached only in Czech and not in Czech and German, demonstrating his own Czech nationalism and proclaiming the important role of Bohemia in God's plan. He also identified himself more fully with the Czech reformation and its ideals, and his preaching was an essential stimulus to the growth and expansion of that movement. Its goals moved beyond the academic and ecclesiastical circle and were adopted by Czech artisans and the Czech middle class. Indeed, as one historian has noted, through his sermons at the Bethlehem Chapel, Hus created the concerns of the reformers and the ecumenical agenda, transforming himself into a 'national religious leader.'[17]

The sermons Hus delivered at Bethlehem Chapel covered a wide range of topics concerned with the moral and institutional reform of the Church. In some of his early sermons, he exhorted his listeners to take up a life of repentance and holiness and to follow Christ. He challenged the laity, including nobles and kings, as well as his fellow clerics, to renounce corruption and immorality and to live a virtuous life without avarice, pride, or other sins, and he taught that the highest goal of the religious life was to love God.[18] In sermons delivered between 1405 and 1407, however, he moved beyond moral exhortation – of laity, clergy, and university masters and students – to address the problems facing the clergy and the Church. From this period on, his sermons became more aggressive and critical. He ferociously attacked the failings of the clergy, denouncing the corruption of the priestly office and demanding reform. In his sermons he proclaimed that corrupt and immoral priests were really the devil's own, and he attacked priests who had concubines or committed adultery. Also of concern to Hus was simony, which, in his treatise on this topic, he defined in traditional terms, as 'an evil consent to an exchange of spiritual goods for nonspiritual.' It is a 'trafficking in holy things,' and 'both he who buys and he who sell [sic] is a merchant, a simoniac is both he who buys and he who sells holy things.'[19] He criticized the clergy for accepting money or gifts in exchange for performing the sacraments and he virulently attacked both the priests and the monks for various financial exactions. In these sermons Hus addressed the hierarchy of the Church as well, and criticized excessive claims to papal power and authority, raising questions, in particular, over indulgences and matters of excommunication. The Church itself was defined as the body of the elect, all those who had been predestined to salvation. Although both the predestined and the foreknown existed together in the Church militant, only the predestined were part of the true Church.

During his tenure as rector at Bethlehem Chapel, Hus continued his scholarly career and worked toward his doctorate in theology. He earned his bachelor's degree in divinity in 1404, and from 1404 to 1406 he gave lectures on the Bible. In 1407 he earned the degree that would allow him to lecture on Peter Lombard's *Book of Sentences*, which he did from 1407 to 1409. He also engaged in academic disputations with other scholars as he prepared for the doctoral degree, and he wrote a commentary on Lombard's *Sentences*, even though other duties prevented him from taking the doctoral degree. It was at this time that Hus also became better acquainted with Wyclif's views, some of which he accepted, others not. Wyclif's teachings would seem to have influenced Hus even though the Czech scholar was never a thoroughgoing disciple of the Oxford theologian. He would, however, defend Wyclif's teachings against the increasingly hostile and irrational attacks on them by the German masters at Prague.

Hus's career at Bethlehem Chapel and at the University of Prague overlapped with broader changes in Czech society and culture, which included increasing tensions between the German and Czech populations. These changes were manifest in the reaction against Wyclif's teachings, led by the Dominican John Hübner and by the German masters at the University of Prague, which broke out in 1403. Hübner petitioned Rome about some forty-five of Wyclif's propositions as well as on the matter of the realism currently taught by the Czech masters of the university. Some twenty-four of the propositions listed by Hübner had previously been condemned at the Blackfriars' Council in England in 1382, and the remaining twenty-one were compiled by Hübner himself. The

Wyclifite teachings included positions on the papacy, on the pope as Antichrist, and on the monastic orders, among other things. Hübner argued that, since some of these propositions had already been condemned, they should be condemned in Bohemia as well. The repudiation of Wyclif's teachings was also sent to the archbishop of Prague, who, in turn, asked the university for an opinion. When the university masters took up the debate, the underlying tensions between the German and Czech masters exploded into the open, since the German scholars had rejected Wyclif's ideas and the Czechs had adopted them as central to their reform program. The Czechs strongly opposed Hübner's condemnation and accused the Dominican of misquoting or taking passages out of context. They asserted that Wyclif's teachings were not in error and declared that they would continue to support these teachings. Despite the vehemence of their opposition to Hübner, the Czech masters lost the university debate when the vote was tallied. The three German nations at the university voted in favor of Hübner's condemnation, whereas the Czech nation voted against it. (A 'nation' was a basic organizational structure of the medieval university, made up of students from the same country or religion.)

The dispute, however, did not put an end to the general interest in Wyclif's ideas. The university did not forbid the study of Wyclif's books but only of the specific articles listed in the condemnation. The archbishop, a well-respected former soldier and noble, Zbyněk, was ill-equipped to render a decision but sympathetic to reform, and he hesitated to make a pronouncement on the matter. The Czech masters, especially Hus, pursued their study of Wyclif more eagerly than before, and some of them went so far as to declare publicly their endorsement of the most controversial of Wyclif's ideas. Although Hus was not among them, he would defend Wyclif and approved of many of the Oxford theologian's positions. In debate with Hübner in 1404, Hus rejected the Dominican's denunciations of Wyclif and accused Hübner of distorting Wyclif's positions. Moreover, Hus ardently maintained that the forty-five articles had been taken out of context and that Wyclif himself was not a heretic. Despite this show of support by Hus and others, the acceptance of Wyclif's teachings faced serious setbacks. In 1407, two of the most active Czech supporters of Wyclif's ideas, Stanislav of Znojmo and Jan Páleč, were called before the pope and forced to recant their teachings. Under papal pressure, they rejected their former advocacy, and when they returned to Prague they were among the staunchest critics of Wyclif. And in 1408, the archbishop prohibited the teaching of the forty-five articles condemned by Hübner, while the Czech masters agreed not to defend the articles 'in their heretical, erroneous, and objectionable sense' – a most ambiguous acquiescence.[20]

Another development of major significance for Jan Hus was King Wenceslas's change of allegiance during the papal schism, which enhanced Hus's standing but also contributed to the estrangement between him and Archbishop Zbyněk. Wenceslas and the university and clergy had supported the popes in Rome, most recently Gregory XII (1406–15), as the legitimate popes against those in Avignon. In an effort to end the schism, however, a number of cardinals withdrew their allegiance to their respective popes and, with the support of the French king and of the University of Paris, agreed to hold a general council to depose the reigning popes and to elect a new one. Meeting at the poorly attended Council of Pisa in 1409, the cardinals elected Peter of Candia, who took the name of Alexander V. Wenceslas, who received promise of support from the French if he backed the Council and the new pope, saw his opportunity to undermine the authority of his brother, Emperor Rupert, and to gain greater power in the Empire. In order to switch his allegiance, the king needed the support of the University of Prague, but he faced the difficult proposition of persuading the German nations, which remained united in their support of Rome. To resolve that dilemma, Wenceslas issued the decree of Kutná Hora on January 18, 1409, which reorganized the nations at the university. The German nations had been divided into three voting blocks, but the decree merged them into one, and the Bohemian block was divided into three blocks from one. The Czech reformers, who made up the majority of the Bohemian nation, hoped to find backing from the conciliar pope, and so they were supportive of the king's move to endorse the Council and the pope it chose, and voted in approval of the conciliar movement. The German nations abandoned the university, returning to new or established universities in other parts of the Empire, where they continued their opposition to Wyclif and to the Czechs at the University of Prague.

Changes of papal affiliation affected Hus and the Czech reformation movement directly, in ways they had surely not anticipated. Rather than support the king and the new conciliar pope, Archbishop Zbyněk refused, as any good soldier would, to break his oath to the Roman pope, Gregory. This enraged Wenceslas, who took steps against the archbishop. Zbyněk was forced to renounce his allegiance to Gregory and declared Alexander to be the legitimate pope; he was also ordered to proclaim that Prague and its university were free from heresy. These humiliations drove Zbyněk away from the reform camp and led to his request that Alexander should issue a bull condemning Wyclif's teachings and prohibiting any preaching outside the cathedral church or monasteries. Issued on December 20, 1409, this bull clearly drove a wedge between the archbishop and Hus, who was obviously the target — if not in the bull, at least as far as Zbyněk was concerned. Hus continued preaching and gained popular support against the archbishop, whose high-handedness alienated not only the people of Prague but also the king. Zbyněk was not going to back down, and on July 16, 1410, he gathered together copies of Wyclif's books and had them burned. Although surrendering his own volumes, Hus protested Zbyněk's actions as unwarranted and arbitrary, especially since Wyclif had not yet been declared a heretic. The archbishop excommunicated Hus and reported the case to the papal curia, which then examined the matter to Hus's disadvantage. Refusing to report to Rome to answer questions concerning his case, Hus was excommunicated in 1411 by the cardinal in charge of his case and by Zbyněk for a second time. The archbishop also placed the city of Prague under an interdict, but the king declared it should not be obeyed. Efforts to resolve the crisis were made by all parties and nearly reached a successful conclusion. Zbyněk was charged with lifting both the interdict and the excommunication of Hus in exchange for concessions from the king, and Hus was to make a full confession of faith, declaring his adherence to orthodox teaching, which he sent to the pope. The archbishop, however, decided to flee Prague for territories of Wenceslas's brother Sigismund, king of Hungary, before fulfilling his end of the agreement and died on the way there, in September 1411.

Hus assumed such a pivotal role in the dispute with Zbyněk in large measure because he, a charismatic preacher, had emerged as the leader of the Czech reformation movement by 1407. Earlier leaders, including some of his own teachers, had begun to pass away, while others, closer in age to Hus, notably Stanislav of Znojmo and Jan Páleč, had defected from the reform camp and turned into harsh critics of the reform and of Wyclif. Preaching from the pulpit at Bethlehem Chapel attracted a large following for Hus from outside the university, but, more importantly still, it allowed him to give voice to his own criticisms of the Church, which coincided with broader reform goals. And since he was also guardedly sympathetic of Wyclifite teachings and open to Czech national-ist ideas, he seemed to be the natural leader of the movement, even though he was not the most radical theologian of his day. His stature was most clearly recognized when the masters at the university chose him as rector on October 17, 1409, an office he held throughout the rest of that year and the next. The election was one of the results of the Kutná Hora decree, which put control of university policy into the hands of the Czech nation.

As leader of the popular reform movement in his capacity at Bethlehem Chapel and as rector of the university, Hus held a unique position at the time of his controversy with Archbishop Zbyněk. Speaking out on behalf of his fellow university scholars, Hus attacked the actions of the archbishop, and found further popular support due to his position at the chapel. Although the compromise brokered between Hus and the archbishop broke down because of Zbyněk's flight and death, and Hus's status at the papal curia remained uncer-tain at best, he surely emerged in an even stronger position in Bohemia than he had before, and his support among the Czech reformers was enhanced when he challenged the anti-Wyclifite John Stokes to a debate over Wyclif's teach-ings — which Stokes declined on the grounds that anyone who read Wyclif was a heretic. Attempts to have the agreement declared valid after the death of Zbyněk failed, but that too seemed to have little impact on Hus's standing. But, having survived the struggle with the archbishop, in the years to come Hus was to face an ever greater challenge over the matter of papal indulgences, which led to an irrevocable break with both pope and king, and over the excesses of the reformation movement he was heading.

On September 9, 1411, the antipope John XXIII issued a bull of indul-gences on behalf of his crusade against King Ladislas of Naples, a supporter of Gregory XII, who had been deposed at the Council of Pisa. Ladislas had aided Gregory to take control of Rome and to force John to flee from the papal city; in response, John sought to raise a crusade. He also ordered all bishops and priests to declare Ladislas 'excommunicated, perjured, a schismatic, a blasphemer, a relapsed heretic, protector of heretics, guilty of the crime of lèse majesté, a conspirator against us and the Church,' and called on all the princes, clergy, and laity to take up the sword in defense of the Church against the heretic Ladislas.[21] In a second bull issued on December 2 of that year, John appointed commissioners to preach indulgences, restated their terms, and proclaimed a crusade against Gregory XII and Ladislas as enemies of the Church. John's call to crusade and offer of indulgences were not enthusiastically supported throughout the Church, and in some quarters they were opposed. They found, however, a ready supporter in Wenceslas, who most likely was guaranteed a part of the proceeds from the sale of the indulgences.

Although the king of Bohemia supported the papal bulls, the Czech reformers did not, and some spoke out quite vociferously against the sale of indulgences. Among the loudest opponents to John XXIII's actions were some reformers who had recently arrived in Prague. One of them, most likely, was Nicholas of Dresden, who published a highly critical treatise on the Church and papacy later on. He and other newcomers were associated with public demonstrations and provocations against the Church. They joined many of those, already living in Prague, who opposed the antipope's proclamation; these included members of the university and even the more conservative masters. The more reform-minded masters and students also rejected the indulgence bull, even though the authorities of the university would not allow protests against it. Despite this restriction, reformers came out against the bull and stimulated popular protest against it. This stoked the king's anger and led to a reaction against the protest. In July, three opponents were beheaded at the order of the magistrates of Prague. Buried at Bethlehem Chapel, they were the first martyrs of the Hussite reform.

It was not just the more extreme wing of the reformation movement that opposed the sale of indulgences and would suffer the king's wrath, but also its more moderate leader, Jan Hus. Indeed, it had been Hus's preaching as much as anything that stimulated the dramatic and sometimes violent popular opposition to the indulgence bull. Although Hus did not deny indulgences in principle – he had, in fact, purchased one when they were offered for sale in 1393 – he denounced the gross and sacrilegious sale of the indulgences for the most unholy cause of war.[22] He was particularly outspoken on this matter and harshly critical of John XXIII's offer of an indulgence to any Christian who would go to war against fellow Christians. In fact, Hus argued that it was not the pope's duty to wage war – nor the duty of any cleric for that matter – because that responsibility was held by the secular power: the temporal sword held by the king was to enter battle, but not the spiritual sword held by the pope.[23] It may also be that Hus, like Wyclif, was distrustful of the crass sale of spiritual gifts;

he clearly believed that forgiveness comes only from God and only to a truly penitent sinner, whereas in the purchaser of an indulgence there was no guarantee of a pure heart. In other words, Hus maintained that God alone can offer an indulgence, through an act of grace to a sinner who repents and confesses his or her sins. And, just as Martin Luther did later during his controversy over indulgences, Hus asked why the pope would not save all Christians.

This daring critique of the papal indulgence proved central to Hus's undoing: it was not just that he lost many friends – his position, after all, was quite popular with the laity and with many of the students at the University of Prague – but he also ran afoul of university administrators and, even more seriously, of King Wenceslas, who stood to benefit materially from the sale of indulgences and also hoped to preserve good relations with John XXIII.[24] Along with his treatise against the papal indulgence, Hus made his position known publicly on a number of occasions, and his sermons against indulgences further inspired the reformers and the people of Prague. He spoke out against the bull in a disputation in January 1412 and again in June 1412, and his second debate was in open violation of the dean's prohibition to discuss the matter. Hus's outspoken views led to popular agitation and to the arrest of the three leaders of the opposition; Hus volunteered to change places with the three, but the magistrate in charge assured him that nothing serious would happen to them – just before he ordered their beheading.

As desperate as the situation seemed at that point, matters worsened still for Hus, who found himself clearly opposed on this matter by the king himself. This left him without the necessary protection from his enemies, who scored repeated successes against him. Various Bohemian bishops and the inquisitor of Prague formally denounced Wyclif's opinions and forbade their teaching. But Hus, who had been away at the time, was unaware of this and openly discussed the ideas of the Oxford theologian. In July, Hus faced further problems when one of the cardinals in Rome excommunicated him; this was the result of an examination of his case by a commission established by the pope in April. Moreover, the ban of excommunication forbade anyone to offer him food, drink, hospitality, or indeed any contact of any kind whatsoever. The town of Prague itself was threatened by an interdict for harboring Hus, once the verdict against him was announced in October 1412. Having lost the support of king, university, and now pope, Hus had little recourse but to appeal to Christ himself, and, while awaiting that verdict, he left Prague, to spare the city and its people of the penalty of the interdict. His departure, possibly orchestrated by the king himself, took place at the same time that the peace treaty concluded between John XXIII and Ladislas was announced in Prague.[25]

Even though Hus was forced to leave the city, he remained in contact with friends there, including Christian of Prachatice, now rector of the university, who consoled him and encouraged him not to lose hope. Hus, as his letters from the time indicate, did not seem to have been overly discouraged by the turn of events and even hoped to regain the good graces of the king. Hoping to overturn the decision rendered against him at Rome, Hus appealed to the royal couple, who accepted his petition and ordered the new archbishop, Conrad of Vechta, to hold a Council at Český Brod in January 1413 to eliminate heresy in the kingdom. The king also invited members of the faculty of the University of Prague to attend, which only served to undermine any chance of success the meeting might have had. Although some of Hus's university colleagues spoke on his behalf at the meeting and defended his teachings, the members of the faculty of theology worked toward a very different outcome. They drew up a consilium which outlined the essential terms for resolving the conflict. The document asserted that all good Christians must believe as the Roman Church does, obey the clergy, and recognize the legitimate authority of the pope and cardinals. The masters of theology also declared that Wyclif's forty-five articles must be acknowledged as either heretical or erroneous. When presented with this consilium, Hus replied with a strongly worded letter which denounced its terms and the faculty members who authored it, especially Stanislav of Znojmo and Jan Páleč. Hus declared that he would rather die than accept the terms of the document; it would be 'better to die well than to live evilly.'[26] The breakdown of the Council revealed the complete failure of a negotiated settlement, even though one further attempt was made.

The commission's failure to find an equitable solution and Hus's refusal to accept any reconciliation with his rivals left him little option but to defend himself as best he could. He spent much of the two years of exile, before his departure for the Council at Constance, writing various responses to the charges and teachings of his enemies. Among his works in Czech and Latin were sermons designed to appeal to the people of Bohemia and denounce the errors of his rivals and the corruptions of the Church. On occasion, he returned to

Prague; he certainly remained in touch with reformers in the city and preached before its people several times. Each time, however, the authorities imposed the interdict and forbade his preaching. Hus noted in one of his letters that, 'when I preached once, they immediately stopped the services, for it was hard for them to hear the Word of God.'[27]

Suppression by the authorities did not silence Hus, however. While in exile, he had recourse to the composition of a number of treatises, which, among other things, attacked the views of his most ardent foes, Stanislav of Znojmo and Jan Páleč, although they, too, had been sent into exile by the king – who was angry over their involvement in the failure to find a peaceful solution at the Council. The three of them indulged in something of a pamphlet war during Hus's absence from Prague; Hus seemed most intent on demolishing their arguments in his written works. It was during this period that he wrote his two most important treatises, the Latin *De ecclesia* ('On the Church') and the Czech *O svatokupectví* ('On Simony').

Published in May 1413, *De ecclesia* offers Hus's mature thinking on the nature of the Church and on the state of the clergy and ecclesiastical hierarchy. Drawing on great Church Fathers such as St. Augustine and Gregory the Great, Hus attacked the views of his rivals and the tenets of the *consilium* compiled by the theology faculty. In *De ecclesia* Hus described his understanding of the true Church, which drew, although not uncritically, on the teachings of Wyclif. For Hus held that the true Church was composed of all the predestined, who included the living, the dead, and those yet to be born. The true Church was invisible, as Wyclif had argued; Hus explained that it consisted in the mystical body of Christ, and Christ himself was the sole head of the Church. All the predestined were bound together in the one true Church and bound to Christ. Hus held, like Wyclif, that the foreknown are excluded from the true Church, even though they are not predestined to damnation but through their own free will turn from God. The foreknown and the elect, however, are joined together in the Church militant, in the Church in the world, and it is not possible to discern the saved from the foreknown. Hus argued further that, even though members of the clergy and laity of the Catholic Church are surely among the predestined, the Catholic Church itself is not to be identified with the true Church of Christ.

In developing his concept of the Church, Hus was clearly influenced by

Wyclif; but he departed from the Oxford theologian on various practical matters concerning the earthly Church and the clergy. Attention to these practical details is the second major theme of his work *De ecclesia* and reveals that Hus was more in the tradition of the Czech reformers than in the line of the more radical Wyclif and his Lollard followers. In one respect, though, Hus did follow Wyclif, albeit in a more moderate form. Like Wyclif, Hus was critical of the claims to papal primacy and authority over the Church and rejected papal claims to a fullness of power over all Christians. Unlike Wyclif, however, Hus did not deny that the pope and the cardinals were the most esteemed and respected figures in the Church. He denied that the pope was the direct successor to Peter, maintaining that the papacy was a human and not a divine institution and that the pope was fallible and could sin.[28] Commenting on Matthew 16: 18–19, which was the traditional foundation of claims to papal primacy and descent from St. Peter, Hus declared that the words 'You are Peter, and on this rock I shall build my church' refer, not to Peter, but to Peter's recognition that Jesus was the Son of God. Peter did not become Christ's vicar but could claim to be the prince of the Apostles because of his virtues and understanding of who Christ was. It was Christ who was the foundation of the Church and remained its head and to claim otherwise, according to Hus, was to deny the ultimate authority of scripture. Indeed, for Hus scripture was the supreme authority in the Church because it was the infallible word of God and not the opinion of flawed humans.

In *De ecclesia*, Hus also touched on other matters concerning the clergy and the Church. Once again asserting the necessity of clerical morality, Hus declared that only those priests who live in accordance with the teachings of Jesus Christ are worthy of the office. They must eschew worldliness and pride and follow the laws of God over the laws of humankind. A true priest is also defined by his devotion to preaching and by a life of apostolic poverty and devotion. Hus also examined the nature and powers of the priesthood, restricting the authority of the priest to spiritual matters and denying him any temporal power, which belongs only to nobles and kings. He noted that no priest, no matter how high in the Church hierarchy, could forgive sins on his own power. It was God alone who could forgive sins for the truly penitent, and the priest was merely God's minister in this matter. Furthermore, like Wyclif, Hus denied that any cleric has the power to bind and loose, to excommunicate or to grant indulgences, because only God may do so and only the sinner can separate himself or herself from God. The priest is responsible for administering the sacraments, but their efficacy is the result of God's grace rather than of any spiritual power possessed by the priest. Hus held, further, that it is better for a sinful priest not to administer the sacraments, but, even if a priest does so in the state of sin, the sacrament is still efficacious because of God's grace. In this, he confirmed his earlier position on the Eucharist. For in his treatise on the Lord's Supper Hus had written that it was not the priest who transformed the bread and wine into the body and blood, but Christ himself was the originator of this miracle. On this matter, Hus clearly turned away from Wyclif's teachings on remanence. But, although rejecting Wyclif's view, Hus used his language to explain what happened to the bread after it had been transformed into the body of Christ, differentiating between the form of the bread and the substance of Christ within it.[29]

Hus's other major work during his exile was focused on the matter of simony, which he had already declared in *De ecclesia* to be one of the worst sins that any member of the clergy could commit. A popular treatise written in Czech between the end of 1412 and February 1413, 'On Simony' attacked one of the most serious problems facing the Church in Hus's day. As he observed, 'there are but few priests who have secured their ordination without simony ... And since simony is heresy, if anyone observe carefully he must perceive that there are many heretics.'[30] Drawing from Gregory the Great and other Church Fathers, Hus, as noted above, defined simony as the 'exchange of spiritual goods for nonspiritual.' It was the buying and selling of holy things as well as the tacit approval of such exchanges, and the source of simony was corruption of the will, that is, an evil will.[31] According to Hus, all ranks of society, both clerical and lay, were guilty of simony. Popes and bishops committed it whenever they strove for office or appointed someone to clerical rank for payment or offered it to the highest bidder. The sale of indulgences by the pope (or priests or bishops) was among the acts of simony described by Hus. It was not only those who sold offices that were guilty of it, argued Hus, but also those who bought them. Any monk who paid to gain entrance to monastic orders or any priest who paid for his ordination was guilty of the crime. Priests also committed simony when they accepted payment for performing their sacramental duties, or when they demanded payment for burying the dead. The laity too committed simony when they paid the clergy for bestowing the sacraments or other spiritual gifts on the laity; kings and emperors were guilty when they appointed clerics to ecclesiastical benefices or offices. Although thoroughly consistent in his denunciations of simony in both clergy and laity, Hus further alienated the king by his attack on royal appointments.

In these late works, just as in sermons and treatises throughout his career as a preacher, university master, and popular leader, Hus provided a sometimes daring reforming program which sought to improve the life and structure of the Church. Although sometimes extreme, in most cases Hus's positions were not altogether unorthodox. Indeed, in many ways he was a very conventional churchman of his day. Critical of numerous aspects of Church life and belief, Hus nonetheless accepted many of the teachings of the Church. He accepted, albeit in a somewhat unique form, the doctrine of transubstantiation as well as the authority of the Bible, of the councils and of the Church Fathers. He approved of the veneration of the saints, especially the Virgin Mary. He believed in purgatory, masses for the dead, sacraments, and other conventional beliefs and practices of the Church of his day. But his teachings on the nature of the Church and on the powers of the pope and clergy set him somewhat apart from the mainstream of orthodoxy. Even more damning was his qualified support for, and public defense of, a number of Wyclif's teachings. His continued preaching while under the ban of excommunication and his sometimes strident criticisms of clerical abuse and corruption also contributed to his identification as a heretic. And his attack on papal indulgences and royal privileges in the Church lost him the support not only of the Church but also of his royal patron and protector. This was indeed a fatal blow.

The last phase of Jan Hus's life coincided with the resolution of the Great Schism at the Council of Constance.[32] Efforts to end the Schism by conciliar decree had not only failed at the earlier meeting in Pisa but worsened the situation by leading to the election of a pope that very few recognized. The meeting at Constance, however, had gained the support of King Sigismund, the younger brother and sometime rival of Wenceslas; this support would be critical to its ultimate success. There was also a great popular support for the Council, which was much better attended than its predecessor. As a consequence, Constance succeeded where Pisa failed. The reigning popes abdicated; they were to be deposed or stripped of any authority if they refused abdication or deposition.

A new pope, Martin V (1417–31), was elected and numerous reforms were implemented to improve the health of the Church. It was also agreed that universal Church councils would be held on a regular basis in the future. And the fate of Jan Hus was finally and tragically determined.

Although anxious about his own fate to the point of writing his will before departing for Constance, Hus welcomed the opportunity presented by the Council hoping that his positions and the Czech reformation movement would gain conciliar sanction. He was granted safe passage by Sigismund himself, and was joined by some thirty companions when he departed for Constance on October 11, 1414. Shortly after his arrival on November 3, John XXIII lifted the interdict against him and granted him the freedom to come and go as he pleased and to participate in the various discussions that were going on at the meeting. But things very quickly turned against Hus, as his enemies worked to his detriment, bringing new charges against him, and, perhaps most ominously, the Council issued its first denunciation of Wyclif's teachings on November 11. Later on, when given the opportunity to reject the forty-five articles, Hus rejected nearly all of them, but enemies such as Jan Páleč undermined his credibility by painting him as one who had been known to disobey the pope and to accept heresy in the past.

Despite promising overtures at the Council, Hus's situation worsened progressively, although his supporters defended him as best they could; they even wrote to Sigismund, making him consider seriously the claim that a decision against Hus would be an insult to the whole of Bohemia. Hus was arrested and imprisoned on November 28, and at times he was kept chained to a wall in the evenings. A commission was formed to examine him and his teachings; this commission included his old and new rivals, such as the noted Parisian theologians Pierre d'Ailly and Jean Gerson, whose theological and philosophical views opposed those of Hus and who arrived at the Council convinced of his guilt and hereticism. A trial was opened against Hus on June 5, 1415, but the judges had already made up their minds against him. Hus was given little opportunity to explain his positions and was routinely forced to give yes or no answers; the first session ended without a decision being reached. Hus's friends had obtained an agreement from Sigismund that no decision could be made against Hus without the king's presence at the session, and on June 7 Sigismund attended the proceedings. As during the previous meeting, Hus was given little opportunity to defend his own teachings and, even worse, he was now forced to defend himself in regard to Wyclif's errors. He was also accused of supporting various teachings of Wyclif and of inspiring unrest in Prague and dissension between the German and Bohemian nations.

At the final session of the trial, on June 8, Hus was presented with a list of errors drawn from his writings. These errors focused on his attitude toward the Church and the clergy; no mention was made of his support of Wyclif, his errors concerning the Eucharist, or his alleged Donatism. As Matthew Spinka notes, Hus's heresy was his conception of the true Church as the association of the elect, and the errors listed in the condemnation were related to this central conception.[33] Those various errors included his understanding of the place of the predestined and of the foreknown in the true Church; his placing of Christ, but not of the pope, at the head of the Church; his conception of the various duties and powers of priesthood; his attitude to matters of excommunication and interdict; and his position on the forty-five articles of Wyclif. By this point it was clear that not only his judges believed him to be guilty of heresy, but Sigismund too, and Hus was commanded to abjure his own teachings. Hus appealed to be allowed to defend himself but, again, was given no opportunity to speak, and it was clear to all that he was to be condemned as a heretic. On June 9 Sigismund allowed the Council to proceed along this line, and on June 18 the final list of charges against Hus and his condemnation were issued.[34]

Although further efforts to convince Hus to accept the decisions of the Council and to abjure his alleged errors were made by his friends, Hus insisted that he must follow his conscience. On July 6 Jan Hus was publicly degraded of his clerical rank and defrocked. One last time he was offered the chance to recant, but according to an eyewitness account he refused, declaring:

> God is my witness that those things that are falsely ascribed to me and of which the false witnesses accuse me, I have never taught or preached. But that the principal intention of my preaching and of all my other acts or writings was solely that I might turn men from sin. And in that truth of the Gospel that I wrote, taught, and preached in accordance with the sayings and expositions of the holy doctors, I am willing gladly to die today.[35]

Hus was then led to the pyre, which was set ablaze as he sang the Credo. He died while offering his last prayers to God.

His executioners broke his bones, so that they would burn completely, and they ensured that his organs were turned completely to ashes, so that the Czechs would not have relics to venerate and so that Hus's movement ended on that day. Despite these efforts, Hus's execution enraged the people of Bohemia; the Hussite reform carried on and eventually led to revolution.[36] Reformers continued his program and introduced new demands, such as for receiving both the chalice and the bread at communion (Utraquism), and the radicals became more outspoken. In 1419, Wenceslas sought to suppress the Hussites. This led to open warfare and the pope himself, at Sigismund's suggestion, called what was to be the first of five crusades against the Hussites and their radical wing, the Taborites. The long struggle finally ended with the defeat of the Taborites in 1436, but concessions were made to the Utraquists that laid the foundation for the emergence of an independent church in Bohemia, foreshadowing events of the next century.

The life and tragic death of Jan Hus brings to a close the history of medieval heresy. Hus may be seen as the last of the great heretics of the Middle Ages, echoing as he did the thoughts of earlier religious dissidents. His teachings addressed some of the most serious problems of the medieval Church; but, as harsh as his attacks may have been, he seems not to have rejected the structure of the Church, even if he advocated its reform and the limitation of papal power. His reforms, however, were not as radical as those of John Wyclif, whose influence on Hus cannot be dismissed; they keep him fully in the tradition of medieval dissent. Moreover, his burning at the stake echoes the common fate of many medieval heretics. But Hus and the movement he inspired foreshadowed the more dramatic events of the sixteenth century and the Protestant Reformation. Like Wyclif before him, Hus set out propositions which would be repeated by Martin Luther and the other reformers of the sixteenth century. Moreover, the establishment of an independent national church in Bohemia after the Hussite wars clearly prefigured the national and sectarian divisions which emerged in the wake of Luther's protest. And so Hus was the last of the great medieval heretics and a forerunner of the reformers of the sixteenth century.

FIVE CENTURIES OF RELIGIOUS DISSENT

*t*he lives of the medieval heretics, as we have seen, had a profound and lasting impact on the development of Church and society in the Middle Ages, and their teachings, at times, foreshadowed the Protestant Reformation of the sixteenth century. Throughout the Middle Ages pious Christians inspired by the Bible, the saints' lives, learned theological treatises, contemporary religious reform movements, or, as they claimed, God above, sought to live the true Christian life as they understood it and rejected the authority of the established Church. At times, these Christians struck at the Church militant, denouncing the abuses and worldliness of the clergy, and at other times, they simply rejected the Church and its ministers in order to follow the apostolic life. Whatever the case, throughout the Middle Ages heretics appeared to offer a distinct understanding of the Christian life, and their emergence was both a response to the changing conditions of their day and an influence on those developments.

From the beginnings of medieval heresy, religious dissidents expressed their discontent with the structure and organization of the Church in the hope that they could restore it to its original purity. Shaped by influences from as far away as Bulgaria and the Byzantine world, heresy in western Europe was also determined by local political, social, cultural, and religious factors. And the rise of heresy in France and other places in Latin Christendom around the year

1000 influenced, in its turn, events which were to develop over the next five centuries: the Crusades, the movement of apostolic poverty, the unification of medieval France, the growth of mysticism, and other important developments in the Middle Ages. The influence of the heretical leaders can be seen in such great events as the Gregorian Reform. Even the absence of outbreaks of heresy in the second half of the eleventh century is often attributed to the Church's adoption of some of the ideas of the heretics of the year 1000.

In the first half of the twelfth century, Henry the Monk and other itinerant preachers embodied the spirit of religious reform and adopted the apostolic life. Henry and other heretical preachers who promoted the emerging ideal of the *vita apostolica* often were virtually indistinguishable from their orthodox and saintly contemporaries, who also adopted the evangelical life and criticized the worldliness of the Church. One of the greatest of the medieval heretics, Valdes of Lyons perhaps best exemplified the apostolic ideal and actively led a life of poverty and preaching despite opposition from the pope himself. Just as earlier orthodox reformers may have adopted some of the ideas of the heretics, so too would the far-sighted leaders of the twelfth and thirteenth centuries; recognizing the appeal of the religious life of poverty and preaching, Pope Innocent III approved the Order of St. Francis of Assisi, whose life was in many ways similar to that of Valdes.

Innocent also called a crusade against the heretics of southern France, thereby redefining one of the great movements of the Middle Ages as a war not only against Muslims in the Holy Land but also against all the enemies of the Church everywhere. His crusade undermined the strength of the Cathar churches in southern France, but may be said to have had a greater impact on the unification of medieval France as a result of the invasion of the northern barons and later participation of the French king. The Cathars also contributed to the formation of the Inquisition as the central tool in fighting heresy; and this fight was itself a part of what the historian R. I. Moore has termed the formation of a persecuting society. Although ultimately suppressed by the Church through sword and fire, heresy repeatedly shaped developments in medieval society between the tenth and the fifteenth centuries.

Heresy also reflected broader developments in the medieval world. The movement of Gerard Segarelli and, especially, his successor Fra Dolcino provides a classic illustration of the peasant movements and uprisings that broke out throughout the Middle Ages. Preaching a radical version of apostolic poverty, motivated by an aggressive apocalypticism, Fra Dolcino attracted a sizeable following, which wreaked havoc in the mountains of northern Italy. Hostile to the Church, which he and his followers identified as false, and to its worldly wealth and power, Dolcino led his peasant followers into open rebellion both against the Church and against its secular allies. This mixture of religious zeal and social and political discontent in his movement echoes that of similar peasant uprisings – in France in 1251 and 1320, in England in 1381, and even in Germany in 1524–25. Dolcino's preaching of a millennial kingdom in this world and his call to establish it can be seen as one of the repeated expressions of the revolutionary and mystical pursuit of the millennium described by Norman Cohn.

Whether or not we can accept this interpretation, Fra Dolcino clearly inspired an important following as a result of his apocalypticism and reputation as a prophet. Another visionary and prophet, who is perhaps more characteristic of medieval developments, is Marguerite Porete. Although addressed to all Christians, her great work, *Mirror of Simple Souls*, reveals a more learned and elitist heresy. In most dramatic fashion, she turned away from the established hierarchy, which she nevertheless accepted as important and necessary, to seek God directly and personally. Her work was an attempt to describe this journey to God and to offer instruction for others to follow. Although it led to her condemnation as a heretic and burning at the stake, the mystical approach was not unheard of throughout the Middle Ages and was advocated by many others who were deemed orthodox, including Hildegard of Bingen, Bernard of Clairvaux and, to a lesser extent, Meister Eckhart. Medieval heretics, therefore, influenced numerous movements and were important examples of the great developments of the Middle Ages.

Indeed, the lives of the heretics provide important insights into the great cultural, political, and especially religious developments of the Middle Ages, but their activities also foreshadowed dramatic events to come. The last of the great medieval heretics, John Wyclif and Jan Hus, offered both a look back to the earlier traditions of medieval heresy and also forward, to Martin Luther's Reformation and to the Protestants of the sixteenth century. Like many of the great leaders of heresy, Wyclif and Hus exercised an important influence on the development of medieval religion and society. Indeed, these great university heretics influenced movements which emerged after their deaths: Wyclif's teachings were of central importance to the Lollard movement in England and Hus's ideas shaped the movement of the Hussites, with their radical wing of the Taborites. In a sense, both of them unleashed wider movements, although neither of them had intended to do more than reform the Church. Their views on the nature of the Church, the role of the clergy, and the definition of the Eucharist were all designed to reform Church doctrine and to return the Church to its apostolic origins. The very nature of these teachings, however, led to their rejection by the Church and prefigured the doctrines of Martin Luther and other Protestant Reformers. The views of Wyclif and Hus on the powers of the papacy in some ways prefigured Luther's more forceful and dramatic criticism of the office of the pope, and Wyclif's theories on the sacrament and on questions of transubstantiation and related matters have frequently been compared to those of Luther. The emergence of a national church in Bohemia after the Hussite wars heralded the emergence of later churches during the Protestant Reformation.

The lives of the heretics, from Bogomil to Hus, therefore are an essential guide to the history of medieval society and the Church, and their devotion to the Christian life stands as testimony to the power of faith in the face of suffering and persecution.

CHRONOLOGY

864	Boris I of Bulgaria converts to Christianity
889	Boris I retires to a monastery and dies
910	*Foundation of the monastery of Cluny*
911	Death of Louis the Child, last of East Frankish Carolingian kings. Charles the Simple grants Normandy to the Viking Rollo
918	Henry the Fowler elected German king
936	Otto I becomes German king
940/50	*Theophylact Lecapenus, patriarch of Constantinople, notes appearance of heresy in Bulgaria*
955	Otto I defeats Magyars at the Battle of Lech
962	Otto I crowned emperor
967	*Gerbert of Aurillac begins study in Spain*
970	*Heresy of Vilgard of Ravenna; Cosmas the priest writes sermon denouncing the Bogomils*
972	Otto II marries the Byzantine princess Theophanu; John I Tzimisces, Byzantine emperor, conquers Bulgaria; Majolus, abbot of Cluny, captured by Muslims
975	Magyar leader Géza converts to Christianity
976	Basil II the Bulgar Slayer becomes Byzantine emperor
983	Otto II defeated by Muslims in southern Italy; he dies December 983
987	Fall of the Carolingian line, Hugh I establishes Capetian dynasty; Bulgaria regains independence
989	Council of Charroux, beginning of Peace of God movement
994	Peace council held at Limoges; plague of firesickness (ergotism) strikes Aquitaine
999	*Otto III appoints Gerbert as Pope Sylvester II*
1000	Stephen crowned king of Hungary
1000	*Heresy of Leutard of Vertus*
1002	Death of Otto III; Conrad II elected king
1003	*Death of Pope Sylvester II*
1009	Fatimid ruler al-Hakim orders attack on the Holy Sepulchre and other shrines
1010	Attacks on Jews in Aquitaine and other parts of Europe
1014	Basil II defeats Bulgarian army, ends Bulgarian resistance to Byzantine authority
1018	*"Manichaean" heretics appear in Aquitaine*
1022	*Heresy of Stephen and Lisois exposed at Orléans*
1025	Death of Basil II
1025	*Heresy in Arras*
1028	*Heresy discovered at Montfort in northern Italy*
1031	Peace Councils of Bourges and Limoges
1033	*Mass pilgrimage to Jerusalem*

1043	*Heretics appear at Chalons-sur-Marne*
1045	*Euthymius of Periblepton notes appearance of Bogomils in Constantinople*
1046	*Synod of Sutri and deposition of popes Gregory VI, Benedict IX, and Sylvester III*
1049	*Council of Rheims; beginning of the Gregorian Reform movement; Hugh becomes abbot of Cluny*
1050	*Berengar of Tours excommunicated for his views on the Eucharist*
1051	*Execution of purported heretics at Goslar, Germany*
1053	Papal forces defeated by Normans at Civitate
1054	*Humbert of Silva Candida and Michael Kerularios declare mutual excommunications initiating the schism between the Roman Catholic and Greek Orthodox Churches*
1056	Death of Emperor Henry III; Henry IV becomes king
1058	*Emergence of the Patarines in Milan*
1059	*Pope Nicholas I publishes papal election decree; Berengar of Tours forced to recant his views*
1064	Death of Edward the Confessor; Harold Godwinson becomes king of England
1064	*Mass pilgrimage to Jerusalem*
1066	Battle of Hastings; William the Conqueror becomes king of England
1071	Byzantine armies defeated at Battle of Manzikert
1075	*Beginning of the Investiture Controversy; Pope Gregory VII compiles the* Dictatus Papae
1077	Henry IV appeals to Pope Gregory VII for forgiveness at Canossa
1077	*Gregory VII officially prohibits lay investiture*
1080	Rudolf of Rheinfelden, antiking, killed in battle; German rebellion ended
1080	*Wibert of Ravenna becomes (anti)Pope Clement III*
1081	Henry IV invades Italy and forces Gregory VII into exile; Alexius I Comnenus becomes Byzantine emperor
1084	*St. Bruno of Cologne founds Carthusian order*
1085	Alfonso IV of Castile captures Toledo
1085	*Death of Gregory VII*
1086	Domesday Book; the Almoravids invade Spain
1087	*Relics of St. Nicholas of Bari stolen from Myra and deposited in Bari*
1088	*Urban II becomes pope*
1091	Norman conquest of Sicily completed
1094	El Cid, Rodrigo Diaz, conquers Valencia
1095	Pope Urban II proclaims First Crusade at the Council of Clermont
1096	Crusaders massacre Jews in the Rhineland; Peasants' Crusade
1098	*Stephen Harding founds monastery at Citeaux and establishes the Cistercian order*
1099	Sack of Jerusalem by crusading armies
1099	*St. Anselm completes* Cur Deus Homo
1100	*Chanson de Roland appears in written form*
1101	*Robert of Arbrissel founds Fontevraux*

1104	Rebellion of future Henry V in the Empire
1111	*Paschal II concedes regalia to secular rulers*
1112	*Bernard of Clairvaux joins the Cistercian order*
1114	*Guibert of Nogent reports heretics at Soissons*
1115	*The heretic Tanchelm preaches in Antwerp*
1116	*First appearance of Henry the Monk*
1120	Sinking of the White Ship
1120	*Peter Abelard compiles the Sic et Non; Norbert of Xanten establishes Premonstratensian order*
1121	*Peter Abelard condemned at the Council of Soissons*
1122	Concordat of Worms
1123	*First Lateran Council*
1130	Roger II crowned king of Sicily and Palermo
1135	Civil war in England between Mathilda and Stephen (ends 1154)
1135	*Henry the Monk brought before the Council of Pisa*
1137	Aragon and Catalonia united under Ramón Berenguer IV
1139	*Second Lateran Council; Henry the Monk begins preaching in the Languedoc*
1140	*Publication of Gratian's Decretum; Peter Abelard condemned at the Council of Sens; death of the popular heretic Peter of Bruis*
1142	*Abbot Suger completes construction of church at St. Denis outside Paris, the first Gothic church; Abbot Peter the Venerable of Cluny commissions translation of the Qur'an into Latin*
1143	Revolution in Rome and establishment of republic
1143	*Arrival of heretics in Cologne*
1144	Zengi captures Edessa
1145	*Henry the Monk imprisoned, dies a short while later*
1147	Crusaders depart on Second Crusade
1151	*Peter Lombard completes his Four Books of Sentences*
1152	Henry of Anjou (the future King Henry II) and Eleanor of Aquitaine marry
1154	Henry II becomes king of England; Nur al-Din captures Damascus
1154	*Adrian IV becomes pope (the only English pope) and reigns until 1159*
1155	*Execution of Arnold of Brescia*
1157	Incident at Besançon; dispute between Emperor Frederick Barbarossa and Pope Adrian IV
1158	Frederick Barbarossa issues the Roncaglia decrees
1159	*Papal schism between Alexander III and (anti)Pope Victor IV*
1163	*Cathars recorded to be still in Cologne*
1164	*King Henry II of England issues the Constitutions of Clarendon*
1165	*Cathars appear in Lombers*
1167	Lombard League forms
1169	Saladin rises to power

1170	Thomas Becket murdered
1171	Saladin ends Fatimid Caliphate of Egypt
1173	*Valdes takes up the apostolic life after hearing the story of St. Alexis*
1174	Frederick Barbarossa defeated at Battle of Legnano
1174	*Cathar Council of St. Félix de Caraman held*
1177	*Valdes attracts disciples*
1177	Peace of Venice
1179	*Third Lateran Council; Valdes seeks papal approval for his life at the Council*
1180	Frederick Barbarossa defeats Duke Henry the Lion of Saxony
1180/1	*Valdes declares profession of faith*
1184	*Pope Lucius III issues Ad abolendam; Valdes and his followers are condemned in the bull*
1187	Crusaders' defeat at Battle of Hattin; Saladin captures Jerusalem
1189	Death of Henry II of England; Richard I becomes king; Frederick Barbarossa departs on Third Crusade
1190	Attacks on Jews in England; Richard I and Philip Augustus of France depart on Third Crusade; Frederick Barbarossa drowns in the River Saleph
1191	Saladin defeated at Arsul
1192	Treaty of Jaffa
1193	Death of Saladin; beginning of Baltic Crusades (end 1230)
1194	Emperor Henry IV conquers Sicily; Raymond VI becomes count of Toulouse
1198	Frederick crowned king of Sicily
1199	Death of Richard I the Lionheart
1201	Fourth Crusade begins
1204	Crusaders sack Constantinople, establish Latin Kingdom; Philip Augustus completes conquest of Normandy
1205	*Death of Valdes of Lyon*
1207	*St. Dominic debates Cathars at Montréal; Durand of Huesca abandons the Waldensians and joins the Catholic Church*
1208	*Peter of Castelnau murdered; Pope Innocent III proclaims Albigensian Crusade*
1209	*Pope Innocent III approves the order of St. Francis; sack of Béziers during the Albigensian Crusade*
1212	Spanish forces defeat the Almohads at the Battle of Las Navas de Tolosa; Children's Crusade
1213	Battle of Muret; death of Peter II of Aragon; King John of England surrenders the kingdom to the papacy and receives it back as a vassal
1214	Battle of Bouvines
1215	King John signs Magna Carta at Runnymede
1215	*Fourth Lateran Council; Innocent III approves the order of St. Dominic*
1218	Beginning of Fifth Crusade (ends 1221); *death of Simon de Montfort at the siege of Toulouse*
1220	Frederick II Hohenstaufen crowned emperor

1221	*Death of St. Dominic*
1223	*St. Francis issues final rule*
1225	*Cathar Council of Pieusse*
1226	King Louis VIII of France invades Occitania
1226	*Death of St. Francis*
1229	Treaty of Paris
1230	*The Beguines first appear during this decade*
1231	*Establishment of the Inquisition*
1242	Alexander Nevsky defeats Teutonic Knights at the Battle of Lake Chud
1242	*Cathars attack and kill a group of inquisitors at Avignonet*
1244	*Cathar fortress at Montségur falls to Catholic forces and 200 Cathars are burned*
1245	Frederick II Hohenstaufen deposed at the Council of Lyon
1245	*Great Inquisition held in Toulouse; Rainerius Sacconi converts from heresy and enters the Dominican order*
1248	Crusade of Louis IX (ends 1254)
1249	*80 suspected Cathars burned at Agen*
1250	Death of Frederick II
1250	*Sacconi writes* Summa on the Cathars and Poor of Lyon
1251	*First Shepherds' Crusade* (Pastoureaux)
1254	Interregnum in the Empire
1258	King Henry III of England accepts Provisions of Oxford
1260	*Gerard Segarelli begins preaching in Parma*
1261	Byzantines retake Constantinople and expel Western knights
1264	Rebellion of Simon de Monfort in England (ends 1265)
1264	*Feast of Corpus Christi instituted*
1267	Louis IX departs on crusade a second time
1270	Louis IX dies on crusade in Tunis
1273	Reign of Rudolf of Habsburg begins in the Empire
1274	*Death of Thomas Aquinas*
1277	*Condemnation of various philosophical and theological theses by Stephen Tempier, bishop of Paris*
1282	Sicilian Vespers
1283	Edward I completes conquest of Wales; the Teutonic Knights complete conquest of Prussia
1285	*Segarelli and his movement, the Apostolic Brethren, are condemned by Pope Honorius IV*
1289	Fall of Tripoli
1290	Jews expelled from England
1290s	*Marguerite Porete begins preaching*
1291	Fall of Acre, last Crusader outpost in the Holy Land
1294	*Pope Celestine V abdicates the papal throne*

1296	King Edward I of England deposed and imprisoned; John de Balliol, king of Scotland
1296	*Pierre and Guilaume Autier enter Italy to begin study to become Cathar perfects*
1299	*Cathar revival under Autier begins*
1300	*Gerard Segarelli burned as a heretic; Fra Dolcino becomes leader of the Apostolic Brethren and issues first prophecy*
1302	*Boniface VIII issues the bull* Unam Sanctam
1303	*Humiliation at Agnani; Boniface VIII captured by King Philip IV's men, is rescued and dies shortly after*
1304	*Fra Dolcino issues his second prophecy; Apostolic Brethren withdraw to mountains and begin attacks on the Church*
1306	Robert the Bruce declared king of Scotland and leads rebellion; Jews expelled from France
1307	Philip IV of France begins persecution of the Knights Templar
1307	*Bernard Gui commissioned as inquisitor in Toulouse; Fra Dolcino and followers captured and executed*
1309	*Papacy moves to Avignon—beginning of Babylonian Captivity of the papacy*
1310	*Marguerite Porete burned at the stake; Pierre Autier condemned as a heretic and burned at the stake*
1311	*Pope Clement V calls the Council of Vienne (lasts until 1312)*
1314	Great Famine; final destruction of the Knights Templar and burning of the last grand master, Jacques de Molay; Robert the Bruce wins the Battle of Bannockburn
1320	*Second Shepherds' Crusade*
1321	Dante completes the *Divine Comedy*
1323	*Pope John XXII condemns Spiritual Franciscan view of poverty; Bernard Gui completes his handbook for inquisitors*
1327	*A copy of Marguerite Porete's* Mirror of Simple Souls *arrives in England*
1328	End of Capetian dynasty in France; Scotland gains independence
1329	*Trial of last follower of Pierre Autier*
1330s	*Birth of John Wyclif*
1331	*Death of Bernard Gui*
1334	*Jacques Fournier, former bishop and inquisitor, becomes Pope Benedict XII (reigns until 1342)*
1337	Beginning of the Hundred Years' War
1346	Battle of Crécy between England and France
1348	Black Death strikes Europe
1354	Ottomans invade the Balkans
1356	Golden Bull issued; Battle of Poitiers between France and England
1358	Jacquerie Rebellion
1372	*John Wyclif becomes doctor of theology*
1378	*Beginning of Great Schism (lasts until 1417)*

1379	*John Wyclif writes* De eucharistia
1381	English Peasants' Revolt; Richard II, king of England, marries Anne of Bohemia
1382	*Blackfriars' Council in England*
1384	*Death of John Wyclif*
1387	*First official use of the term "Lollard"*
1398	*Jan Hus lectures on the writings of John Wyclif*
1399	Deposition of Richard II, king of England
1401	*Statute passed in England for burning heretics*
1407	*Lollard Bible is banned in England; Jan Hus emerges as reform leader in Bohemia*
1409	*Council of Pisa*
1410	Teutonic Knights defeated at the Battle of Tannenberg
1410	*Copies of John Wyclif's writings burned in Prague*
1411	King Sigismund of Hungary elected king of Germany
1413	*Jan Hus writes* De ecclesia
1414	Rebellion of Sir John Oldcastle
1415	Henry V wins Battle of Agincourt
1415	*Jan Hus condemned as a heretic at the Council of Constance and burned at the stake*
1417	*Martin V elected pope, restores papal authority in Rome and ends Great Schism*
1420	*Crusade against Hussites proclaimed*
1427	*Hussites defeat crusaders; Second Hussite Crusade proclaimed*
1428	*John Wyclif's body exhumed and burned*
1429	Rise of Joan of Arc
1431	Death of Joan of Arc
1431	*Council of Basel; Hussites defeat crusade again*
1434	*Taborites defeated by moderate Hussites and Catholics*
1436	*Hussites sign peace treaty; Bohemian Catholic Church established*
1439	*Pragmatic Sanctions of Bourges; Council of Ferrara-Florence meets*
1440	*Thomas à Kempis completes* Imitation of Christ
1440s	Invention of moveable type by Johannes Gutenberg
1444	Ottomans defeat Christian armies at the Battle of Varna
1453	Fall of Constantinople to Mehmed II the Conqueror; end of the Hundred Years' War
1455	Wars of the Roses begin
1483	Richard III usurps the throne of England
1483	*Torquemada becomes grand inquisitor in Spain*
1485	Battle of Bosworth Field and end of the Wars of the Roses; Henry VII founds Tudor dynasty
1492	Fall of Granada and expulsion of Muslims from Spain; Jews expelled from Spain
1516	Thomas More publishes *Utopia*
1517	*Martin Luther posts 95 Theses*

NOTES

Introduction

1. 'The Letter of Heribert,' translated by Guy Lobrichon in 'The Chiaroscuro of Heresy: Early Eleventh-Century Aquitaine as Seen from Auxerre,' in *The Peace of God: Social Violence and Religious Response in France around the Year 1000*, Thomas Head and Richard Landes, ed. (Ithaca, NY: Cornell University Press, 1992), p. 85.
2. Ibid.
3. Ibid. R. I. Moore, *The Origins of European Dissent* (Oxford: Blackwell, 1985), p. 198, notes that this formula is similar to one which, according to Cosmas the Priest, was used by the Bogomils.
4. 'The Letter of Heribert,' p. 85.
5. Ibid.
6. Ibid. The meaning of the miracle of the wine vat is explored fully in Claire Taylor, 'The Letter of Heribert of Périgord as a Source for Dualist Heresy in the Society of Early Eleventh Century Aquitaine,' *Journal of Medieval History* 26 (2000): 313–49.
7. Malcolm Lambert, *Medieval Heresy: Popular Movements from the Gregorian Reform to the Reformation*, 3rd edn. (Oxford: Blackwell, 2002), p. 36.

Chapter 1

1. John V. A. Fine, Jr, *The Early Medieval Balkans: A Critical Survey from the Sixth to the Late Twelfth Century* (Ann Arbor, MI: University of Michigan Press, 1993), pp. 106–81, provides a useful survey of events in ninth- and tenth-century Bulgaria.
2. Dmitri Obolensky, *The Bogomils: A Study in Balkan Neo-Manichaeism* (Cambridge: Cambridge University Press, 1948), p. 92.
3. Ibid., p. 112.
4. 'To Peter, King of Bulgaria, from Theophylact the Patriarch, Composed by John, *Chartophylax* of the Great Church,' in *Christian Dualist Heresies in the Byzantine World, c.650–c.1405*, trans. and ann. Janet and Bernard Hamilton (Manchester: Manchester University Press, 1998), p. 99.
5. The classic statement of this can be found in Steven Runciman, *The Medieval Manichee: A Study of the Christian Dualist Heresy* (New York: The Viking Press, 1961). A more recent survey of the history of medieval dualism, which does not posit an unconnected chain, is that of Yuri Stoyanov, *The Other God: Dualist Religions from Antiquity to the Cathar Heresy* (New Haven and London: Yale University Press, 2000).
6. For a general overview of the Paulicians, see Runciman, *The Medieval Manichee*, pp. 26–62, and Obolensky, *The Bogomils*, pp. 52–69. A different view of the Paulicians is offered by Nina Garsoian, *The Paulician Heresy: A Study of the Origin and Development of Paulicianism in Armenia and the Eastern Provinces of the Byzantine Empire* (The Hague and Paris: Mouton, 1967).

7. Peter of Sicily, *History of the Paulicians*, in *Christian Dualist Heresies*, p. 67.
8. For a translation of the anathemas, see *Christian Dualist Heresies*, p. 100.
9. The sermon has been translated in part or whole several times, most recently under the title 'The Discourse of the Priest Cosmas against Bogomils (after 972),' in *Christian Dualist Heresies*, pp. 114–34. The standard edition and translation into French is that of H.-C. Puech and A. Vaillant, *Le Traité contre les Bogomiles de Cosmas le Prêtre* (Paris: Institut d'Etudes Slaves, 1945).
10. Fine, *The Early Medieval Balkans*, p. 173.
11. Obolensky, *The Bogomils*, p. 104.
12. For the various translations of the Greek name 'Theophilos' see Stoyanov, *The Other God*, 164. The latest one can be found in *Christian Dualist Heresies*, pp. 114–34; the translation of 'Bogomil' is at p. 116.
13. 'The Discourse of Cosmas,' p. 116.
14. Ibid.
15. Ibid.
16. Ibid., p. 127.
17. Ibid., p. 126.
18. Ibid., p. 127.
19. Ibid., p. 128.
20. Ibid.
21. Stoyanov, *The Other God*, pp. 163–64.
22. 'The Discourse of Cosmas,' p. 130.
23. Ibid., p. 117.
24. Ibid., p. 118.
25. Ibid., p. 123.
26. Ibid., pp. 123–24.
27. Ibid., p. 131.
28. Ibid., p. 123.
29. Ibid.
30. Ibid., p. 125.
31. Ibid., p. 118.
32. Ibid., p. 125.
33. Ibid., p. 121.
34. Ibid., p. 119.
35. Ibid., p. 120.
36. Ibid., p. 129.
37. Ibid., p. 116.
38. Ibid., p. 132.
39. Ibid., pp. 132–33.
40. Ibid., p. 130.

Chapter 2

1. *Heresies of the High Middle Ages*, ed. and trans. by Walter L. Wakefield and Austin P. Evans (New York: Columbia University Press, 1991), p. 74. I have corrected the translation slightly.
2. The classic statement of this view is Runciman, *The Medieval Manichee*. It has recently been revived by Jean-Pierre Poly and Erich Bournazel, *The Feudal Transformation: 900–1200*, trans. Caroline Higgit (New York: Holmes and Meier, 1991), pp. 272–308.
3. This process is best described in Georges Duby, *The Three Orders: Feudal Society Imagined*, trans. Arthur Goldhammer (Chicago: University of Chicago Press, 1980), and in Poly and Bournazel, *The Feudal Transformation*.
4. Uta-Renate Blumenthal, *The Investiture Controversy: Church and Monarchy from the Ninth to the Twelfth Century* (Philadelphia: University of Pennsylvania Press, 1988), provides the best introduction to religious reform in the eleventh century.
5. Rodulfus Glaber, in *Rodvlfi Glabri Historiarum Libri Quinque: Rodulfus Glaber, The Five Books of the Histories*, edited and translated by John France (Oxford: Clarendon Press, 1989), 3: 6.9, pp. 126–27.
6. *Heresies of the High Middle Ages*, p. 75.
7. *Heresies of the High Middle Ages*, pp. 76–81, is the best translation of the account of Paul of St. Pere de Chartres.
8. Ibid., p. 77.
9. Ibid., p. 78.
10. Ibid., pp. 78–79.
11. Ibid., p. 81.
12. Ibid.
13. Heinrich Fichtenau, *Heretics and Scholars in the High Middle Ages, 1000–1200*, trans. Denise A. Kaiser (University Park, PA: Pennsylvania State University Press, 1998), p. 38.
14. *Heresies of the High Middle Ages*, p. 81.
15. Ibid., p. 76.
16. R. H. Bautier, 'L'Hérésie d'Orléans et le mouvement intellectuel au début du XIe siècle,' in *Actes du 95e Congrès National des Sociétés Savantes* (Rheims, 1970): *Section philologique et historique* (Paris, 1975), Vol. 1, pp. 63–88.
17. The growth of literacy after the year 1000 is the subject of numerous studies, the most important of which are those of Michael Clanchy, *From Memory to Written Record: England 1066–1307*, 2nd edn. (Oxford: Blackwell, 1993), and especially Brian Stock, *The Implications of Literacy: Written Language and Models of Interpretation in the Eleventh and Twelfth Centuries* (Princeton: Princeton University Press, 1983). Stock provides a useful analysis of the heresy at Orléans at pp. 106–20.
18. Stock, *The Implications of Literacy*, pp. 88–243.

Chapter 3

1. This matter is fully explored in Michael Frassetto, *Medieval Purity and Piety: Essays on Medieval Clerical Celibacy and Religious Reform* (New York: Garland Publishing, Inc., 1998).
2. *Self and Society in Medieval France: The Memoirs of Abbot Guibert of Nogent*, ed. John F. Benton (Toronto: University of Toronto Press, 1991), Book 3, Chapter 17, pp. 212–14.
3. The identification of Henry as a heresiarch was made by Moore, *Origins*, p. 83.
4. Marbod of Rennes describing Robert of Arbrissel, cited in Moore, *Origins*, pp. 84–85.
5. *Heresies of the High Middle Ages*, p. 109.
6. Ibid., pp. 108 and 109.
7. Ibid., p. 109.
8. Ibid.
9. Ibid., p. 110.
10. Ibid., pp. 110–11.
11. Ibid., pp. 111–12.
12. Ibid., p. 113.
13. Ibid., p. 114.
14. Ibid., p. 115.
15. Ibid., p. 116.
16. Cited in Moore, *Origins of European Dissent*, pp. 95–96.
17. *Heresies of the High Middle Ages*, p. 116.
18. Ibid.
19. Ibid., p. 117.
20. Ibid., p. 116.
21. Ibid.
22. Ibid., p. 117.
23. Ibid.
24. Ibid.
25. Cited in Moore, *Origins*, p. 95.
26. *Heresies of the High Middle Ages*, p. 122.
27. Ibid., p. 125.
28. Ibid.
29. Ibid.

Chapter 4

1. M. D. Chenu, *Nature, Man, and Society in the Twelfth Century: Essays on New Theological Perspectives in the Latin West*, ed. and trans. Jerome Taylor and Lester K. Little (Chicago: University of Chicago Press, 1968), p. 243.

2. Lester K. Little, *Religious Poverty and the Profit Economy in Medieval Europe* (Ithaca, NY: Cornell University Press, 1978), p. 120.
3. Ibid., p. 121.
4. Selections from the Laon Anonymous concerning the conversion of Valdes are translated in *Heresies of the High Middle Ages*, pp. 200–202.
5. Ibid., p. 201.
6. Ibid.
7. Ibid.
8. Quoted in Lutz Kaelber, *Schools of Asceticism: Ideology and Organization in Medieval Religious Communities* (University Park, PA: Pennsylvania State University Press, 1998), p. 138.
9. *Heresies of the High Middle Ages*, p. 210.
10. Ibid.
11. Ibid.
12. Ibid., p. 203.
13. Ibid., p. 204.
14. Ibid.
15. Ibid., p. 203.
16. Ibid., p. 206.
17. Ibid.
18. Ibid., p. 207.
19. Ibid.
20. Ibid.
21. Ibid.
22. The decree is translated in *Heresy and Authority in Medieval Europe: Documents in Translation*, ed. Edward Peters (Philadelphia: University of Pennsylvania Press, 1980), pp. 170–73.
23. Ibid., p. 172.
24. Ibid., p. 171.
25. Ibid.
26. *Heresies of the High Middle Ages*, p. 204.
27. Quoted in Euan Cameron, *Waldenses: Rejections of Holy Church in Medieval Europe* (Oxford: Blackwell, 2001), p. 42.

Chapter 5

1. A translation of this account appears as 'An Appeal from Eberwin of Steinfeld against Heretics at Cologne,' in Wakefield and Evans, *Heresies of the High Middle Ages*, pp. 127–32.
2. A translation of this account from the *Acta concilii Lumbariensis* appears under the title 'A Debate between Catholics and Heretics' in *Heresies of the High Middle Ages*, pp. 190–94.

3. Quoted in Jonathan Sumption, *The Albigensian Crusade* (London and Boston: Faber, 1978), p. 74.
4. Quoted in Dana C. Munro, *Urban and the Crusaders* (Philadelphia: University of Pennsylvania Press, 1985), p. 18.
5. Quoted in Joseph R. Strayer, *The Albigensian Crusades* (Ann Arbor, MI: University of Michigan Press, 1992), p. 90.
6. Quoted in Strayer, *The Albigensian Crusades*, pp. 90–91.
7. Particularly useful in the preparation of this chapter has been Lawrence Marvin's forthcoming study of the Albigensian Crusade and career of Simon de Montfort. I would like to thank him for sharing his work with me.

Chapter 6

1. 'The Summa of Rainerius Sacconi,' in Wakefield and Evans, *Heresies of the High Middle Ages*, p. 336.
2. Malcolm Lambert, *The Cathars* (Oxford: Blackwell, 1998), p. 151.
3. Quoted in Malcom Barber, *The Cathars: Dualist Heretics in Languedoc in the High Middle Ages* (London: Longman, 2000), p. 154.
4. The full story of the fall of Montségur is most dramatically told in Zoé Oldenbourg, *The Massacre at Montségur: A History of the Albigensian Crusade*, trans. P. Green (New York: Pantheon Books, 1962).
5. Barber, *The Cathars*, p. 182.
6. Quoted in Jean Duvernoy, *Le Catharisme*, Vol. 2: *L'Histoire des Cathares* (Toulouse: Edouard Privat, 1979), p. 322.
7. Lambert, *The Cathars*, p. 236.
8. René Weiss, *The Yellow Cross: The Story of the Last Cathars' Rebellion Against the Inquisition, 1290–1329* (New York: Vintage Books, 2002), p. 155.
9. Ibid., p. 108.
10. Ibid., pp. 108–109.
11. Ibid., pp. 109–10.
12. Lambert, *The Cathars*, pp. 250–51.
13. Barber, *The Cathars*, pp. 90–91.
14. Duvernoy, *Le Catharisme*, Vol. 2, p. 209.
15. Lambert, *The Cathars*, p. 246.
16. Quoted in Barber, *The Cathars*, p. 187.
17. Quoted in Barber, *The Cathars*, pp. 187–88.
18. Lambert, *The Cathars*, p. 239.

Chapter 7

1. Dante, *The Inferno* Canto 28, pp. 53–57, trans. Robert Pinsky (New York: The Noonday Press, 1994), p. 239.

2. Marjorie Reeves, *The Influence of Prophecy in the Later Middle Ages: A Study of Joachimism* (Notre Dame, IN: University of Notre Dame Press, 1993), p. 242.

3. Bernard Gui, *Manuel de l'Inquisiteur*, ed. and trans. by Guy Mollat (Paris: Champion, 1926), Vol. 1, 3:2, pp. 84–86. A helpful introduction to the activities of Bernard Gui is James Given's study 'A Medieval Inquisitor at Work: Bernard Gui, 3 March 1308 to 19 June 1323,' in *Portraits of Medieval and Renaissance Living: Essays in Memory of David Herlihy*, ed. Samuel K. Cohn, Jr and Steven A. Epstein (Ann Arbor, MI: The University of Michigan Press, 1996), pp. 207–32.

4. Lambert, *Medieval Heresy*, p. 221.

5. Joachim's ideas and influence are best studied in Reeves, *The Influence of Prophecy*.

6. Jeffrey Burton Russell, *Dissent and Order in the Middle Ages: The Search for Legitimate Authority* (New York: Twayne Publishers, 1992), p. 76.

7. Gui, *Manuel de l'Inquisiteur*, p. 78.

8. Ibid., p. 80.

9. Gordon Leff, *Heresy in the Later Middle Ages: The Relation of Heterodoxy to Dissent, c.1250–1450* (New York: Barnes and Noble, Inc., 1967), Vol. 1, p. 193.

10. Gui, *Manuel de l'Inquisiteur*, pp. 80–82.

11. Ibid., pp. 82–84.

12. Ibid., pp. 88–90.

13. Ibid., p. 90.

14. Russell, *Dissent and Order in the Middle Ages*, p. 76.

15. Reeves, *The Influence of Prophecy*, p. 246.

16. Gui, *Manuel de l'Inquisiteur*, p. 98.

17. Ibid., pp. 94–96.

18. Ibid., pp. 96.

19. Reeves, *The Influence of Prophecy*, p. 246.

20. Gui, *Manuel de l'Inquisiteur*, pp. 96–98.

21. *Popular Protest in Late Medieval Europe*, ed. and trans. Samuel K. Cohn, Jr (Manchester: Manchester University Press, 2004), p. 57.

22. Cohn, *Popular Protest*, p. 55.

23. Ibid., p. 56.

24. Ibid.

25. Gui, *Manuel de l'Inquisiteur*, p. 100.

26. Leff, *Heresy in the Later Middle Ages*, Vol. 1, p. 194.

27. Gui, *Manuel de l'Inquisiteur*, p. 106.

28. Ibid.

29. Gui's manual, pp. 108–18, contains a Latin edition and French translation of the letter.

30. Reeves, *The Influence of Prophecy*, p. 247.

31. Leff, *Heresy in the Later Middle Ages*, Vol. 1, p. 195.

Chapter 8

1. H. C. Lea, *A History of the Inquisition in the Middle Ages*, 3 vols. (New York: Harper, 1887), Vol. 2, p. 123.
2. A brief but useful summary of her life is Ellen L. Babinsky's 'Marguerite Porete,' in *Medieval France: An Encyclopedia*, ed. William W. Kibler and Grover A. Zinn (New York: Garland Publishing, Inc., 1995), pp. 588–89.
3. Peter Dronke, *Women Writers of the Middle Ages* (Cambridge: Cambridge University Press, 1984), p. 217.
4. Robert Lerner, *The Heresy of the Free Spirit in the Later Middle Ages* (Berkeley and Los Angeles: University of California Press, 1972; reprinted Notre Dame, IN: University of Notre Dame Press, 1991), p. 233.
5. Lerner, *The Heresy of the Free Spirit*, p. 203.
6. Quoted in Lerner, *The Heresy of the Free Spirit*, p. 1.
7. Lea, *History of the Inquisition*, Vol. 2, pp. 122–23; and Lerner, *The Heresy of the Free Spirit*, p. 5.
8. The best discussion of the early history of the Beguines is in Brenda M. Bolton, 'Mulieres Sanctae,' in *Women in Medieval Society*, ed. Susan Mosher Stuard (Philadelphia: University of Pennsylvania Press, 1976), pp. 141–58.
9. The best introductions to the Beguines are Herbert Grundmann, *Religious Movements in the High Middle Ages*, trans. Steven Rowan (Notre Dame, IN: University of Notre Dame Press, 1995), pp. 139–52, and Ernest W. McDonnell, *The Beguines and Beghards in Medieval Culture, with Special Emphasis on the Belgian Scene* (New Brunswick, NJ: Rutgers University Press, 1954).
10. Quoted in *Marguerite Porete: The Mirror of Simple Souls*, trans. and intro. Ellen L. Babinsky (New York: Paulist Press, 1993), p. 11.
11. Babinksy, 'Introduction,' *Mirror of Simple Souls*, p. 11.
12. Lerner, *The Heresy of the Free Spirit*.
13. Leff, *Heresy in the Later Middle Ages*, Vol. 1, p. 371.
14. *Mirror of Simple Souls*, ch. 140, p. 221.
15. Quoted in Babinksy, 'Introduction,' *Mirror of Simple Souls*, pp. 23–24.
16. Babinsky, 'Introduction,' *Mirror of Simple Souls*, p. 26, and Lerner, *The Heresy of the Free Spirit*, pp. 72–75, discuss the question of the copies and translations of Marguerite's *Mirror*.
17. Norman Cohn, *The Pursuit of the Millennium*, 3rd edn. (New York: Oxford University Press, 1970), p. 164.
18. Lerner, *The Heresy of the Free Spirit*, p. 75, and Babinsky, 'Marguerite Porete,' p. 588.
19. The figures are from Lerner, *The Heresy of the Free Spirit*, p. 201.
20. Dronke, *Women Writers*, p. 218.
21. Ibid.
22. Lerner, *The Heresy of the Free Spirit*, p. 202.
23. *Mirror of Simple Souls*, p. 79.

24. Ibid., ch. 1, p. 80.
25. Ibid., ch. 61, p. 138.
26. Ibid.
27. Convenient summaries of the stages can be found in Cohn, *The Pursuit of the Millennium*, p. 185, and in Lerner, *The Heresy of the Free Spirit*, pp. 202–203.
28. *Mirror of Simple Souls*, ch. 61, p. 138.
29. Ibid., ch. 118, p. 189.
30. Ibid.
31. Ibid., ch. 118, p. 190.
32. Ibid., ch. 118, pp. 190–91.
33. Ibid., ch. 118, p. 193.
34. Ibid., ch. 5, p. 83.
35. Ibid., ch. 85, p. 160.
36. Ibid., ch. 9, p. 87.
37. Ibid., ch. 52, pp. 129–30.
38. Lerner, *The Heresy of the Free Spirit*, p. 203.
39. *Mirror of Simple Souls*, ch. 43, p. 122.
40. Ibid., ch. 122, p. 200.
41. Lambert, *Medieval Heresy*, p. 204.
42. Leff, *Heresy in the Later Middle Ages*, p. 370.
43. Lerner, *The Heresy of the Free Spirit*, pp. 68–71, raises this possibility, but it has not been uniformly accepted, and Babinsky rejects the connection in her introduction to Porete's *Mirror*, pp. 24–26.
44. For general introduction to Philip, and for a discussion of the persecutions of Boniface and the Templars, see Joseph Strayer, *The Reign of Philip the Fair* (Princeton: Princeton University Press, 1980). The best studies of the Templars are those of Malcolm Barber: *The New Knighthood: A History of the Order of the Temple* (Cambridge: Cambridge University Press, 1995) and *The Trial of the Templars* (Cambridge: Cambridge University Press, 1993). On Philip's struggles against Boniface and the Templars, see James Given, 'Chasing Phantoms: Philip IV and the Fantastic,' in *Heresy and the Persecuting Society in the Middle Ages: Essays on the Work of R. I. Moore*, ed. Michael Frassetto (Leiden: Brill, 2006), pp. 271–89.
45. Lerner, *The Heresy of the Free Spirit*, p. 68.
46. Babinsky, 'Introduction,' *Mirror of Simple Souls*, p. 20.
47. Given, 'Chasing Phantoms,' p. 289.

Chapter 9

1. Quoted in Margaret Deanesly, *A History of the Medieval Church, 590–1500* (New York: Routledge, 1972), p. 222.
2. *Selections from English Wycliffite Writings*, ed. Anne Hudson (Toronto: University of Toronto Press, 1997), p. 1.

3. Russell, *Dissent and Order in the Middle Ages*, pp. 82–83.
4. A brief but useful survey of Wyclif's life is Anne Hudson, 'Wyclif, John,' in *Dictionary of the Middle Ages*, ed. Joseph Strayer (New York: Scribner, 1982–89), Vol. 12, pp. 706–11. H. B. Workman, *John Wyclif*, 2 vols. (Oxford: Clarendon Press, 1926), and Anthony Kenny, *Wyclif* (Oxford: Oxford University Press, 1985), are good full-length biographies.
5. Lambert, *Medieval Heresy*, p. 254.
6. K. B. McFarlane, *John Wycliffe and the Beginnings of English Nonconformity* (New York: The Macmillan Company, 1953), p. 70.
7. McFarlane, *John Wycliffe*, pp. 24–25.
8. Deanesly, *History of the Medieval Church*, 222.
9. *Medieval Philosophy*, ed. John Marenbon (New York: Routledge, 1998), p. 433.
10. Cited in Lambert, *Medieval Heresy*, p. 252.
11. *Medieval Philosophy*, p. 433.
12. Hudson, *English Wycliffite Writings*, p. 2.
13. Lambert, *Medieval Heresy*, p. 254.
14. Leff, *Heresy in the Late Middle Ages*, p. 496.
15. McFarlane, *John Wycliffe*, p. 60.
16. Lambert, *Medieval Heresy*, p. 253.
17. McFarlane, *John Wycliffe*, p. 63.
18. Ibid., p. 76; Kenny, *Wyclif*, p. 53.
19. Quoted in McFarlane, *John Wycliffe*, p. 78.
20. Ibid.
21. 'Pope Gregory XI to the Masters of Oxford: On Wyclif,' in Peters, *Heresy and Authority in Medieval Europe*, p. 271.
22. 'Pope Gregory to the Masters of Oxford,' p. 271.
23. McFarlane, *John Wycliffe*, p. 81.
24. Kenny, *Wyclif*, p. 59.
25. McFarlane, *John Wycliffe*, pp. 97–98.
26. Kenny, *Wyclif*, p. 91.
27. Quoted in Kenny, *Wyclif*, p. 91.
28. Quoted in Kenny, *Wyclif*, p. 92.
29. Michael Wilks, '*Reformatio Regni*: Wyclif and Hus as Leaders of Religious Protest Movements,' in *Schism, Heresy and Religious Protest* Studies in Church History, Vol. 9, ed. Derek Baker (Cambridge: Cambridge University Press, 1972), pp. 126–27.
30. McFarlane, *John Wycliffe*, p. 117.
31. Kenny, *Wyclif*, p. 94.
32. Quoted in McFarlane, *John Wycliffe*, p. 120.
33. Lambert, *Medieval Heresy*, p. 259, and Stephen E. Lahey, *Philosophy and Politics in the Thought of John Wyclif* (Cambridge: Cambridge University Press, 2003), p. 4.
34. Kenny, *Wyclif*, pp. 52–53.

35. Leff, *Heresy in the Later Middle Ages*, p. 546.
36. Ibid., p. 516.
37. Quoted in Kenny, *Wyclif*, p. 71.
38. Leff, *Heresy in the Later Middle Ages*, p. 518.
39. Kenny, *Wyclif*, pp. 70–71.
40. Quoted in Kenny, *Wyclif*, p. 76.
41. Quoted in McFarlane, *John Wycliffe*, p. 91.
42. Hudson, *English Wycliffite Writings*, p. 162. Selections of the Wyclifite Bible can be found in Hudson's volume, pp. 40–72, and the complete text can be found in J. Forshall and F. Madden, *The Holy Bible, containing the Old and New Testaments, with the Apocryphal books, in the earliest English versions made from the Latin Vulgate by John Wycliffe and his followers* (Oxford: Oxford University Press, 1850).
43. Quoted in Kenny, *Wyclif*, p. 62.
44. Leff, *Heresy in the Later Middle Ages*, p. 513.
45. McFarlane, *John Wycliffe*, pp. 94–95.
46. Leff, *Heresy in the Later Middle Ages*, p. 556.
47. Ibid., p. 559. For full accounts of the Lollards, see Lambert, *Medieval Heresy*, pp. 257–305; Leff, *Heresy in the Later Middle Ages*, pp. 559–605; and especially Anne Hudson, *The Premature Reformation: Wycliffite Texts and Lollard History* (Oxford: Oxford University Press, 1988).
48. Lambert, *Medieval Heresy*, p. 270.
49. Ibid., p. 273.
50. McFarlane, *John Wycliffe*, pp. 127–36.
51. The Council's condemnations have been translated in Peters's *Heresy and Authority in Medieval Europe*, pp. 274–77.
52. McFarlane, *John Wycliffe*, p. 120.

Chapter 10
1. Matthew Spinka, *John Hus: A Biography* (Princeton: Princeton University Press, 1968), p. 3.
2. Leff, *Heresy in the Later Middle Ages*, p. 608.
3. Ibid.
4. Lambert, *Medieval Heresy*, p. 313.
5. Spinka, *John Hus*, pp. 6–7.
6. Ibid., p. 19.
7. Kenny, *Wyclif*, p. 102.
8. *John Hus at the Council of Constance*, trans. Matthew Spinka (New York: Columbia University Press, 1965), pp. 26–28.
9. Russell, *Dissent and Order in the Middle Ages*, p. 89.
10. Spinka, *John Hus*, p. 22.
11. Ibid., pp. 23–24.

12. Ibid., pp. 24–25.
13. Quoted in Spinka's *John Hus*, p. 28.
14. Spinka, *John Hus*, p. 40.
15. Ibid., pp. 45–46.
16. Lambert, *Medieval Heresy*, p. 319.
17. Leff, *Heresy in the Later Middle Ages*, Vol. 2, p. 620.
18. *John Hus at the Council of Constance*, pp. 31–32.
19. 'John Hus: On Simony,' in *Heresy and Authority in Medieval Europe*, pp. 282 and 283.
20. Quoted in Lambert, *Medieval Heresy*, p. 322.
21. Quoted in Spinka, *John Hus*, p. 132.
22. Leff, *Heresy in the Later Middle Ages*, Vol. 2, p. 635.
23. Spinka, *John Hus*, p. 137.
24. Wilks, 'Wyclif and Hus as Leaders of Religious Protest Movements,' pp. 128–29.
25. Ibid., p. 129.
26. Quoted in *John Hus at the Council of Constance*, p. 45.
27. Quoted in Spinka, *John Hus*, p. 165.
28. Cohn, *The Pursuit of the Millennium*, p. 207.
29. Leff, *Heresy in the Later Middle Ages*, Vol. 2, pp. 658–59.
30. 'John Hus: On Simony,' p. 284.
31. Ibid., pp. 282–83.
32. For a full discussion of the Council, see C. M. D. Crowder, *Unity, Heresy and Reform, 1378–1460* (New York: St Martin's Press, 1977), *The Council of Constance*, ed. L. S. Loomis (New York: Columbia University Press, 1961).
33. *John Hus at the Council of Constance*, p. 73.
34. The list can be found in 'The Council of Constance, 1415: The Condemnation of Hus's Errors,' *Heresy and Authority*, pp. 286–89.
35. 'Peter of Mladoňovice: An Account of the Trial and Condemnation of Master John Hus in Constance,' in *John Hus at the Council of Constance*, p. 233.
36. For a full discussion of the revolt, see Howard Kaminsky, *A History of the Hussite Revolution* (Berkeley and Los Angeles: University of California Press, 1967). For the apocalyptic character of the revolt, see Cohn, *The Pursuit of the Millennium*, pp. 206–34.

BIBLIOGRAPHY

Arnold, John H. *Inquisition and Power: Catharism and the Confessing Subject in Medieval Languedoc.* Philadelphia: University of Pennsylvania Press, 2001.

Audisio, Gabriel. *The Waldensian Dissent: Persecution and Survival, c. 1180–c. 1570.* Claire Davison, trans. Cambridge: Cambridge University Press, 1999.

Babinsky, Ellen L. 'Marguerite Porete.' In *Medieval France: An Encyclopedia*, William W. Kibler and Grover A. Zinn, eds. New York: Garland Publishing, Inc., 1995, 588–89.

Babinsky, Ellen L., trans. and intro. *Marguerite Porete: The Mirror of Simple Souls.* New York: Paulist Press, 1993.

Baker, Derek, ed. *Schism, Heresy and Religious Protest.* Studies in Church History, Vol. 9. Cambridge: Cambridge University Press, 1972.

Barber, Malcolm. *The Trial of the Templars.* Cambridge: Cambridge University Press, 1993.

Barber, Malcolm. *The New Knighthood: A History of the Order of the Temple.* Cambridge: Cambridge University Press, 1995.

Barber, Malcolm. *The Cathars: Dualist Heretics in Languedoc in the High Middle Ages.* London: Longman, 2000.

Bautier, R. H. 'L'Hérésie d'Orléans et le mouvement intellectuel au début du XIe siècle.' In *Actes du 95e Congrès National des Sociétés Savantes* (Rheims, 1970) – Section *philologique et historique.* Paris, 1975, Vol. 1, 63–88.

Benton, F., ed. *Self and Society in Medieval France: The Memoirs of Abbot Guibert of Nogent.* Toronto: University of Toronto Press, 1991.

Biller, Peter. *The Waldenses, 1170–1530.* Ashgate: Variorum, 2001.

Biller, Peter and Anne Hudson, eds. *Heresy and Literacy, 1000–1530.* Cambridge: Cambridge University Press, 1994.

Blumenthal, Uta-Renate. *The Investiture Controversy: Church and Monarchy from the Ninth to the Twelfth Century.* Philadelphia: University of Pennsylvania Press, 1988.

Bolton, Brenda M. 'Mulieres Sanctae.' In *Women in Medieval Society*, Susan Mosher Stuard, ed. Philadelphia: University of Pennsylvania Press, 1976, 141–58.

Bredero, Adriaan. *Christendom and Christianity in the Middle Ages.* Grand Rapids, MI: William B. Eerdmans Publishing Company, 1994.

Cameron, Euan. *Waldenses: Rejections of Holy Church in Medieval Europe.* Oxford: Blackwell, 2000.

Chenu, M. D. *Nature, Man, and Society in the Twelfth Century: Essays on New Theological Perspectives in the Latin West*, Jerome Taylor and Lester K. Little, eds. and trans. Chicago: University of Chicago Press, 1968.

Clanchy, Michael. *From Memory to Written Record: England 1066–1307*, 2nd edn. Oxford: Blackwell, 1993.

Cohn, Norman. *The Pursuit of the Millennium: Revolutionary Millenarians and Mystical Anarchists of the Middle Ages*, 3rd edn., revised and expanded. New York: Oxford University Press, 1970.

Cohn, Norman. *Europe's Inner Demons: The Demonization of Christians in Medieval Christendom*, revised edn. Chicago: University of Chicago Press, 1993.

Cohn, Samuel K., Jr., ed. and trans. *Popular Protest in Late Medieval Europe*. Manchester: Manchester University Press, 2004.

Crowder, C. M. D. *Unity, Heresy and Reform, 1378–1460*. New York: St Martin's Press, 1977.

Deanesly, Margaret. *A History of the Medieval Church, 590–1500*. New York: Routledge, 1972.

Dronke, Peter. *Women Writers of the Middle Ages*. Cambridge: Cambridge University Press, 1984.

Duby, Georges. *The Three Orders: Feudal Society Imagined*. Arthur Goldhammer, trans. Chicago: University of Chicago Press, 1980.

Duvernoy, Jean. *Le Catharisme. I: La Religion des Cathares; II: L'Histoire des Cathares*. Toulouse: Edouard Privat, 1976 and 1979.

Fichtenau, Heinrich. *Heretics and Scholars in the High Middle Ages, 1000–1200*. Denise A. Kaiser, trans. University Park, PA: Pennsylvania State University Press, 1998.

Fine, John V. A., Jr. *The Early Medieval Balkans: A Critical Survey from the Sixth to the Late Twelfth Century*. Ann Arbor, MI: University of Michigan Press, 1993.

Forshall, J. and F. Madden. *The Holy Bible, containing the Old and New Testaments, with the Apocryphal books, in the earliest English versions made from the Latin Vulgate by John Wycliffe and his followers*. Oxford: Oxford University Press, 1850.

France, John, ed. and trans. *Rodvlfi Glabri Historiarum Libri Quinque: Rodulfus Glaber, The Five Books of the Histories*. Oxford: Clarendon Press, 1989.

Frassetto, Michael. *Medieval Purity and Piety: Essays on Medieval Clerical Celibacy and Religious Reform*. New York: Garland Publishing, Inc., 1998.

Frassetto, Michael, ed., *Heresy and the Persecuting Society: Essays on the Work of R. I. Moore*. Leiden: Brill, 2006.

Garsoian, Nina. *The Paulician Heresy: A Study of the Origin and Development of Paulicianism in Armenia and the Eastern Provinces of the Byzantine Empire*. The Hague and Paris: Mouton, 1967.

Given, James. 'A Medieval Inquisitor at Work: Bernard Gui, 3 March 1308 to 19 June 1323.' In *Portraits of Medieval and Renaissance Living: Essays in Memory of David Herlihy*, Samuel K. Cohn, Jr. and Steven A. Epstein, eds. Ann Arbor, MI: University of Michigan Press, 1996.

Given, James. *Inquisition and Medieval Society: Power, Discipline, and Resistance in Languedoc*. Ithaca, NY: Cornell University Press, 1997.

Given, James. 'Chasing Phantoms: Philip IV and the Fantastic.' In *Heresy and the Persecuting Society in the Middle Ages: Essays on the Work of R. I. Moore*, Michael Frassetto, ed. Leiden: Brill, 2006, 271–89.

Grundmann, Herbert. *Religious Movements in the Middle Ages*. Steven Rowan, trans. Notre Dame, IN: University of Notre Dame Press, 1995.

Gui, Bernard. *Manuel de l'Inquisiteur*. Guy Mollat, ed. and trans. Paris: Champion, 1926.

Hamilton, Bernard. *The Medieval Inquisition*. New York: Holmes and Meier, 1981.

Hamilton, Janet and Bernard Hamilton, eds. and trans. *Christian Dualist Heresies in the Byzantine World, c. 650–c. 1405*. Manchester: Manchester University Press, 1998.

Heymann, Frederick G. 'The Crusades against the Hussites.' In *A History of the Crusades* (Editor in Chief, Kenneth Meyer Setton), Vol. 3: *The Fourteenth and Fifteenth Centuries*, Harry W. Hazard, ed. Madison: University of Wisconsin Press, 1969–89, pp. 586–646.

Hudson, Anne. *The Premature Reformation: Wycliffite Texts and Lollard History*. Oxford: Oxford University Press, 1988.

Hudson, Anne. 'Wyclif, John.' In *Dictionary of the Middle Ages*. Joseph Strayer, ed. New York: Scribner, 1982–89, Vol. 12, 706–11.

Hudson, Anne, ed. *Selections from English Wycliffite Writings*. Toronto: University of Toronto Press, 1997.

Kaelber, Lutz. *Schools of Asceticism: Ideology and Organization in Medieval Religious Communities*. University Park, PA: Pennsylvania State University Press, 1998.

Kaminsky, Howard. *A History of the Hussite Revolution*. Berkeley and Los Angeles: University of California Press, 1967.

Kenny, Anthony. *Wyclif*. Oxford: Oxford University Press, 1985.

Lahey, Stephen E. *Philosophy and Politics in the Thought of John Wyclif*. Cambridge: Cambridge University Press, 2003.

Lambert, Malcolm. *The Cathars*. Oxford: Blackwell, 1998.

Lambert, Malcolm. *Medieval Heresy: Popular Movements from the Gregorian Reform to the Reformation*, 3rd edn. Oxford: Blackwell, 2002.

Lansing, Carol. *Power and Purity: Cathar Heresy in Medieval Italy*. Oxford: Oxford University Press, 1998.

Lea, Henry Charles. *A History of the Inquisition in the Middle Ages*, 3 vols. New York: Harper, 1887.

Leff, Gordon. *Heresy in the Later Middle Ages: The Relation of Heterodoxy to Dissent c. 1250–c. 1450*, 2 vols. New York: Barnes and Noble, Inc., 1967.

Le Goff, Jacques and Herbert Grundmann, eds. *Hérésies et sociétés dans l'Europe pré-industrielle, 11–18 siècles*. Paris: Mouton, 1968.

Lerner, Robert. *The Heresy of the Free Spirit in the Later Middle Ages*. Berkeley and Los Angeles: University of California Press, 1972; reprinted Notre Dame, IN: University of Notre Dame Press, 1991.

Le Roy Laudurie, Emmanuel. *Montaillou: The Promised Land of Error.* Barbara Bray, trans. New York: Vintage Books, 1979.

Little, Lester K. *Religious Poverty and the Profit Economy in Medieval Europe.* Ithaca, NY: Cornell University Press, 1978.

Lobrichon, Guy, trans. 'The Letter of Heribert' (in 'The Chiaroscuro of Heresy: Early Eleventh-Century Aquitaine as Seen from Auxerre'). In *The Peace of God: Social Violence and Religious Response in France around the Year 1000,* Thomas Head and Richard Landes, eds. Ithaca, NY: Cornell University Press, 1992, 85.

Loomis, L. S., ed. *The Council of Constance.* New York: Columbia University Press, 1961.

Loos, Milan. *Dualist Heresy in the Middle Ages.* Prague: Academia, 1974.

McDonnell, Ernest W. *The Beguines and Beghards in Medieval Culture with Special Emphasis on the Belgian Scene.* New Brunswick, NJ: Rutgers University Press, 1954.

McFarlane, K. B. *John Wycliffe and the Beginnings of English Nonconformity.* New York: The Macmillan Company, 1953.

Marenbon, John, ed. *Medieval Philosophy.* New York: Routledge, 1998.

Marvin, Lawrence. *The Occitan War: 1209–21* (Cambridge: Cambridge University Press, forthcoming).

Moore, R. I. *The Origins of European Dissent.* Harmondsworth: Penguin, 1977; reissued Oxford: Blackwell, 1985.

Moore, R. I. *The Formation of a Persecuting Society: Power and Deviance in Western Europe, 950-1250.* Oxford: Blackwell, 1987.

Moore, R. I., ed. *The Birth of Popular Heresy.* New York: St Martin's Press, 1976.

Mundy, John. *Men and Women at Toulouse in the Age of the Cathars.* Toronto: Pontifical Institute of Medieval Studies, 1990.

Munro, Dana C., ed. *Urban and the Crusaders.* Philadelphia: University of Pennsylvania Press (Translations and Reprints from the Original Sources of European History, Vol. 1:2), 1985.

Obolensky, Dmitri. *The Bogomils: A Study in Balkan Neo-Manichaeism.* Cambridge: Cambridge University Press, 1948.

Oldenbourg, Zoé. *The Massacre at Montségur: A History of the Albigensian Crusade.* P. Green, trans. New York: Pantheon Books, 1962.

Pegg, Mark. *The Corruption of Angels: The Great Inquisition of 1245–1246.* Princeton: Princeton University Press, 2001.

Peters, Edward. *Inquisition.* New York: Free Press, 1988.

Peters, Edward, ed. *Heresy and Authority in Medieval Europe: Documents in Translation.* Philadelphia: University of Pennsylvania Press, 1980.

Poly, Jean-Pierre and Erich Bournazel. *The Feudal Transformation: 900–1200.* Caroline Higgit, trans. New York: Holmes and Meier, 1991.

Reeves, Marjorie. *The Influence of Prophecy in the Later Middle Ages: A Study of Joachimism.* Notre Dame, IN: University of Notre Dame Press, 1993.

Roach, Andrew P. *The Devil's World: Heresy and Society, 1100–1300*. London: Longman, 2005.

Runciman, Steven. *The Medieval Manichee: A Study of the Christian Dualist Heresy*. New York: The Viking Press, 1961.

Russell, Jeffrey Burton. *Dissent and Reform in the Early Middle Ages*. Berkeley and Los Angeles: University of California Press, 1965.

Russell, Jeffrey Burton. *Dissent and Order in the Middle Ages: The Search for Legitimate Authority*. New York: Twayne Publishers, 1992.

Southern, R. W. *The Making of the Middle Ages*. New Haven: Yale University Press, 1953.

Spinka, Matthew. *John Hus: A Biography*. Princeton: Princeton University Press, 1968.

Spinka, Matthew, trans. *John Hus at the Council of Constance*. New York: Columbia University Press, 1965.

Stock, Brian. *The Implications of Literacy: Written Language and Models of Interpretation in the Eleventh and Twelfth Centuries*. Princeton: Princeton University Press, 1983.

Stoyanov, Yuri. *The Other God: Dualist Religions from Antiquity to the Cathar Heresy*. New Haven and London: Yale University Press, 2000.

Strayer, Joseph. *The Reign of Philip the Fair*. Princeton: Princeton University Press, 1980.

Strayer, Joseph. *The Albigensian Crusades*. Ann Arbor, MI: University of Michigan Press, 1992.

Sumption, Jonathan. *The Albigensian Crusade*. London and Boston: Faber, 1978.

Taylor, Claire. 'The Letter of Heribert of Périgord as a Source for Dualist Heresy in the Society of Early Eleventh-Century Aquitaine.' *Journal of Medieval History* 26 (2000): 313–49.

Taylor, Claire. *Heresy in Medieval France: Dualism in Aquitaine and the Agenais, 1000–1249*. Woodbridge: The Boydell Press, 2005.

Wakefield, Walter L. *Heresy, Crusade and Inquisition in Southern France, 1100–1250*. London: George Allen and Unwin, Ltd., 1974.

Wakefield, Walter L. and Austin P. Evans, eds. and trans. *Heresies of the High Middle Ages*. New York: Columbia University Press, 1991.

Waugh, Scott L. and Peter Diehl. *Christendom and Its Discontents: Exclusion, Persecution, and Rebellion, 1000–1500*. Cambridge: Cambridge University Press, 1996.

Weiss, René. *The Yellow Cross: The Story of the Last Cathars' Rebellion against the Inquisition, 1290–1329*. New York: Vintage Books, 2002.

Wilks, Michael. '*Reformatio Regni*: Wyclif and Hus as Leaders of Religious Protest Movements.' In *Schism, Heresy and Religious Protest*, Derek Baker, ed. Studies in Church History, Vol. 9. Cambridge: Cambridge University Press, 1972, 126–27.

Workman, Herbert. *John Wyclif: A Study of the English Medieval Church*, 2 vols. Oxford: Clarendon Press, 1926.

INDEX

Passagini 70

Patarini 70

Patriarch of Constantinople 8

Paul, Apostle 10

Paul of St. Pere de Chartres 30–34

Paulianism/Paulicianism 9, 10, 11, 16

Peasants' Revolt (1381) 163

Pelagian heresy 49

penance 50, 88, 122, 123

Percy, Lord, Marshal of England 158

Périgeux 2, 53

Périgord 1, 2, 5

Périgord heresy 28

 apostolic life of heretics 1–2, 5; conversion of laity and clerics 1, 2; criticism of ecclesiastical materialism 5; denial of the value of alms 1, 2, 4; rejection of Catholic doctrine 2; rejection of Church authority 5; rejection of the Eucharist 4; rejection of images of Christ on the cross 2, 4; rejection of meat 1, 4; teachings based on the Gospels 3, 4–5; and wine-drinking 1, 4; 'wondrous feats' 2

Peter of Benevento 97, 98

Peter of Candia see Alexander V, Pope

Peter of Castelnau 83, 84, 88

Peter, St. 25, 40, 57, 63, 125, 193

Peter I, Tsar of Bulgaria 8–12, 21

Peter II, King of Aragon 90, 92, 94, 95, 96

Peter III, King of Aragon 128

Peter of Bruis 41–2, 76

Peter of Sicily 10

Peter the Venerable, Abbot of Cluny 42, 47

Peyre, Guillaume 118–19

Philip IV the Fair, King of France 130, 140, 148, 149

Philip Augustus, King of France 82, 85, 86, 87, 91, 98

Philip of Marigny, Bishop of Cambrai 140, 142

Philippa of Hainaut 143

Philippe of Alairac 119

Pierre Raymond of Saint-Papoul 109

Pieusse: Cathar council (1225) 102

'Piphles' 77

Poor of Lombardy 74–6

Poor of Lyons 62, 63, 67, 68, 70, 71

 see also Waldensianism

Pope, the

 claims ultimate authority 40; Dolcino's four popes of the last days 130–31; Dolcino's prediction 128–9; Hus and 193, 198, 202; involvement in political disputes 59; leading juridical figures in society 59; papal reform 40; sends out special missions 80; successor to the Apostle Peter 40; and the Waldenses 64; Wyclif and 156, 161, 167, 168, 173, 179, 185, 193, 202; see also Great Schism

population growth 58

Porete, Marguerite 5, 134, 135–50

 background 136; as a Beguine 136, 139, 145; deliberations of two commissions 140–42; execution 135, 136, 142, 201; and Heresy of the Free Spirit 136, 139, 143; ordered to stop spreading her teachings and writings 140; promotion of a spiritual elite 149; refuses to answer inquisitor's questions 140, 142, 148; sent to Paris 140; teachings 136, 140, 142, 148; work gains a substantial following 149–50; Mirror of Simple Souls 5, 135, 136, 139–49, 201

Prachatice, Bohemia 180

Prague 177, 187, 189, 190, 191

Prague, Archbishop of see Zbynek

Prague Cathedral 178

Premonstratensians 76

Priscillianist heresy 66

prodigal son, parable of the 15

prophets, rejected by Bogomilism 18

Protestant churches, and Waldensianism 74

Protestant Reformation 175, 198, 199, 201, 202

Protestant reformers 57, 169, 201, 202

Provence 99

purgatory 52

Queen's College, Oxford 153

Quercy 98, 106

Raimond de Rodes, Friar 110

Ramsbury, William 172

Raymond V, Count of Toulouse 80

Raymond VI, Count of Toulouse 75–101

 attempted reconciliation with the Church 87–8, 91–2; Battle of Muret 96, 97; becomes

ACKNOWLEDGEMENTS

Although it would be rather contrary to a volume on heresy, not to recognize those responsible for its completion would be most heretical indeed, and so I must thank those who have made it possible. I should like to thank all those at Profile Books for the assistance they have provided and their efforts to correct the many infelicities of style I have committed in these pages. I would like especially to thank John Davey and Peter Carson for their patience and continued support for a project that has taken longer than expected. I owe a debt of gratitude to Claire Taylor, who suggested that I take up this project and who has helped me shape my own understanding of heresy in the Middle Ages. I would not have been able to complete this volume without the continued support and encouragement of Jill and Olivia, who have suffered more than a few interruptions in family life so that I could finish this book, and it is to them that I am most thankful.

A THOUSAND CONSOLATIONS

twins, Trillium and Fern—grab for it, each determined to be the one to give it to their teacher. "I thought naming them after plants would make them docile," Diane likes to say. "Turns out I should have named them Snap, Crackle, and Pop." Each has Diane's husband Randy's flaming red hair, and a fiery personality to match. They end up carrying the package together, each clutching on to it with one hand in order to be fair. Diane and I follow, me wishing I had thought to change out of my wax-splattered jeans and at least glance in the mirror before I came. I try to comb my hair quickly with my fingers.

Héctor is encircled by admiring parents, but Diane's girls bulldoze their way through the crowd shouting, "Señor Vargas! Señor Vargas!" and present him with the gift. To my embarrassment, he opens it right away.

"Ah, a candle. Thank you, girls," he says.

"Héctor, this is my friend Paula. She made the candle," Diane says.

Héctor offers his right hand. I resist the impulse to look at it first before allowing him to take my own. His grasp is large and encompassing, despite the missing digits.

"A candlemaker?" he says. "Like the butcher, the baker—"

"That's a candle*stick*maker," I say.

"That's true. You don't make sticks," he says.

"Actually, Paula's a pianist too," Diane says.

"Used to be," I say.

Héctor nods and sniffs the orange-and-cinnamon-scented candle. "Now you make music for the nose."

"You could say that," I say. "Etude for the nose, for pianists with *no* fingers at all."

Diane shoots me a horrified look, but Héctor laughs. He reads the label on the candle. "*Christmas Spirit*—orange for harmony, cinnamon for strength," then asks, "Does it work?"

He doesn't mean will it burn evenly or will it smoke. Like every customer who visits my studio, he wants to believe that sending a particular combination of scents into the universe will accord his wish power. As paroxysms of magical thinking grip the world in the weeks leading up to Christmas, people buy candles not just as gifts, but to meet their personal needs. Of course, the *Christmas Spirit* candles are among the most popular at this time of year; surprisingly, so are *Fidelity* and *Unrequited Love*.

"Can you make one for conceiving a child?" I've been asked.

"Can you help me get into medical school?"

I've made customized candles for everything from passing a driver's test to passing kidney stones. One man asked for a candle that would make his Christmas turkey come out moist.

"Whether they work depends on your perspective," I tell Héctor.

Héctor nods. "Most things do. They say nothing exists at all without an observer."

I glance over my shoulder. "Are they observing us now?" I ask.

"They must be," he says. "Because I'm quite certain we're both here."

I'm certainly aware of Diane observing us, and listening, her mouth slightly open, her head bobbing back and forth like she's watching a tennis match.

"You're very confident about the nature of reality," I say to Héctor.

"It might be an illusion," he replies.

"Which? Your confidence? Or reality?"

Héctor smiles and offers me his hand again.

"I already shook your hand," I say, taking it nonetheless.

"I know," he says.

The girls, who have been distracted by a classmate who's developed a voluminous nosebleed, suddenly burst back between us, clamouring for Señor Vargas's attention. "What about these?" Héctor indicates the sisters. "The Three Furies, I like to call them. They could be a myth."

Diane snorts. "I wish!"

Juniper screeches and points at Trillium. "You've got nose-blood on your dress!"

"Eeeuuuw!" Trillium moans. "I think I'm going to puke."

"That's it!" Diane claps her hands together. "We're off. Say goodbye to Señor Vargas."

I wish I could do more than join the girls' loud chorus of goodbyes, but as I try to catch Héctor's eye, he is already being introduced by the school principal to another group of admirers.

"DO YOU WANT to come in for coffee?" I ask Diane as she pulls up in front of my studio to drop me off. I want a chance to ask her about Héctor.

"A quick one. They'll be screaming for their supper soon." The girls burst into the studio like Tasmanian devils and rummage wildly through my inventory, sucking in the scents with deep, exaggerated sniffs.

I make coffee in the percolator I keep in my studio and pour us each a cup. "Was he a pianist before he lost the fingers?" I ask.

"Yes. A very successful one, I'm told. This was in Mexico."

I shudder. "How did it happen?"

"A knife accident," Diane says. She glances over her shoulder at the girls, who are squashing their faces and tongues against the inside of the front window and squealing at the responses of passersby.

"A knife accident?"

"Girls, go to the bathroom!" Diane orders.

"All of us?" Trillium asks.

"Yes."

"But I don't have to go," Fern says.

"If you turn on the tap it will make you have to pee," Diane instructs.

The girls race down the back hall and into the bathroom.

"And close the door," Diane shouts, then moves closer to me and speaks quietly. "A knife accident is what we tell the kids. It was actually members of a drug cartel. They tortured him and cut off his fingers."

"Why did they want his fingers?" I ask, assuming she is having me on.

Diane gives me a look. "I don't think obtaining the severed fingers was the point."

"They might be some kind of talisman," I say.

"Only you would think of that." She objects to what she calls my morbid fascinations, like my fondness for gory BBC crime dramas, or my refusal to kill spiders.

("Refusing to kill spiders makes me a nice person, not a morbid one," I told her once.

"I'm only a nice person *after* the spiders are dead," she replied.)

"I assume they wanted to scare him," Diane continues. "That's why he fled to Canada."

"Wait a minute. You're serious?" I say, feeling a delayed jolt of shock go through my body. "So he's mixed up with a Mexican drug cartel?"

"Laura—that's the principal—assures us that he had nothing to do with the drug trade," Diane explains. "There's no way she would have hired him to work with kids if it were otherwise. But I don't know the details. Apparently, he doesn't like to talk about it. Understandable. My speculation is that he must have known or witnessed something."

The toilet flushes.

"When was this?" I ask.

"I'm not sure. I think he came to Canada late last winter. He started teaching at the school in May. The regular music teacher went into labour early. Twins—God, they're like a plague! Laura had met him at some refugee centre. Her son was volunteering there and Héctor started teaching him piano."

"So he's a refugee?"

"I think it's all still in process. Apparently the first lawyer he had wasn't very good, but Laura convinced a mother from the school who is a big immigration lawyer—her kid's a total hooligan—to take Héctor on pro bono."

The toilet flushes again.

"But he will be approved," I say. "He was tortured. How can he not be approved?"

"I'm sure it's just red tape." Diane shifts and looks at me quizzically for a moment, then smiles. "You're showing a healthy interest in Señor Vargas."

"Most people would characterize interest in human rights abuses as healthy," I concede.

"I sense something more."

"I'm not sure *sense* is one of your strengths, Diane."

"I'm going to ignore that," she says, taking a big sip of coffee. "Because as your best friend, I'm aware that certain events in your life have resulted in an overdeveloped cynicism."

I snort. The toilet flushes a third time.

"Notice I refrained from using the word *bitter*," she adds.

"How sensitive of you."

"Come on, you and Héctor would be perfect together. You've got so much in common, your experience both performing and teaching. He's a great guy. You have to admit, he's attractive, and the kids adore him," she says. "And he was obviously interested in you."

"Why would he be interested in me?" I say, but I can feel myself blushing.

"Ahhh!" Diane points a gotcha finger at me as the toilet flushes for the fourth time. "Girls!" she hollers. "Get out here!" The girls come thundering down the hall from the bathroom, as Diane takes out her phone. "What do you want on your pizza?"

I raise my eyebrows. "Takeout pizza?" Diane is a chef who hosts a popular weekly podcast cooking show called *No Excuses*.

"Shut up!" she tells me, then places her order. As she

hangs up there is a burst of excited screams from across the room. The girls have discovered some of last year's Valentine's Day stock. "Sump-too-us Sex," Juniper reads from the label. "Trillium needs one of these for her boyfriend."

"I don't have a boyfriend!" Trillium screeches.

"Yes, you do. Kissy Connor!"

Diane rolls her eyes.

"Do they even know what sex is?" I ask.

"I'm going to have to explain it to them now, aren't I? Thanks a lot!" She attempts to steer her daughters to the door. "Let's go, guys! The pizza will be ready for pickup in ten."

I follow to lock the door behind them, but before she steps out, Diane turns to me. "I'm serious about you and Héctor, Paula."

It's my turn to roll my eyes.

"Paula." She puts her hand on my arm. "Why not? All joking aside, you deserve some happiness, you really do!"

Only the happy believe that people get what they deserve, I think, but all I say is good night.

THE FRIDAY AFTER the Christmas recital falls just a few days before the winter solstice; it's already dark by late afternoon. Business is brisk early in the day, but it peters out. I begin turning things off, preparing to lock up and retire to my apartment on the second floor for the night. With only the light of several candles and the string of Christmas lights outside, I sink into the canvas deck chair I keep in the studio for moments like this. Snow has begun to fall. Through the storefront's glass expanse, I can follow each flake's descent for several feet.

I don't know how long I've been sitting before a man approaches, hesitantly, looking up around the door as if to verify the address. My heart starts pounding before my head catches up. Héctor. He tries the door, finds it latched, then cups his hands against the glass to peer inside. He can't see me sunk in my chair in the relative dark. *If I stay perfectly still*, I think, *he won't see me.* He steps back again, peers up, and hesitates for several moments before reluctantly turning to walk away. Instead of calming down, my heart pounds even harder. An urgent voice in my head says, *Don't let him go.* I leap from my seat, open the door and call out breathlessly, "Héctor!"

"Paula." He stops and smiles. "I thought you were closed."

"I was. I mean, I was about to. Please, come in."

He steps inside and stops, as many do, to suck in the combined scents of hundreds of spells. "What a beautiful, tranquil place. And you live here too?" he asks.

"Yes, upstairs."

"I hope you don't mind my arriving unannounced," Héctor says. "The address was on the candle label."

"Of course I don't mind," I say. I reach for a light switch, but Héctor stops me.

"Don't. It's perfect like this." He peruses the candles, looking up at me as he inhales each scent. "It must be a busy time of year for you," he says.

"It's much busier in October and November when I make the Christmas stock. Most of it goes wholesale to other retailers. In December I get to relax a bit," I explain. I only open the studio to walk-in customers in the lead-up to special holidays, and even then, given my studio's residential location, I get only a handful of shoppers a day.

He nods. "That's one advantage of teaching music too. Time off at Christmas."

"You wish you didn't have to teach," I say, knowing all too well. In addition to teaching young children, I used to lead a high school drama club, teaching teenagers. Working with older, more capable children was more rewarding than teaching the little ones in many ways; their successes were so much more than stodgy showpieces to please their parents. But at the same time, it was difficult to work with young singers and actors in whom drive and ambition were beginning to take hold, alongside the sheer joy of performance. A day didn't go by that I wasn't privy to a gigantic and deeply held dream. Usually it was the student's dream, sometimes a parent's vicarious ambition on the child's behalf—either way, it was always vastly unrealistic. It was a struggle to find a balance between encouragement and tempering expectations, especially when I harboured those same unrealistic hopes and expectations for myself. Whenever I was tempted to laugh at a young girl telling me her goal was to win an Oscar one day, I bit my lip, nodded gravely, and agreed that anything could happen.

It was this very sentiment on which I capitalized to launch my own change of profession and become a candle maker. The school board had slashed its funding for several programs including the drama club I taught. The cuts would have eliminated a quarter of class time as well as the twice-yearly productions that were the focus and showcase of all our efforts, if the students and teachers hadn't rallied to

fight back. The students were passionate about their opportunities to perform, so they organized a Hope Sale to raise
money. Students, parents, and faculty were all expected to
contribute some kind of baked goods or crafts—there was
no getting out of it.

"Isn't there a secret recipe in your family you could
whip up?" the sale organizer, mother of an Oscar-hopeful,
asked me.

"If there is a secret family recipe, they know better
than to share it with me," I told her. "I'm hope*less* when
it comes to baking."

"What about a craft?"

I wrinkled my nose. "All I've ever made with my hands
were a few candles. My sister and I tried it when we were
teenagers. The candles turned out fine, but we stupidly
dumped the excess hot wax down the kitchen sink. Wreaked
havoc with the plumbing. Our parents barred us from ever
doing it again," I explained.

"You don't live with your parents now, do you?" the
mother pressed on, clapping her hands together. "Candles
would be fabulous. The perfect symbol of hope."

That afternoon, I went to the library and found some books
on candle making, including one about the magical properties
of scent. The next night, I bought supplies and got to work.
The process was surprisingly soothing, full of peace and calm,
the opposite of a frenetic improvisation class. The scent of
vanilla—which I chose for its apparent qualities of promoting
confidence and stamina—filled the kitchen, and despite my
skepticism, seemed to work. By the day of the big Hope Sale I
had three dozen candles, which to my great surprise sold out

before the sale was even halfway over. It wasn't the colour or form of the candles, or even their delicious smell that attracted buyers; it was the labels: *Perfect Performance*—crafted to instill confidence, clarity, and calm. Young actors and musicians, or rather their parents, snapped them up, could hardly wait to get home and light them, setting my candles to work on their dreams. Meanwhile the sight of the proceeds from the sale filling the school's coffers was a genuine inspiration for me, a way to finally leave teaching behind.

"Teaching can be tiresome," Héctor concedes. "But I enjoy the children." He picks up a *Releasing Regret* candle and reads. "Amber for forgiveness, gardenia for newfound joy. It's like being a priest, or a psychotherapist."

"I don't require people to tell me their secret wishes when they buy a candle," I say.

Héctor chuckles. "Perhaps you should."

"Okay," I say. "What is it you wish for?"

"I wish to take you out for dinner."

My stomach flutters. "When?"

"We could go right now."

"Now?"

"Why not?"

I laugh nervously. "I guess there's no reason why not. But I'd like to get changed first this time."

"This time." He looks confused. "Isn't this our first date? I'm sure I would remember if we'd had dinner together before."

I'm glad he can't see me blush in the dim light. "Of course, yes. Just give me five minutes." I run upstairs to my bedroom, where I can barely manage buttons and zippers because my hands are shaking so much. Since Teddy died, I've only gone on two dates. The first was a blind date Diane arranged, contrary to my explicit wish, with a librarian named Floyd who enrolled repeatedly in cooking courses she taught through the city's Life-Long Learning program. I went to dinner with Floyd only to discover it was Diane he was obsessed with. He spent the whole meal quizzing me about her life. "He asked me if you have any tattoos," I reported back to Diane, who was aghast. "And are you aware that he has a Little Mermaid tattoo on his bicep?"

"A mermaid? Really?"

"Not *a* mermaid—the Little Mermaid."

"As in *Disney*?" She accused me of making that up, but I hadn't.

"He rolled up his sleeve in the restaurant to show me," I explained. "It was quite good, actually."

Diane had to cancel her next class because she couldn't prevent Floyd from enrolling again. That's when she decided to move online instead.

The other date since Teddy happened accidentally, at least on my part. I'd met Errol a few times at craft fairs when I first started selling candles. He made jewellery from fish bones. He was so soft-spoken that you had to lean your ear to within a few inches of his face to catch anything he said. When he asked if I would meet him for coffee to advise him on getting his (hopeless) jewellery into retail locations, it seemed unkind to refuse. We had coffee and talked—whispered, in his case—about how best to sell his wares. We were about to part on the sidewalk out front when he pulled me to him and kissed me full on the mouth.

I stepped back and told him he had misunderstood, that I was not interested in that kind of relationship. I don't know what he replied. He did speak, but I couldn't hear him and didn't dare lean in lest he take that as a signal and try to kiss me again. So I gave an idiotic little wave, said, "Well, bye then," and walked away. I didn't see or hear from him again.

There can be no such misunderstanding with Héctor. He's already called it a date, and I've already agreed. I look at myself in the mirror. The clean blouse I've changed into suddenly looks too low-cut. I hesitate, then change into a turtleneck sweater, before returning to the studio. I lock the door behind us as we emerge into the snow-globe evening.

"What about Portuguese?" Héctor suggests.

"Fine with me."

We walk several blocks north where we catch the Dundas streetcar and travel east to Little Portugal. At the restaurant, we sit in a semicircular booth, so that our elbows touch. While Héctor is reading the menu, I spot a woman pointing out his fingers—or absence thereof—to her date, but Héctor doesn't appear to notice.

"What do you think of crisped fresh sardines with olives and lemon as an appetizer?" he asks.

"That sounds good," I say, suddenly realizing that I am ravenously hungry.

"Sardines have a special place in my heart," Héctor says. "There's a village near the town where I grew up that is famous, because in 1924, a shower of sardines rained down on it for six minutes straight."

My eyebrows rise. "A shower of sardines?"

"From the sky, yes. I had a part-time job there when I was in high school. A tour guide for the pilgrims."

"Pilgrims," I repeat.

"Of course. It was a miracle."

"Not for the sardines," I observe.

"That's true." Héctor smiles and looks at me thoughtfully. "It was quite a sacrifice on their part. There have been dozens of reports of fishes or salamanders falling from the sky all over the world, going way back."

"Which is more miraculous? Salamanders or fish?" I ask.

"Well, salamanders are more evolved."

"So it would be even more auspicious if, say, raccoons fell from the sky."

Héctor nods. "That stands to reason, but it would also be more dangerous."

We both laugh loudly, and the gawking woman glares over at us again. Héctor waves to her with his maimed hand and her eyes nearly bulge out of their sockets, which only makes us laugh more. I wonder how he would respond if I asked about his hand, the experience that brought him to Canada. The terror he must have experienced. And the loss—of his home, his country, and his career; he is a professional pianist who's lost his fingers. Diane said he didn't like to talk about it, but maybe that's just with nosy parents at the school. This is a date. It might seem rude *not* to say anything, as if I'm not interested in something of such significance in his life. It's a dilemma I've seen others chew on when they encounter me and wonder whether they should say anything about Teddy's death.

Héctor, it seems, has no such qualms. "Your friend Diane tells me you are a widow," he says.

I make a mental note to berate Diane for failing to tell me that Héctor was asking about me. Like we're in high school. To my horror, I realize this thought has made me smile.

Héctor looks at me quizzically.

"Oh, excuse me. It's not being a widow that makes me smile," I say, turning a deep red. I'm saved from further explanation by the plate of sardines.

After an appropriate interval of tasting and exclaiming about the delicious fish, I continue. "So, yes, a widow. Teddy died of a brain tumour five years ago."

"He was young," Héctor says, more statement than question.

"Yes. Twenty-six."

"I was married once," Héctor says. Before I can ask, he shakes his head. "No, nothing tragic. Just a mistake. We separated after only a few months."

When he says this, I feel a pang of jealousy. Jealousy because whatever else happened, she had him for those months, and all I've had, at this point, is an appetizer. *I must be going completely insane*, I think. Once again, I realize I am smiling inappropriately.

"I'm sorry," I say, grasping for some kind of convention. "That must have been hard for you."

Héctor smiles inappropriately back. "Yes, it was awful, thank you."

We laugh again, though I'm not sure either of us knows why.

"What about other family? Did you have to leave them behind?" I ask.

He shakes his head. "My parents have both died. My mother when I was a child, of breast cancer. My father more recently, just three years ago. I was an only child, so no siblings. Just friends, lots of friends in the orchestra, though many of them left before me, to the States or wherever they could go."

"Are you still in touch with any of them?"

"My former roommate, Jorge. He's a violinist. I speak to him sometimes, but it's dangerous, so not too often."

I get the feeling that he'd rather not continue on this topic, and we eat for several seconds in silence.

The gawking woman and her companion rise to leave. When they exit the restaurant, a swirl of snowflakes enters on a gust. "Had you ever seen snow before you came to Canada?"

"Once," he says. "When I was a child. The mayor of my town arranged it."

"Arranged for it to snow?"

He nods. "His daughter wanted snow for Christmas. He'd told her she could have anything she wanted. He was very rich, of course. Friends in high places."

"The highest, it seems," I said.

He nods again. "A general, I think. It arrived in a gigantic cargo plane. The whole belly loaded with snow. The soldiers used whatever they could find—forklifts, golf carts, what-ever—to unload it in a heap on the airfield. We played in it, all the town's kids, until there was nothing left but soggy ground. It was magical."

"It sounds wonderful," I say. "Where did the snow come from?"

"They told us it came from Montreal, which we understood to be very close to the North Pole."

"Yes, it is."

"Incidentally, I have to catch a train to Montreal early tomorrow morning," he says.

"Really? What's in Montreal—besides snow?"

"The school band won a cross-Canada competition to perform an ecumenical medley at a big charity benefit," he explains. "The Montreal Symphony Orchestra will be there."

"An ecumenical medley?" I ask.

"Yes, you know, a little Christmas, a little Hanukkah, a little Kwanza, a little Eid. Though I think Eid happened in August," he says. "I did the arrangement myself."

"Does this mean you'll be travelling with all the kids in the band?"

"Yes." He smiles widely, as if to say *lucky me*. "And a few parent-volunteers. And as a reward for all our hard work, we get to spend the following day downhill skiing."

"Have you ever skied before?" I ask.

"Never," he says. "I'm sure it's not as dangerous as it looks."

The main course arrives—porcini-crusted roasted black cod and grilled octopus with roasted pepper salad—and we eat. I eat like I haven't eaten in years, even devouring a sweet and heavy coconut custard tart for dessert. It all tastes so startlingly good.

When we leave the restaurant, the snow has thinned to flurries. Héctor insists on seeing me home, even though it means he'll have to double back on the same streetcar to his apartment in Little Italy. On the streetcar, he takes my left hand in his right, and this time, I look. The index and middle fingers have been sheared off at the knuckle and the ring finger ends at the second joint. I turn his hand over and notice that his thumb, although intact, is also scarred, as if it had been cut deeply just above the knuckle. The skin over the stumps looks smooth. I touch it. "Does it hurt?"

"Not at all," he says. "You know, I can still feel the missing fingers. Phantom limb syndrome. In fact—" he raises his hand to my face as if to stroke my cheek with the missing fingers' ghosts, "they can still feel your skin."

I shiver, my eyes widen, as if I have really felt his touch, but Héctor bursts out laughing. "Got you!" I have to laugh too.

"Yes," I concede, "you got me, but only for a second."

"I hope I have you for much longer than that," he says.

We continue holding hands as he walks me down Sorauren Avenue, stopping at my front door.

"Good night, then, Paula," he says. He leans in and kisses me lightly on the lips and my heart flutters wildly. "Can I call you when I'm back from Montreal?"

"Yes," I manage to whisper.

He waves and turns back north.

I lock the door behind me and make my way to the back of my studio without turning on any lights. Halfway up the stairs, I stop and steady myself; the strength of my wish to see and speak to Héctor again is disorienting. I haven't allowed myself to want anything for so long. After years of being if not content, then self-contained, it feels like there's a force inside of me trying to expand beyond the border of my skin. Not to separate from my body, but to inflate it, as if with helium.

My apartment is freezing. I turn up the thermostat, make tea and huddle on the couch in a blanket while I wait for the rooms to warm up. Though I tell myself repeatedly to stop, my mind continues to cast its thoughts ahead to Héctor's return. Crawling into bed only fuels more fantasies; when I finally fall asleep I dream I'm caught in a blizzard of sparkling sardines. A miracle.

TO MY SURPRISE, his call comes sooner than I'd expected, from Montreal, on Sunday night.

"Paula, I'm dying," he says. There are children shriek-ing in the background and a blast from what sounds like a trombone. "It's quite possible I'm already dead."

"It sounds like you've arrived in hell," I say. Another blast from the trombone, this one so loud I hold the phone away from my ear.

"Please let it be purgatory," he says. "Then there's hope. Will you make a candle, for the salvation of my soul from purgatory?"

"I'm more worried about your ears," I say.

"What?"

"Very funny. But would that help—making candles? I mean, I've heard of indulgences, but I'm not Catholic, so I don't know all the ins and outs of purgatory."

"Paula, if I survive, I will be more than happy to teach you all the ins and outs."

I laugh and remember, viscerally, what it felt like to kiss him. I'm taken aback, and a little bit scared, by how strong my desire for him is. It's been so long, and this is happening so suddenly. "I look forward to learning," I say. "How was the concert?"

"Fantastic! The audience was so moved by my ecumenical medley that there were mass conversions on the spot," he says. "The Jews became Muslims, the Muslims became Christians, and the Christians became Kwanza-ists."

"What did the Kwanza-ists do?"

"Alas, they alone were unmoved."

"How was learning to ski? Did you break a leg?" I ask.

"Both of them. I am so covered in bruises that I look like a plum," he says.

"Ha! Look at this one!" a boy shouts nearby.

"Wow, fantastic, Tyler," Héctor says. Then to me: "Every time I wiped out, they whipped out their phones and snapped a photo. Now they're comparing to see who has the most embarrassing shot of Señor Vargas."

"You can actually see the snow packed into his nostrils," the boy shouts, then laughs hysterically.

I laugh. "Sounds like one for Facebook."

"They've already created a page dedicated to my humiliation," he says.

"Is it tomorrow that you return?"

"Yes. One more night in purgatory. Then five hours on the train," he says.

"I'll pray for you."

"Please do, Paula. I'll call you when I get home. The train gets in around four thirty."

I am happy, and it scares me. I can't allow myself to feel this way about something that might not be real.

When five o'clock Monday passes, then six with no phone call, my spirit rapidly deflates. I berate myself for being so gullible and stupid. After all I've seen and been through! Of course it was too good to be true. *At least no one can read my mind,* I think, *and know just how much of a fool I've been.* At seven thirty, I put on my pajamas and settle in for a long evening with a grisly police procedural, thinking, *now* this *is reality.*

When the phone rings at ten to ten, my heart leaps nonetheless.

"Paula, I'm sorry I'm late," he says. "The train was delayed four hours."

"They're always delayed," I say casually, as if that's what I've been thinking all along. "Was it snow?"

"They just told us something was obstructing the tracks. They wouldn't say what," he says. "Very mysterious."

"Sardines?"

"Quite possibly. The kids figured it was a school bus."

"The kids! Oh boy, nine hours on a train. They must have been climbing the walls."

"Actually, they were quite relaxed. There were these nuns in our car who kept passing around an enormous box of chocolates. No matter how many the kids ate, there was always another layer underneath," he says.

"Like the loaves and fishes," I suggest.

"Exactly."

"But wouldn't chocolate have made the kids more hyper?" I ask.

"They were full of brandy," he says. "Nuns are very clever, you know."

"I know now."

Before hanging up we arrange to meet for dinner at a sushi place near his apartment the following evening.

Tuesday is overcast, almost dark, dark enough that I light several candles in the windowed front of my studio to make it look inviting. I often light a stick of incense just outside the door—the candles' scents are not strong enough; they dissipate in the open air—but incense will waft over to the sidewalk and catch the odd customer by the nose. I step outside to try to light a bayberry stick, but clumps of wet snow begin falling rapidly, extinguishing the flame from my lighter.

It's noon before I have my first customer, a woman.

"Do you sell candles?" she asks as she enters.

I resist the urge to peer around at my candle-making studio and the display of candles in front of her. Nor do I point out the sign in the window that she just passed, which reads "Spellbound Candles Christmas Sale." Any one of these clues might have indicated to the discerning consumer that I sell nothing but candles. Instead, I nod sweetly. Her hair fans out from her face against an acrylic fur hood in an extraordinary display of static electricity. She buys three *Magi* candles—frankincense and myrrh, with gold sparkles rolled onto the surface.

An hour later two women arrive. I've seen one of them in the studio before. As they enter, she says to the other woman, who is certainly her sister, possibly a twin, "Don't worry, this will work. Everything will be fine this year."

"Excuse me," she says to me. "I think I saw some here before to help people get along? Harmony, or something?"

I point out the *Christmas Spirit* line.

"Orange for harmony, cinnamon for strength," she reads. "Perfect. That's exactly what we need. See?" She turns to her sister. "I told you!"

"Our mother is coming for Christmas," the sister tells me. "Last year we had to get a restraining order."

I should warn them that essential oils are not a suitable substitute for police; I sell them five candles instead.

INSTEAD OF MEETING inside the restaurant as planned, I find Héctor waiting at the streetcar stop at College and Grace. Without a word, as I step off, he takes me in his arms and kisses me.

"Here we are," he says moments later, at the door to the sushi restaurant. We sit in a booth, adjacent to each other again.

"I feel so happy and at ease when I'm with you, Paula," Héctor says. "Why do you think that is? I'm usually more nervous when I meet a woman."

"I'm not a woman," I say. "Did you not notice the tailfin?"

He leans back and looks at my feet. "Those boots must be very painful, then."

He looks back at my face, examines it for several seconds. "I think it's because you remind me of something, something I've never actually experienced before."

"There is an aboriginal community somewhere in South America," I say, "that sees the future as being behind us. They imagine themselves looking forward into the past. Because of course, you can see the past, whereas you can't see the future. But it also suggests the future is a return of some kind, a homecoming." I shrug. "I heard it on the CBC."

"Then it must be true," he says.

"Do you think our lives are predestined, part of a plan that someone or some part of ourselves makes for us before we're born?"

"Paula, you ask such difficult questions," he says. "Don't you want to know my favourite colour?"

A waitress interrupts us with menus. We order warmed sake.

"I was raised Catholic," Héctor says. "I don't understand this concept of predestination. It seems to eliminate the possibility of hope."

"That depends on what you mean by hope. If hope is just wishful thinking, then it isn't real. It's simply delusion," I say.

"That's a funny thing," he replies, "for someone who makes wish-candles for a living, to say there is no hope."

I smile. "I didn't say there is no hope. And you misunderstand my candles. I used to think if you just wanted something enough, it was inevitable. But now I think the only real hope is being receptive to whatever comes your way, not deluding yourself into thinking you can manipulate the future with your thoughts. You have to pay attention to what is real. Hope requires awareness; in fact, hope *is* awareness."

"I see. So that is how one must understand your candles," he says. "They don't make wishes come true. They symbolize attention, a metaphoric turning-on-the-lights, so you become receptive to whatever comes, even if it's the opposite of what you wanted."

"Exactly," I say. "Just don't tell my customers that."

"Don't worry, I won't give you away." He takes my right hand in both of his, linking my palm to his left while he strokes the back with the remaining fingers of his right. His touch makes me shiver.

The sake arrives, followed shortly by an assortment of sushi and maki rolls.

"Can you use chopsticks with your hand?" I ask as I take up my own.

"Watch and be amazed," he says. He manoeuvres the plastic sticks between his maimed fingers, raises them in the air with a flourish, and I expect a feat of dexterity to match his performance at the keyboard, but instead he signals to the waitress: "May I please have a fork?"

IF HOPE IS receptivity and attention, then I'm the most hopeful person alive tonight. I receive Héctor's every touch and word as if I have no skin, as if every filament of my nervous system is exposed and listening. I am keenly aware each time his arm brushes mine, or his knee bumps my leg under the table. When we finish our meal and he helps me into my coat, I stop myself from leaning back into him, to be engulfed by him instead of mere fabric.

When we step out onto College Street, the temperature has dropped and there are flurries in the air. He offers me his arm and I slip my hand through the crook of his elbow. We turn and walk south on Grace Street.

"My place is there," he says, pointing to a house on the west side, across from St. Francis of Assisi church. "But there's something I want to show you first."

He leads me to the side entrance of the church that opens onto Mansfield Avenue, where there is the largest nativity scene I've ever seen. A star that looks suspiciously like a pentagram dangles over the whole display, suspended from a small crane parked beside the church. There are half a dozen sheep gathered around, as well as two donkeys, a cow, and a rabbit.

"I don't remember any bunnies in the Bible," I say.

The three magi—one white, one black, and one who might be Chinese—are in attendance on life-sized horses, which means they are actually taller than the roof of the three-sided stable. Inside, Joseph is smiling like the Cheshire cat, with all of his teeth showing; Mary, on the other hand, looks like she's been crying.

"Is that a Cabbage Patch doll?" I lean closer to confirm that yes, indeed, baby Jesus bears those trademark chubby cheeks.

"It's fantastic!" Héctor says.

I laugh. "Maybe it is perfectly appropriate. I mean, there is something fundamentally ridiculous about the divine becoming flesh."

Héctor nods. "Lovely and ridiculous."

We return to Grace Street and cross. Héctor's apartment is on the second floor of a house. He leads me up the stairs, one hand reaching behind to hold mine, still gloved. At the top, instead of letting go, he pulls my hand forward and places it on his side, as if for safe-keeping, while he engages both of his to unlock his door. He retrieves my hand, but then he drops his keys, which clatter noisily down to the next step. As he stoops to pick them up, the door at the bottom of the stairs opens and an elderly woman in a long pink nightgown begins scolding us in what I assume is Italian.

"I'm so sorry, Mrs. Bartolamiol," Héctor says. "So sorry we woke you. It was an accident. We'll be very quiet now, I promise."

She gives a dismissive wave and closes her door again.

"My landlady," Héctor says, once we're inside his apartment. "She gets up early every morning to go to Italian mass across the street. Laura, my principal, is also a member of the congregation. That's how I was able to rent this apartment."

"I hope she's not going to be upset with you," I say.

"It might be worth it. Seeing her solved a mystery I've been wondering about."

"What's that?"

"She's been a widow for more than thirty years. In all that time, Laura claims, she's never worn a stitch that was not black. But now we know she cheats at night."

His words shake me, momentarily, not with grief and certainly not from any old-fashioned notions about a widow's role, but rather as a flicker of warning about the nature of longing and its power to betray. It must show on my face, because Héctor stops as if startled, and I fear the spell is broken.

"Oh, Paula, I'm sorry. I didn't mean to suggest—" he says.

"It's okay, it's fine," I say.

But Héctor still looks concerned. "Would you like some brandy?" he asks.

I nod and he goes into the kitchen while I look around

the small living room that contains a couch, a television, and a desk and chair. A large front window overlooks Grace Street. I wish desperately that I could rewind to when Héctor placed my hand on his waist, before I allowed a fleeting thought about my past to spoil the mood.

He returns from the kitchen with a bottle and two glasses, which he places on the coffee table. He sits down on the couch, still smiling, but deferential now, cautious, allowing me to decide whether I will sit down beside him, which I do. He pours the brandy and hands me a glass. I take a sip, then put the glass down—quickly, because my hands are shaking so much—and lean in close to kiss him.

AT THREE O'CLOCK in the morning I wake, aching with longing for Héctor, even though he is right beside me. Like that poem of Basho's, "Even in Kyoto / hearing the cuckoo's cry / I long for Kyoto."

How have I allowed this to mean so much so quickly?

THERE IS JUST enough light in the room for me to see his face as he opens his eyes a few minutes before seven o'clock.

"Paula," he says. "Have you been awake long?"

"No," I say. "I've been asleep most of my life. Before now."

I make coffee in his tiny kitchen while he showers. I'm peering into his fridge when he enters the kitchen and puts his arms around me from behind.

"What do Mexicans eat for breakfast?" I ask. "Huevos rancheros, or something?"

"Something far more exotic," Héctor says. He goes over to a cupboard and takes out a jar. "Nutella."

He takes half a loaf of bread from the freezer and puts two slices in the toaster. Just as I'm about to spread Nutella on my slice, a door slams downstairs, startling me, and a gloop falls onto the red blouse I wore last night, landing on my left breast.

"Let me get that," Héctor says. He wets a tea towel and rubs my breast, looking into my eyes instead of at the stain.

"Mrs. Bartolamiol would be scandalized," I say.

"I would be too," he says. He kisses me and continues to caress my breast. "But I'm going to be late for work."

AS I UNLOCK the door to my studio, I realize that the whole way home—the ride on the streetcar, then walking down Sorauren amid the clutches of people rushing to get their kids to school and themselves off to work—I've been imagining Héctor beside me. In my head, I've been narrating for him all of the mundane details of my day as it is unfolding. It's as if I want to explain myself to him in every possible way.

Even as I go upstairs and undress to get in the shower, I catch myself mentally telling him that, although I love to paint my toenails, which are currently navy blue, I can't abide putting polish on my fingernails, because I can feel the weight of it at all times and it drives me nuts. It's an absurd impulse, this narrating. Yet I continue to do so almost unconsciously.

I'm setting up the studio to open for the day when Diane calls.

"Tell me everything," she orders.

"I'm very smart, Diane," I say, "but even I don't know everything. Try God."

"I have a right to know," she insists. "I introduced you, after all. I saw him when I dropped the girls off at school, so I know you saw him last night."

I pause, but then I can't help giggling. "As a matter of fact, I saw him this morning too."

Diane gasps dramatically. "And when will you see him again?"

"I don't know," I say breezily, as if it doesn't matter.

"It's no use pretending to be all casual about this, Paula. I can hear how huge it is," she says. "Your voice is different."

"Different how?"

"There's a ting."

"Maybe I have a loose filling."

"A ting of happiness."

"What, you've never heard me happy before?"

"The last time I saw you happy was a very, *very* long time ago," she says.

"What was the occasion?" I ask.

"I don't know, but you were wearing green," she says. "Don't try to change the subject, because you know exactly what I'm talking about. It was before Teddy got sick. Since then, jokey? Good-natured? Sure. But not happy. Sad. Always closed up and sad beneath the surface."

I don't resent her words, as I might once have done. Because she's right. I'm aware of the largeness of the transformation; in fact, it is much larger even than Diane suspects. So large that it terrifies me.

When I first laid eyes on Héctor less than a week ago, I felt as though I recognized him. Is this what they call love at first sight? It feels more like love *is* first sight: the propensity to look past all potential barriers, the illusions and deceptions of personality, to the true essence of another being; the total empathy that reveals that other person's essence and your own are one.

Yet I know so little about Héctor and his life.

✳ CHAPTER TWO ✳

I FIRST MET TEDDY BACKSTAGE AFTER playing the lead role in a gruesome production of *Medea*. It was my last performance as a theatre student at York University. A month later I would graduate and begin what I had no doubt would be my swift rise to stardom.

But that was not my first sight of Teddy. Three years earlier, he'd played a goofy teenage snowboarder in a CBC television comedy set in a less-than-spectacular small-town Ontario ski resort. It was a running joke on the show that the mountains were barely taller than the mall. The show was cancelled after only one season, so Teddy's was hardly a household name, but aspiring actors enrolled in local theatre schools—I was in my second year at York at the time—were keenly aware of any and all productions that might become opportunities to take a step up to the big league. Some of my classmates had even auditioned for Teddy's role. So when Teddy subsequently enrolled in the theatre program at Humber College, he was something of a minor celebrity, and the news spread through the tight-knit theatre community, to the York campus as well. We students were still young enough to be awed by his foray into television and fame. We spoke in hushed, admiring tones of the deep commitment to improving his craft Teddy demonstrated with his decision to continue with school instead of just grabbing the next television role we presumed must be on offer. As we learned and experienced more about the industry, we began to real-ize the road to success is seldom that easy or straightforward, but that didn't dampen Teddy's popularity. He had an aura of success that people latched on to, assuming, sometimes unconsciously, that it would help their own careers.

I was struggling to wipe the fake blood from my face and hair—I didn't want to attract horrified stares on the bus ride home—struggling because my hands were shaking violently. Some actors shake with fear and nervousness before a performance begins. Not me. It was only at the end, when the audience and my colleagues stood and cheered for me, and I knew that I had nailed it, that my body began to tremble with terror.

I had been determined to play Medea; so had every other girl in the graduating class. Of course we all wanted to play her, a woman struggling to take charge of her life in a male-dominated world. We all felt passionately about it, even though, at that age, the full force of that struggle was still well ahead of us. Bitter rivalries flared during auditions, but in the end, I won. The director said I had a "subtle but convincing darkness."

While I was shaking too hard to remove my makeup, Teddy and his Humber classmate Greg came backstage into the green room. They were looking for their friend Anwar, who was my co-star in the role of Jason. Not finding Anwar, Greg returned to the hall, but Teddy approached me and took my fluttering hands in his. "You've got the *I was brilliant* shakes," he said. He didn't look as goofy as he had on television; his lopsided grin was quite charming.

I laughed. "Just a delayed nervous reaction."

"No," Teddy insisted. "Because you *were* brilliant." His eyes were startlingly blue.

Instead of catching the bus home, I joined the three of them, at Teddy's invitation, at a nearby campus pub for a drink. Greg and Anwar soon left. I was exhausted and should have left too, but Teddy persuaded me to have one more drink and we ended up staying until the pub closed. We rode the bus together, and then the subway. Although he had farther to go, he insisted on getting off the train to walk me the rest of the way home. I was living in a tiny basement apartment in the home of my former piano teacher, Mrs. Gaskell.

"Wouldn't it be easier to live close to campus?" Teddy asked.

I explained to him that I was paying my way through university by teaching piano lessons. Mrs. Gaskell was approaching seventy and retirement. Apart from a couple of older students, she'd handed most of her pupils over to me, allowing me to use her front room and piano to conduct lessons. She was happy to be rid of the aggravation of moulding stubborn young minds and fingers but would have missed the presence of young children in her home. She still met them at the door with a tin of cookies before they began their lessons with me.

"So you play piano too," Teddy said admiringly.

"I'm no concert pianist. Merely competent. The biggest advantage is that I can accompany myself singing."

"Wow. I wish I could. And teaching kids is a lot better than waiting tables, which I used to do until I started doing magic shows, for birthday parties and things. Not exclusively for children, but most of the time."

"You do that in the summer?" I asked.

"Year-round, but it's busiest in the summer."

"That's the problem with piano lessons. Most kids take the summer off, so I usually have to do some waiting on tables as well. Of course, this year I'm finishing school, so I'll be going to auditions, and hope— What?"

Teddy had stopped suddenly to face me and was looking at me intently. The streetlights were bright enough that I could see the blue of his eyes.

"Would you mind being beheaded?" he asked.

I thought for a moment before replying, "Probably not *after* the fact."

Teddy laughed loudly, even slapping his thigh. "It's a

magic trick," he explained. "A variation on sawing the lady in half."

"And you need a lady?"

"Exactly!" Teddy became very excited and grabbed hold of my upper arms. "If we worked together, I could expand into all sorts of tricks, not just the guillotine. It could be a much bigger show!"

His face was so animated with child-like delight that I couldn't help but smile and agree to be his partner. Then we kissed, and continued to stop at intervals to kiss again until we reached Mrs. Gaskell's door. Teddy kissed me one last time and said, "You know, you might mind after the fact—being beheaded, I mean. They say Anne Boleyn haunts the Tower of London with her head held under her arm."

The kids loved the guillotine trick, especially when my apparently severed head started to scream—my personal touch. But they were even more impressed by Teddy's closing act in which he stabbed a foot-long needle through the flesh of his inner forearm. The fake blood spurting from the wound really got the little barbarians going.

Teddy truly was a wizard. He grabbed the children's awestruck attention the moment he stepped into the room. His zeal combined effortlessly with the energy of a roomful of children, and the result was intoxicating. I genuinely enjoyed those gigs. More importantly the shows provided respite, if only for an hour or two at a time, from the stress of auditioning for parts.

I'd always prided myself on being well prepared for auditions, carefully researching the best possible pieces to prepare and consulting with professors for their opinions.

Then I rehearsed until I could have done the pieces in my sleep (and sometimes did do so, according to Teddy). Still, I was always much more nervous about auditions than performances. Then the waiting and waiting for word, only—usually—to be disappointed, stressed me out even more.

Teddy could not have been more supportive. He would stay up all night to rehearse with me, even when he said my performance was already perfect. He went solo at any magic shows that conflicted with my schedule, while insisting I still accept my cut of the pay. And he never ceased to reassure me that my day would come, and come soon.

Teddy was not the kind of man I'd ever expected to find myself with. He was younger than me, for one thing—only by a year, but his unselfconscious exuberance sometimes made me feel like a wise older sister or aunt. Still, when he looked at me with his blue eyes so utterly open and adoring, my stomach fluttered like it did at the end of a performance that I knew had gone well and after which the audience members showed by their applause that they knew it too. It didn't hurt to be in receipt of envious looks, when we were out for dinner or walking hand in hand, from other women who recognized Teddy from TV. We spent Labour Day on Toronto Island, and as we rode the ferry back, he gave me a ring with two tiny rubies and told me he was more madly in love with me than he'd ever imagined he could be with anyone. When I told him I loved him too, his eyes welled up with tears.

Teddy returned to class in the fall. He had little time for anything aside from his schoolwork, which had become more fast paced and urgent, given that he was in his final year. By the time they got through the flurry of mid-term assignments and graded performances, he and his classmates were desperate for a chance to let off steam and unwind.

"I want to have a party," Teddy said. His roommates at the townhouse he shared near the college campus agreed to hold one there, but Teddy wasn't satisfied with a regular college bash.

"I want it to be truly memorable," he said.

"Everyone could bring a cat?" I suggested.

"Something meaningful," he continued. "Something that gets at the heart of the human condition."

"We all know the human condition is a tragedy," I said. "So tell everyone to come dressed as their favourite tragic character."

I meant it no more seriously than I had the cats, but Teddy gasped with excitement and kissed me. "Paula, you're a genius!"

Guests' interpretations of "tragic character" varied widely—from classical heroes (Herakles, Antigone), to comic book characters (Batman, the Hulk), to actual people (James Dean, Sylvia Plath). As one might expect from a theatre-school crowd, many of the costumes were over-the-top. There was an Oedipus with gory bleeding eyes, a Joan of Arc encircled by construction-paper flames, and an Ophelia who arrived dripping wet. She excused herself at intervals to renew the effect by stepping under the shower. I chose to be Dido, because dressing as her allowed me to incorporate a collapsible sword, one of Teddy's magic tricks, and appear to plunge it into my heart.

Teddy, to my surprise, dressed as Willy Loman from *Death of a Salesman*. I had expected him to choose something more flamboyant. Instead he wore a plain old brown suit and a fedora, and as he made his way among the guests he started mumbling to himself. He grew increasingly morose as the evening wore on until I found him sitting on the second floor landing, head and shoulders resting on the beat-up briefcase he'd been carrying all night, tears running down his face.

I suggested we go to my place for the night; he did not resist, but trudged the block to the subway station so slowly, with dragging feet, that I had to take his arm and keep coaxing him along.

"Teddy," I said. "You are not Willy Loman."

"Aren't I?" he said, stopping dramatically and opening his arms in a gesture of despair.

"No, you're Teddy plus a few too many beers."

He just shook his head sadly and followed me down the stairs. I gripped his elbow tightly as the train came speeding into the station, just in case he was thinking of following Willy's example. I tried to cheer him up on the train by demonstrating a new trick—swallowing the collapsible sword—but that only made a child sitting across from us with her father start screaming, and I had to apologize and show her how the sword really worked.

I had hoped I could just roll Teddy into my bed and let him sleep off his misery, but once we'd tiptoed down the basement stairs to avoid waking Mrs. Gaskell, Teddy sat down on my bed and dropped his head into his hands. "I'm scared, Paul," he said in a stage whisper. He'd recently taken to shortening my name to Paul.

I sat beside him and rubbed his back. "What are you scared of?"

"There's so much I want to do, so much I want to give, but what if I never succeed in reaching my audience. What if I end up dying without leaving anything behind?"

"Then your life will have had no meaning," I deadpanned.

But Teddy didn't laugh; he nodded and whispered, "Exactly."

I gave him a playful swat. "I was joking, Ding-dong. You really do love a good tragedy, don't you?"

Again, no smile; another nod. "It's the highest art form," he said. "It's big and noble. It gives meaning to suffering."

"I'm sure you'll find tomorrow's hangover very meaningful indeed," I said. I convinced him to take two Tylenol with a large glass of water before he passed out on my bed, his cheeks still damp with tears.

Alarmed by Teddy's state, I had pointedly remained bright and playful all evening, but underneath I was feeling resentful and annoyed. He'd been moaning on and on, feeling sorry for himself about something that hadn't even happened yet. He was still a student. Whereas I had graduated six months earlier and had yet to land a significant role.

I'd auditioned with great and incredibly naive expectations for a major production of *Mamma Mia!*, then for a number of smaller companies with equally disappointing results. I was cast in a life insurance commercial, appearing in one brief shot seated at a desk in a stuffy suit. No lines. When I described it to Diane, she realized she'd seen the commercial several times without even recognizing me. I made a few hundred dollars, paid in cash, appearing in a student film about zombie-vampires. When I asked the filmmaker how a vampire could become a zombie when vampires never die, he responded that it was the other way around: the zombie had become a vampire. Not wanting to lose the cash, I pretended that made more sense. Finally, there was one small role in a strange contemporary play about a skyscraper rooftop garden collective, which closed after only two shows due to lack of ticket sales. This was a relief, because the stage set gave me vertigo.

I had hoped by the end of the summer to have enough acting work to give up some of my returning piano students. Instead, to continue to pay rent and begin to pay back student loans, I had to take on quite a few more. I also started teaching a lunchtime drama club for teenagers at a nearby high school. All this teaching curtailed my efforts to book auditions—a full-time job in itself. I began to feel scared, panicked that this world I wanted so much to be a part of was going to pass me by. I hadn't felt this way since I was twelve, when my mother took my sister Miranda and me to see *Les Misérables*, which had just opened in Toronto.

It was not the show that had filled me with panic; quite the opposite, it thrilled me to my bones. Every second I found myself simultaneously watching from the audience and imagining myself on stage in all the best roles: Fantine, Cosette, Éponine. It was when I was back at home, poring over the program notes and humming under my breath, that I became afraid. The bio for the girl who played Young Cosette described a list of credentials and accomplishments I didn't even know were possible. And she was only nine! Throughout my years of elementary school, I had vied for and usually won leading roles in every class play or performance and any school-wide productions that came up, beginning with Cindy Lou Who in *The Grinch Who Stole Christmas* when I was in Grade 3, and culminating with the lead in a musical version of *Snow White* earlier that year. But it had never occurred to me to look beyond these in-school opportunities.

Young Cosette was a veteran of several Toronto stage productions and had even played the daughter of a single teenage mom on *Degrassi Junior High*. What's more, she'd been attending the Kleinburg School of the Arts since she was six, studying dance, drama, and voice. Voice! Did one actually *study* voice? I already knew how to sing. It wasn't like learning to play the piano—or was it?

My parents were also skeptical about the concept of voice lessons when I asked, but they were willing to let me give them a try. It was Mrs. Gaskell who referred me to a voice coach, and it was also Mrs. Gaskell who reassured me, on learning of my aspirations, that it was not necessary to achieve such success while still a child. In fact, she explained, most child stars burned out young and failed to continue with the same success into adulthood. It was much better to focus on learning and aim to get into a good theatre program after high school.

"Which will be much easier," she added, "if you already have your Grade 8 in piano."

Up until then, I'd been an average, rather plodding piano student. When I realized it could have a bearing on my future career, I got to work, and began advancing through the Royal Conservatory grades at a decent pace.

In my first year of high school I won the role of Abigail Williams in *The Crucible*. Later I would look back and cringe at the overblown melodrama with which I played that role, but my classmates thought it was great. I employed more subtlety the following year when I got to play Emily in *Our Town*. My voice teacher suggested I read the play in advance; before that it hadn't occurred to me that one should prepare for an audition in any way other than to show up with one's talent. I read the play and was so determined to play the role of Emily, no one else had a chance. I thought I understood Emily when she observed, from beyond the grave, that living people don't "realize life while they live it," because when I performed—when I was in the zone—all my senses were heightened, and I could see what others did not. When I-as-Emily mourned, "It goes so fast. We don't have time to look at one another," I didn't have to fake my tears.

The theatre program at York University was intense and nerve-wracking, especially as it meant auditioning again at the end of each year, before passing through to the next. I witnessed the heartbreak of those classmates who failed to make the cut and move on. I told them, and myself, that it could just as easily have been me, but deep down, I didn't believe that. How could I, when my dream was more real than my life? Emily and Medea were more real than Paula. It was inconceivable that I would fail, and as long as I was still in school, experience confirmed this. I went from success to success, always lauded by my teachers for my performance skills.

It was at York that I met Diane, in a psychology elective called Sensation and Perception I took to fulfill degree requirements. In a discussion about synesthesia, Diane and I found ourselves in a passionate debate about the colour of the letter *G*. (She, absurdly, insisting it is red. It's actually green.) The professor finally intervened, assuring us that the colour of the letter *G* would not be on the exam; the rest of our classmates simply looked baffled. After class, Diane suggested we settle the issue over a cup of coffee. We never did settle the issue, but we did become best friends. And at every one of my public performances, she gave me a standing ovation, no matter if she was the only one on her feet. We celebrated afterward with a meal at an Italian restaurant whose only signage was a giant three-dimensional nose sticking out over Yonge Street.

Teddy's exaggerated *Death of a Salesman* despair triggered the fear I'd been repressing since graduation, the worry that grew with each subsequent disappointment— that I might not succeed in the world of theatre after all. I always knew it was a difficult, nearly impossible business, that the odds were stacked against even the most talented person. Yet somewhere deep down, I'd continued to believe I would be an exception. As I lay awake all night listening to Willy Loman snore, I began to doubt.

IN MARCH, I landed the minor role of Birdie in a production of *The Little Foxes* that ran in a small downtown theatre for two weeks. Teddy came to see it opening night, then met me at the stage door afterward to go out for some food. Instead of congratulating me, he seemed distracted and bemused.

"What's wrong?" I asked, a flicker of fear in my stomach. "Was I terrible?"

"No, of course not. You were amazing. You were perfect. It was the actress who played Regina who was terrible. Why weren't you cast in that role? You would have been so much better!"

"You're biased," I said, though I very much agreed with him and was gratified by his observation. "Anyway, she was bound to get the lead role. The director is her sister."

As I said those words, it was as if a light switched on in my head. At York, we'd studied all aspects of theatre production, including fundraising, the everyday issues involved in running a theatre company, and all of the technical issues involved in lighting, stages, and sets. This approach acknowledged the fact that precious few performers have the luxury of sitting back and choosing from a multitude of plum parts. I'd finished school secretly thinking I might be one of those precious few, but another fruitless round of auditions in late winter for the summer festival season proved how unrealistic I had been. I finally began to realize that the only way to guarantee myself opportunities to play interesting roles would be to create those opportunities myself. Of course, this wasn't something I could do entirely alone.

"Teddy, what do you think of the idea of starting our own theatre company?" I asked him a few nights later, when he arrived at my basement apartment and flopped down on my bed with exhaustion. They'd just begun rehearsals for the graduating class's year-end production of *You're a Good Man, Charlie Brown*. Teddy was to play Snoopy.

"I think it's a great idea!" he said, bolting upright with

sudden energy. "Then we could play the parts we want, the parts we were born to play. I wouldn't always have to be the stoner, or the dumb jock, or, you know, the dog." It was a source of much frustration for Teddy that he was consistently cast in comic roles, both in school productions and in his few professional gigs. One glimpse of his goofy smile and they wouldn't even let him audition for serious roles. Personally, I agreed with his teachers, that comedy really was his forte; he just didn't have the shadow side an actor needs to inhabit darker roles. But I didn't want to burst his bubble; I needed his enthusiasm.

"I'm picturing a core group of five or six actors," I explained. "We'd have to be a self-directing ensemble, so we'd want really creative people who aren't just good performers, but good writers and improvisers as well."

"Writers! Yes!" Teddy said even more enthusiastically. "You know I've always wanted to write my own plays!"

I didn't know that, before that moment, but I agreed that it would be good to do original work if we really wanted to make a splash.

I set to work making plans, first identifying other candidates to join the company. My former classmate and co-star Anwar was my first choice, and Teddy agreed. Teddy suggested his classmates Greg and Tamsin, whom I'd come to know and admire. We rounded out the list with an actress named Aurelie whom I'd encountered at several auditions since she graduated from George Brown College.

Despite being extremely busy with his final weeks of school, Teddy, unbeknownst to me, was making plans as well. In the second week of May, the day after his final performance as Snoopy, he called me. He was so excited, he could barely get the words out, but even when he did, I didn't understand.

"I found the perfect place," he said.

"The perfect place for what?" I asked.

"The perfect place for our theatre company."

"We're looking for a place?"

Teddy paused for a moment, as if he were now the one confused, then said, "Of course. I've found one that's perfect, both for living in and running the company. But we have to go right now!"

I knew that Teddy had to move out of his student co-op at the end of the month. I didn't realize he was thinking about finding a place that would accommodate the company as well, and I felt quite taken aback. The prospect seemed far too expensive. But I agreed to meet him at Ossington Station, where we transferred to the northbound bus. The perfect place was a coach house. In behind a block of Victorian row houses, it backed onto the railway just north of Dupont Street. We entered through a regular-sized door near one corner, but nearly the entire front wall comprised huge wooden doors that could be opened, like a garage, presumably at one time to admit a coach. The ground floor was one open space except for a tiny room walled off under the stairs. The floor in this space was concrete, with several area rugs laid on to give the illusion of warmth. The walls and the inside of the large doors appeared to be insulated, but not, I suspected, very well. Although it was a warm May day, I shivered.

"Is it heated?" I asked the middle-aged Portuguese

woman who was showing the coach house on behalf of her elderly father, the owner.

She pointed to inadequate-looking baseboard heaters along three walls. "Electric," she said. "But depending on what you want to use this space for, you may not want to heat it too much in winter. The living quarters are upstairs."

We climbed the steep wooden staircase to the small apartment. There was a good-sized living–dining–kitchen area. The bathroom had an old-fashioned claw-footed tub, with two shower curtains you had to pull all the way around a loop to create a stall. There were proper windows in the main space, but the bedroom had only a wooden shutter, about three feet from the floor, that opened, alarmingly, to open space.

"That looks dangerous," I said.

The woman shrugged. "As long as there are no small children."

"It's fantastic!" Teddy said. "Look at the view!" It faced northwest, encompassing the railway stretching out in the distance. Teddy was nearly vibrating with excitement, but I was worried.

"Could you give us a few minutes to discuss?" I asked the woman, who shrugged and told us she would be downstairs. "The rent," I began, but Teddy interrupted.

"The rent is a steal," he said. "For all that space downstairs? And think about it. If we open the doors downstairs and set up chairs outside, we could even use the space for some performances."

"Only in the summer, when there's no threat of rain. The winters will be very cold. And with all electric heating, the hydro bills will be insane," I said. "And it's already a lot more than what you're paying now. Where will the extra come from?"

"But don't you get it?" Teddy said. He stepped in front of me and took both my hands in his. "Both of us would move in. If we combine the rent we're paying now, well, it wouldn't be too much more than that. And we'd be able to claim half of it on our taxes as company expenses."

My automatic inclination was to say no, it was too impractical, but Teddy's confidence and enthusiasm were infectious. I stopped and looked around, and to my amazement, I started to see it as he did. Suddenly, the possibilities seemed endless and my hopes soared. We went downstairs to tell the woman we'd take it. Teddy ran into the open area where he leapt with glee, clicking his heels together in the air.

We signed the lease. I made arrangements with Mrs. Gaskell to continue to meet students at her house until they went on hiatus at the end of June. Come September, I would have to make different arrangements, because as it turned out, she was planning to sell her house and downsize to a condo. She had been wanting to do so for some time but held off because she didn't want to turn me out. So instead of being upset by my move, as I had feared, Mrs. Gaskell was pleased. Everything was falling into place. It seemed like fate.

Then, two days before we were scheduled to move into the coach house, the unthinkable happened: I got a phone call from the Shaw Festival. One of their junior cast members, a young woman I knew and had auditioned with, had fractured her pelvis in a water-skiing accident, and they needed a replacement. She was officially cast in only a small, non-speaking role but was the understudy for small, speaking parts in three other plays. There was no guarantee of actually taking the stage in any of those roles, but there was a chance. And it was an opportunity to be seen by some of the most important people in the Canadian theatre scene. But it would mean moving to Niagara-on-the-Lake for the summer, abandoning Teddy and our fledgling theatre company.

"Not exactly abandoning," said Diane, who happened to arrive just minutes after I got the call. She'd come by to drop off a stack of folded bankers boxes she had left over from a move of her own. "You'd just be postponing for a few months."

"But what about the coach house?"

"Couldn't Teddy find a roommate for the summer? There must be students who could use a place," she said.

"I don't know, it might be too late," I said. "And Teddy will be devastated. He has so many plans."

"He'll understand. He should understand. It's a great opportunity for you."

All afternoon, as I packed, I played and replayed in my head possible conversations with Teddy. He was busy helping one of his classmates move, knowing that classmate would help us in return, but I expected him in the evening.

When I did finally tell him, I was taken aback by his response.

"You're not actually considering it, are you?" he said. He looked incredulous.

"Well . . ." I sputtered. "It is the Shaw Festival."

"But it's not even a real part. You'll be standing back-stage watching all summer."

I was very surprised that he would dismiss the offer this way. The chance to work with a prestigious company even as an understudy wasn't spectacular, but at least it was a step on the traditional ladder to success. Or so I thought.

"Paul, you're so much better than that! You're meant to play leading roles—Antigone! Cleopatra! Not to mention the roles I'm going to write for you. You're meant to be a star, not a prop." He told me about his teacher at Humber who'd spent twenty years at Stratford without ever playing anything more than a chorus member or a footman.

"Of course it's no guarantee of success," I said. "But there's no success without some chance opportunity, and so few people get that. Diane thinks it would be foolish to turn it down."

"Diane?" Teddy looked suddenly stricken. "You told Diane before you told me?"

"Well, I didn't mean to, she just happened to be here."

He sank dramatically into a chair, face in hands, sud-denly, utterly defeated. When he looked up at me again, there were tears in his eyes. When he spoke, his voice was hoarse. "I guess if this is what you really want to do, I can't stop you," he said.

"Teddy," I said, trying to put my arm around him. I felt terrible. His disappointment was palpable.

"I just can't believe it," he said. "All our plans. I never imagined we'd have to mount our first production with-out you."

I frowned. It hadn't occurred to me that Teddy and the

other members of the theatre company might proceed in my absence. I thought they would just postpone.

I tossed and turned all night. In the morning, I told Teddy that I'd decided to turn down the offer. The joy on his face was so overwhelming and intense that any doubts I still harboured melted away.

AS SOON AS Teddy and I moved into the coach house, we called together the colleagues who had agreed to join the company. The first order of business was to come up with a name.

"Something that declares who and what we are, that captures the essence of what we are all about," Teddy said.

"Which is?" Tamsin asked.

"Passion! Above all else, we are passionate about what we do," Teddy said. "That's why I was thinking Passionfruit. The fruits of our passion. The Passionfruit Theatre Company."

"Ugh," I said, wrinkling my nose with distaste.

"What's wrong with it? It's perfect!" Teddy said.

"It's terrible," I said. "It's mawkish."

We turned to the others to see whose side they'd take.

"It's a bit . . ." Tamsin struggled to find the word.

"Gooey?" Aurelie suggested.

Teddy frowned.

"She's right, Ted," Greg said. "It's a bit sentimental."

"Cloying," Tamsin added.

"Okay, okay!" Teddy put up his hands. "I get it. So, does anyone else have a suggestion?"

"What about something neutral, like Coach House Theatre?" Anwar suggested.

"Why would we want to be neutral?" Teddy asked.

"That's the last thing we want! We want something strong that conveys the extremes of human emotion, the peaks and the valleys!"

"The Psych Ward Theatre Company?" Aurelie said. The rest of us laughed, but Teddy was becoming exasperated.

"The Rollercoaster Theatre Company," said Tamsin.

"The Salt-and-Pepper Players," said Greg.

"No, no," Teddy moaned. "Those are so obvious and clichéd. It's got to be something smart and sharp, as well as meaningful."

"What about Gamut," I suggested. It was what I'd been thinking all along.

Teddy frowned, but the others cocked their heads with interest.

"As in runs the gamut?" Greg asked.

"In musical terms, gamut refers to the complete scale or full range of a voice or instrument," I explained.

"I like it," said Tamsin, and the others nodded in agreement.

"Yeah, it's catchy and original and it does actually mean what we want it to mean," said Anwar.

Teddy was the lone holdout. "That's true, but it's not a passionate name."

"Passion belongs on the stage," Tamsin said. "Not in the letterhead."

And so we officially became the Gamut Theatre Company. We went out for falafels to celebrate.

WE ALL FELT it was very important that Gamut's first production be an original. But no one was more surprised than me when at our next meeting Teddy told us he'd already been working on a concept.

"A tragedy of passion," was how he described it. "Like *Romeo and Juliet* but taken up another notch. Shakespeare on steroids. You see, Romeo and Juliet's passionate love is defeated by hate and prejudice and tradition. But what could be more tragic than love defeated by love?"

There were blank stares all around.

Teddy continued, "What if you were passionately in love with someone who dies, or you think they are dead. You mourn and eventually move on and fall passionately in love with someone else, only to have the first person turn up alive. You're now passionately in love with both, which destroys the possibility of passionate love with either."

There was silence for several seconds before Anwar spoke up. "I'm not sure, but I kind of think that's been done before."

"But I don't think it's really been done well," Teddy said. "Quintessentially, I mean. We need to make it edgy and new. Up to date. No, beyond up to date—prophetic!"

"You mean set in the future?" Aurelie asked.

"I hadn't thought of that specifically, but that's a possibility," Teddy said. "We need a specific scenario."

I had an idea. "There was something on the radio the other day about the founder of the first cryogenics company that deep-freezes people in the hope that they can be awakened once humans have figured out how to achieve immortality. I thought it was very funny, although they just mentioned in passing that in addition to having himself frozen on the occasion of his death, the founder had also frozen both his first wife *and* his second wife. I couldn't help wondering what will happen when all three are resurrected together. Who will be the legitimate wife?"

"It's perfect!" Tamsin said. "It's exactly what you want. What does he do if he's passionately in love with both of them?"

Teddy was unsure, at first, but was soon swept up in the wave of excitement and ideas that burst forth. As Tamsin and I discussed possible clashes between the resurrected wives, we realized we had the seeds of one of the play's key scenes, and began writing it down immediately.

Try as we did in those early writing sessions, we could not stop Teddy's grand tragedy from spiralling—deteriorating, Teddy would say—into all-out comedy. Then it deteriorated even further into, of all things, a musical. He finally gave in to this comic shift when he realized how well it was working, and in the end, his performance as the befuddled bigamist would be the best in the show.

We all had parts: Tamsin, as the first wife, was a sarcastic harridan to whose barbs Aurelie, as the sweet and harebrained second wife, was completely oblivious. Anwar played the slightly mad doctor responsible for thawing them out; Greg was a destitute descendant hoping his frozen forebears knew of some hidden treasure he was entitled to inherit. I actually had the largest role. I played a wise and ghostly narrator or master of ceremonies—ghostly because I had sensibly refused the promise of cryogenics back in my day and allowed my body to die—and doubled as pianist to accompany whichever character felt the need to burst into song.

The troupe worked on the play every free minute we could scrounge away from our various jobs: driving a taxi (Greg), waiting on tables (Anwar, Aurelie), and reading tarot cards (Tamsin). Teddy and I hauled out the guillotine and the giant needle and added several new tricks to our repertoire, including one in which he appeared to extract spiders from my ear. Our energy seemed endless. In addition to writing and rehearsing, and composing and practising the musical numbers, we built the set from scratch.

Opening night, for the play we'd finally agreed to call *Frozen Assets*, was at the end of July. We prayed there wouldn't be a thunderstorm; when we set up the fifty chairs we'd rented, only half fit under cover of the coach house roof. The rest spilled out into the alley. We had canvassed the neighbours a week earlier with an information flyer—and handed out lots of free tickets—to discuss any concerns about noise. It was a neighbourhood full of artists, and there were several artists' and musicians' studios along the alley, so we encountered nothing but enthusiasm for our venture. In contrast to the title of the play, the evening was ferociously hot. We set up electric fans in every available space and had to strain our voices to compete with the whir of the motors. Like clockwork, a passing train's whistle interrupted Teddy's climactic song—"I Can't Decide" to the tune of "I Will Survive." Even so, it was an inspiring success. Teddy was radiant, like a live wire crackling with energy. Everyone raved about his performance in particular, and I found myself feeling both proud and a little envious at the same time.

On the first night, the audience was mostly family and

friends of the cast members. My parents attended with equal parts curiosity and trepidation. They were already a little nervous after driving into the busy downtown core from their home in North York, a trip they didn't like to make very often. All those one-way streets and impatient taxi drivers! But when I found them after the performance, they were relaxed and beaming. "I even got all the jokes," my mother said with pride. "Well, most of them."

They'd expressed grave doubts when Teddy and I moved into the coach house, worried about our ability to pay the bills. Now my father did a head count and announced with satisfaction that we'd clearly made a bundle. (I refrained from pointing out that most of that audience—himself included—had received comps.)

I was touched that my sister Miranda also came, with her husband Gordon, despite being mere days away from giving birth to their third child, Harriet. Five-year-old Hunter and four-year-old Phyllis were having a sleepover at Gordon's parents', something Miranda was loath to allow since the time her mother-in-law let them play with a Ouija board.

"That was fantastic," Miranda told me as she gave me a hug. "The baby must have thought so too, because she's been kicking up a storm all evening. Look," Miranda said, pulling the cotton fabric of her sundress tight over her belly. Sure enough, there was a ripple of movement followed by a distinct bulge—ankle? elbow?—that moved from right to left.

Miranda and Gordon left soon after, as did my parents, but Teddy's family stayed to celebrate. Teddy was the youngest of six siblings. Aside from his sister Louise, all were married—Fiona to Michael, Colleen also to a Michael (henceforward known as Second Mike, like a book in the Bible, since Fiona's had turned up first), his brother Roy to Moira (henceforward known, at least to Teddy and me, as Moira-oind-Roy), and the eldest, Callum, to Yvonne. Each couple had at least two kids; all were in attendance that opening night. Teddy's parents, Clive and Vivian, were there as well.

Surprisingly, even without family members swelling the ranks, our audience for the second performance grew. Word of mouth spread, and despite a continuing heat wave, we had a full house on the third night. We decided to extend the run for another three nights before the forecast called for torrential rain.

After the final performance, we had a party in the studio that went nearly all night. When the last remaining guests, including several members of Teddy's family who had returned for the festivities, finally straggled off, dawn was breaking across the rail lands behind the downtown core, turning the gathering storm clouds deep red. Teddy and I went up to our bedroom, entwined ourselves together in a beanbag chair by the glass-less window, and stuck our bare feet out into the rapidly cooling air.

I was utterly exhausted, yet I'd never felt more awake, never felt happier. The thrill of performing and feeling the audience's response, the magical heightened consciousness that develops among performers when they are in sync and on fire—I felt drunk with it. It was all I'd ever wanted. After a year of disappointments, I felt, like the characters in the play, resurrected from a deep freeze. And it would not have happened without Teddy. I turned my face around to his and kissed him deeply.

"Paul," he said, "there's something I want to ask you."

He scrambled out of the beanbag chair and knelt beside it. "Paul," he began, then hesitated. "I think you have to stand for this," he said.

"Why?" I asked, teasing. I thought I knew what was coming; a huge smile twitched at the corners of my mouth.

"Because I'm trying to ask you to marry me," he said.

"Try harder!"

His blue eyes sparkled and he held up a finger. "Wait here."

He left the bedroom and ran down the stairs to the ground floor, where I could hear him rooting around backstage. When he returned, he approached the beanbag chair, put his hands under my arms and pulled me to my feet while I pretended to resist. He sank to his knees in front of me and tried to adopt a straight face as he began again.

"Paul, I love you more than anyone or anything in the world," he said, and then attempted a magic trick I'd seen him perform hundreds of times—producing a bouquet of flowers as if from thin air (actually from a contraption hidden in his sleeve). But this time, as the flowers burst into bloom, one of the blossoms, a plastic pink rose, popped off and hit him in the eye. "Aagh!"

I fell back onto the beanbag chair laughing. Teddy climbed on top of me and proceeded to kiss me.

"Wait a minute, I haven't said yes yet," I protested.

"You will."

SO THE SECOND production of the Gamut Theatre Company, at the end of the summer, was the Wedding of Paula and Teddy, and it was a production. Having the theatre in his blood, Teddy was no reluctant groom when it came to making plans. He wanted to be involved in everything, including the wardrobe for the entire cast. He arranged for us to meet up with Diane and Miranda, who would be brides-maids, and four-year-old Phyllis, who would be flower girl, for a shopping expedition in Kensington Market. At a vintage store for children—I didn't even know such a thing existed—Phyllis chose a yellow tutu with a skirt as wide as she was tall. She refused to take it off and left the store wear-ing it. (Miranda later informed me that there was a colossal tantrum at bedtime when she insisted Phyllis finally take it off.) Teddy then took us to another vintage store specializ-ing in 1940s-style women's wear. Diane and Miranda were skeptical, at first, but once they saw themselves looking, as Teddy put it, "like Barbara Stanwyck and Joan Crawford," all doubt was gone. Diane chose a lilac-coloured, knee-length wiggle dress; Miranda found a tailored, emerald-green skirt suit with padded shoulders that was pleasingly slimming. She hadn't had a chance yet to lose the extra weight from her recent pregnancy.

"Now for hats," Teddy said, and Diane actually squealed with excitement.

"Wait a minute!" I said. "What about me? I haven't even tried anything on yet!"

Teddy stared at me like I was crazy. "But I can't help you with that, Paul. It's bad luck for the groom to see the bride's outfit before the wedding."

I frowned. It was a surprising nod to traditional super-stition given the all-around unconventional nature of the event, but Diane and Miranda insisted he was right. I was on my own, and I felt the pressure.

In the course of making our plans, a lively sort of rivalry had sprung up between Teddy and me over who could come up with the most colourful and unconventional ideas. I had hired an ordained pagan minister to officiate; Teddy had convinced Greg's jazz accordionist sister to provide accompaniment. The ceremony would include a Greek chorus (Teddy's idea) and some ornamental sword-play (mine) by the male members of Teddy's family, who would all, including Teddy, be dressed in kilts and the full regalia of their Scottish ancestors. At one point I suggested stringing a series of trapezes from the coach house ceiling and conducting the ceremony mid-air. Teddy's eyes grew briefly wide with excitement before I burst out laughing and he realized I was joking. Deciding on food, however, was purely an economic matter. Cilla, a former classmate of Teddy's from Humber College, offered cut-rate catering services as long as we could round up a couple of gas bar-becues for her to use.

Everything was arranged, but a week before the wedding, I still had nothing to wear and I was starting to panic. I had to find something magnificent and outrageous that would top all of the other shenanigans. I was the bride, after all.

In desperation, I called Clara, the head costume designer at York University, and explained my conundrum. "I've got just the thing!" she said.

I took the bus up to my old campus the next day. Clara

led me into the costume storage room and with a grand "Ta-da!" pulled from the rack a glorious dark-red rococo Marie Antoinette period gown from a production a few years back. She held it up to me. "Exactly your size!"

I was so relieved to have the dress that I completely forgot about footwear until the day of the wedding. I ended up wearing flip-flops, but it didn't matter, as my feet remained hidden under the wide, floor-length hoop skirt, and only someone listening very closely would have heard them slapping against my feet. When Teddy first saw me emerge from the coach house stairway and begin my way down the makeshift aisle, he bowed down and touched the floor, eliciting guffaws of laughter from me and all of our guests.

My parents, undoubtedly, would have preferred a normal church wedding, but they'd already come to accept that Teddy and I were "different" from their more stolid and conventional daughter and son-in-law, Miranda and Gordon. My family participated in the celebration with wide-eyed amusement, collecting quirky stories about their "artistic" offspring to share with incredulous friends. Teddy's family was relatively impervious to the occasion's special charms, more concerned with the quantity of beer and spirits available at our makeshift bar.

Over the course of the evening, I noticed several neighbours and passersby peering in at the spectacle from the double doors of the coach house, propped open to release the heat, and joining in with the party when it spilled out into the humid August evening for sparklers and Cilla's barbecue in the alley. The festivities continued late into the night, long after my family left, a wilted Phyllis sound asleep in Gordon's arms and baby Harriet screaming in Miranda's. It was nearly dawn when I overheard one of our drop-in guests say, "What? This was a real wedding? I thought it was another play."

✳ CHAPTER THREE ✳

A WEEK BEFORE CHRISTMAS, THE CUSTOMERS dropping by the studio look ever more harried. I'm keenly aware of what a luxury it is to know that I can simply relax. With the bulk of my Christmas sales finished before December, anything I sell directly from the studio is extra. Nor do I have to worry about travelling. My newly retired parents bought a condo in Florida last summer and have now joined the ranks of the snowbirds who migrate south for the cold half of the year. Miranda and Gordon and the three kids are driving down for Christmas, and to go to Disney

World. They invited me to come along, but I declined. It isn't just the horrifying prospect of Disney World that deters me. Though they encouraged me to come, I know they'll have a much better time without me. They spent the last four Christmases walking on eggshells around me, so careful not to mention Teddy, or anything that might remind me of Teddy, or basically anything that could trigger any sad thought at all. Miranda was particularly annoying, speaking to me in a slightly louder than necessary voice—as if being a widow made me hard of hearing—and with an artificially upbeat tone. When Phyllis last year began to recall one of the magic tricks Teddy used to do for her, my sister put her hand over her daughter's mouth to shush her and hustled her into the bathroom for a talk to warn her off upsetting Aunt Paula. Phyllis knew I wasn't the least bit upset. Later, when her mother was busy in another room, she went ahead and asked me to explain the guillotine trick.

It is Miranda and my mother who are uncomfortable talking about Teddy; they maintain the fiction that they fear upsetting me for their own sakes. On balance they were probably relieved when I told them I was spending Christmas at Diane's, satisfied that it was my own preference. But I'm suddenly wondering if it wouldn't have been wiser to go. I don't want to; my heart and body scream against the prospect of separating myself from Héctor for a week. But that's precisely what makes my mind uneasy. What if I'm just caught up in a fantasy, and at Christmas of all times, when I know too well how hard reality can fall?

When Héctor calls at six, my concerns are immediately overwhelmed by desire for him.

"Paula," he says, "I'm on the College streetcar just past Bathurst. I don't usually use my phone on the streetcar, because it's likely to distract me and make me miss my stop."

"Your stop is coming up soon," I say, shifting easily into the rhythm of his banter.

"Indeed. There is a grave risk that I will be so engrossed in this conversation that I will continue riding long past Grace Street," he says.

"I see. You might get as far as Sorauren before you realize your mistake. What would you do then?"

"I would be in need of some comfort, I think," he says. "It's a long, cold walk back."

"I've been known to offer the odd bit of comfort."

"I would be very grateful for it, Paula."

My heart races when he knocks at the studio door ten minutes later. It's already dark outside and big wet flurries are falling fast.

"This time, I'm going to show you upstairs," I say.

His eyes widen. "Is it as sexy as downstairs?" he asks.

We nearly stumble on the stairs because we can't stop kissing. In the living room, I realize the curtains on my front window are still open, but when I reach up with both arms to close them, he presses up behind me and puts his hands on my breasts. He slides one hand down my belly and under my waistband just as I pull the curtains together. We find our way to the bedroom, which is still dark. My body feels raw, chafed in places from last night, but this only arouses me more, like we're closer to breaking through the skin that divides us. We both come quickly, intensely. I pull the comforter up over us, suddenly realizing how cold it is in the room. I always close the heating vent in the bedroom during the day, opening it only in the evening before I go to bed. We lie in the dark for several minutes.

"Are you hungry?" I ask finally.

"Famished."

We dress and walk up the street to Vicky's Fish and Chips and Thai Food, where we order sweet potato curry and spicy deep-fried oysters, then find seats at the narrow table that lines the front window. The world outside is invisible from our side of the steamed-up glass, where the air is thick with cooking oil, the fluorescent lights overhead harsh. What registers is his body beside me, each of us perched on a high stool, light points of pressure at shoulder, hip, thigh, and calf. I don't want to stop touching him; my body seeks constant contact with his.

When they call our number, Héctor carries the food over from the counter, and we eat voraciously, again, as if in each other's presence, we can't get enough of anything.

"Remarkable," Héctor says, looking at me as he bites into an oyster with a big, satisfied sigh.

"Are you referring to me, or the food?" I ask.

"Both," he says. "You have many similar qualities, actually. Though you're a little more talkative."

"The oysters may have had plenty to say before they were tumbled into a vat of hot oil," I suggest. "Who knows?"

"Only Vicky."

We ponder Vicky's many secrets in silence for several seconds, before hauling our stuffed bodies down from the stools and heading back out into the cold. Back at the studio, instead of going upstairs, Héctor sinks into the canvas chair by the front window and says, "Let's stay down here for a bit. The scents are so relaxing."

"How about some coffee?" I ask.

"That would be lovely."

I light a few candles and turn on the percolator behind the counter. When I turn around, Héctor is seated at my piano, opening the keyboard cover. I freeze, my body suddenly stiff with tension at the sight. I am struck by a memory of sitting side by side with Teddy at the piano on a particularly cold winter's night. I'd demanded he give me the green wool sweater he was wearing, lest the blood flowing into my hands grow too cold for me to continue playing. He removed the sweater and helped it over my head without a moment's hesitation, though it must have left him cold. When I sold the coach house, I wanted to get rid of the piano too. It was Diane who persuaded me to keep it. "Someday you'll remember that you love playing and singing," she said. It was too difficult to get it up the narrow stairs to my apartment, so the movers left it in a corner of the studio. I haven't touched it since.

Héctor launches into what can only be his ecumenical medley. The piano is slightly out of tune. I try to focus on making the coffee, but I can't help turning back to watch him. It is fascinating to see how he compensates for the missing fingers, even using what's left of the knuckle of what used to be his ring finger to play some keys. More amazing, he appears to be improvising on the spot this piano version from what he previously composed for the middle-school band. I recognize "It Came Upon a Midnight

Clear" and a Hanukkah tune I can't name. I can guess the religions affiliated with other sections until he shifts into what is certainly the theme from *The Pink Panther*. I laugh, then, and approach with two cups.

"Is that a religion?" I ask.

"It should be," he replies.

"You should be on YouTube," I say.

"I'm already on YouTube. With fingers intact."

I wince. "Oh God, I'm sorry."

Héctor chuckles. "No need to be sorry. It's a better image for the world to remember me by. I mean, that and the clips with snow up my nose, of course."

I invite him to stay the night, but he says it will be all over Facebook by noon if he wears the same clothes two days in a row. Although my body aches for him as soon as he leaves, I'm also a little relieved. So many thoughts and emotions are roiling up inside me. After washing the coffee things, I go upstairs, turn on my computer and go online. I find three videos of him performing, two with a small orchestra, one solo. The two with orchestra turn out to be from the same concert; the quality of both recordings is poor, though Héctor's virtuosity at the piano comes through clearly. It is the solo performance, however, that I find myself watching repeatedly, with its clear view of his face. He looks much younger, though the date on the video is from only four years ago. There is no sign of the grey hair that now graces both temples and extends along the sides of his head, or of the deep lines etched on either side of his mouth, like two sets of brackets.

I recognize the expression on his face: widest-awake

exhilaration. Some call it the zone. I've felt it myself many times. The realization hits me like a truck: for myself, losing the capacity to enter the zone was like losing one of my senses—of taste, maybe, a unique mode of understanding. How much greater must it have been for Héctor! It must have felt like his heart was being cut out as his fingers were cut off, so suddenly and irreversibly. Although the truth is, I still don't really know how it happened.

I don't understand how he can continue to play now, happily and with such grace. I start to cry, bitter, voluminous tears for his loss, and, as I've not allowed myself in years, for the loss of my own measly career.

I'M STILL UPSTAIRS in my apartment at nine the next morning when someone knocks on the glass door of the studio. Imagining it is the woman in need of more harmony, I try to ignore it, but the knocking persists, and I finally make my way down to find Diane peering in. I point to my hours-of-operation sign and shrug to mime my inability to change the rules. She leans forward and presses her face and mouth grotesquely against the glass, just like her daughters did last week, until I give in and let her in.

"I got in a fight this morning," she says.

"Not the crossing guard again."

"Oh, don't get me started on him!" She rolls her eyes. "No, this time it was a three-way fight: myself, this mother who is some kind of granola alt-rock-folk singer known simply as Em—I like to call her Ah-Em." Diane coughs to demonstrate. "And also the gym teacher."

"The gym teacher?"

"Heather something-or-other. Scary muscles. Anyway, the fight was all your fault. You and your paramour," she says gleefully. "Seems he's quite in demand."

"How can it be my fault?" I ask.

"I invited him for Christmas dinner," Diane says, then prompts: "This is where you thank me."

I roll my eyes.

"I had to fight for him. Seems Heather was planning a Mexican theme so Héctor would go to hers, and Ah-Em was counting on him so they could have a jam session and sing-along. But I made sure he knew *you* would be at mine. So of course he chose me—I mean, he chose you."

I should feel flattered, and I do, but I can't help wondering, *why has he chosen me?* Once upon a time I was confident of my ability to attract admiration and love, when I could command an audience's attention and hear their applause, but now it all seems so much more mysterious and uncertain. Do we really have free choice, or is there only fate? Should I feel reassured by the fact that Diane, always clear-eyed and unsentimental, has no reservations about my relationship with Héctor, or should I be alarmed that even she has fallen victim to his charms?

"Now, I need one more candle," she says. "For the crossing guard."

HÉCTOR CALLS ME at noon. "Paula, I have something urgent to ask you."

My stomach tightens a tiny bit: is this something real, or a joke?

"What is an Ugly Sweater Party?" he asks.

I sigh with relief and explain. "Christmas tradition. You have to wear the most humiliatingly ridiculous sweater you can find. Preferably with a seasonal theme."

"Is this from the Bible?" he asks.

"Yes," I say. "The wise men. You know, brainy, but no fashion sense."

"I see. Well, I've been invited to one of these parties tonight. My lawyer and her husband. They're also my student Tyler's parents. Would you like to come with me?"

"Sure," I say nervously. I can't remember the last time I went to a party. "But do you have an ugly sweater?"

"No. Unfortunately, I have both brains and impeccable taste," he says.

"There's a Salvation Army store just down on Queen Street. We can look there if you have time after school."

He arrives at my studio at three, classes having finished early today since it's the last day before the break. I hang the "Closed" sign on the door—to heck with desperate shoppers—and we head down the street.

It takes some digging, but we finally find a cream-and-brown homemade sweater with an image of a cooked turkey on the front. It's a little big for Héctor, but otherwise irresistible. For myself, I find a pink and red number, with fluffy poofs at the neck and cuffs, that looks distinctly like something Dr. Seuss's Whos would wear.

When we return to the studio, two women, seemingly mother and daughter, are peering in the dark window, cupping their hands over their eyes. I let these customers in and leave Héctor to tend to them while I run down to the basement and throw the sweaters in the washing machine.

Returning to the top of the stairs, I hear Héctor explaining to the women how the candles "work."

"It's all a matter of physics," he says. "The force of desire that is released when you light this candle actually changes the nature of reality at an atomic level."

The mother nods gravely.

Her daughter, browsing nearby, snorts. "You should make one for world peace then." But the mother, completely mesmerized by Héctor, buys six candles.

"Do I get a commission?" Héctor asks after they leave.

"On the contrary. You are going to pay my legal bills when I get sued for false—" I shut up because more customers are already entering the store. They continue to come, as people get off school and work for the day, and Héctor continues to regale them with stories of the candles' miraculous properties. I finally manage to stem the tide and lock up at seven thirty, which gives us just enough time to don our ugly sweaters and head out.

Tyler and his parents, it turns out, live in a condo on the twenty-fourth floor of a glass tower overlooking Toronto Harbour. We're greeted by a man dressed like an elf in a long green sweater with zigzag collar and cuffs, the bottom edge lined with bells. "Hi, I'm Walter," he says. He shakes my hand, but Héctor gets a hearty bear hug.

"Barbara's been trying to reach you," Walter says. Before he can explain, a woman in a matching jingly sweater taps Héctor's back. He turns and leans in for another hug.

"Paula, this is Barbara," Héctor introduces us. I recognize her from the school recital. She's tiny, with a neat asymmetric haircut and sharp, black-framed glasses.

"You haven't been answering your phone, Héctor!" she reprimands. "I've been trying to get hold of you all afternoon."

"I'm sorry, Barbara. What is it?" Héctor asks with a smile, so calmly, as if the matter at hand—a decision that will determine his entire future—holds no urgency whatsoever. It is my brow that contracts with concern.

"The judge who is reviewing your case has asked for a meeting," Barbara says. "Monday at eleven. He's in Ottawa, but we'll teleconference from my office."

"A meeting about what?" Héctor asks, again with maddening calm.

"I don't know exactly. He wants more information, details on a few points," Barbara says. "That's all they would say."

"That sounds reasonable," Héctor says.

"Actually, it's unheard of," Barbara says. "I've never known a judge to ask for a meeting like this before."

"Do you think it's a bad sign?" I ask. I can hear the alarm in my own voice.

Héctor puts his hand on my back, not looking at me, but drawing me slightly closer to his side as he says, "I think it's probably good news, Paula. If they want more information, they're not slamming the door, right?"

Barbara just smiles and raises her eyebrows, as if to say that if she does have an opinion on the matter, she's not going to share it right now, or not with me at least.

I'm suddenly struck by the fact that, as large as Héctor looms already in my own life, Barbara and Walter have known him longer and certainly know far more about the details of his case. They might see me as someone Héctor has dated a few times, someone temporary. Perhaps he has introduced them to other women, who have come and gone.

"The bar is over there," Barbara says, gesturing across the room. "It's help yourself."

I had thought, on entering the apartment and spotting only a handful of others, that we were among the first to arrive. But beside the bar are sliding glass doors to an enormous balcony where I can now see at least twenty people, mingling and talking. Despite several large heaters set on the balcony's perimeter, there is a fresh bite to the air outside. The sweaters, it turns out, though ugly and ridiculous, are also quite practical.

I recognize Laura, the school principal, and the singer-songwriter Em. Most of the guests seem to be parents from the school, and they all greet Héctor enthusiastically. The women are particularly happy to see him; I can feel their appraising glances as Héctor and I make our way together through the crowd. A small drone sporting a spring of mistletoe starts buzzing around overhead, and several women try to position themselves close to Héctor at the drone's approach.

"You have some very exotic traditions in this country," he says when Em explains the significance of the hovering drone, but he gamely gives her a peck on the cheek.

As more people approach Héctor, I find myself nudged farther and farther away from him until I'm right next to the chest-high concrete wall that encloses the balcony. I avoid vertigo by not looking over the edge. I'm already experiencing a strange sense of dislocation. It's as if I have at once gone back and forward in time, where all is both familiar and new. Sensations I was once accustomed to—the frisson of sexual jealousy, the constant physical awareness of the presence of a particular other even when not touching—are a shock to me now as they flood my senses after so many years, years during which, had I given it any thought, I'd have declared such feelings dead forever, impossible to reignite. I'd have dismissed them as something characteristic of youth, of naïveté.

Despite Héctor's confidence, I'm troubled by the conversation with Barbara. In the middle of the crowd, he looks entirely at ease (though I do notice him watching for the drone from the corners of his eyes and attempting to stay clear of its path). He seems to be at ease in any circumstance. Is it a gift, or an act? Suddenly he turns and looks directly at me, as if he's felt me watching him. We lock eyes for a moment and he smiles widely. I smile back instinctively, and experience a surge of intense longing.

It's late by the time we escape. We tried to leave earlier, but parents marvelling about the wonders Héctor had worked with their kids repeatedly detained him. I'm chilled from too long spent on the balcony and can't stop shivering, even once we're back at Héctor's apartment, huddling beside the space heater Mrs. Bartolamiol has forbidden him to possess.

Héctor makes a pot of tea and pours two shots of brandy, which we decide to drink in bed. Only then, drinking the warm liquid and wrapped in blankets and Héctor's arms, do I begin to thaw.

"Héctor," I whisper, nervous but determined to find out.

"Can you tell me what happened, with your fingers? Can you tell me why?"

I can't see his face clearly. We've turned off all the lights, chosen to drink our tea by what little brightness seeps through the thin curtains from the streetlights outside. He remains silent for several seconds and I fear I've made a mistake with my request, but when he speaks, it is with the same mischievous warmth he has when he tells all his stories.

"There is a congressman from Juárez, where I lived. His name is Martín Ochoa, but he's known as El Poeta," he says.

"He's a poet?"

"He thinks so," Héctor says. "He writes poems in honour of everything from Independence Day to National Garbage Collectors Appreciation Day. Then he reads them aloud in Congress, or at press conferences, before getting to the business at hand."

"Are they good?"

"They're terrible. They all begin with the weather at dawn somehow portending the importance of the day's commemoration."

"What kind of weather portends a happy garbage collectors' day?" I ask.

"Windy, I think," Héctor says. "Carries off the fumes."

"So this politician is ridiculed?"

"Not at all," Héctor says. "He's actually very much admired, for a number of reasons. First of all, he's quite possibly the only politician in Mexico who is clean."

"Clean?"

"Of any influence—narcos, army, police—he's not

beholden to any of them, and he's determined to keep it that way. Of course, that's easier to do when you're born with the kind of wealth he was born with. He inherited a tomato empire."

"Congressman, Poet, Tomato Emperor," I say. "That's quite an impressive business card."

"The second thing is, he's more than just flowery talk. He heads a committee to reduce crime through positive incentives, including promotion of the arts. He believes that art of all kinds—music, painting, poetry, dance—is an effective way to counter violence and corruption. He's established dozens of arts schools and programs in and around Juárez, often seeded with his own money. Including the academy where I was teaching before I left. Just a few advanced students, not like now. I could choose them entirely on the basis of talent. It didn't matter where they were from or if they could afford it. El Poeta's programs took care of all that. One of my last students was from a slum in Chihuahua City. He used to draw keyboards on the asphalt with chalk and practise on that when he didn't have access to a piano. He said he could hear every note in his head as if it were real. If he played a wrong key on the asphalt, he would hear it."

For the first time, I hear a wistful note in Héctor's voice, a hint of what he has lost.

"This congressman," I say, "you knew him."

"Yes, he sponsored a concert series in which I performed with the Juárez Symphony Orchestra. He admired my playing."

"Did he write a poem about it?"

Héctor laughs. "If he did, I never heard it."

"But you got to know him," I say.

Héctor hesitates, clears his throat. "Yes. His house—his mansion—is like Fort Knox. He's very smart. He refuses to have any police, or army, or professional security forces to guard him or his house. He knows how corruptible they all are. He hires every person individually, based on his own assessment."

"You mean whether they appreciate his poems," I say.

Héctor laughs. "I'm not sure if that's on the test, but whatever is works. His staff is known to be totally loyal and incorruptible."

"The narcos can't get to him."

"Yes."

"But why would they want to get to him?" I ask. "A politician who's big on art can't be that much of a threat to them, can he?"

"The arts programming is what gets the committee the most attention and praise. Even international politicians come to talk to him about it all the time because it's good press. It's one of the committee's other proposed 'positive incentives' that has the cartel worried. Other politicians keep promoting negative ways to crack down on corruption of local police being bought by the cartels, like longer prison sentences. Ochoa is promoting a complementary proposal to significantly increase police pay and benefits for their families. The idea is that this makes them harder to corrupt."

"And the narcos think this could work?"

He shrugs. "Maybe."

Tiny snowflakes have begun to fall outside, leaving droplets on the bit of the window I can see between the not-quite-closed curtains. I set my empty cup on the bedside table and settle closer into Héctor's side. I wish I could just fall asleep and pretend there is no more to the story, that it is something far, far away. But my mind won't stop racing.

"Somebody wanted to use you," I speculate, "to get to the congressman. Who?"

Héctor is quiet for several seconds before he speaks again. "He wasn't even a real narco, just a wannabe narco really. Young. I'd known him since he was just a kid, when I first moved to Juárez. His uncle was my landlord. Now he, the landlord, was the real thing. A big player in some gang associated with the Juárez cartel, but I had nothing to do with any of it. I just rented an apartment from him. Half of the tenants seemed to be extended family of his. He had sons—I don't even know how many—all set to follow in their father's footsteps. And then there was this one scrawny kid—the poor cousin, I guess. I don't know what happened to his parents. He lived there with his uncle's family, but he was always the scapegoat, the butt of their jokes. They used to send him down the building's garbage chute on a regular basis. They called him a *suricata.*"

"What's that?"

"I don't know the English. An African animal, looks like a cat that walks on its hind legs, long neck, no chin."

"A meerkat?"

"Yes, maybe."

"Why did they call him that?"

"Because he had a long neck and no chin," Héctor says. "And he ate bugs."

"He ate bugs?"

"Actually, I think his cousins made him eat bugs after they found out that's what suricatas do. But he cultivated it, a kind of act to impress people."

"Poor kid."

"I felt sorry for him too. I offered to teach him to play guitar because he told me he wanted to be a rock star. But he was useless, couldn't or wouldn't follow a simple instruction. He just wasn't very bright. And he was unpleasant, not some sweet, naive thing. Sneery and rude. And when I let him take a guitar I borrowed from the school to practise, he smashed it to bits, deliberately. No remorse. He thought it was funny.

"I didn't have much more to do with him after that, but I would see him around. As he got older, and the war between the Sinaloa and Juárez cartels was heating up, his cousins were making their way up the ranks, and he wanted desperately to do the same. Then there was an article in the paper about Congressman Ochoa attending a concert in which I performed. I guess he figured he knew me, I knew the congressman, here was his chance to get noticed, to prove himself. Ochoa is flamboyant, often in the news. It would have been a real coup for the poor cousin to be the one to take him down."

Héctor shifts his body beside mine. For the first time, I sense some discomfort on his part, in telling me these things.

"What did he want from you?" I whisper. "Did he want *you* to kill him?"

Héctor chuckles. "No. Even El Suricata knew that would be hopeless. He wanted me to get him inside the congressman's house, through the gates."

Héctor yawns. It's nearly two o'clock. I feel bad keeping him awake, stirring all this up, but I have to know.

"So he threatened to cut off your fingers if you didn't help him, and you refused?" I say.

"It was a little more civilized to begin with," Héctor says. "He offered me money."

"And you refused."

"Worse. I laughed," Héctor says. "I didn't take him seriously. The little brat who ate bugs. But then he came back with his cousins. Four of them."

I cringe. Maybe I don't want to know. "But why your fingers?" I ask. "Wouldn't it have made more sense to cut something else?"

"Something else!" Héctor says with alarm. He shifts as if to look at my face. "Like what?"

"I don't know . . . like your nose, or your ear or something. Isn't an ear more traditional?"

"Have you considered becoming a narco yourself, Paula? You might have a vocation."

"You know what I'm saying. Without your fingers . . . if you're no longer a pianist, you might lose access to this Poet guy. Didn't they consider that?"

"Consideration was not their strong point," Héctor says.

"I know, but still. Why did it have to be your fingers—" Unexpectedly, my voice breaks. I appreciate the levity Héctor has interjected throughout this difficult story, but suddenly it's too much. My eyes fill with tears.

Héctor kisses the side of my head. "Who knows? Maybe it was standard procedure to start with the fingers. Or maybe it was a kind of twisted revenge for El Suricata's failure to become a rock star. I didn't think he'd follow through, actually. First he just cut my thumb, that's why I have a scar there. I didn't think he had the courage to do worse. Then suddenly, chop! Two and a half fingers gone."

I shudder. "Okay. I think I've heard enough for now," I say.

It seems only moments later that Héctor drops off to sleep; I hear the moment his breathing shifts. But sleep continues to elude me. Careful not to wake him, I slip out of bed, find my phone in my coat pocket and take it into the living room. A search for Congressman Ochoa turns up a few articles that are in English. All, like Héctor said, praise his championing of arts programs to steer children away from lives of crime. There's even one about a Canadian MP who visited the barrios to see if such programming could have any application here. The stories of young people whose lives were transformed not by achieving fame and success, but simply through the love of music or art, make me feel desolate, like I've lost hold of something precious.

The battery is low, so I turn the phone off and climb back into bed beside Héctor.

When sleep does finally come to me, sometime after three o'clock, it brings a series of disturbing dreams. In the last, I am probing the contents of an enormous jar of Nutella with my fingers. I don't know what I'm looking for, except that the search fills me with dread. Finally, something hidden in the chocolate spread snaps hold of my index finger, something tight and metallic like a finger cuff, and I wake up with a soft yelp.

It's only seven thirty. Héctor is still sound asleep, but

I know falling back to sleep is hopeless for me, so I get up. Not wanting to face the Nutella jar after my nightmare, I get dressed and sneak downstairs, careful to leave the doors unlocked so I'll be able to get back in. The sky is just beginning to show some light when I reach College Street, but there are already quite a few people bustling around. The Pan European Bakery is brightly lit and oozing warmth onto the street outside. As I enter, a man is sliding a pan of fruit turnovers, just out of the oven, into the display counter. I buy several, which he puts into a large paper bag.

As I head back down Grace Street, people, mostly older women, are climbing the stairs to enter the church. When the doors open I can hear that the mass has begun. Suddenly curious, I slip inside. I enter the sanctuary thinking that I'll just sit on the edge of a back pew, away from the other congregants and unnoticed. But several other latecomers have done exactly that; the aisle seats are all taken. I must sit among them.

The service is in Italian. I concentrate on the words, to see if there is anything I can recognize; I attended a Presbyterian church with my parents as a child. I give up trying to understand and let the sounds fall to a less atten-tive part of my awareness instead, like soft background music. There is no organ accompaniment, just the voices, cracked and off-key but totally uninhibited. The pattern of their responses is so familiar and engrained. Not a flicker of hesitation or uncertainty. I follow their lead, standing when they stand, but I do not try to sing. In the nave of the church is a gigantic mural of Christ on the cross; strangely, he is hanging there dressed in white robes. Unlike the austere Presbyterian sanctuary of my youth, this church is full of efforts toward beauty, acknowledging perhaps that the sensuous is a possible opening to God. But it's as if they became afraid of the full implications of this recognition and pulled back, covered Christ's nakedness, settling for phoney frills, like the plastic flowers on the altar. Yet the congregants around me are participating in this service with intense sincerity.

About halfway through the service members of the congregation are invited to greet each other. "*Pace,*" says a woman sitting down the pew from me as she takes my hand. "Peace," says another older, more observant woman sitting behind me. A waft of fresh turnover smell reaches my nose from the paper bag on the pew beside me. When everyone moves out of the pews into the main aisle to line up for communion, I grab the turnovers and slip back outside.

Héctor's apartment is still silent when I climb the stairs. I turn on the coffee machine and take the bag of turnovers into the bedroom. He sighs and stretches when I sit down beside him on the bed and slide a turnover out of the bag.

"I've just been to mass," I say. He opens his eyes with surprise, in time to see me take a bite. The blueberry filling squirts against my upper lip; I have to lap it with my tongue, like a cat.

He smiles and lifts himself up onto one elbow. "Why did you do that?"

I hold out the turnover and he takes it from my hand.

"I wanted to see what it was like," I say.

He takes a bite of blueberry, moves as if to hand it back, then changes his mind, taking a second bite instead. I reach into the bag for a cherry one.

He swallows. "Was it like anything other than mass?"

"I can't even say whether it was like mass or not, as I've never been to a Catholic mass before. But it's funny, isn't it? How we go through life looking for similes."

"Wasn't it like a Protestant mass?"

"Not at all. There we get turnovers, instead of measly, thin wafers." As he finishes the blueberry, I offer him the second half of the cherry, and he takes it, greedily.

"So that's what the Reformation was all about." He licks cherry filling from his fingers.

"Um-hum. Pastries for the people."

He chuckles and kisses me. We never get to the coffee. We make love lazily, then, heavy with the sweet pastries, fall back to sleep. When we wake again, it is nearly noon and the apartment smells of the scorched coffee that has turned thick and tarry in the pot. I dump it and make a fresh batch. When Héctor opens the cupboard with the Nutella, I tell him about my dream. He laughs and closes the cupboard again.

"Don't you ever have nightmares?" I ask him, thinking of how deeply he slept, while I tossed and turned all night.

"Not about sandwich spreads," he says.

"What about, then?"

"I used to have nightmares about the flying monkeys," he says.

"So did I!" I say. "But seriously, don't you ever have nightmares about . . . it?"

"I used to, but I don't seem to have them when I'm with you," he says.

I would think he is just saying this to be charming, but he looks thoughtful as he says it, as if he's just realizing it for himself.

"We could go out for lunch," he suggests.

"I should go back to the studio. Open for a few hours at least," I say. "I have a duty to the desperate. But maybe we could do something tonight?"

"Okay. You know what I would like?" Héctor says. "I'd like to experience a typical evening with Paula. An ordinary evening doing whatever it is you usually do."

I feel myself blushing. In the years since Teddy died, I've become progressively more of a homebody, a hermit, holed up alone most evenings with a glass of cheap wine and a television box set, retiring to bed by ten. Most recently, it's been *Inspector Morse*, a set Diane gave me for my birthday.

"God knows why I'm encouraging you," she said at the time. "If I was a good friend, I'd sign you up for ballroom dancing instead."

"Lucky for me you're the worst friend ever," I said.

I'm embarrassed to admit to such a boring, spinsterish life, so I try to pinpoint something interesting in the experience. "British mysteries," I tell him.

"What is a British mystery?" Héctor asks dramatically, as if it might involve actually spying for MI6.

I blush more deeply. No choice now but to admit that I'm talking about watching television. But if Héctor is any less enthusiastic about that prospect, he doesn't show it. "I'll bring wine!" he says.

As it turns out, the program captivates Héctor; he is particularly intrigued by the cool, stiff-upper-lip manner in which various characters receive terrible news, even of a loved one's gruesome murder. Yet there is something of that very spirit in him, I think. I wonder if I could still enjoy watching crime dramas if I'd been through what Héctor endured.

CHAPTER FOUR

THE EUPHORIA OF OUR FIRST summer in the coach house evaporated quickly after the wedding. Proceeds from *Frozen Assets* had barely covered the cost of the rental chairs. Wedding expenses had been mostly covered by credit card, which we now, in addition to everything else, had to pay off. There was no question of moving forward with a new theatre production. We had to double down and earn some money first.

Teddy got a job as a tour guide at the Royal Ontario Museum. I resumed teaching the high school lunchtime drama club when school started again, but I had to scramble to figure out how to accommodate my returning piano students, who provided the bulk of my income. I didn't even own a piano. Luckily, I was able to locate a used one online; the owners didn't even want payment as long as we hauled it away, a task Teddy's brothers happily undertook, picking it up and delivering it to the coach house with Moira-oind-Roy's pickup truck.

I realized that the little room under the stairs on the ground floor of the coach house was the only viable space in which I could teach my students. Once winter came, the large room would be far too cold, and there was no chance of getting a piano up the narrow, rickety stairs to the second floor. We covered the concrete floor with a thick under-pad and carpet, which Teddy's parents were getting rid of, before moving the piano in. Teddy and I scavenged the neighbourhood the night before garbage pickup and found a small couch for those parents who liked to stay during their child's lesson. The room had to be warm and comfortable to keep students coming. With the baseboard heater on high and the door to the rest of the coach house closed, it would be just cosy enough to do the trick.

When the cold weather did arrive, the piano room was the *only* space that was cosy and warm. We took refuge there many a winter evening, seated at the piano side by side, singing anything and everything I could manage to plunk out in some recognizable way. It was an essential outlet for our creative energy, given the temporary lack of opportunity to get onstage and perform. As fall stretched into winter, we grew increasingly frustrated by our inability to make any headway with our acting careers. In February, I got word of an open casting call for *Wicked*, but when I mentioned it to Teddy, he grew visibly upset.

"Paul, you can't audition. Gamut needs you. I need you. I just know something will happen and we'll be able to move ahead soon. I can feel it."

Something did happen: Teddy's great-uncle Morris died. Teddy had only ever met Morris once, when he was ten years old and his family travelled to Scotland. Morris lived in what had seemed to Teddy at the time to be an ancient castle, though it was probably just a crumbling old house, with his life partner, Tom. The fact that Morris was gay and still something of a scandal in his small village and among older family members didn't even register with Teddy at the time. He simply recognized in Morris a true kindred spirit. The week they spent together was one of the happiest of Teddy's childhood. Though Morris was already in his mid-sixties at that point, he had every bit as much flamboyant energy as his great-nephew. Every day they subjected the rest of the family to a spectacle of some kind—scenes from *Henry V* or the musical *Oliver!* or *Singin' in the Rain*. For the latter, Morris actually taught Teddy to tap dance.

"I always meant to go back and visit him," Teddy said after hanging up with his mother, who had phoned with the news. "He seemed like someone who would live forever. It never occurred to me that at some point, it would be too late."

A few weeks later, even more startling news: Morris had left Teddy a significant sum of money in his will, along with a personal note. "Dear Teddy," the note read. "Thank you for the fabulous wedding photo you sent. It reminded me a great deal of that glorious week we spent together. Times have certainly changed; still, living a life true to yourself, as you are clearly doing, means you will always face obstacles and opposition. It is my hope that this gift will help to ease your way a little. May you and Paul have a long and blessed life together. Morris."

"Wow," Teddy said, wiping away tears. "You know he always wanted to be a professional actor too, it just never happened for him."

"It's funny that he calls me Paul," I said. "Just like you do."

"I likely signed the card to him that way, Teddy & Paul, when I sent the photo," Teddy said.

"Wait a minute," I said. "What photo did you send?"

"It was one with the full cast, so to speak," Teddy said. "I thought he'd appreciate that."

"Show me which one," I insisted.

Teddy flipped through our wedding album and finally pointed to a group shot in which we are surrounded by the whole wedding party, the chorus, the accordion player, the sword fighters, and a few random neighbours. Although Teddy and I are side by side, more or less in the centre of the photo, Teddy actually has his best man, Greg, at his other side, in a loose chokehold and they are both beaming at the camera.

"Teddy," I said, looking at him steadily. "Morris thought you married a man!"

"What?"

I jab my finger at Greg's face. "*Paul.*"

"That's impossible," Teddy said, peering at the photo. "It's totally obvious that you are the bride."

"No, Teddy, look. It's not obvious at all, not in this crazy bunch," I said. "I might just be the requisite Marie Antoinette. Every gay wedding has one."

Teddy stared at the photo in astonishment for several seconds before we both started laughing and couldn't stop.

Needless to say, we did not disclose our suspicions about Morris's mistake lest one of Teddy's numerous siblings and cousins contest his good fortune. After paying off all of our debts, there was still a significant amount of money left over, and Teddy knew exactly what he wanted to do with it. Our elderly landlord's health had been declining and his daughter had already warned us that they were planning to sell the coach house. It didn't take Teddy long to convince them both that if they sold it to us, we could all avoid paying real estate agents, and it would save them a lot of hassle. Teddy's inheritance made a substantial down payment; the bank, to my surprise, granted us a mortgage on the basis of my teaching income and Teddy's ongoing job at the ROM.

More financially secure, it seemed possible finally to press on with our next theatre project. We called together the other members of Gamut, minus Tamsin, who had landed a recurring role in a CBC television drama. Of course, though we'd held off auditioning elsewhere ourselves, we could not have expected her to turn down such a role for the sake of what might or might not happen with us. I began the meeting by suggesting that our next logical step would be to seek funding for a larger production of *Frozen Assets* at a bigger venue.

"But we can't do the same play," Teddy protested. "We have to show that we are progressing, demonstrate our range. We can't get stuck doing only comedy. We've got to aim higher, with something more serious."

To my surprise, the others agreed. I felt a little bit stung. Though we'd all collaborated on the script, I secretly thought of *Frozen Assets* as my own, since I'd come up with the original idea. I firmly believed it had greater potential than our short stint the previous summer.

"I take it you have a specific idea in mind," Anwar said to Teddy, who grinned.

"I do," he said, shifting forward to the very edge of the couch. When he grew animated, he used a lot of hand gestures that reminded me of his magic tricks, as if he were conjuring something. "Basically *Othello* but with a modern psychological twist. You see, in Shakespeare's version, Iago's evil scheming strikes a chord with Othello's own insecurity, hence the tragedy. But imagine how much more intense it would be if they were one and the same."

He paused for dramatic effect.

"The twist is, Iago and Othello *are the same person*," Teddy said. "Othello with multiple personality disorder."

I frowned, then quipped, "Why not make Desdemona one of the personalities too. Then Othello/Iago/Desdemona would have to kill him/herself?"

It was Teddy's turn to frown. "It's not supposed to be funny," he said.

"Not *supposed* to be but—"

Everyone looked confused; it slowly dawned on me that

the others did not consider the idea as patently ridiculous as I did.

"It's a very interesting idea," said Aurelie.

"I like the idea of taking a classic and completely radicalizing it for modern times," Greg said. "It could become part of our mission as a company."

"Yes!" Teddy said, pumping his fist in agreement.

"But how will the audience know when you're being Othello and when you're being Iago?" I asked Teddy, presuming he meant to play that double role himself.

This time Teddy looked not just confused, but a little hurt. "What do you mean, how will they know?" he said. "By my *acting!*"

While the others pitched in with helpful ideas of their own, I could think of nothing but objections.

"It might not go over very well," I said, "a blue-eyed Scotsman playing Othello?"

Teddy thought for a moment. "Well, I think that would be one of the psychological aspects. The Iago personality colonizing, in a sense, the Othello personality," he explained.

My frown only deepened. I felt sure that if Tamsin had been present, she would have backed me up, but the others were clearly under Teddy's spell, nodding avidly at his explanation. I knew Teddy could be persuasive; I'd just never seen it from the outside before, because previously I'd always been among the persuaded. As my own misgivings grew, the others only became more enthusiastic. Finally, Anwar expressed some concern about the shortage of parts, if Teddy was to take both leading roles.

"Well, there's Desdemona," Teddy said, nodding toward

me. "We could adjust things, consolidate the other parts into three characters, or play multiple parts."

"Aurelie should play Desdemona," I blurted.

"What?" Teddy looked very surprised.

"Aurelie would make an excellent Desdemona," I said.

Aurelie smiled so hopefully that Teddy couldn't object, though I knew he wanted to play opposite me. When he asked me privately that night why I didn't want to play Desdemona, I stuck with my explanation—that I thought Aurelie should have the opportunity. I didn't tell him that, in fact, I had grave doubts about the whole play.

As the play developed, my doubts only grew. At times, I was tempted to just wash my hands of it, refuse to play any role at all. But we were supposed to be a collective, which sometimes meant compromising one's own ego; I didn't want to be the childish one who turned her back as soon as something didn't go her way. Unlike Tamsin, I had no other offers of work on the table that might have excused me. So I went along, and tried to give suggestions that would give the whole muddled concept of the play the tiniest bit of clarity. Increasingly, the others received these suggestions as unhelpful criticism, so I began keeping my thoughts to myself.

When we opened the coach house to an audience again, almost a year after the premiere of *Frozen Assets*, expectations were high. Nearly everyone present on opening night had seen our first production and come back for more of the same. Their confusion and disappointment were palpable by the time we reached intermission. I overheard one conversation when I slipped out from backstage and upstairs to our apartment to use the washroom.

"Maybe it's all a setup and it'll turn funny in the second half," a man said.

"Maybe it *is* funny and we just don't get it," a woman replied.

As the play reached its climax in the second half, someone came to that exact conclusion. Othello/Iago had Desdemona in a stranglehold. Teddy was flipping his head from side to side as he alternated ever more rapidly between his two extremes—angel and devil—of personality, when there was a loud, unmistakable snicker from the audience. For a moment, Teddy froze; I could see the sudden panic in his eyes from where I stood behind the curtain just a few feet away. Then he managed to pull through, to finish Desdemona off and bring the play to its close, but I already knew he was devastated.

TAMSIN RETURNED FOR the Dr. Othello and Mr. Iago post-mortem. (Her CBC drama character had died in a freak curling accident.) She had seen the production, so I was hopeful she would back me up on my observations. There was a part of me that just wanted to scream, "I told you so! I told you so!" at them all. But after holding and comforting Teddy all night as he sobbed like a child over his humiliation, I knew that would only make things worse.

Before Tamsin and I could say anything, Teddy launched into a teary apology to us all. "It's totally my fault," he said, then began a litany of details he felt he should have handled differently: he should have changed this line to that, used one gesture instead of another, and so on. He'd written all of these details down, filling several pages with notes, while obsessing about the failure in the weeks since the production.

I sighed. "Teddy, I'm not sure the problem lies in all these details. I think it has more to do with larger choices about the production as a whole," I said.

Tamsin nodded in agreement. "People came to this play expecting something more like the last one," she said.

"But we don't want to just meet expectations," Teddy said. "We want to explode them."

"There are explosions, and then there are explosions," Tamsin muttered.

"The concept of this play," I said, "was very, very ambitious."

"I am ambitious!" Teddy said. There was a new edge of anger to his voice.

"Of course. We all are," I said, trying to think of a way to soften my criticism. "Maybe it was too big a leap at this point in our development. We need to begin with our strengths and take it more slowly."

"And you know, our greatest strength at this point is really *Frozen Assets*," Tamsin said. "We should think about taking that to another level, a bigger scale."

My triumphant inner imp cooed another "I told you so!" while the others began murmuring in agreement as they mulled it over. Only Teddy looked like he might cry again.

"It is a good idea, Teddy," I coaxed him. "Surely the best one for us right now."

"But that could take forever, to find funding and a bigger venue." Teddy threw his hands up in a dramatic gesture of despair. "I just want to act."

"It's true," Tamsin conceded. "It will be a long haul. Probably next year at the earliest. What if we did another play here in the meantime. Something more modest—"

Teddy tried to break in with a protest, but Tamsin shushed him and continued to speak.

"By modest, I refer only to scale, not quality. What if we chose one of the timeless classics, and did it straight? Spare ourselves the stress of writing and just focus on great performances. Then people would have at least some idea of what they were coming to see."

This was met with a chorus of agreement from the others, though Teddy still looked a bit lost. Aurelie wanted to do *The Importance of Being Earnest*; Anwar wanted *Heartbreak House*. But eventually, the only way we could win Teddy over was by agreeing that the choice would at least be another tragedy.

"Do you have a specific tragedy in mind?" Tamsin asked.

"Yes," he said, and looked at me. "*Antigone*. Paula would be a spectacular Antigone."

I was unexpectedly moved by his suggestion and felt more than a little bit sheepish, given my previously traitorous thoughts. The others, to my shame and glee, were immediately in favour of the motion.

I had always wanted to play Antigone. I threw myself into it, allowing my hopes and fantasies about finally being discovered to soar again, as they had back when I was a student. Rehearsals went remarkably well, given the previous friction. Maybe it was because we'd stopped trying to outdo the text, were less distracted by gimmicks and extras. When I performed, I felt that pure flame of passion shining through me again that I hadn't felt in a long time. There was a moment, when our coach house audience rose to their feet and applauded, when I believed everything possible again, just like I had at eleven, imagining myself centre stage at *Les Misérables*.

Yet nothing changed. We got a good review in a local weekly—one that specifically praised my performance—but after a week, the size of the audience dwindled to a handful, and it seemed prudent to end the run. Nothing had changed. Our one hope remained with the remount of *Frozen Assets*.

We found a venue, a two-hundred-seat theatre downtown near Queen and Bathurst, for a week-long run the following May. But then Tamsin announced her permanent departure from Gamut. She'd landed roles in not one, but two major American films that would be shooting in Toronto over the winter, and she just wouldn't have time for anything else. We tried to be happy for her sake, but it was only natural that we were envious. It also left a hole in the cast. Aurelie wanted to take Tamsin's place as the caustic first wife, so we recruited Justine, another former classmate from Humber College, to fill the vacated second wife role. We worked long and hard getting ourselves up to speed with both old and new roles and adapting our performance to the new venue.

Nearly everyone who saw the first production in the coach house bought tickets to the second, which should have been a good thing. But despite all our efforts, we just couldn't match the electric excitement of the first run. Aurelie didn't have Tamsin's comic timing and appeal; her first wife came off as merely whiny and shrill. Justine was a bag of nerves and stumbled several times with her lines. But the biggest disappointment was Teddy. It was impossible to put a finger on exactly why. He went through all of the same motions, with the same frenetic level of energy he brought to every role, yet it still fell flat. His heart wasn't in it.

With each performance, I grew more frustrated. It seemed to me that Teddy wasn't even trying. The audience's response was polite, but muted, more muted, I thought, on each subsequent night. After the curtain fell on our final performance, we decamped to the green room in silence. All of us, that is, except Teddy.

"So who's for drinks at Fionn MacCool's?" he asked. "We should celebrate."

"I don't know what we have to celebrate," I said bitterly. I wasn't looking directly at Teddy, but could see the confusion on his face in the mirror.

"What do you mean? We just finished a successful run," he said. "What's not to celebrate?"

"'Successful' is a bit of a stretch," said Anwar. There were murmurs of agreement from the others.

"Well," said Teddy—I watched him in the mirror as he threw up his hands—"maybe we should have tried something new, instead of looking backward and doing something we'd already done."

I stood and turned to face him. "So that's what this was— you didn't want to do *Frozen Assets* again, you didn't get your own way, so you decided to sabotage the whole thing!" To my astonishment, I realized I was shouting. I'd never shouted at Teddy in private, let alone in front of others. My astonishment was nothing compared to the shock on Teddy's face. The others squirmed with discomfort.

"Sabotage?" Teddy said incredulously.

"Oh, come on! You were like a sleepwalker out there; you were barely going through the motions," I said. I knew I was going too far, exaggerating wildly, but it felt good to hurl my frustrations on someone else. At least, it felt good for a few moments, then it felt worse than ever.

Justine and Anwar slipped out of the room, but Greg and Aurelie remained.

"Come on, Paula, that's not fair," Greg said. "There was nothing wrong with Teddy's performance. The play just didn't click as well this time."

"I can't believe you think I would . . . sabotage us," Teddy said. He still looked confused, like he was trying to understand all the implications of my words and couldn't. But there was an edge of anger there as well.

I turned away and sank back into the chair. "I'm sorry, I didn't really mean that," I said with my face in my hands. But I only backed down and hid my face because I was so embarrassed about losing my temper and felt the need to defuse the situation. I tossed and turned all night with the anger and resentment that continued to roil through my body. It was dawn before I finally fell asleep, and when I woke mid-morning, Teddy had gone out. Wanting a sympathetic ear, I got on the subway and headed east to visit Diane.

"What are you doing here?" Diane asked, with her usual tact, when she found me unexpectedly on her doorstep.

"Why wouldn't I be here?" I said. "Maybe I enjoy visiting you."

"Do you see that?" She pointed to a garbage bag beside

the door. "There are three hundred dirty diapers in there. And this?" She rubbed at a crumbly stain on her knee. "This baby barf is at least three days old. Trust me. No one enjoys visiting me these days."

Diane had given birth to the twins in May, just two days after Juniper's first birthday. "Not just an accidental pregnancy," she liked to say, "a fifty-car pileup pregnancy."

I followed her into the kitchen.

"I can offer you tea or breast milk," Diane said. "Or tea with breast milk."

"I'll pass, thanks."

"Your choice. So, tell me why you're really here," she demanded.

"To do your laundry?" I suggested.

"I'm going to take you up on that," she said. "But you still have to tell me." With a baby on each arm, she made her way around the house pointing with her head at every blanket, cloth, or piece of clothing that needed washing.

I sighed. "Teddy and I had a fight about the play, which was a flop," I said as I gathered the indicated items into a laundry basket. Diane had been understandably excused from attending this time. "What's worse, it happened backstage, with the others in the room."

Diane gave a low whistle, which Juniper immediately tried to imitate.

"I always looked down on couples who were willing to fight with an audience. It's embarrassing for everybody. So undignified."

"Dignity is overrated," Diane said. "Can you take off my pants?"

She lifted the babies away from her hips so I could slide her track pants down and add them to the load of laundry I'd collected. I went downstairs and put the clothes in the machine in the basement. When I returned upstairs, Diane had managed to put on fresh clothes, although the tag on her T-shirt was visible under her chin.

"What was the fight actually about?" she asked.

"Teddy didn't really want to do this play again. So he pretended to go along but gave a mediocre performance, just to prove us wrong."

Diane frowned. "I find it hard to believe Teddy would do that."

"You didn't see the play."

"I had three excellent reasons," she said. "But even if he wasn't entirely on his game, maybe it was subconscious. It can be hard to fake enthusiasm if you don't really believe in something."

"He's an actor. It's what actors do," I said. But as much as I wanted to hold on to my anger, which felt simpler than frustration, I knew she was probably right. "All right," I conceded, "so maybe he didn't do it intentionally, but denying the possibility that he even did it subconsciously just makes it worse. The way I see it, failure can be useful if you see it clearly and learn from it. Denial is a dead end."

"I don't know, I think denial has its uses," she said, as she pushed a baby into my arms. "Especially in a business like acting."

"What? You mean it's obviously hopeless, so I should just pretend it's not and get on with it?"

"Exactly."

"I'm not just talking about acting, I'm talking about us, Teddy and me."

"Whoa, wait a minute, Paula," Diane said. "Don't go confusing professional differences with marital difficulties. You and Teddy both have big actor-egos. You're bound to clash when it comes to your work."

I frowned. "I don't have a big actor-ego."

"And I don't have stretch marks," Diane said. "Your marriage is about a lot more than a working partnership, isn't it? I mean, so Teddy is unrealistically optimistic. Isn't that what you love about him?"

I did once love the great optimism he harboured for both of us, but that was before I began to understand how unrealistic it was. Still, Diane was right about confusing career and marriage, and I felt suitably admonished.

I rehearsed my apology on the subway ride home, and thought maybe if I made something nice for supper, we could at least begin to move on, to find a way forward. But when I entered the coach house, it was already filled with cooking smells. Teddy had prepared an elaborate Chinese meal that included spring rolls from scratch. He had also bought fortune cookies, then extracted the fortunes with tweezers and replaced them with personalized love notes. Unable to wait until after the meal to show me this trick, he handed me a cookie as soon as I came in. The fortune, when I broke it open, read, "I wish there were olives in Chinese food, because *olive you*."

"What's all this for?" I asked.

"To say sorry," Teddy said.

I sank into a chair and surveyed the elaborately set table.

He'd even bought flowers and arranged them in a vase. In fact, he must have bought the vase too, because we didn't have one when I left. Any remaining bit of anger disappeared in a rush of affection for Teddy.

"Look, Paul, I think we're both disappointed with where we are in our careers right now. We need to make sure as we move forward that we do what's right for both of our careers, that we really talk things through, just the two of us, before we commit to the next production."

It was unclear when, and if, that production would ever come about. Our box office takings for *Frozen Assets* had covered costs, but only just. There was no profit to invest in future projects of any kind, comedy or tragedy; the very future of the Gamut Theatre Company was in doubt.

Meanwhile, it was summer. With schools closed and most of my piano students on holiday, we needed to launch another season of magic shows to make ends meet. Teddy seemed to have an unending supply of energy, performing day after day for crowds of screaming children, while still managing a few shifts at the ROM each week. But I felt increasingly drained. I lay awake night after night, unable to sleep, and my exhaustion accumulated. I was so tired I started making mistakes during the magic shows, and in the last week of August, at one of our largest birthday parties yet, I messed up the guillotine trick.

Teddy had expressed concern days earlier about the shadows under my eyes and my haggard look; now he insisted I take a break. He would do the last few shows we had scheduled for the summer on his own. Miranda and Gordon had rented a cottage in Muskoka, so I decided to take a bus north from the city and join them for the remainder of the week and through the weekend.

After several days of sitting by a peaceful lake, and nights teaching Phyllis and Hunter silly songs by a campfire, I was sleeping again and much more relaxed. I arrived home late Monday afternoon. When I came into the kitchen there was a bottle of Prosecco in the sink packed in ice.

"What's this?" I asked.

"We're celebrating!" Teddy said and kissed me. His eyes were as bright as I'd ever seen them.

"Celebrating what?"

"I got a role in a TV show!"

I stared at him, not understanding, "What?"

"It's a new CBC drama about time travel. I play a magician. It's a small role but ongoing. I'll appear at least briefly in every episode, so it'll be a lot of work."

"But . . . how?"

"Greg called on Wednesday, just after you left. He saw the casting call that said they wanted someone with real sleight-of-hand skills. The audition was Thursday—"

I interrupted him. "The audition?"

"Yeah." Teddy stopped suddenly, confused.

The calm and serenity I'd found at the cottage disappeared in an instant, replaced by slow-burning, red-hot fury.

"You auditioned," I said, trying to keep my voice from shaking. "When I wanted to audition for *Wicked* last year, you talked me out of it, said we had to focus on Gamut."

"But that was different. I mean *Wicked*, those roles always go to really big-voiced singers," he said. "Whereas this, Paul, I was a shoo-in! How many actors do you know who can do sleight of hand like me?"

"So the real reason you told me not to audition was because you didn't think I had a chance?"

"No, I didn't mean—"

"What happened to being committed to work that's good for both of us?" I said.

"But this will be good for both of us!" he said, lighting up with a smile again. "I'll be making so much more money! More than your teaching and my job at the ROM combined!"

"Great," I said. "So you won't object if I quit teaching then?"

"Oh," Teddy said, surprised and then flustered again. "Well . . . I guess . . . if that's what you really want to do."

"Good, because I think that would be good for *both* of us," I said.

"Paul, I thought you'd be happy for me," he said, his brows drawn together, like he might cry.

"I am, Teddy. Absolutely ecstatic," I said. I ran back down the stairs and let the coach house door bang shut behind me.

I DIDN'T ABANDON my piano students after all, but I did resign from the daily drama club, as it was the most problematic in terms of scheduling conflicts with possible auditions. I had decided to put all my energy into advancing my own career. At first, it seemed to work. I was motivated and focused. But when Christmas arrived without even a single callback, that energy started to wane.

Teddy, meanwhile, was greatly enjoying his role in the television series *Chronology*. His character was a kind of soul guide whose sleight-of-hand skills were more than just tricks; they were metaphors for otherworldly manipulation in the lead character's life. He nearly always appeared mysteriously, in darkness, his blue eyes lit in sharp, unnerving contrast. Once again, when we went out, people started recognizing him. On one occasion someone even asked for his autograph.

"You should be careful," I said to him bitterly. "You might become too closely associated with the quirky magician character. No one will want to cast you as anything else." I felt gratified by the worry that crossed his face.

With a new round of casting calls for the summer festival season approaching in late winter, I had to decide whether to try out again for the Shaw Festival. What if they remembered me, remembered that I had turned them down three years ago and held it against me? The thought of trying again made me thoroughly miserable, but in the end, I decided I had to take every chance I could get, so I went to the audition. When I stood up in front of the panel making the call, a wave of fear went through my stomach. I'd never experienced stage fright before. Nervous excitement, yes, but that was always just excess energy that channelled smoothly into my performance as I got underway. I told myself the fear would dissipate as I began my monologue, but it didn't. It spread into my limbs, down my legs, until I could feel my knees trembling. I continued to recite by rote for several seconds as I thought, *I'm not going to be able to do this.* My voice cracked finally; I burst into tears and ran from the room in a panic.

How could I have been so stupid as to let Teddy convince me to turn down Shaw's original offer? Had he really believed the offer wasn't worth my while, or had he just said that so I wouldn't go and mess up all his great plans? Why had I listened to him? I found myself fantasizing in great detail what might have happened if I had gone to Niagara-on-the-Lake. I might have had the chance to play one or more of the roles I was understudying. I might subsequently have been cast in something bigger, even a lead, and never become mired down with Gamut. I might not have married Teddy. What would my life have been like then? What would it be like now if he were suddenly, magically gone?

TEDDY'S SCENES IN *Chronology* were always set at night, so he often worked until well past midnight. His character proved popular with viewers. So as the season progressed, the writers expanded his part, and he was away from home even more. I became used to spending most evenings alone once my students left.

In April we received an invitation to the opening of one of Tamsin's films. I barely gave the card a second look, but Teddy thought it was important to show our support.

"I'm filming Friday, so I can't go," he said. "But you could go, couldn't you, Paul? You could represent us both."

I shrugged. "I've got nothing else to do," I said. My last student on Fridays finished at five.

"Please tell her I'd be there if I could," he said. "I'm sure she'll understand."

"Of course," I said. "You successful people understand each other."

Teddy frowned, but did not respond. He had to leave or he'd be late for work.

Friday arrived and I felt strangely energized about attending the opening and the reception that was to follow. I made a point of dressing up in a skirt and a top that dipped low in the back, baring my shoulders and spine nearly to the waist. The reception was at a hotel just up the street from the cinema. I took a martini from a tray proffered by a waiter just inside the door, and downed more than half in the first few minutes. I had always hated such events and usually made my appearance as brief as possible before slipping out. This time I stayed, sipping a second martini and a third, engaging in conversations with people I didn't know. I wasn't actually enjoying myself, but I felt a sense of urgency, as if there were something there I needed to find and couldn't leave until I did.

The crowd had begun to thin when I sat at the bar and accepted a fourth drink. A man in his mid-fifties sat beside me. I knew who he was. His name was Mark Slate, and he'd been one of the producers on the television series Tamsin had had a role in a year or so earlier. I'd caught his eye briefly earlier in the evening and had thought in that moment that he was clocking me, though I wasn't sure. He'd removed the jacket of his tailored suit and rolled up his sleeves, showing off what looked like a very expensive watch—though it could have been a glaring fake, for all I could tell.

As we chatted, I became aware of the potential opportunities on offer should I reciprocate his interest. I'd encountered such chances a few times when I was a student, yet always disdained them, and those who did give in to the temptation. But this time—perhaps it was the gin haze or my desperation for something to change—I just couldn't tear myself away. Mark managed to touch my bare back several times, and despite myself, I shivered. He raised his hand at one point to stroke my face, and I allowed myself to lean in briefly to his touch, before I jerked away in shock. Across the room, paused by the entrance to the women's washroom, was Tamsin, and she was staring directly at me. We locked eyes for a moment before she continued through the door. In a panic, I grabbed my purse, slid off the barstool and hurried away, barely even acknowledging Mark with a goodbye. All I could think was that I had to get out of there before Tamsin emerged from the washroom, as though not seeing me when she came out would erase what she had already seen. I managed to get into a taxi just as I thought I saw Tamsin exit the hotel.

To my great relief, Teddy wasn't home when I arrived at the coach house. In fact, he was there very little in the following days, as he worked overtime shooting the season finale. When he was home, he was usually catching up on sleep. I did my best to avoid him. Shame over my behaviour with Mark sat in my stomach like solidifying tar. I prayed that Teddy would never get wind of it.

The cast and crew of *Chronology* were waiting on ten-terhooks to hear if the series would be renewed for another season. On Thursday afternoon, Teddy texted me to say the news was good. They were all going out for a celebratory dinner party and would I please come. I told him I couldn't, that Thursday was my latest night with piano students. It was a lame excuse—my last student finished at nine, at which point the party would just barely have gotten underway. But I just couldn't face another party of industry insiders.

Halfway through that last lesson, I was surprised to hear Teddy come in, his footsteps sounding on the stairs overhead. Why wasn't he at the party? After seeing my student off, I climbed the stairs myself and was more surprised to find Teddy sitting in near darkness. When he looked at me his eyes were rimmed with red, as though he'd been crying.

"Paul, are you having an affair?" he asked. He didn't seem angry; he seemed scared.

I sat down heavily across from him. "No," I said, then asked, "You talked to Tamsin?"

"She said she saw you."

"She saw me at the bar with Mark Slate, the producer. I was drunk and . . . well . . . flirting. There was nothing more, I swear to you, Teddy. It was stupid. It was ugly."

"Tamsin says he's got a reputation," Teddy said. "Getting involved with younger actresses, promising them things."

I winced. "Does Tamsin think I'm having an affair with him?"

"She didn't know. She was worried. I mean why would you—" His voice broke. "Do you *want* to have an affair?"

"No, no. Of course not," I said as my own tears started to fall. "I wasn't interested in him at all. I'm just so frustrated. You're moving on with your career and I'm going nowhere. I'm sorry, Teddy."

He came and sat beside me. "I'm sorry too. I've been completely absorbed with the show. The truth is, I wouldn't be where I am without you. I don't think I'd be anywhere. Honestly, Paul, I don't think I could live without you." He hugged me and I could feel him crying in earnest again. "Please don't leave me," he said into my ear.

"I won't. I'm not going to leave you," I said. I felt ashamed, both for the stupidity of my behaviour and the pain it was causing him.

Over the next couple of weeks, we were excessively kind and considerate to each other. It was a busier spring than usual, as several of my students were preparing for Royal Conservatory exams and had booked extra lessons. Aside from a few work meetings, Teddy spent most of his time alone upstairs, jotting things down in a notebook, or just sitting, apparently deep in thought.

Early one evening, when I came upstairs, he picked me up by the waist and twirled me around.

"I have a new idea for a play!" he said.

"Let me guess," I said. "*Romeo and Juliet* with a twist."

"Exactly!" he said. "You know it's what I've wanted to do all along, but this time it stays firmly in the realm of the tragic. A modern *Romeo and Juliet* that is just about their passion, their relationship. Picture it, Paul. Just two actors—just the two of us, no one else—in a psychotherapist's office."

"Romeo and Juliet get therapy?"

"Just Romeo, actually. Juliet is the therapist."

"I see. So this will be a classic case of transference. Patient falling in love with his therapist."

Teddy snapped his fingers with excitement. "That's it! That's the title! *Transference*. Paul, you're brilliant. So this is what I was thinking: A heartbroken man named Roman turns to therapy after the death of his fiancée, Rosaline. After a few sessions with Dr. Caplet, he realizes that what he thought was love with Rosaline was shallow compared to what he begins to feel for his therapist, especially as she begins to share as much of her own inner life as he does of his. Dr. Caplet, too, feels the intensity of their growing bond but is bound, by professional ethics and fear of censure by her profession's governing body, to refuse to act on her feelings, even though her refusal threatens to drive her patient—and herself—to despair."

Until this point, I thought he was joking. I suddenly realized, with a tiny shiver of dread, that he was not.

"It's an interesting idea. I suppose you could start working on it, and maybe sometime in the future—"

"If we really get down to work, I think we could mount a production at the end of August," Teddy said.

"But that's impossible. You said shooting for season two of *Chronology* was starting earlier this year, in July."

"I'm not going to be shooting season two," he said.

"What?"

"I quit. I told them I wasn't signing on for season two. I want to concentrate on our work together, like I should have done all along. I want to concentrate on us," he said.

I stared at Teddy in horror. "Teddy, no, you can't do that! What did you say to them? You have to call them back, tell them you made a mistake."

"It's not a mistake. When I thought there was a chance I might lose you, Paul, I felt more scared than I've ever felt in my life. I don't ever want to feel that way again," he said.

"But I'm not going to leave you. I was never going to leave you! I was just jealous because my career was going nowhere!"

"Now it will go somewhere, both our careers together," he said. "And you know it's true, what you said, about being forever identified as a bit character actor if I stay in the role too long. That's not what I want to do. It's not what I'm meant to do!"

"No, it's not true, Teddy. The part is good. You might not get an opportunity like that again."

But he remained maddeningly calm and sure of himself. Nothing I said would persuade him. His colleagues and friends railed at the insanity of his decision. His family was utterly dismayed. His sister Louise came by, a freshly baked loaf of her signature zucchini bread in hand, intent on convincing him to change his mind. Of all his family, Louise was Teddy's biggest fan, to the point, at times, of fawning. She'd had a photo of Teddy as the soul guide/magician blown up to nearly poster size and framed. It hung just inside her apartment door, so that it was the first thing anyone entering saw. She tried flattery, telling him how brilliant and unique his portrayal of the magician was, and progressed to dire warnings about how he'd be blacklisted by the industry for quitting. Nothing, not even warm zucchini bread spread with butter, would dissuade him from his belief that he'd made the right choice.

When Louise left I followed her down the stairs to lock the coach house door behind her. She was visibly distressed. As she stepped outside, she turned back to me and said angrily, "This is your fault! Teddy told me."

I felt like I'd been punched. Could Teddy really have told her about Tamsin seeing me with Mark? "Told you what?" I asked breathlessly.

Louise paused before speaking, more with annoyance now than anger. "He said he wanted to concentrate on your 'joint career.'" She made air quotes with her fingers. "Don't pull him down just because you're having trouble, Paula. It's not fair."

Out of a deep sense of guilt, I began working on the new play with Teddy. How could I refuse when I was the cause of him sabotaging his own career? He was more confident and excited about the project than I'd ever seen him before. He seemed to buzz with an almost frenzied energy, much more manic than his usual zeal. His colour was unnaturally high, as if he'd always just come in from a run. I, on the other hand, was filled with dread and a terrible sense of déjà vu.

The script was uneven and overwrought. Teddy had inserted verbatim from Shakespeare several of Romeo's and Juliet's speeches, as well as dialogue between the two, at crucial points throughout, including the final double-death scene. I told him it was confusing, the shifts from modern to Shakespearean diction were disruptive, and the references didn't make sense in the therapeutic context. He insisted it was the symbolism that was important, that the audience was smart enough to get it.

As summer progressed, I did everything I could to clarify and simplify and make the play work. But Teddy was rarely willing to give an inch. He exuded ecstatic conviction. Whenever we reached an impasse, I backed down, silently remembering my guilt. It didn't help that Louise started attending our rehearsals. She had offered to make the Renaissance-era Veronese costumes Teddy had his heart set on.

Opening night arrived. Certain I was going to be sick to my stomach, I lingered upstairs near the bathroom while the audience found their seats. I retched a few times over the toilet, but nothing came up; the nausea remained and I could no longer delay getting into position backstage. I was surprised Teddy hadn't come upstairs looking for me. Normally, he would have been frantic. But when I made my way downstairs and into the narrow strip behind our stage, I realized in an instant that nothing was normal.

Teddy was leaning over a stool, heaving and seemingly rocking in pain.

"Teddy?" I said.

He looked up at me, his face terrified. He clutched at his head with both hands and let out an agonized howl so loud, it was heard over the buzz of the crowd outside, and there was a sudden hush. Later I would learn that most of the audience thought this was just the unorthodox beginning of the play. When I ran onto the stage and shouted for someone to call an ambulance, they still weren't sure. It was Louise who called 911 as we both rushed back behind the stage to find Teddy out cold on the floor, though his eyes remained eerily open.

Teddy regained consciousness in the ambulance and immediately started crying, sobbing like a young child, because, he said, his head hurt so much he thought it was cracking open. He insisted I inspect his scalp for crevices;

nothing would reassure him that his skull was still intact. I followed the stretcher as the paramedics wheeled him through the emergency room. People looked and kept looking. I was dressed as Juliet, after all, in a flowing gown of several diaphanous layers. With a circlet of flowers in my hair and dramatic eye makeup starting to smudge into thick black shadows, I must have made a strange sight.

I was allowed to go with Teddy into an examination room to wait. He clutched at my hand so hard his nails left little red crescents in my skin, but we didn't have to wait for long. His symptoms must have made him a priority, because an ER physician arrived within minutes. He conducted a few tests on Teddy's reflexes and eyes. When he asked Teddy to rate the pain on a scale of one to ten, Teddy said, "A gazillion!"

I laughed, and then immediately started to sob. It was such a typically child-like Teddy response.

They bundled him off for a CT scan, so I had to return to the waiting room. As I was about to re-enter, I had a strange sense of unreality and felt confused and frightened. It was as if I were still onstage, mistaking a role for my life. When the waiting room audience lifted their eyes to stare at me once more, I felt panic. What came next? I'd forgotten all my lines.

Then familiar faces coming toward me broke the spell. Teddy's parents and Louise had followed the ambulance in their car, as had Diane in hers. I told them what little I knew and then we waited. I urged Diane to go home to the babies, but she refused.

"Randy'll be going nuts with all three of them on his own," I said.

"I know," Diane said and grinned.

Teddy's other siblings began to arrive, some with spouses and children in tow. The MacGregor clan had always seemed to me like a kind of swarm. The swarm grew steadily and filled the waiting room with concerned buzzing.

Finally, his parents and I were allowed in to see him. He'd been given a big dose of painkiller and was groggy but awake. He reached for my hand.

"There's a mass in my brain," he told us, with no apparent perturbation.

His parents reacted immediately, in rising, fearful voices. I felt as if a pitcher of icy water were being poured over my head, and I couldn't move.

"What do you mean?"

"A mass of what?"

The ER doctor spoke in a very calm voice. "We won't know exactly until we can test a sample. Unfortunately, given the location of the tumour—"

"Tumour!" Teddy's mother gasped, suddenly understanding what was meant by the term "mass."

"Given the location within the brain," the doctor continued, "even a biopsy will require an invasive procedure. Surgery," he added, looking pointedly at Vivian. "We will attempt to remove the tumour at the same time, but only subsequent tests will tell us what we're dealing with."

"You mean whether it's malignant," Clive said grimly.

"Yes," the doctor said. He looked as if he were about to say more, but thought better of it.

"When?" I asked.

"As soon as possible," he said. "Given the severity of Teddy's condition, we think it's best."

I looked at Teddy to see how he was taking this, but though he was still holding tight to my hand, he appeared to have drifted off into a deep and seemingly peaceful sleep. I wasn't sure I would ever sleep again.

"Yes, he's not likely to wake again until morning," the doctor said. "We've given him a pretty powerful painkiller. You really should go home and get some rest, and—" he nodded specifically in my direction, "a change of clothes."

I refused to leave, despite my outlandish costume. Going home alone to the coach house would make it all real, and I wasn't ready to face that yet. Better to continue as I was, on with the show. Teddy's own costume had been removed and stuffed haphazardly into a plastic shopping bag that was now on the floor. The collapsible dagger I was supposed to take from his belt and plunge into my heart at the end of the play was on his bedside table. A nurse had dressed him in a flimsy blue and white gown. There was a shadow on one side of his face that I thought was the beginning of a bruise; once the others were gone, I took a closer look and realized it was dirt. Dust, I thought, from the stool he'd been doubled over on when I found him backstage. I soaked some paper towels in warm water in the bathroom and washed it off. He didn't even stir. Like Romeo finding Juliet in the vault, I might have mistaken him for dead.

⁕ CHAPTER FIVE ⁕

As I PREPARE TO OPEN the studio on the Sunday following the Ugly Sweater Party, Héctor tells me he needs
to head out to do, among other errands, his Christmas shopping. Only after he leaves does the dilemma present itself:
are we getting each other Christmas gifts? On Christmas
Day we will have known each other precisely two weeks.
From an objective perspective, a two-week acquaintance
would not suggest an exchange of gifts, but there's nothing
objective about our two-week acquaintance. And we will
be together on Christmas Day. All afternoon, as customers

come and go, I worry over the questions in my mind. Do I get him something significant, or something casual, like a box of chocolates? What if I get him something significant and he chooses something casual? Or vice versa? (When we were in university, Diane gave a boy she'd been dating for a month an old-fashioned hand-carved shaving kit she'd had specially monogrammed for him; he gave her two movie vouchers, one of which he obviously planned to use himself. The relationship didn't last past Boxing Day.) In either case, what would I get him?

Héctor inadvertently gives me an idea when he calls later that evening.

"Are you worried?" I ask, when he yawns and tells me he's going to bed early to be well rested for Monday's teleconference with the judge.

He says no, but for the first time I sense that he is. "You should make one of your magic candles to ensure my success," he says.

I laugh off the suggestion, but after we say good night and hang up, it occurs to me that a customized candle—something funny—would be the perfect solution to the gift dilemma. Significant *and* casual. A meaningful joke.

I head downstairs early on Monday morning aiming to mix Héctor's candle before opening to customers. I'd hoped the perfect formula, something both touching and comical, would come to me overnight, but I'm still drawing a blank. I turn the stove on to begin melting a small block of wax, then turn to the shelf of books I keep behind the counter. The titles include *Advanced Aromatherapy, Candle Magick, The Scent of Success,* and *Spellcasting for Dummies.*

Whenever a customer asks me how I know which scents to combine, I point to this shelf and say, "Research."

As I flip through a volume awkwardly called *Es-scents-tials*, the heading "Mexican Blends" catches my eye. Nothing beyond the heading substantiates the claim that the recipes are rooted in any particular Mexican tradition, but the synchronicity is intriguing, and when I turn the page and see that among the Mexican blends is one called, "Opening the Road," I feel a little shiver. "To clear the road of any obstacles and open the door to new opportunities," is its described effect. Like so many of my customers, I find myself entertaining the hope that burning a candle can change the course of the universe.

I decide to go ahead with the Mexican blend—it's a complex one with four ingredients: jasmine, hyacinth, cinnamon, and bay—and come up with my own title and description later, something that will make Héctor laugh. I toss around phrases like "greasing the wheel" and "bureaucratic laxative" as I add stearin and red dye (it is a Christmas gift, after all) to the molten wax.

The handle on the saucepan I'm using is coming loose. It's a very small pan that I rarely use, since I usually make candles in larger batches. All it really needs is for the screw to be tightened, but my screwdrivers are upstairs in a kitchen drawer, and can't be bothered to go up. I figure if I hold the handle with two hands, it will be steady enough. I'm wrong. As I lift the pot to pour the wax into a star-shaped mould, it tips, turns on the loose screw and pours hot wax over the fingers of my left hand. I've suffered hundreds of mild wax burns doing my work, but not like this. Never with wax so hot, and never with so much sticking to my skin so that it continues to burn even as it cools. It is worst on the pinky and ring fingers; the heat feels like it's penetrating to the bone. I plunk down the pan, turn on the tap and hold my hand under cold water, which solidifies the wax on my fingers like a second skin. Once it is cooled, I dry the hand with a towel and begin to peel off the wax. To my horror, a layer of blistered skin peels off with it. Panic wells up through my abdomen. I'm fighting back sobs when the phone rings. I pick it up with my right hand.

"What's wrong?" Héctor asks as soon as he hears my voice.

"I burned myself. My hand. With hot wax."

"How bad is it?"

"I don't know. Worse than I've ever had. There's still wax on it, and I can't get it off without the skin."

"What do you mean, 'without the skin'?"

"The skin comes off with the wax."

"Paula, you've got to get it looked at! What's the nearest hospital?"

"Saint Joseph's, on the Queensway," I say. "Yes, I guess I better."

"Yes. Go now. Take a taxi. I'll meet you there as soon as I can."

Now that I have instructions to follow, the panic subsides. I make sure all of the burners in the studio are off, turn off the lights, and go upstairs for my coat. I push the burnt hand into the sleeve without thinking and gasp at the pain. Once the coat is on, I hesitate. Should I cover the hand with something? It seems wrong somehow to go out with the injury exposed, but to touch it with anything makes it hurt more. Instead I hold it up protectively in front of me, careful that it doesn't touch the zipper of my coat.

As I climb into the back of the taxi, telling the driver I need to go to emergency, he glances first in his mirror, then turns and looks at my arm with great alarm. Only then do I realize how it appears at a glance. The dried wax is bright red; it must look a bloody mess. I explain to the driver that it is wax and not blood, but I give no such assurances to the other patients in the waiting room who look up from their chairs with horror as I walk over to the triage desk. *Besides*, I think, *if they manage to get the wax off, there might be a bloody mess underneath.* Another shock of adrenalin panic goes through me at this thought, but then Héctor arrives, and I experience a wave of relief.

The first sight of my hand startles him, until he is close enough to perceive the red wax. He sits down beside me, on the injured side, and takes hold of my arm gently, up away from the burn, to manoeuvre it into view. Gingerly, he touches one finger to the wax. "Does this hurt?" he asks.

"Yes," I say.

He nods sagely. "Good, then I know not to do that."

"It's strange, isn't it? I mean, I know a burn isn't nearly as bad as—" I nod toward his right hand. "But it's an odd coincidence, don't you think? What do you think it means?"

He examines my hand, careful not to put any pressure on the painful parts. "It's hard to say for sure until the wax is removed, but I think your burn is the exact shape of the Virgin Mary."

"I think it's a punishment."

He leans back and looks at me curiously. "Punishment for what?"

I sigh. "I've taken things for granted," I say vaguely. "Not paid attention to what's really import—" I break off, realizing with horror that, in the midst of my own mini-drama, I've completely forgotten about Héctor's meeting with the judge. He must have been calling to tell me about it when I interrupted with news of my burn. "Héctor, the judge! What did the judge say?"

He gives a dismissive wave. "It was fine. The judge just wanted more details. He wanted to know more about my friendship with Congressman Ochoa."

I frown. "What details? Why? Doesn't he believe you?"

"It's fine, Paula. It's just red tape," he says.

Why is he so reticent about it? Is it just because he doesn't want to worry me?

He lifts my hand and kisses the tip of my index finger, a patch that escaped the wax. "We all have regrets, Paula," he says. "The only thing you're being punished for is being so clumsy."

A nurse with a clipboard calls my name.

THE DOCTOR, A young resident, has no better idea how to remove the wax than I have. But she is gentle and patient as she peels it off bit by bit with a kind of tweezers. Each time a bit of skin comes away with the wax I tense, pulling involuntarily against the grasp of the nurse who is trying to hold my arm steady. The young doctor stops and smiles at me. "Maybe it would be better if you looked the other way," she says.

I agree and find that when I'm not watching, I can't actually tell when skin is peeling or not. Which is not to say it does not hurt, but that the pain spreads uniformly over the entire burn. When she has finished removing the wax, she bathes the burn in a solution that stings sharply, bringing tears to my eyes.

"Will there be permanent damage?" I ask her. "I mean, once it heals."

"I suggest you make an appointment with your GP to keep an eye on it over the next couple of weeks. You'll want to keep the skin supple as it heals. But I see no reason why it shouldn't eventually get back to normal."

I see no reason. Her words repeat in my head as she leaves me with a nurse who bandages my hand. Does reason ever have anything to do with what happens, or what one sees? Still, her words are reassuring. My relief must be evident on my face; Héctor smiles widely when I return to the waiting area.

He holds out his hands as if to present me to myself. "You see?"

I laugh. "I see."

We walk home to the studio, stopping at a pharmacy to fill a prescription for some steroid cream, then at a bakery for some fresh buns, and at a specialty foods shop where they sell tubs of "homemade" broccoli soup.

"I just want to double-check that everything is off," I say as we come in the door. It is not until this moment that it occurs to me to wonder what effect the burn might have on the work by which I make a living. The spilled wax has solidified in a red splotch on the counter, vaguely the shape of a guitar, I think. I leave it for now. I'll have to leave it all for a few days and then reassess how well I can use the hand. Valentine's Day orders will be due soon.

When I join Héctor upstairs, he's already heating up the soup on the stove and setting the table for lunch. He has also put a CD in the stereo. His choice is unexpected: sixteenth-century settings of the *Lamentations of Jeremiah*. The effect is not cheering, but sharpening. The table, the bowls, the whole kitchen look suddenly like a painting in which every detail is deliberate, as do Héctor's movements, slicing the bread, ladling the soup. The simple food is rich and comforting. When we finish, I rise to carry dishes to the sink, but he tells me no.

"You need some rest." He takes me by the good hand down the hall to my bedroom and leads me over to the bed to lie down. He picks up a little round velvety cushion that has uselessly adorned my bedrooms since I was a teenager, ceremoniously puffs it up, puts it beside my left shoulder, then lifts my burnt hand so that it lies against the cushion palm up. He sits on the bed beside me and unbuttons my blouse; I shiver each time his fingers brush my skin. He takes hold of the right sleeve, so I can pull my arm out, then he slips a hand under my back, gently lifting me up, pulling my blouse out from beneath me, and unclasping my bra while he's there. Tenderly, he removes the sleeve and strap from my left arm and sets my hand back on its pillow. He kisses my lips, my neck, my breasts.

When my left hand moves involuntarily to his hair, he lifts his head. "No. The hand must rest. It must not move," he says, putting it back on the cushion.

"Kinky. It's like a kind of bondage," I say.

He grins as he unbuttons and unzips my jeans. I lift my hips for him to slide them off.

CHRISTMAS EVE DAY, and after yesterday's candle fiasco, I still don't have a gift for Héctor.

"I need to go over to Roncesvalles and get a few things," I tell him.

"Make me a list and I'll go," he says.

It's tempting; I could just give him a list that says "Héctor's Christmas gift." Problem solved. "No, no, that's okay," I say instead.

"But your hand!" he says. He's been solicitous and caring from the moment I woke up, putting fresh steroid cream and a new bandage on my hand before he'd let me out of bed, then making pancakes, which he carefully cut up into bite-sized pieces. He tried to feed them to me, but I drew the line there.

"I'll go with you then," he continues. "To carry everything. I'll be your beast of burden."

I'm still wondering how I'm going to shake him off when the doorbell rings below, followed by loud rapping on the front window. I look out from the second floor to see at least three people waiting outside the studio. One of them sees me looking and shouts. Despite closed windows, I can hear him asking when I'll be opening.

"Héctor," I say, holding up my uninjured hand to indicate *five minutes* to the man below. "You know how you can really help me?"

"Anything for you, Paula," he says from the sink where he's washing the breakfast dishes.

"Watch the shop for me for a little while."

Héctor is genuinely happy to comply. As he regales last-minute customers with outrageous stories of my candles' success, I manage to slip out and walk a block over to Roncesvalles Avenue, optimistic that the perfect gift for Héctor will quickly make its presence known, though I've still no idea what that gift might be.

The sidewalk is very busy with shoppers who clearly still have quite a few items to tick off their lists before tonight's and tomorrow's festivities, yet a sense of that celebration is already in the air. People are friendlier, more willing to hold doors open or step aside patiently while someone more encumbered moves by. Traditionally a Polish and German neighbourhood, there are still many family-owned bakeries, delis, and cafés along this stretch. But in recent years, among them have sprung up all sorts of trendy little shops selling specialty items, like bathware crafted from bicycle parts, or everything you might need to be in a cowboy movie. As I finger a bicycle chain toothbrush holder, then a set of spurs, my optimism begins to wane, and I wonder if I will have to resort to chocolates after all. In a store devoted exclusively to hand wear—mittens, gloves, and muffs of every kind—I consider asking if they have any three-fingered styles, but realize the joke will be lost on anyone other than Héctor. Finally, I come upon a small bookstore, one of the last such independent bookstores in the city. *A book*, I think. A respectable gift, at least. I browse the season's crop of novels. Nothing seems interesting or significant enough. I am at the point of despair when a large hardcover book on display catches my eye. It's a bilingual volume of the poetry of Fernando Pessoa. Portuguese, I think. To commemorate our first date. I open it at random:

You who are a mystic see a meaning in all things.
For you everything has a veiled significance.

I buy the book. Then I walk a little farther north to a German import store that's been there as long as I can remember, since long before I was born, I'm sure. It's run by two German women, sisters I think, who must now be in their eighties. There I buy a box of brandy-filled chocolates and an assortment of beautiful foil-wrapped chocolates shaped like ladybugs, teddy bears, and European-style Santas whose robes and headdresses make them look more like the pope than a North American Santa. I stop at Sobey's for a few groceries—nothing will be open tomorrow, after all—then hurry back to the studio to relieve Héctor.

Though there are nearly a dozen customers in the store, Héctor is in no need of relief of any kind. Some are perusing the candles, but most are gathered around the piano, watching Héctor play, uttering exclamations of astonishment and praise. As I enter, he is nearing the end of Bartók's "Etude for the Left Hand." I feel a stab of nostalgic longing. How I envy Héctor's ability to put pain and disappointment behind him, to enjoy the music for what it is, not what he is. I wish I could do the same. The store erupts with cheers and applause as he finishes the piece, but instead of giving a bow, he launches into "Jingle Bells" and the customers start singing. Over the next hour I sell a remarkable number of candles, purchased almost as an afterthought by people drawn in by the music and mirth spilling out into the street.

By mid-afternoon the crowd dwindles, and I finally convince Héctor to allow me to close the shop. We eat the rest of the soup and buns, then retreat to the bedroom for another round of careful lovemaking, my burnt hand relegated once again to its velvet perch. Afterward, we doze off.

When I open my eyes again, it's dark and the clock reads 6:20. I'm confused for several seconds before I realize it is 6:20 in the evening, Christmas Eve. For the first time in many years that thought, the simple fact of it being Christmas, gives me a thrill, like it did when I was a child. I could stay like this, curled up against Héctor's sleeping side, forever.

"Paula," he says, and my whole body jumps with the start. I thought he was asleep. "I thought you were awake," he says.

"I was," I say. "I am awake."

"You seem uncertain," he says.

"Well, that's true." I laugh. "We'd better get dressed."

Our plan is to return to Héctor's neighbourhood to attend mass at St. Francis of Assisi church. Laura recommended the Christmas Eve service as one of the rare times the historic pipe organ is played, and Héctor is keen to hear it.

He helps me with the buttons on my blouse and insists on tying a festive ribbon around my bandage. We catch the streetcar east to Grace Street. The entrance to the church is lit up, and organ music is already pouring out as people make their way inside. Despite the crowds in the foyer waiting for ushers to lead them to empty seats, Laura spots Héctor the minute we enter and waves us over.

"What's this?" she asks, gesturing to my hand.

"Burn," I say.

"She rescued a puppy from a burning building," Héctor explains.

Laura looks at me. "Several puppies, actually," I say.

She laughs and introduces me to her husband, Malcolm, and her teenaged son, Christopher. "I hope you are aware of just how fabulous our Héctor is. Do you know what he did for Christopher?"

"I did hear that he met Christopher when he was volunteering at the refugee house," I say.

Malcolm snorts. "Court-ordered community service," he says. "Not *voluntary* volunteering. Tell Héctor's girlfriend what you did, son," he says to Christopher, who has earbuds in his ears—despite, or maybe because of, the organ music—and is bobbing his head to that alternative beat.

"He got in with the wrong crowd," Laura says, not defensively, but with a smile, as if it's a family joke.

"He stole a gargoyle from the neighbour's porch roof," Malcolm continues. "Why, you ask? After all, his loving parents would happily have bought him a gargoyle if it had been his wish. But no, because he friends *dared* him. How was it exactly, son?"

Christopher pointedly ignores him, fiddling instead with the volume on his phone.

"The dare was sent by text. Three simple letters: *idy*, which is apparently more compelling than stone tablets engraved on Mount Sinai," Malcolm explains. "Do you know how he got caught?"

"How?" I say, when I realize Malcolm is waiting for me to respond.

"He left his phone behind," Malcolm says with a bark of laughter, though it's clear he's told this story many times before. "Dropped it on the roof."

Laura sighs. "Yes, yes, teenage boys do stupid things. The point is, it was Héctor who helped him turn things around."

"Saved him from a life of crime, mate," Malcolm says, ostentatiously shaking Héctor's hand. "Stealing gargoyles is just a gateway crime. Who knows what it would have been next—garden gnomes? Bird baths?" He cracks up and this time even Laura laughs.

"Seriously though," Laura says, laying a hand on my arm, determined to tell her story. "Christopher always loved playing piano and singing when he was young. Of course, we pushed him to practise and do well, but he loved it. He hurt himself more than us when he quit. His friends thought it was stupid. It was seeing Héctor play that rickety old piano at the centre that got him back into it. Héctor taught him—what is it called?"

"The walking bass line," Héctor says.

"Something to do with blues or jazz," Laura says.

"Paula knows. She's a pianist too," Héctor says. *Used to be*, I think, with a twinge of regret.

"Anyway, Héctor started giving him lessons, and I can't tell you how much of a change there's been. Not just with the music, but in every aspect of his life," Laura says. "Héctor, I'm not sure if Chris has told you this, but his friend Logan—the one who dared him—is taking guitar lessons. He figures with Chris on keyboard, they can start a band."

Héctor laughs. "He'll have a long way to go to catch up with Christopher. He's a good musician."

"He is," Laura says. "Oh, here they are!" She begins waving wildly to a couple with two small children who've just entered the foyer.

"Ah! Dusan! Violetta!" Héctor says as they approach. He shakes the man's hand, kisses the woman's cheeks, and pats the heads of the two kids, who smile up at him. "Paula," he says, "these are friends I met at the refugee centre. They are from the Czech Republic."

We reach the entrance to what looks like an already packed sanctuary. "We're going to have to split up," Laura says. The Czech family, along with Malcolm and Christopher, find an empty stretch of pew together; Laura, Héctor, and I squeeze onto the end of a pew farther back.

"I want them to have at least one good Christmas in Canada," Laura says to me, nodding in Dusan and Violetta's direction. "It's not looking good for them at all. They're Roma, but it's almost impossible to prove they experienced persecution because it's so systemic. Without a specific threat—like in Héctor's case—the chance their refugee claim will be approved is very small."

I don't even want to consider the possibility that this could be Héctor's only Christmas here. The service begins. I've always loved Christmas songs, but as I join in, my voice cracks, I haven't sung in so long.

When Laura joins the congregants filing forward for

communion, I look at Héctor to see if he will join them. He remains seated, holding my hand in both of his.

"Aren't you going up?" I whisper.

"I haven't been to confession in a very long time," he says.

"You mean you have a guilty conscience," I joke.

He smiles and kisses my temple.

The service over, the organist launches into "Joy to the World" again and people continue to sing as they spill out into the cold December night. Héctor and I find ourselves beside the crazy outdoor crèche again.

"It's too bad there are no real animals here," Héctor says. "According to legend, all animals around the world kneel down to the Christ child at the stroke of midnight."

"If we walk up to College Street, we might find some pigeons," I suggest.

"Unfortunately, birds may be the one exception," he says.

"Why?"

"Because they don't have knees."

We find Laura in the crowd and say our farewells, then head across the street to Héctor's apartment. We can still hear the organ playing as we undress.

AT THREE O'CLOCK I wake up from a dream in which Teddy's parents have called me to wish me a merry Christmas. I'm confused, because Clive and Vivian always do call me on Christmas Eve, but last night, for the first time since Teddy died, they did not. Then I realize with queasy dread that I turned my phone off before going into the church, and never bothered to turn it back on. I tell myself to leave it until morning. There's nothing I can do about it now anyway; I can't call them back at 3:00 AM. I toy with the idea that maybe, by some miracle, they too had been busy and hadn't actually called, but it's no use. I won't get back to sleep without knowing, so I slip into the living room and check. Sure enough, a missed call at 9:05, and a message. As always, each is on a different extension of their landline. They're clearly surprised to have reached my voicemail—it's the first time since Teddy's death that I haven't picked up their call—but they recover quickly. "I suppose you're busy with some Christmas do," Vivian says, "so we wish you the best. But it can still be a hard time, dear, so you know we're thinking of you."

Clive breaks in: "The whole family sends their wishes, Paula. So merry Christmas, and best for the new year."

There is some awkward coughing and a few "well thens" before they hang up.

I know Clive and Vivian wouldn't begrudge my moving on. If they were initially disconcerted about getting my voicemail, it will not have troubled them for long. I'm sure it will satisfy them if I simply call them back tomorrow. But the realization that I forgot does disturb me. I lie awake for several hours after that, dozing off only as dawn light is beginning to show around the edges of the curtains. Héctor wakes me some time later when he brings me a cup of coffee, along with a soft, tissue-wrapped package. "Merry Christmas, Paula," he says. I unwrap the paper to find an exquisitely crocheted black silk shawl, the design spidery and delicate. "It's beautiful," I say.

"Isn't it? Violetta made it."

"Violetta from last night?"

"Yes. A genuine Roma shawl," he says.

"I have something for you too," I say. I climb out of bed, find my bag in the next room, and dig out the book of poetry, sliding my phone, which I left on the coffee table last night, into a pocket. "It's nowhere near as spectacular as this shawl, I know," I say handing Héctor the package. But he appears to be delighted. He kisses me on the forehead.

After coffee and a few slices of toast, I get dressed and pack up my gifts for Diane's girls. Héctor removes a garbage bag from his closet containing something large and bulky.

"What is that?" I ask.

"A surprise," he says. "For the girls."

He refuses to reveal the nature of the surprise, tying the bag tightly at the top so I can't peek.

Outside the world is hushed in a way that strikes me as being particular to Christmas Day, as if the world were cognizant of and has decided to respect the buzz of happy activity going on behind closed doors. I wish more than anything that I could participate in the buzz, but a sense of unease from those wee hours lingers. We walk up to College and catch the streetcar heading east.

A surprising number of people get on, and by the time we reach Queen's Park, the streetcar is quite crowded. Héctor holds his unwieldy package protectively on his lap, craning his neck to see over the top. Only after Yonge Street and an exodus of riders transferring to the subway does the crowd diminish. As we cross the Don Valley, flurries begin to fall and grow thicker when we get off at Carlaw. We walk the half block north to Diane and Randy's house. The three girls, peering expectantly at our bags, meet us at the door. The living room is already awash with torn wrapping paper, boxes, and plastic packaging threatening to bury Diane's parents, Arnie and Magda, who have to swim through the mess to greet us.

I distribute my packages, each adorned with several of the German foil-wrapped chocolates, to the girls before even removing my coat.

"They better not be candles," Juniper says, eliciting a yelp of laughter from Héctor, a muttered expletive from Diane.

The girls are, however, genuinely pleased enough with the contents of their packages—electronic hamsters known as ZhuZhu Pets—that they don't need to be ordered to thank me and give me a hug, though they steer clear of my bandage. When I tell them I have a burn, Trillium jumps back with alarm and says, "You mean it's hot?"

With all other gifts opened, they turn their attention to Señor Vargas's mysterious package.

"What's in there?"

"Is it for us?"

"Is it alive?"

Héctor carries the package to the centre of the room so as to unveil it to greater effect. "This is a Christmas tradition in Mexico," he says. He reaches inside the garbage bag and pauses dramatically before pulling out a brightly coloured papier mâché donkey. The three girls gasp in unison; it's as if he's conducting a choir. "A piñata!" he announces.

"Oh heavens," Diane mutters.

The girls jump up and down, shrieking with excitement, clearly aware that the piñata is full of goodies.

"Now where shall we hang it?" Héctor looks up and around the room.

Randy gets up to help secure the piñata to the ceiling fan, ignoring Diane's precautions.

"Now, Diane, do you have a broom?" Héctor asks, flashing an angelic grin.

Diane reluctantly takes a broom from the hall closet. "Someone's going to lose an eye," she says to me as she hands the broom over.

"Probably just some fingers," I murmur.

"Now, who's the youngest?" Héctor asks, pulling a red bandanna from his pocket. "The youngest goes first."

"I am!" Fern shrieks.

"Only by ten minutes!" Trillium protests. "It's so unfair!"

Héctor ties the bandanna over Fern's eyes, then stands her within broom's reach of the piñata. No sooner does he place the broom handle in her hands than she starts swinging it wildly every which way as if she has no memory of where she saw the piñata before her eyes were covered.

Everyone ducks, Magda lets out a scream, a lamp hits the floor, and a water glass is shattered across the coffee table before Héctor manages to grab Fern from behind and close his own hands over hers to stop the swinging. He turns her back toward the piñata and, keeping his own grip on the broomstick, helps her guide it to its mark. A couple of swings and a small wound opens up on the burro's backside.

"I can see the loot!" Trillium squeals.

It's her turn next, and Héctor keeps hold of the

broomstick as she makes her first hit. After that, she is able to make contact on her own and does so with surprising force, grunting with the effort.

"Good grief!" Diane says. "She sounds like Maria Sharapova."

A second wound gapes in the donkey's middle. It's about to be disembowelled, when Juniper takes hold of the stick. It only takes two strikes before the piñata splits open and the goodies shower onto the floor. Juniper begins grabbing blindly at the loot, not wanting to stop even to take off the bandanna for fear her sisters will get a jump on her.

I choose that moment to slip upstairs to the bathroom, making sure my phone is in my pocket. When I reach Clive and Vivian, the sound of overexcited children shouting and opening gifts in the background is even louder than the cacophony downstairs from me. Our exchange is cordial and brief, as they are eager to get back to their grandchildren. I stay in the bathroom a little while longer, just trying to get my bearings.

Seeing Héctor entertaining the children with the piñata, reminding me as it does of the countless holidays when Teddy entertained his family and mine with magic shows, has been disorienting, setting thoughts and feelings swirling inside me. In those first years with Teddy, happiness seemed so solid, the trajectory of its growth and our continued success a certainty. As it turned out, it was as fleeting as the flower bouquet that vanished into thin air with a puff of the magician's breath. I splash cold water on my face and return to the festivities, determined to enjoy myself and make sure it is a good Christmas for Héctor.

A few hours later we sit down to dinner. Diane, as usual, has outdone herself. She sets an enormous turkey on the table.

"It looks magnificent, Diane," Héctor says.

"Thank you," she says. "Mind you, my mother is responsible for the—bleh!—sausage stuffing. I want to make sure I don't get blamed for that."

"The recipe for this stuffing is a priceless family heirloom," Magda says.

"What does that mean?" Fern asks.

"It means it's been passed down from mother to daughter for generations. My great-great-grandmother made this stuffing, and one day, when you are grown up and have children of your own, you will make it too," Magda says.

"You'll be dead by then, right?" Fern says matter-of-factly.

"Why is it called stuffing?" Juniper asks.

"Because we stuff it in the turkey's bum," says Diane.

The girls erupt in hysterical giggles.

Once we finish dessert, a remarkable Christmas pudding with hot caramel sauce that even the children savour, Diane slumps back in her chair. "Okay, folks, I'm going into a coma now."

"Can I come?" Trillium asks.

I too am feeling a little faint and claustrophobic.

Héctor puts his hand on my knee. "Are you okay?"

"I think I could use some fresh air."

"What a great idea!" Diane says. "Take the kids, will you?"

"We can't leave you with all the washing up," I say.

"Not only will I happily do the dishes alone," Diane says, "but I will also sign over the deed to my house if you will just take my children away!"

The girls open a closet by the door and within seconds it looks like it's been disembowelled as they dig through a heap of pink and purple snow pants, ski jackets, and scarves.

"Anyone else want to join us?" Héctor asks.

By way of response, Arnie collapses into a recliner, and Diane, Randy, and Magda begin ferrying plates to the kitchen.

The air outside is cold and crisp. The snow is falling more thickly now, not just flurries, but heavy wet clumps that are rapidly covering the ground.

"Look, it's perfect packing snow," Héctor says, stooping to the ground as soon as we step outside.

"Where did you learn that term—'packing snow'?" I ask.

"It's in the citizenship study guide," he says.

The girls begin pummelling him with snowballs, aiming, with uncanny accuracy, for his head.

"Mercy! Mercy!" he shouts, trying to shield his face with his arms.

"Let him speak," Juniper says imperiously, gesturing to her sisters to hold their fire.

As he slowly lowers his arms from his face, he gasps and points down the street ahead of us. "Look!"

Sweetly gullible, they all turn to look. "What? What is it?"

"I just saw a reindeer run behind that hedge!"

"No way," Juniper says, but her sisters have already started running. Weighing her slightly more mature skepticism against the fear that her sisters will spot a reindeer she has missed, sibling rivalry wins out and she bolts after them.

"Quick thinking," I say, "but it will probably backfire."

"Not if there really is a reindeer," he says.

"I saw it! I saw it!" Fern shouts from down the street, jumping up and down with excitement.

Héctor smiles at me. "Ye of little faith."

When we catch up to them, Juniper is crouching down, examining the ground beside the hedge. "You couldn't have seen it. There are no footprints," she says.

"That's because reindeers fly," says Fern. "Right, Señor Vargas?"

"I've never known a reindeer who didn't," he says.

Somehow we move on from the phantom reindeer, and the girls engage in a new game of following behind us, stepping only in Héctor's footprints. He deliberately takes very long strides, then very short ones, to challenge them, which makes it difficult for me to keep pace beside him. He reaches for my hand, remembering too late about my burn.

"I'm so sorry, Paula," he says when I yelp with pain. "Here." He stops me with his hands on my elbows, then steps around to my left side, making a little ceremonial dance of the manoeuvre. The girls shriek with delight as they try to follow his steps, circling around us as we link our two good hands, my right and his left, together.

"Señor and Paula, sitting in a tree," Juniper chants. "K-i-s-s-i-n-g."

Héctor grins, leans toward me and kisses me full on the mouth.

"Eeeeuuuuuw!" the girls screech.

Though it's still early in the evening, we leave Diane's soon after we return from our walk, as even the girls look ready for bed. Randy gives us a lift home. Before we know it, we're climbing the stairs to my apartment, shockingly quiet after the bedlam at Diane's.

The dark bedroom is lit up with the many coloured lights that decorate the house across the street, twinkling on and off in a frantic pattern. I reach up to close the curtains, but Héctor stops me. "Don't," he says. We undress in the dark and climb into bed, lit up by hundreds of tiny points of light.

※ **CHAPTER SIX** *※*

T HE SURGEON WAS ABLE TO remove only a small portion of the tumour in Teddy's brain. He recommended
starting chemotherapy immediately, even before the biopsy
results were in, based on what he said was evidence of
recent rapid growth that was damaging surrounding tissue.
Teddy's mother wailed loudly on hearing this assessment.
I wanted to wail too; for a few seconds, I felt panicked and
thought I might faint. But Teddy took the doctor's news
with surprising equanimity, without a shred of doubt as
to his ability to overcome. He was just as confident of this

as he was when he stood in front of a group of children in his magician's hat, certain he could make them exclaim with awe. His unwavering belief convinced me too, in part because I needed it to be true. I decided that if I could help him get through this, all could be well again. If we could fix this, we could fix everything else that had gone wrong.

"So this mass is still here, inside my head," he said.

"Like an alien implant," I suggested, knowing humour was the best way to keep his spirits up. "Maybe it's transmitting signals back to the mothership."

Teddy laughed, then winced in pain. "It feels more like an actual alien with a personality, not just a computer chip or transmitter."

"Then we should give it a name," I said.

"How about Ripley?" he said, and winced again as he laughed at his own joke.

"We don't want to encourage him," I said. "It should be something belittling."

"Like what?"

"How about 'Les'?"

They kept Teddy in hospital for his first round of chemotherapy, because of his pain and the potential for seizures. It was September by this time, and though we could ill afford it, there was no question of me returning to my teaching duties. I distributed my individual piano students among a number of my colleagues who were happy to help, on a temporary basis. The extra money Teddy had made during his television gig would do for another month or two. I had no idea what I would do after that. Teddy's parents and various other members of his family were at the hospital every day, but there was no way I was going to entrust Teddy's care to them. I knew Teddy and what he needed better than anyone.

We were all temporarily expelled from Teddy's room one day while the oncologist instructed a group of residents on Teddy's case. Colleen raised speculation about whether it was the tumour's early growth that had provoked Teddy's decision to quit *Chronology*—a decision they still inter-preted as completely insane. I avoided Louise's eyes, praying she wouldn't tell them that I was the real reason Teddy had quit. The knowledge filled me with shame even more now that Teddy was ill. Though I knew it was irrational, what was happening to Teddy seemed inextricably linked to his decision several months ago. If I could get him through this ordeal, it would atone for so much.

When Teddy's hair fell out, the downy white fuzz that replaced it made him look years younger, despite the strain he was under. His eyes seemed bigger and brighter, his lopsided smile even goofier. Seeing him like that made my heart nearly break, he seemed so vulnerable. At the same time it reminded me of the incredible child-like energy he'd always had, and gave me hope that the same would fuel his recovery.

"I look like a giant Pampers baby," he said one day as he emerged from the washroom.

"Maybe they're holding auditions," I said. He laughed loudly and later I overheard him repeat the joke to his mother, who told him it wasn't remotely funny.

A scan after the first round of chemotherapy showed no significant shrinkage of the tumour, but the doctors were confident that the regimen of painkillers and anticonvulsant drugs he was taking was effective enough for him to go home to await the next stage of treatment. Teddy was ecstatic, and so was I. I had no doubt his own home would be a more healing-inducing environment than the hospital. I also thought it would give us more time alone, but his parents and siblings treated the coach house much like the hospital waiting room, coming and going as they pleased. The one advantage to this arrangement was that they almost always brought food: baked goods, frozen lasagnas, fruit baskets, and at least once a week Teddy's mother's signature casserole (and Teddy's favourite) made with macaroni, canned tuna, Campbell's mushroom soup, and onion soup mix as garnish.

I knew Teddy would do better if he had something to occupy him, something he loved. Discovering that his favourite sleight-of-hand magician had published a new book of tricks, I bought it for him as a surprise. As I'd hoped, he loved it and threw himself into learning the new moves. It meant that I had to be his attentive first audience—something I'd never been keen on. The truth was, card tricks bored me silly. Once you knew, in theory, how they were done, with palming and distraction, the outcome ("How did you know the exact card I randomly picked? It's as if you read my mind!") ceased to amaze. But I was determined not to reveal my irritation or impatience in any way. I picked a card when he asked me to and praised the miraculous result. I told myself it was helping to restore his health, as if his learning to make cards disappear was also making his tumour vanish.

THE NEXT STAGE of Teddy's treatment, radiation this time, began on Halloween. His parents wanted to drive him to and from his appointments, but he insisted that he and I go alone. He told them it was to save the outrageous cost of hospital parking. He told me that his mother's fussing made him feel sicker than he actually was. "I feel much stronger when I'm with you, Paul," he said. I agreed that anything that made him feel better was worthwhile—even as it increased the weight of responsibility on me—no matter what his parents wanted.

We were both optimistic about this new round of treatment and were eager to get it underway. "Wasn't it radiation that turned Peter Parker into Spider-Man?" he said as we rode the subway to the hospital.

"Yes. That is one of the potential side effects," I said. "Others include X-ray vision and glowing in the dark."

"Cool," he said. "Do you think Les knows what's coming, that he's about to be zapped by a radioactive death ray? I mean, he can probably read my thoughts, can't he? Since he lives right inside my brain."

"How do you know it's you and not Les who is actually thinking those thoughts?" I said.

Teddy's eyes grew wide. "That's true," he said. "But that would make Les suicidal."

"All cancers are suicidal," I observed. "Once they kill their hosts, they obviously die too." As soon as I said it, I regretted it. I'd been trying to avoid any mention of death. I looked carefully at Teddy's face to see if my suggestion had disturbed him, but he just looked thoughtful, intrigued by the twist of philosophy.

"I never thought of that before," he said.

The appointment went ahead on schedule. I was not allowed into the room where the radiation was administered, but they did let me watch, along with the technician, from behind the protective glass. Teddy lay on his back on a table; after much careful adjustment of the position of his head, he was told not to move a millimetre.

"What if I get the hiccups?" he asked.

"Don't," said the technician.

When it was finished, I asked Teddy how it felt. "Okay," he said tentatively. "I didn't really feel anything. How did it look?" he asked.

"It was wild," I told him. "A mini mushroom cloud rose from your head."

"Really?" Teddy said.

The technician laughed loudly; Teddy laughed then too, but I could tell he was disappointed to realize the mushroom cloud was just a joke.

We made our way down to the ground floor in a crowded elevator and through the hospital lobby to the automatic revolving door. As we emerged into the sunshine and surprising warmth of Indian summer, Teddy said, "You know what? I feel more than okay. I feel really good."

"No nausea?" I asked.

"None at all," he said. "In fact, I'm starving. You know what I really want to do? I want to go out for lunch. Can we go out for lunch?"

"Of course."

We walked up University Avenue to College Street, then decided to continue walking—Teddy insisted he felt strong enough—to a restaurant on Harbord Street that used to be one of our favourites. Neither of us could remember when or why we had stopped going. As we crossed one of the fields on the University of Toronto campus, Teddy grabbed my hand and started swinging it. I was surprised that he didn't start to skip.

We had a long, leisurely lunch that included Teddy's favourite sticky toffee pudding with ice cream for dessert. By the time we emerged back into the sun, schools had let out and streams of brightly costumed kids were making their way home, already buzzing with excitement about the evening ahead. I was worried that he might be getting tired, but Teddy insisted we continue to walk, zigzagging our way home through the neighbourhoods, eavesdropping on the children's lively exchanges, and witnessing the exquisitely pale yellow sun that bathes Toronto each October.

"Whoa! Now that's really scary," Teddy said as we passed a little girl dressed as a clown.

The girl looked up at Teddy and said, "What are you supposed to be? A zombie?"

Despite his energy and cheer that day, Teddy's skin still looked pasty white; there were deep dark circles under his eyes, and the scar from his operation was plainly visible through the wispy fuzz on his skull. He laughed so hard at the girl's comment that he had to stop and lean on a fence, clutching at a cramp in his side. When he could stand again, he made to walk like a zombie, charging after another cluster of kids, several of whom were dressed as Spider-Man, who ran ahead shrieking with glee.

On Bloor Street we passed a small grocery store with a

display of pumpkins outside. "Paul!" Teddy gasped. "We need a jack-o'-lantern! How did we forget?"

We hadn't bothered to carve a pumpkin the previous year because no trick-or-treaters ventured around the back of the houses to knock on the coach house door. Now we were doing it for ourselves, for the joy of it; I vowed that in the coming years, once Teddy got well, we would always have a pumpkin. We bought a large one, realizing too late that we should have waited and bought one closer to home, as it proved quite awkward and heavy to carry. But we took turns, passing it back and forth like a baby, and by the time we arrived at the coach house, it had been christened Teddy Junior.

"Actually, I'd like to start him off right and call him Theodore," Teddy said. "I always wished people would call me by my proper name instead of Teddy, which, face it, is basically the name of a stuffed toy. But nobody would do it. I once went a whole month refusing to acknowledge anyone unless they addressed me as Theodore; it still didn't work. My family would just pinch me instead to get my attention, so I finally gave up the campaign."

"I could never think of you as anything but Teddy," I said.

"That just hurts," he said.

His parents' car was parked in the alley, and when we opened the door to the coach house, his mother came running down the stairs. "Where have you been? I've been sick with worry! Your appointment ended hours ago."

"We went out for lunch. And we found this little guy. Theodore Junior." He held the pumpkin up next to his head. "The resemblance is uncanny, isn't it?"

Vivian didn't laugh. She glared at me. "Why weren't you answering your phone?"

I'd turned it off at the hospital. Since Teddy was with me, it didn't even occur to me to turn it back on. "I'm sorry," I said. "We didn't realize you were coming over."

"Well of course I was coming over," she said. "Of course I want to see my son when he's just been zapped with dangerous whatchamacallit!"

Upstairs, Clive was on the couch reading a newspaper.

"Hey, Dad," Teddy said. "Which part of the paper are you finished with? I need it."

Clive handed over the Entertainment section, which Teddy spread out on the kitchen table. He set the pumpkin on top and began rooting around in the drawers for a suitable knife.

Vivian was desperate to know more about the radiation session, but Teddy couldn't be distracted from the task at hand.

"Aha!" he said, holding up a large butcher knife. "My turn to be the surgeon." He sawed vigorously in a circle around the stem until he was able to pop off the top of Theodore Junior's head.

I reached inside and began scooping out the orange guts.

"Do you think that's what Les looks like?" Teddy asked.

"More or less," I said.

Teddy guffawed and Vivian gasped. "Teddy, be careful with that knife! You're waving it every which way."

Teddy set the knife down. "What I need now is a marker."

He went into the bedroom where I kept my desk. I scraped the remaining innards from the pumpkin with a tablespoon, then began extracting the seeds from the pile of gloop for roasting.

"Do you really think this is a good idea?" Vivian asked. "Shouldn't he be resting?"

"Ta-da!" Teddy emerged from the bedroom with a black marker and began drawing guidelines for Theodore Junior's face.

"I think we'd better get going," Clive said, rising from the couch, "or the trick-or-treaters will be rioting at our front door."

Vivian sighed deeply and shook her head. She kissed Teddy and told him to take care of himself.

"Paula's taking care of me," he said.

She sighed again and they left.

Teddy carved a jack-o'-lantern that looked like an evil baby and set it on the kitchen windowsill facing inward, so that as we sat on the couch with plates of warmed-up tuna casserole, we could see its diabolically toothless grin leering at us. The 1963 version of *The Haunting* was on television. We couldn't tear our eyes away and watched to the end, though it had us clutching each other in genuine fear. We were still holding on when we moved to our bed and fell asleep curled up close.

At about three o'clock I awoke to what I thought was a loud bang in the kitchen. Teddy remained asleep, so I wondered if I had dreamed it. I waited through a full minute of silence before slipping out of bed to check. There was still a tiny flicker of light coming from the jack-o'-lantern. I'd forgotten to blow out the candle; it had burned down to little more than a puddle of wax that would have snuffed itself out shortly anyway. When I put it out, the smoke from the wick was sharp and pungent in my nose. It reminded me of something, though I couldn't quite grasp what. Nothing else in the room was amiss or out of place, so I returned to bed. Glancing at Teddy, I realized his eyes were now open. He was lying flat on his back, looking up.

"Did you hear that?" I asked.

"No," he said.

He didn't ask, "Did I hear what?" He just said no, which struck me as strange. But before I could ask him about it, his eyes were closed again, his breathing deep and steady as if he was already sound asleep.

TO MY DISMAY, Teddy was far less upbeat about his second radiation session the following morning. He seemed rather agitated and irritable. When I asked him if he felt okay, he just said he was tired because he hadn't slept well. I worried that Vivian was right and I had tired him out too much.

This time I stayed in the waiting room and tried to read while he underwent his treatment. Afterward we headed straight for the subway and home again. Teddy didn't want any lunch. He went to the bedroom instead for a nap. Wednesday he was the same, and on Thursday when he emerged from the session, he felt too nauseated to risk taking the subway. I had to give in and call his parents to ask for a ride.

Painful burn blisters appeared on the side of his head where the radiation was directed. I was rubbing salve into his scalp one night to soothe the burns when I noticed Theodore Junior still sitting in the window, now caving in on one side. I quietly disposed of the pumpkin in the green bin before Teddy saw it. The analogy was just too grotesque.

A scan following the first round of radiation showed disappointing results: the tumour still had not shrunk. I refused to believe in any outcome other than Teddy's full recovery. What worried me more was the look in Teddy's eyes: he was beginning to doubt. He gave up on magic, not just learning new tricks, but practising any sleight of hand. This only aggravated the restlessness that seemed to take him over at this time. Card tricks had always been a good outlet for his fidgety energy, but now he didn't seem to know what to do with his hands; he developed a habit of running them repeatedly over his fuzzy skull.

He started behaving oddly in other ways too. I never actually saw this behaviour, only its aftermath. I would find that he had moved things all over the house, leaving them or putting them away in strange places. I'd find my pillow on the kitchen counter, or a fork in the medicine cabinet. Teddy denied all responsibility. At first, I just laughed it off as absentmindedness, understandable given the circumstances. I once emerged from the bedroom to find every cabinet and drawer in the kitchen standing open, like in a movie about poltergeists. Again Teddy said he didn't do it. As incidents occurred more frequently, I became worried by his persistent denials. It wasn't like Teddy not to lay claim to a prank. I mentioned it to his oncologist when I was able to pull her aside for a moment outside Teddy's hearing, but she dismissed it, saying the stress and trauma to his brain were bound to cause lapses and moments of confusion.

On the last night of November, I woke suddenly at about three o'clock. Teddy was lying beside me, wide awake.

"What's the matter?" I asked.

"Les is keeping me awake," he said.

"I'll get you one of the painkillers," I said as I began to swing my legs out of bed.

"No!" he nearly shouted, and grabbed my arm to hold me back, then more quietly said, "It's not pain. It's just Les, he's telling me things."

"You're hearing voices?" I ask, trying to disguise my alarm.

"Just his," Teddy said. "Only it's not really a voice per se. It's more just his perspective."

"Teddy," I said very quietly, "Les is not a person. He . . . it is not an entity of any kind. Just some aberrant cells."

Teddy said nothing.

Suddenly there was a loud thump from the kitchen, like someone had dropped a heavy book on the floor. It was just like the one I'd heard a month earlier, only this time I was awake. "What the hell was that?" I said, fear and adrenalin rushing through my veins. I turned again to get out of bed, but Teddy clutched harder on to my arm, hurting it.

"No!" he said again. "Please stay here with me, Paul," he pleaded.

"But what if there's an intruder?" I said. I could hear the panic in my voice.

"It's just Les," he said, and would not let go of my arm. I couldn't shake him off; he seemed to have superhuman strength. And so we stayed like that for several seconds, me splayed awkwardly with my legs half out of bed, torso twisted toward Teddy, who was still holding my arm in a vise-like grip. I was afraid but also concerned about not alarming Teddy and making him even worse. Maybe this was just another odd but not unexpected symptom of his brain stress. I listened intently for more sounds from the kitchen but could hear only my rapid breaths. Finally, I lay back down. Teddy fell asleep, only barely loosening his grip on my arm. Eventually, I too must have drifted off, because the next thing I knew, Teddy was standing next to the bed, shaking me awake.

"Time to get up, Paul," he said. "We've got a busy day ahead."

"What?" I looked at the clock. 7:08. "Is that *bacon?*"

"I made breakfast," Teddy said. "We need to fuel up. Today's our last chance to rehearse, and we still need to iron out so many things."

"What are you talking about?"

"The play! *Romeo and Juliet.* Come on, get out of bed, sleepyhead!" He returned to the kitchen.

With an overwhelming sense of dread, I got up and dressed quickly in the first pair of jeans and sweater I could find, and followed him. Not just bacon. He'd also made pancakes. He ordered me to the table and placed a plate full of food in front of me; this time, I felt too nauseated to eat, but Teddy polished off both his own plate and mine.

"I'll do these later," he said, dumping the dishes in the sink. "I can't wait to get started." He opened the door to go downstairs, then stopped and looked back at me. "Aren't you coming?"

"I'll be down in a minute," I said. "You go ahead."

He left. I picked up my phone. His parents were scheduled to arrive to pick us up at 8:15. I texted asking them to come as early as possible, then went downstairs. It was freezing. Teddy hadn't bothered to turn on the electric heaters, though it hardly made any difference once I did.

The stage remained as we had left it that night in August when Teddy was first rushed to the hospital. I hadn't wanted to upset him by dismantling it in his absence—though now I wished I had. When he did return home, he said nothing about it. In fact, until that moment I don't think he'd mentioned the play once. Now he was pacing the stage, reciting Romeo's lines.

"It is the east, and Juliet is the sun!" he called out when he saw me. "Come!" he said, patting the seat of the therapist's armchair.

I stepped onto the stage tentatively. Teddy seemed to be surrounded by an energy field of some kind, electricity, or maybe radioactivity. I had the feeling that if I touched him, I would get a nasty shock. I sat in the armchair; Teddy lay back on the couch. "Dr. Caplet," he began, and continued with the opening scene of *Transference: A Tragedy*. I fumbled, trying to remember my own lines, could barely get them out when I did, but Teddy didn't seem to notice. He was completely absorbed in his own performance, which grew increasingly bizarre. He stood up when he should have remained sitting and frequently approached the edge of the stage, making grand gestures with his arms as he addressed an invisible audience. Then, as he launched into Romeo's next speech, he began circling the couch, faster and faster, until he was practically jogging. And as he did, his speech sped up accordingly, until it was no longer coherent.

Panic rose in my chest as I took out my phone. Teddy was running in circles so fast now, I was afraid he was going to tumble off the stage. A car pulled into the alley outside. Clive and Vivian. Teddy stopped, looked out at me with wide-eyed terror, said, "Paul?" and then collapsed.

TEDDY REMAINED UNCONSCIOUS for several hours, during which time they conducted several tests, including a scan showing the mass had grown. When I was finally allowed into the room to see him, he was sitting up. He looked pale and gaunt, but relaxed. "Paul," he said, holding out his hand for mine. Then he smiled sadly and said, "It looks like Les is more."

I was determined to be strong for him, though I felt like I might disintegrate. "Your family is outside," I told him. "The *whole* family."

"Okay," he said. "But there's something I want to ask you first."

"Anything."

"Can you get me a notebook?"

"Of course. Which notebook?"

"A new, blank one. For writing in. I want to write in longhand. It's more authentic."

"Okay," I said, wondering why his family had to be absent when he made this perfectly normal request.

"When I was asleep, I had this dream. More of a vision," he said, looking over my shoulder as if he were seeing the vision again. His eyes found their way back to my face. "Paul, I know there's a good chance I'll never be onstage again."

I started to protest, "Don't be ridiculous—" but he stopped me.

"Paul, please. I know I can't say this to them," he said, nodding toward the hall outside, "so I have to be able to say it to you. There's a good chance that my only legacy now will be what I write between now and . . . the thing is, this dream I had . . . it's an idea, a really brilliant idea!"

And there it was again, that flash of excitement in his blue, blue eyes that he got with every new idea. Deep down inside me a tiny voice sighed *not again*, but I slammed the door shut on the very thought. I knew what I had to do: I had to cultivate that excitement no matter what. As long as I could keep his dreams alive, I just knew he too would live. I took his hand. "I'll get you a notebook."

He grinned. "Thank you."

Everyone, including Teddy, insisted I go home to sleep that night. Teddy was to stay in hospital again while undergoing another, more aggressive round of radiation treatments. So I complied, but I got up early, left the coach house at seven thirty and took the subway an extra stop south on University Avenue where there was a large Staples store open early for the business district. As I entered the brightly lit store, I was stopped suddenly in my tracks. Christmas music. Of course, I knew the holidays were just a couple of weeks away. If I'd still been teaching, I'd have hauled out my stash of Christmas songs for the kids to learn. But here, now, was the realization that for the people around me, the other shoppers in the store, the people hurrying to work outside, the regular Christmas season was underway, regular life continued. The thought was so disorienting that I felt dizzy for a few seconds.

An employee approached to ask if I needed help finding anything. I felt like I was looking at him through the wrong end of a pair of binoculars. I finally managed to stammer, "Notebooks."

He pointed me to the correct aisle. I found myself surveying a huge selection of notebooks of different colours, styles, and shapes, everything from whimsical (Hello Kitty on the cover, or shaped like a watermelon) to seriously boring (brown lizard skin). How on earth was I to choose the book that would save Teddy's life? More problematic than aesthetics was the question of length. Too many pages might be discouraging for him; on the other hand, too few could reinforce his notion that he had little time left. I finally settled on a plain red, medium-sized spiral-bound notebook with a cardboard cover sturdy enough for Teddy to fold it open and write while sitting in bed.

The cashier at the checkout counter, a woman about my age, was wearing reindeer antler deely-boppers. "A red notebook," she said. "Let me guess—it's for your Christmas wish list!"

"A two-hundred-page wish list?" I said.

"Dream big, baby," she said. "That's my motto. D-B-B!"

As I walked up University Avenue toward the hospital, I remembered how Miranda and I used to fight over the Sears Christmas wish catalogue each year from the time it arrived in late November right up until Christmas Eve. My mother had to put a calendar on the fridge, marked on alternate days with Miranda's and my initials, indicating whose turn it was to take the catalogue to bed to pine over before sleep.

To my surprise and relief, when I arrived at the hospital, none of Teddy's family was there yet. I found him sitting on top of the covers, seemingly deep in thought as he gazed over at the window. "The barbecue is at nine," he told me, referring to that morning's radiation session. He shifted his body and patted the bed beside him for me to sit where he could put his arm around me. I sat down and took the notebook out of my bag.

"Perfect," he said. "The ideas have been flying around in my head and I need to get them down before I forget."

A nurse arrived with a wheelchair to take him away. "Do you want me to come?" I asked.

"Nah, I'm a veteran," he said. "Besides, you'd better stay and tell Mom where I am. She'll have a heart attack if she arrives and finds my bed empty."

The more aggressive radiation took its toll on Teddy. In the immediate aftermath he felt the worst, nauseated and dizzy, needing help to get to the bathroom and back. The burns on his scalp became more severe this time and required regular salving. By mid-afternoon, he'd start feeling stronger and more clearheaded. This was when he'd take out the red notebook and work. We were all forbidden to look at the notebook, even to glance over his shoulder.

Though I was not allowed to see what he wrote, he liked it best if I stayed in the room with him while he scribbled away, bent over the page with furious determination in his eyes. I tried to read or work on my laptop, but found it very difficult to concentrate. Sometimes he would murmur aloud and laugh. It was as if I were hearing a conversation coming from another room but couldn't quite catch the words. Other times, I would get a prickly feeling and look up to find Teddy staring at me intently, yet not quite registering my presence, as if he were looking at a painting of me instead of my face. I found myself glancing frequently at the clock, then berated myself lest Teddy should notice. My neck and shoulders grew increasingly tense with the ongoing effort to tamp down my restlessness. By the time a nurse arrived each day with Teddy's evening medications in a tiny paper cup, I was exhausted and craved unconsciousness. Even so, when I arrived at the empty coach house, it was a struggle to settle down and sleep. I'd return the hospital the next day still tired and unrefreshed, but I was determined to keep going, for my own sake as much as Teddy's.

On the winter solstice, the shortest day of the year, I slept in and arrived at the hospital late. Teddy had already returned from his radiation session and was waiting for me in his room. When I apologized, he looked at me with concern and said, "Paul, you're losing weight."

I shrugged, but he looked thoughtful. "Isn't today Diane's birthday?" he asked.

"Yes," I said. "The twenty-first." I was surprised that Teddy remembered.

"How is she doing?" he asked.

"Still pretty much housebound, with all those babies," I said. "But you know Diane."

"You should go see her," he said. "Today, I mean."

I had already spoken to Diane that morning and she'd invited me to do just that. She and her husband had big plans: Randy was going to pick up Thai food on the way home from work. "We might even stay up past eight!" Diane said. I'd told her I couldn't possibly leave Teddy alone, but the desire to go, to get away even for a short while from the oppressive cycle of hospital and home, was suddenly overwhelming.

"You wouldn't mind?" I asked Teddy.

"Of course not," he said.

Mid-afternoon I kissed Teddy goodbye and took the College streetcar east across the valley. Looking down at the highway and the Don River below, I was shocked to note that it was now actually winter. The seasons were progressing even while I was in limbo. It was as if I expected them to halt as well until my life was back on track. I wasn't even wearing a proper winter coat, or hat and gloves, as the temperature (I realized while walking up Diane's street) clearly warranted.

I rang the bell and the front door was promptly opened by one of the twins wearing nothing but a diaper.

"Wow, she's learned to work the door handle," I said.

"You're surprised that my offspring have opposable thumbs?" Diane asked.

"Isn't it a bit dangerous? She's not even two."

"Try to think of the positive side of things, Paula," Diane said. "The child is a prodigy, already showing signs of a brilliant career as a butler. Sweetheart, take Paula's coat for her."

But Trillium or Fern—I wasn't sure which one—was now speeding away on a wheeled plastic duck, stopping only when she crashed into her sister on an identical plastic duck. They began to argue in their secret twin language, their voices rising until Juniper, also fluent in their twin gibberish, as well as speaking perfectly formed English—"already bilingual at two and a half!" Diane liked to brag—stepped in to break them up.

"Happy birthday," I said, handing Diane a plastic bag. "And yes, I did buy it at the hospital gift shop."

Diane opened the bag. She looked puzzled. "What is it?"

"A travel pillow. You have to blow it up," I said. "You told me last week you kept getting kinks in your neck from falling asleep sitting up. This holds your neck straight. Here, let me." I took it back and blew it up for her, then fitted it on the back of her neck.

"This is amazing," she said, tilting her head from side to side to test it. "I'll even be able to sleep standing up. I can't tell you how many times I've wished I could do exactly that— you know, catch a few winks in line at the grocery store."

"Just don't try it while cooking," I said.

"Oh, I can cook in my sleep, no problem. This is really amazing, Paula," she repeated. "Even if you're about to tell me it's a birthday-slash-Christmas gift."

Diane was always ranting about how having her birthday so close to Christmas meant she got cheated out of half her rightful gifts. If it was a birthday-slash-Christmas gift, it had better be twice as good. She sat on the couch, leaned back against her travel pillow, and closed her eyes. Juniper immediately climbed onto one knee; Trillium claimed the other. "The only thing that could improve on this birthday present would be earplugs," she said. "That and Randy getting back with my wine."

"How about some tea?" I said, going ahead and filling the kettle.

Fern stood in front of Diane, tiny hands on tiny hips, and, finding her mother's lap already full of her sisters, scolded them all in her twin gibberish.

"What is she saying?" I asked.

"That I should have used birth control," Diane said.

I made two cups of tea and carried them over, but was trepidatious about where to put them down.

"What you've got to do," Diane said, her eyes still closed, "is put the cups on the table, then very quickly—very, very quickly!—get the brat in a lock hold so she can't touch them."

I placed myself between Fern and the coffee table before I set the tea down. Fern made a beeline for the cups, but I managed to scoop her up while she squealed with evident delight. I sat down beside Diane with the child in my lap. She busied herself pulling the drawstring out of my hoodie. I looked up to find Diane observing me, though her head still rested on the pillow.

"So how are you really?" she asked. "You look like you could use one of these thingies."

"I could, but the chairs at the hospital don't have high enough backs."

"But how are you coping. Feeling," she said. "Only you're not really saying anything to anyone."

I frowned. "Who's anyone?"

"Miranda, actually."

"You talked to her?"

"She phoned me," Diane said. "They're worried, I guess. You seem to be going along, coping fine."

"They're worried that I'm coping fine?"

"Worried you're only pretending to be coping fine," she clarified.

"Is there a difference?"

Diane shrugged. "Probably not," she said, "come to think of it."

"Anyway, it doesn't matter how I'm feeling day to day. It won't matter at all once we get through this."

She narrowed her eyes at me. "But it does matter, especially since you don't really know what this is, I mean, how things are going to turn out, or how long . . ."

"The radiation is clearly working better this time," I said. "He's starting to look better."

Having successfully removed the cord from my hood, Fern tried looping it around Trillium's neck. To distract her, I showed her how to weave it around her bare toes instead. "You once warned me about mistaking professional problems for relationship ones, and you were right," I said quietly, "but I went on making that mistake anyway, and I have to make that better. So Teddy has to get better." Despite myself, I started to cry. With no arms free to hug me, Diane and babies leaned in against my side.

"I'm sure he will," she murmured.

When Randy arrived home, we were still there, huddled together in a heap of babies on the couch. Juniper ran and latched on to her father's leg while he set the food out on the dining table.

"Here, can you take Fern so I can get up?" Diane said, handing me a twin.

"But this is Trillium, isn't it? I thought I already had Fern."

"Oh God, who knows," Diane said. "I can't tell them apart."

THE MACGREGORS' CHRISTMAS EVE PARTIES were legendary. They involved vats of beer and scotch, mountains of food, and musical instruments of all kinds, including at least one set of bagpipes, and usually resulted in a number of minor injuries from drunken attempts to imitate *Braveheart*. If the youngest MacGregor son could not make it to the party this year, they were determined to bring at least some version of it to him.

"We have to give him a good Christmas, just in case," I overheard Fiona say to one of the nurses a few days earlier, as she outlined the family's plans. She didn't spell out in case of what, but I knew what she meant, and it made me angry. I thought Teddy was looking remarkably well. The radiation sessions had ceased the previous week as the regular hospital staff was reduced to a minimum over the holidays. Teddy's doctors planned to reassess his condition on their return. This meant Teddy was less nauseated, and able to get on with his work earlier in the day. He appeared to be writing at a frenzied rate, though he still allowed no one to see what was on the page.

"Don't let Teddy hear you say things like that," I told Fiona. She and the nurse exchanged a glance, but said nothing.

Teddy was still writing mid-afternoon on Christmas Eve. When I returned to his room with my coffee, he barely glanced up from his notebook. I wandered over to the window. The slice of University Avenue I could see from that angle was monochrome grey. It started to rain. I recalled one very rainy Christmas Eve when I was a child.

"Don't worry," my father had said to Miranda and me as we watched the weather anxiously. "Santa will just have to use his boat this year instead."

I went to bed that night utterly reassured by the nonsensical picture in my mind: a big red boat perched on the roof of our bungalow, while Santa got on with the task at hand. The resilience of the human imagination.

I suddenly felt someone's eyes on me and turned around. Teddy was looking at me, the notebook closed and held close to his chest, and smiling, no, actually beaming. "It's finished, Paul," he said. "I'm finished my play."

I felt a flicker of dread that was twofold, first about the nature of the play itself. Would it be another untenable idea I would have to pretend to like? More worrisome was what the play's completion would mean for Teddy's state of mind. Would the momentum toward healing slow, or God forbid cease, now that he'd finished this task? I'd have to make sure he remained motivated, whatever it took.

"Now I can tell you what it's about," he said. He held out his hand for me, clutching mine when I came over and sat on the bed. "It's the greatest love story. Orpheus and Eurydice, husband and wife," he said. "Only in this case, it's Orpheus who dies, and his wife who has to retrieve him. It's about us, Paul."

I gasped silently and tears sprang to my eyes. "Teddy," I started to say, but then his sister Colleen entered the room, followed by her two young sons and Second Mike carrying a three-foot-tall Christmas tree in a pot, already decorated with a tartan theme.

"Let the party begin," Teddy said. He gave me a wink, then put his notebook into the drawer in his bedside table, while I hastily wiped my eyes and tried to compose myself.

Moira-oind-Roy and family arrived soon after, followed by Teddy's parents. By late afternoon the entire clan was there, children and babies included, and none came empty-handed. They managed to smuggle in all sorts of Christmas treats: mince-meat tarts and pumpkin pie, and of course, scotch—carefully concealed in soft drink bottles and Thermoses.

My parents and Miranda and Gordon came as well, though they looked a bit overwhelmed by the MacGregors' merriment. Teddy presided like a king at the centre of the gathering. He sat upright on the bed, his legs stretched out on top of the blankets, chatting animatedly as his family pressed in, trying to get close to him. I watched him from a corner of the room. Every once in a while, he would look up from whomever he was talking to and find my face. We'd lock eyes for a moment and he'd smile.

As the party grew more noisy and raucous, and the true nature of the beverages being consumed became more evident, the hospital staff intervened. It was time for the partiers to leave so patients could take their evening medications and turn in. MacGregor voices rose in protest, and there might have been a riot but for Teddy taking charge. He rose up on his knees on the bed and called for everyone's attention.

"Please, everybody, thanks for coming. You really have made this an amazing Christmas for me. But we sick people need our sleep. Don't make the nurses haul you away, because they will."

So one by one, they kissed him good night and wished him a merry Christmas before taking their leave. The night manager insisted they take every last bit of food and drink, as well as the Christmas tree, which she said could trigger allergies. It was a bit like the Grinch's famous Christmas Eve clear-out, not a crumb was left behind. Last to leave were Teddy's parents and Louise.

"Can we drop you off, Paula?" Clive asked.

But Teddy reached for my hand and squeezed it tight. "Please stay with me," he pleaded. He'd never asked me to stay like that before, but I dismissed my apprehension, telling myself he was just being sentimental because it was Christmas Eve.

The staff gave me a blanket and pillow with which to try to make myself comfortable in my chair, but once Teddy was settled, and the light turned off in his room as the nurse left, I quietly climbed into his bed.

The ward was unusually silent; perhaps it just seemed so after the cacophony of the party. I thought for a moment that Teddy had already drifted off, but then he whispered my name. "Paul," he said. "Eurydice."

I snuggled up close, tucking my arm under his.

"I want you to play her," he continued.

"Teddy—"

"Please," he said. "Promise me you'll do the play. Even if I can't play Orpheus."

"Don't be ridiculous, of course you'll get to play him."

"Please, Paul," he said. His voice was urgent, no longer whispering, his body tensed against mine. "Promise me that if I can't, you'll do it."

"Teddy, that's not going to happen—"

"Please!"

I sighed. "Okay," I said. There was no way he was going to calm down unless I did.

"You promise?"

"Yes, I promise."

His body relaxed and he kissed the side of my head. "Thank you," he said, whispering again. "I knew you would. I know you're the one who'd come and find me in the underworld." His breathing started to shift as he muttered, "I love you, Paul," and then he slept.

All night, I drifted in and out of dreams: of having to move back into Mrs. Gaskell's basement; of catching the streetcar the wrong way, rushing away into empty fields north of the city; of suddenly realizing the sidewalk I was walking on was actually a dizzyingly high bridge.

At six in the morning, stiff from my awkward position in Teddy's bed, I eased myself out, carefully so as not to wake him. His breathing sounded oddly shallow, but steady. I found my bag and some toiletries and went to the bathroom to brush my teeth and wash my face. Looking at myself in the mirror, I was a fright. There were dark circles around my eyes. My greasy hair stood up every which way. I wondered if Teddy would mind if I popped home for a shower. If I took a taxi, I could be back before the cavalry returned for the day. Given their hungover state, they'd probably straggle in later than usual. From the bathroom, I could hear activity in the ward ramping up, as it always did at that hour, and figured Teddy would be awake soon. But when I re-entered the room, I could see that he was still. Perfectly still. He was no longer breathing at all.

THERE WAS A brief attempt to resuscitate him after I alerted the nurse, but it was quickly deemed futile. They lowered his bed and pulled up a sheet to cover his head, but I motioned to stop them. I had to be able to see him, to touch him, or I would never be able to believe it was true. They left us alone. The skin of his cheek already felt chilled, and his eyes seemed to have sunk deeper into his eye sockets. I accepted a nurse's offer to call his parents for me, accepted as well her offer to call my own. I was literally dumbstruck, unable to speak. I responded to questions with nods and gestures, or just did not respond at all. A hole in my stomach was expanding inside me, the black hole that had just swallowed a whole world.

I could hear Vivian weeping from down the hall well before she and Clive and Louise entered the room. They all stood around his bed and cried, but I still could not.

A doctor, actually a third-year resident who had the misfortune to be on call on Christmas Day, entered the room. She was a young, soft-spoken woman, but she spoke with calm authority. She explained that although she did not yet know exactly what had caused Teddy's death, given the nature of his tumour, we always knew a devastating brain "event" was a possibility. *We always knew.*

More MacGregors started to arrive, crying loudly as they insisted on entering the room where Teddy's body still lay. My parents arrived too, quieter but no less stricken. The hospital staff grew agitated. It was Christmas Day. They needed to remove the body from the ward quickly, with as little upset as possible to the other patients and their families, many of whom would soon be arriving to celebrate the day. They did not need to be met first thing Christmas morning by a corpse.

We were all banished from the room. In the waiting area, Clive suggested that everyone regather at their house. Those MacGregors who were still en route to the hospital were called and redirected. I was about to leave with my parents when I suddenly remembered the notebook—my first real thought since I found Teddy not breathing.

"Wait," I croaked, and ran back to the room. The bed

was now empty, stripped of its sheets. A nurse was emptying the contents of Teddy's bedside cabinet into a plastic shopping bag.

"Oh, good," she said. "I was going to come looking for you. I think this is everything." She handed me the bag. Books, phone, iPod, pens, and the notebook. Everything.

MY PARENTS DROVE me to the coach house so that I could pack myself some clothes. They insisted I come to their house for the next few days.

Miranda and Gordon and the kids were already at my parents' home when we arrived. When we entered, I remembered with a bit of a shock that it was Christmas morning. The kids, though upset about Teddy, were also clearly put out that they'd not yet been allowed to open their gifts, which were still piled around the base of the Christmas tree. The smell of turkey was beginning to waft through the house.

"I went ahead and put the turkey in," Miranda said with a little shrug. "I mean, we'll still need to eat."

Though I knew it was absurd, I felt as though I should apologize to them for ruining Christmas. I excused myself to take a shower instead. I spent as long as I could in the bathroom and then in my childhood bedroom getting dressed. From the living room I could hear the kids' voices rise to their usual cacophony, only to be shushed at intervals to a more subdued tone. They'd been allowed to go ahead and open their gifts. When I rejoined them in the wrapping-paper strewn living room, they looked up guiltily.

"I hope you don't mind . . ." Miranda said.

"Of course not," I said. "Teddy wouldn't have wanted them to miss Christmas."

Teddy would/wouldn't have wanted. Over the next few days, I would hear those words uttered countless times, as I met with his family several times to arrange the funeral and burial.

Teddy's parents actually lived quite close to mine in North York. It had been a point of marvel for Teddy and me when we first met to realize that we'd grown up in practically the same neighbourhood. I posited that we'd probably seen each other on at least one occasion, but he insisted that if we had, he would have known, would have sensed a "cosmic connection."

To my relief, his parents presumed from the start that they would pay. Even so, I had no objections to their plans. Teddy had always liked the pomp and ceremony of the high Anglican church of which they were members, though they only ever attended a few times a year. The only point of contention arose, and that within his family, around the matter of Teddy's clothes. Clive thought he should be buried in the same ancestral regalia they'd all donned for our wedding.

"I don't know, Dad," Colleen said. "It's a bit undignified to buried in a kilt, isn't it?"

Clive bristled. "How can it be undignified? It's my family heritage! Your family heritage!"

"Yes, but when you guys all dress up like that, you mean it a little ironically, don't you?" Colleen said, looking to Roy and Callum for support. "I mean, I think Teddy did, at least."

An argument ensued until it was finally put to me to settle: did Teddy wear his kilt ironically, or not?

"Well," I said slowly, realizing wearily that I didn't actually know the answer. "Only the top half of the coffin will be open, so it doesn't really matter what he's wearing from the waist down."

"What are you saying, just bury him in his underwear?" Fiona asked.

"It doesn't matter what we can see, it matters what he's actually wearing when he . . . when he . . ." Clive sputtered.

"Enters the pearly gates," Callum finished. "Better give him trousers."

Unbeknownst to me or to Teddy's family, his former classmates and acting colleagues decided that in honour of Teddy, they would attend the funeral dressed as their favourite heroes. So among the MacGregor kilts (worn with varying degrees of irony), the clergy and choir members' robes, and my own family's sober suits and dresses were a full cast of superheroes and celebrities of the theatre world. Some reprised their roles from Teddy's legendary party; others chose a lighter tribute—I spotted at least three Snoopies.

Greg, dressed as the Silver Surfer, delivered the eulogy. Another group of friends put together a slide show of Teddy's career to project on a screen above the pulpit. There were shots of him as a child, including one of him tap dancing with his great-uncle Morris, and his appearances in school plays from kindergarten through college. Then, with a shock, I realized I was looking at photos of myself: in *Frozen Assets*, at our wedding, doing magic shows—including one of Teddy displaying my apparently severed head, which elicited many chuckles and a few appalled gasps. In photo after photo, there I was at Teddy's side. I felt like I was looking at two people who had died.

There were lots more stories and anecdotes about Teddy's shenanigans shared at the noisy wake that followed the funeral. The MacGregors' house overflowed with family and friends who grew increasingly drunk and loud as they remembered him. Everyone was relentlessly kind to me, telling me over and over again how much I had meant to Teddy. I felt more exhausted than I'd ever been in my life. I'd already told my parents that I'd be returning to the coach house that night. No matter that they thought I still shouldn't be alone; being alone was the only thing I wanted.

I was scanning the crowded living room for Miranda and Gordon, who had promised to drive me home, when Louise took my arm and pulled me aside.

"I just want you to know, Paula, that I'll do everything I can to help you," she said.

"Thank you," I said, a little confused.

"I mean with the theatre company. I know Teddy would have wanted to keep it going," she said. "What was he working on in the hospital? It was a new play, wasn't it?"

"I don't know, Teddy was always writing stuff," I said sharply, suddenly irritated as well as exhausted.

Louise looked affronted.

"Look, I can't even think about that now," I said, pushing past her. That was when the tears finally came, and they came voluminously. I wasn't sure they would ever stop. Miranda and my parents closed in around me and obligingly steered me out to the car to take me home.

Miranda expressed consternation about leaving me alone

at the coach house; I assured her I was fine. But once she and Gordon had driven off and I locked the door behind me, I started shivering violently. The main floor was dark and cavernous; the stage set seemed sinister.

I hurried upstairs. I turned up the thermostat, but I still couldn't stop shivering. My teeth chattered. Just as I had when I was a child, I hummed a note to hear it staccatoed by the clattering. *What a strange thing to be doing*, I thought, as I continued to do so. But what did it matter if I behaved strangely? I lived alone now; no one else would see.

I forced my teeth to stop. I put the containers of food Vivian had packed for me in the fridge. In the bedroom I removed the navy-and-white dress Miranda had lent me for the funeral, put on a pair of Teddy's track pants and a hoodie, and crawled into bed. After what seemed like hours, I fell into a light, restless sleep, but kept waking myself with the sound of a sharp intake of my own breath. Finally, I got up, went into the kitchen, and put the kettle on. The shopping bag of Teddy's stuff from the hospital was on a kitchen chair. I could see the outline of the red notebook through the translucent plastic. I made myself a cup of tea and stared at the bag for several minutes before reaching inside and removing the notebook. There was nothing on the cover but a few lines of squiggling, as if he'd been testing his pen for ink. I sat with the notebook for some time, until long after my teacup was empty, and I still could not bring myself to open it, to look inside. Instead, I put it back into the shopping bag and returned to bed. This time, instead of my breath, I kept hearing sounds from various corners of the coach house, creaks and rustles that would wake me as soon as I began to drift off. I got up and went back to the kitchen. The shopping bag was where I'd left it, undisturbed. I removed the notebook again and put it inside a kitchen drawer on top of a stack of tea towels. Back to bed.

This time, though I told myself it was insane, I thought I heard the drawer slide open. It hadn't; when I got up again to look, the drawer was firmly shut, but I didn't want to take any more chances. I took the notebook out, opened the apartment door, and crept down the stairs to the freezing-cold ground floor. I turned on the light in the music room under the stairs. I hadn't set foot in there in weeks, since before Teddy's last trip to the hospital. That it hadn't changed was somehow shocking, and not in the least bit comforting. I opened the seat of the piano bench and put Teddy's notebook inside, underneath a pile of music. Then I turned off the light and returned to the stairs. A few steps up, I started running, just as Miranda and I used to do climbing up from the basement in our parents' home, as fast as we could, so as not to be grabbed by the bony hands of whatever fearful creature lurked beneath.

THE MOST FEARFUL creature threatening to stalk me in the new year was my growing mountain of debt. Unbeknownst to Teddy, or to anyone but the bank, I had taken out a line of credit in the fall. It had covered December's mortgage payment and all other expenses to the end of the year; now, even though I was returning to work with the drama club and my piano students, it would have to cover January's mortgage payment as well. I wasn't at all sure that I could continue paying for the coach house on my own, nor was I sure that I wanted to. Every time I entered or left, I had to pass through the space, so cavernous and cold in winter, that had been the site of extremes of both triumph and defeat, from *Frozen Assets* to the *Othello* fiasco, from the Wedding of Paula and Teddy to *Transference*. It felt like an admonition. Whenever a good memory arose or something happened that I wanted to tell Teddy about, it was knocked back by a twinge of guilt.

In the second week of January, my individual students began returning to the coach house for their lessons. Each time I sat beside a student on the piano bench to demonstrate, I was keenly aware of the presence of Teddy's notebook beneath the seat. As soon as the last student was gone, I turned out the lights of the music room and hurried upstairs. I could no longer play the piano for pleasure or stand to remain alone in the room with the piano bench.

Louise called me regularly. I had to force myself to answer when I saw her name, remind myself that she was genuinely devastated by Teddy's death and not deliberately hounding me. "Continuing with the Gamut Theatre Company," she told me, "is not just about honouring Teddy's memory. It's about your own future, Paula. I mean, have you thought about *your* career? What are you going to do?"

The thought of any kind of future at all seemed monstrous. I couldn't imagine anything that could begin to fill the vacuum that was my life.

I made an appointment with the bank. The personal finance advisor was a young woman named Destiny who looked to be only in her early twenties. She reminded me of my young drama students, the ones with ADHD, who could display fantastically intense emotions but never concentrated long enough to continue in character for an entire scene. Destiny greeted me with such a sombre expression of condolences for my loss that for a moment I feared she would actually cry. Moments later, however, her usual positive perkiness was poking through as she pulled up my financial details on her computer screen. "Let's take a look-see," she said. She clicked through a few more screens, moving her lips as she read, before turning back to me. "Are you aware of the terms of your mortgage insurance?" she asked.

"I'm . . . not sure," I said, wondering if it was possible that things were even worse than I thought.

"The mortgage was taken out jointly by you and your husband. At that time, you opted for an insurance policy that would pay off the mortgage in full should one of you die."

I stared, not comprehending.

"And since that has now happened," she began enthusiastically with a giant smile, remembering too late that she was talking about my husband's untimely death. She quashed the smile quickly and repeated in her sombre voice, "Since one of you has now passed, the mortgage is paid off. You won't actually need to make any more payments, at least, not once the paperwork is all sorted."

I was unable to speak as I tried to process what she had said. Everything suddenly seemed unreal. Destiny gave me a quizzical look. "Were you not aware of this provision?" she asked.

"I—" I stammered. Had I really not known? Not only could I no longer trust my perception of the present, but suddenly it seemed that my memory was also unsafe, and with it the integrity of my self. I felt panicked and started to breathe rapidly.

"Are you okay?" Destiny asked, half rising from her chair. "Do you want some water?"

"Yes, water," I managed to say, and once she left the room, I started to calm down. I put my palm flat on Destiny's desk for a moment. Solid, real. When she returned, I accepted the paper cup of water gratefully and gulped it down. It was icy cold.

Aside from having confirmed that I now owned the coach house outright, mortgage free, I registered little else from the meeting. I nodded and signed where Destiny told me to sign and shook her hand on my way out to begin a different life.

I NEVER TOLD Louise or any member of Teddy's family that his death had eliminated my financial debt. It felt instead as though I'd incurred a debt of another sort, which only deepened my feelings of guilt. Aside from Louise, who was angry about my failure to carry on Teddy's legacy, his family would not have begrudged me financial security; to the contrary, they would have said I deserved it. His parents often took the opportunity to tell me how much I'd meant to Teddy, which only made me feel worse. They called me regularly, at first, and duly invited me to family gatherings. Gradually the invitations stopped coming, and the calls dwindled to a few times a year, to my relief.

When I announced my intention, in the summer fol-lowing Teddy's death, to sell the coach house and start a candle-making business, I was surprised—and perhaps a bit hurt—by what little resistance my decision met. No one, apart from Louise, ever suggested I try to continue a career in the theatre without Teddy. Only Diane had reservations about my giving up that life. I allowed her to persuade me to keep my piano, to move it with me into the candle-making studio, though I was glad it would have to remain on the main floor. I duct-taped the piano bench closed for the move, so that I would not have to remove Teddy's notebook.

There it remains, untouched and unread.

❋ CHAPTER EIGHT ❋

IN THE SECOND WEEK OF January, school starts again; Héctor goes back to teaching and I return to my studio. Our New Year's Eve came and went early—literally—at Diane's house. Diane and Randy's New Year's Eve parties are legendary among her friends. Not for being wild and crazy, but for the exact opposite reason: they allow all of the parents, exhausted from a week and a half with their holidaying, hyperactive, sugar-fuelled kids, to go to bed early and get one over on the little brats at the same time. Everyone has to swear to obey the same rules. They must order their children to take an afternoon nap in preparation for a very late night. While the kids are asleep, or at least alone in bed, they put every clock in the house forward three hours, and hide any phones or devices that might give them away. When they all get to the party, they do the midnight countdown at nine. The kids are thrilled at being allowed to stay up so late, and the parents can be home in bed by ten. "They may not believe in Santa Claus anymore," says Diane. "But I swear they're going to believe in the nine o'clock New Year until they're thirty!"

Héctor and I were only too happy to be in bed early and asleep before the cheers and fireworks that officially welcomed the new year. We were exhausted after weeks of parties and dinners and get-togethers; so many of Héctor's students' parents were adamant that their children's favourite teacher stop by for at least a drink. I'm looking forward to a slower schedule. In all the flurry of holiday activity, I've barely had time to think. But instead, a blow—a not unexpected turn of events, but a blow nonetheless: Dusan and Violetta are issued a deportation order.

Laura hastily organizes a farewell potluck dinner party at the refugee centre. Determined to contribute his "world famous" stuffed peppers, Héctor dictates over the phone a list of ingredients for me to collect. I can hear the middle-school band warming up their instruments in the background. Once I have all of the groceries on his list, I head over to his apartment to meet him after school, ready to play sous-chef. Just as I arrive, Diane's minivan pulls up and Héctor climbs out.

"He pleaded for a ride," Diane rolls down her window to tell me. "Says he's on an urgent mission to cook a dish taught to the Aztecs by otherworldly visitors."

"Really," I say. I look at Héctor and hold out one of the shopping bags. "This is the recipe that includes ranch-flavoured Doritos?"

Héctor nods. "The secret ingredient. The otherworldly travellers came from the future."

Diane leaves and we spend the rest of the afternoon cooking the peppers before preparing to leave, while I try to avoid thinking about Dusan and Violetta.

The refugee centre is a three-storey house on Dundas West. It's dark and snowing when we arrive, but the windows of the house are all brightly lit.

"It was just like this when I first arrived here," Héctor says, stopping to take it in. "Almost a year ago now."

He is smiling, as though the memory is a pleasant one, although it's hard to imagine it was anything but daunting to land in this city in the middle of winter, homeless and utterly uncertain about even the immediate future.

The front door is opened by Laura's son, Christopher, who is wearing a large apron. "Guess what?" he says as Héctor slaps his shoulder in greeting. "My band cut a demo. I can play it for you on my phone."

"Fantastic!" Héctor says. "What's your band called?"

"Sweaty Fungus," Christopher says grinning. "Inspired by Logan's athlete's foot."

The front hall opens into a large living room with several couches and a piano along one wall. A man with a small child of about five or six is sitting on one couch with a chess board set up between them. Two women are examining a pile of paperwork together on another.

"Hello, everybody," Héctor calls, giving a general wave as he carries the pan of peppers through the room and into a large kitchen with a table big enough for at least two dozen people. The kitchen is warm, buzzing with activity and already full of savoury food smells. Barbara and Walter are both stirring pots, one on each of the two stoves. Other people I don't recognize are slicing bread and setting out dishes and cutlery on the table.

"Héctor and Paula! Wonderful to see you!" Laura says, opening her arms to greet us. She takes the pan of peppers and puts it into one of the ovens. "Paula, you've never been here before, have you. Would you like a quick tour?"

Héctor has already been co-opted by Christopher, who is handing him earbuds to listen to Sweaty Fungus, so I follow Laura up the narrow staircase.

"This house can accommodate twelve people, give or take a few young children. This is the largest room here," she says, pointing in through the open door of a bedroom. A woman wearing a headscarf is changing a baby's diaper on one of the beds. She smiles and murmurs hello. "We reserve this room for families," Laura continues. "This is where Dusan and Violetta stayed when they arrived."

The other two bedroom doors on this floor are closed; Laura explains that the rooms have two beds each, so occupants have to be paired with a roommate. At the top of the stairs to the third floor, another bedroom door stands open. On one of the twin beds sits a young man who could be anywhere from twelve to twenty, I think. He's thin and delicate-looking, and although he smiles at us, the expression in his eyes is one of total, disoriented shock.

"Abdi arrived from Somalia late last night," Laura explains. "You'll come downstairs and join us for food, Abdi?" she asks, making gestures to indicate eating.

"Yes, yes," Abdi nods and mimics Laura's gestures to indicate he has understood.

The ceiling slopes down toward the end of the hall where there's a tiny door, only about three feet high. "That leads to our roof-top balcony," Laura says. "It's lovely in the summer. Right now it's just buried in snow."

Abdi still sits motionless on the bed when we pass his room on the way back down. Héctor must have felt much the same as Abdi, it suddenly occurs to me, though it's hard to imagine Héctor being scared.

Laura and I return to the main floor to discover that Dusan and Violetta and their children have just arrived. Violetta seemed stern and aloof when I met her at Christmas, but the wide smile she gives me when she sees I'm wearing the shawl she made makes me realize she is probably just shy.

"Beautiful," she says.

I hold out a stretch of the shawl and agree, "Yes, it is very beautiful. You do very beautiful work."

"No," Violetta says, and makes an impatient gesture as if she doesn't know the words.

"She means you are beautiful wearing it," Héctor says.

Violetta nods yes, that is what she means, and I feel myself flush with pleasure.

Several more people arrive who stayed here at the

same time as Héctor, and they greet one another loudly, with enthusiastic embraces. The celebratory mood belies the sombre nature of the occasion as visitors and current residents of the house move into the kitchen where volunteers have set out the food. We all squeeze in around the giant table. There's a wide assortment of dishes: in addition to Héctor's peppers, there are pans of cannelloni, goat curry, vegetable samosas, and schnitzel, as well as heaps of fresh bread.

Barbara compliments Héctor on his peppers. "There's a distinct flavour that I can't quite put my finger on."

"That would be the secret ingredient," Héctor says. "Paula knows what it is, but if she tells, I will have to kill her."

"Why, is it cocaine?" Christopher asks.

"Christopher!" Laura gasps. Héctor and I laugh.

"Well, it is Mexican," Christopher says, making Laura gasp again and Héctor laugh even harder.

"Racial stereotypes are not allowed in this house," Laura says.

"Says my bossy Italian mother," Christopher mutters, and this time everyone laughs, including Abdi, though it's unclear how much he understands.

"Héctor," says the young mother I saw upstairs, whose name is Nahlah. "At what age must a child start learning to play an instrument like piano or violin?"

Héctor turns to the baby sitting in an old-fashioned high chair at the corner of the table between himself and Nahlah. The child grips Héctor's finger in her little fist. "We could start after supper," he says.

The others laugh.

"I was thinking of Adam," Nahlah says, indicating the little boy at her other side, who is feeding himself samosas with both hands. "If we had not left Syria, he would have had lessons already. I think he needs to start soon or it will be too late to have a chance at real success."

"The music is important for its own sake," Héctor says. "It's never too late to begin."

"I'll say. Look at this one," Malcolm says, indicating his son, Christopher. "Saved from a life of crime."

"But realistically," Nahlah persists.

"Ah, realistically," Héctor says. "That is something else entirely."

There are still heaps of food left once everyone is stuffed. I stay back in the kitchen with some of the volunteers to clean up and pack away the extra food while the guests move into the front sitting room. Laura follows them with trays of coffee and tea and brandy. We are nearly finished with the dishes when we hear piano music coming from the front, a sad tune that sounds like some kind of Eastern European folk music. Then Héctor is joined by the most haunting voice I have ever heard. Stepping through the archway, tea towel still in hand, I see that it is Violetta, singing in her language. Her voice seems to come from a place deeper than could be contained in her petite frame. Her whole body is gripped by the song; the previously shy and awkward woman now has none of that self-consciousness. Everyone else is utterly silent. Even Nahlah's baby is quietly rapt. They finish the song and begin another, equally sad and powerful. There is no need to understand the words; the story, Violetta and

Dusan's story, vibrates in her tone. Early tomorrow morning they will begin their journey, their return, to what? To the end of a dream.

ALTHOUGH HÉCTOR'S CASE is very different from Dusan and Violetta's, as Laura and Barbara have reassured me, their deportation feels like a warning, a reminder of just how untrustworthy desire can be, how untrustworthy it can make me be. So in the days following the farewell dinner, I find myself putting Héctor off, telling him I can't see him because I've fallen behind on my Valentine's Day orders and need to catch up.

It's not entirely untrue. Usually I begin making Valentine's Day candles the day after Boxing Day. This year my injury has delayed me. The burn covers most of the back of my hand, but not the palm, which is good, because it means I can pick things up without pain. But the skin of the back of my hand is still tender. I have to be careful pulling it through sleeves and avoid putting it in hot water. I still wear a long yellow rubber glove in the shower, which Héctor professes to find very sexy. The healed skin seems tighter, more rigid than it used to be. When I stretch my fingers around something or make a fist, there is a slightly unpleasant pulling sensation across my knuckles, but after a few days back in the studio, I got used to it and am now able to work unhindered. So my explanation to Héctor is really just an excuse.

It seems easier, feels like a relief, to simply decide that a future with Héctor is impossible. It just can't be real. Easier to never again face the devastation of dashed dreams, whether by forced separation or some other disillusionment.

Friday morning Héctor calls and I promise to get back to him about supper. By late afternoon, I still haven't called. With snow threatening outside, the studio is dark, and I have to turn on several lights. I'm finishing a new batch of candles, *Rekindling the Romance*—mimosa to enhance imagination, honeysuckle to instill tolerance, for couples who've been together too long—when Héctor knocks on my front window. Despite everything, my heart leaps.

"Paula, please let me in," he calls through the glass. "I've come bearing gifts." He's carrying a bag of groceries from which he takes an enormous gnarly root vegetable of some kind and holds it up proudly for me to see. I open the door.

"What is that?" I ask.

"It's Beethoven," he says. "Look." He traces, with the ring finger of his right hand, a pattern of lines and bulges in the vegetable's wrinkly flesh.

I lean in to examine it more closely. "I think you're right," I say, recognizing the scowl, the high forehead and wild hair. When I raise my face he kisses me, and I realize it's no use fighting it. The longing is too powerful. How can something I yearn for in every part of my body and soul not be real?

I turn off the lights in the studio and we head upstairs with the groceries, which include, it turns out, some recognizable foods as well: mushrooms, red peppers, zucchini, and a slab of tilapia. I turn on my computer, since it turns out neither of us has any clue how Beethoven should be cooked, while Héctor begins washing vegetables.

"I once found a meteorite that looked like Barbra Streisand," he says, then he sings a few bars: 'Love soft as an easy chair / Love fresh as the morning air / One love that is shared by two / I have found with you.' My mother loved Barbra Streisand."

"Really? She didn't prefer classical music?"

"Bach, Beethoven, they were all well and good, but Barbra. Barbra was the pinnacle of musical achievement. Unfortunately, I had a terrible singing voice, as I've just demonstrated, so classical music it was," he says. "But every night, after I'd done my homework and practised my scales and all my assigned pieces, and practised them again, only then, she'd haul out a little turntable and her Barbra Streisand records, and we would dance and sing along until bedtime. That's when my mother was happiest. It didn't matter what else was going on, whatever worries, troubles, sickness, pain—when Barbra sang my mother was transported, forgot all about it."

"I think it must be celeriac," I say, after entering the phrase 'strange root vegetables' into a search engine. "Also known as knob celery."

Héctor peers over my shoulder at the photo of celeriac roots on my screen. "I don't recognize any of these ones," he says. "Though that could be Bob Dylan." He points.

"So where did you find the meteorite?"

"In La Zona del Silencio," he says. "The Zone of Silence. It's a patch of desert in Durango."

"Why is it silent?"

"Because there's some kind of energy there that inter-rupts radio waves and all kinds of communications. Any aircraft or vehicles passing through lose radio contact. Something like the Bermuda Triangle. In fact, I believe it lies at the exact same latitude as the Bermuda Triangle."

"I've heard whole boats and planes disappear in the Bermuda Triangle," I say. "It might be a portal to another time, or another dimension."

"It's the same with La Zona del Silencio," Héctor says. "Well, there are no boats, because it's the desert, but a variety of strange phenomena has occurred there: mutant plants and animals, UFO sightings, mysterious encounters. And meteorites, of course. More meteorites land there than anywhere else on earth."

"Did you go to collect them?" I ask.

"I only went once. After my mother died, my father and I went on a bit of a road trip. We had this ramshackle old station wagon, baby blue. Sometimes we stayed in a cheap motel, but mostly we'd just pull off the road and sleep in the back of the car. My father had always been fascinated by the zone. He collected books and articles about it, and never tired of speculating about what caused the strange phenomena. My mother told him he was crazy. She was of the tribe that believed the strangeness was caused by radioactive material left behind when an American test missile went off course and crashed there in 1970. But my father argued that the strange occurrences predated that crash by decades. He'd heard about the zone already when he was a child. He believed it was the area's nature that likely caused the missile crash. And in all the speculation, he'd come to the conclusion that there was a metaphysical significance to it. My mother said that was nonsense. 'The only thing more I want to hear about La Zona del Silencio is *silencio*,' she would say, but she'd be laughing. Obviously, I took my father's side. I mean, UFOs, mutant animals— what kid wouldn't? I was excited when he said where we were going. That was the first thing I got excited about again, after her death, which I suppose was the point. It was a good distraction after so much sadness. It was great. As soon as we passed the sign marking the beginning of the zone, the car radio went haywire."

"Not silent?"

"Mostly just static, yes, but we left it on, because every once in a while, something strange would come through, a bit of music or a voice saying a few suddenly clear words or a sentence. My father made me write down everything we heard. He wanted to see if there was some kind of pattern or meaning he could decipher. But the only thing resembling a pattern I could find was that the number thirty-seven was mentioned frequently, as were the names of several kinds of cheese."

"That does sound suspicious," I say. "Did you see anything strange?"

"Everything we saw was strange. Blue cacti, Siamese snakes."

"Siamese snakes?"

"Conjoined. Two heads, two tails. They were paralyzed because the two heads wanted to go in different directions. But the best show was when it got dark."

"You stayed overnight?"

"My father built a fire and we lay down on top of our sleeping bags to watch," he says.

"Ah, yes, the UFOs."

"I can't say for certain what they were, Paula. Falling stars? Alien invaders? Satellites? What I do remember is that the sky was alive with moving lights that night. It was the most glorious sight. I fell asleep watching it and it continued in my dreams. My father must have moved me into the car at some point. When I woke up in the morning, I got out and walked over to where I had been lying, and that's where I found it."

"Found what?"

"The meteorite that looked like Barbra Streisand."

"Of course," I say. "It was a message from your mother."

Héctor leans over my chair, tilts my face away from the screen and toward him, and kisses me. "My father would have liked you, Paula."

When we finish eating, Héctor opens the door at the top of the stairs and gestures for me to follow him down. I hesitate only briefly. In the studio, he leaves the overhead lights off, but turns on the small lamp on the piano. He pulls out the piano bench and for a split second of terror, I think he's going to open it up, but he merely puts it in place and sits down.

"Come sit with me," he says, patting the bench beside him.

"Héctor, I—" I shake my head, holding back.

He looks confused. "Why not? Here," he says, stretching out his hand to me. I take a deep breath and take it, allowing him to guide me into place beside him. I haven't sat on that bench at the piano in over four years.

He takes my burnt hand in his and examines it. "Does it still hurt?" he asks.

I shake my head.

"You know, together we make a complete pianist," he says. "One good hand each. We could play together."

"Oh, no," I say, feeling panicky. "I'm much too rusty. I haven't played in years."

"Why did you stop playing?" he asks. "I know why you stopped teaching, but why did you stop playing?"

"Didn't you find it hard to play again, after your fingers," I say. "I don't mean physically or technically. I mean emotionally. I'm not sure I could have borne it."

"But you didn't lose your fingers," he says.

"No." How can I explain to him? Unlike mine, his loss is pure tragedy, unmarred by guilt or his own murky complicity. The happiness I felt those times when Teddy and I sang at the piano, and more importantly the happiness Teddy felt, was not stolen by members of a drug cartel, but by me.

Héctor waits for me to continue; when I don't, he begins to play. I recognize the heartrending song Violetta sang. I watch his fingers move on the keyboard. It's still amazing and disconcerting to watch, the shock of the missing fingers all over again. He plays to the end of the piece and stops.

"Give me your right hand," Héctor says.

I lift my hand and he lays his over top and lowers it to the piano. Like a teacher might with a small child just learning to play.

"You could be my ghost player," he says. "Something like a ghostwriter."

The slight pressure on my knuckles from the stumps of his missing fingers indicates where I should press. It's unwieldy, awkward, but then for a few seconds, the first few bars of the sad song, the notes do flow.

"Paula, you're trembling," he says. He stops and closes his hand around mine.

I close my eyes and lean against him.

"The first time I played with the Juárez Symphony Orchestra," he says, "I was so scared and nervous, I nearly ran away before the concert."

"I don't believe it," I say. "You're never nervous."

"I was, I was," he insists. "I even smoked a cigarette in the men's room to try to relax."

"Did it work?"

"No. When I got on stage, I was sweating so much, my hands were sweating so much, that when I started to play, my fingers slipped off the keys. I was terrified I was going to miss a note. Just when I thought I was going to have to stop, stop playing, stop the performance, the sprinkler system in the building went off and the auditorium had to be evacuated. The concert was cancelled. Everyone got soaked, which was fine with me, because I was already drenched in sweat."

I laugh. "So what happened the next time you had to play?"

"Well, that's the thing. The incident with the sprinkler made me realize that the universe will have its way no matter what. On that occasion it happened to save my ass. And then I wasn't nervous anymore. What's the point—what will be, will be. The next concert went perfectly. No sprinklers, no sweat."

"Did they find out why the sprinklers went off in the first place? Was there actually a fire?"

"Yes, in the men's room," Héctor says. "Someone left a lit cigarette in the garbage can."

I laugh again. *The universe will have its way indeed.* Héctor closes the lid on the keyboard and turns off the light, as we rise and return upstairs.

THE WEEKEND BEFORE VALENTINE'S DAY I open the studio to customers again. Héctor happily reprises his role at the piano, taking requests for romantic songs. He amazes with his ability to play anything, even pop songs I'm sure he has never considered trying on the piano before, including a rendition of Beyoncé's "All the Single Ladies," to raucous cheers from a trio of women who've banded together in defiance of the holiday's conventions.

By late afternoon, the stream of customers dwindles and I consider closing up. Héctor is playing "Memories," in honour of Barbra Streisand, when a woman enters the studio. I don't recognize her immediately; her hair is shorter and she's gained a bit of weight. Only as I approach to ask if I can help her do I realize that it is Louise.

"I thought it must be you playing, Paula," she says, "when I heard the music from outside."

"Oh, no," I say, suddenly flustered. "This is Héctor." Seeing me gesture in his direction, he stops playing and comes over. "Héctor, this is my, ah, former sister-in-law."

"I think we can always consider ourselves sisters-in-law," Louise says. She says it warmly, without any sort of accusation or bitterness. Noticing the bulge beneath her coat, I realize that she is pregnant.

Louise was angry and hurt when I sold the coach house. It didn't help that she found out when she dropped by one day, a loaf of freshly baked pumpkin bread in hand, hoping to coax me into moving forward with the next production, only to find a "For Sale" sign outside. She actually threw the pumpkin bread across the room. She didn't throw it hard enough, or the loaf just wasn't aerodynamic enough to fly as far as the opposite wall. Instead, it fell in a slow, descending arc and thudded, virtually undamaged in its tinfoil wrap, onto the floor. (It was, in fact, still quite edible, as I discovered after she left.)

"How long have you been planning this?" she demanded to know.

I shrugged guiltily. It was true that I had allowed her to continue believing in the future of the theatre company, not with any outright lies, but by evasion, repeatedly putting her off when she called or stopped by to discuss it.

"But Paula, it was Teddy's dream, his vision. You're trampling all over his memory."

"I'm not trampling on anything. You're right. It was *his* dream, *his* vision. I can't live his dream for him," I said. *I can't even live my own*, I thought.

"I don't think you ever really cared about him at all," she said angrily and burst into tears. She stormed out before I could respond, which was good, because I had no idea what more to say.

We did eventually speak again, and Louise did apologize for that last comment, but even after the coach house was sold, she didn't entirely give up. Months, even years later, she'd still, on occasion, bring it up: the idea of mounting a small production somewhere, maybe as part of the Fringe Festival.

"Are you sure there wasn't something, even an outline or idea in his notes, that we could work on?" she'd ask.

I evaded, and eventually her questions stopped.

Standing with her in my studio now, on Valentine's Day, I can't remember when we last spoke. A look of speculation crosses her face, as Héctor offers his hand, about the nature of our relationship, no doubt. It changes briefly to alarm as she registers the missing fingers in his grip, but she recovers quickly.

"I was just in the neighbourhood, so I thought I'd drop by," Louise says.

I doubt this; I feel certain she has a specific mission in mind. Surely it can't be about the theatre company still, not now with a baby on the way. She seems more settled, less anxious than a few years ago when she was so desperate to continue Teddy's legacy. And she isn't carrying any baked goods to throw.

"How have you been?" I ask, unconsciously glancing down at her belly.

"Oh, well, this," she says. "Yeah, good. I'm really good. Apart from puking a lot."

"Maybe Paula can make a candle for that," Héctor says, then asks me, "Can you?"

"Sure," I say. "What shall I call it? *Vomit Not?*"

"It's catchy," he says.

We laugh. Louise looks a little bewildered, but continues to smile.

"Louise, would you like some tea?" I ask.

"No, thank you," she says. "I'll have to make eight pit stops on the drive home if I do. I just wanted to stop by and tell you—" She hesitates. I wonder briefly if I do want her to go on, but I nod encouragingly anyway.

"I know that the baby is a boy," she continues. "And I think I'd like to name him Teddy." She pauses again, glancing briefly at Héctor. "I just wondered if that would be okay with you. My parents love the idea, so . . ."

"It is a lovely idea, Louise," I say. "Of course it's fine with me."

"Good," Louise says, clearly relieved. "And he will be Teddy MacGregor. He'll have my name, not—well, the father isn't in the picture, so Teddy MacGregor the Second."

"You know he always wished people would call him Theodore instead of Teddy," I say unexpectedly even to myself.

Louise laughs. "Funny, I could never think of him as anything but Teddy."

"You don't talk about Teddy much," Héctor says after Louise takes her leave.

"I don't *not* talk about him," I say.

"What was he like?"

"Youthful," I say.

"You were both young," Héctor says.

"Teddy would have been young even if he'd lived to be old," I say. "And there were bad things about that as well as good. Or maybe bad is the wrong word. Difficult, perhaps. But you never talk about your ex-wife."

"Dolores," Héctor says. "Technically, she's not my ex-wife."

"What?" I say. "You mean you're still married?"

"No, we were never actually married," he says. "I mean, we were, but it was annulled, so in retrospect, we weren't."

"Well, hindsight is twenty-twenty."

"Yes, and we were very young too, just graduated from university music programs."

"Was she also a pianist?"

"No, she played the tuba, because she was only four foot nine."

"She played tuba *because* she was four foot nine?"

"Exactly. She was something of a contrarian. Born thirty years later, I think she'd have been diagnosed with Oppositional Defiant Disorder. Whenever someone told her she shouldn't or couldn't do something, she'd make a point of doing it. Her middle-school teacher told her the one instrument she couldn't play was the tuba. At that time, she weighed less than the instrument. Mind you, she became very good. One of the best tuba players I know."

"Why did you get married?"

"Because her mother hated me," Héctor says. "Her mother used to throw things at me when I came by. Anything that came to hand: shoes, casseroles, mops."

"Why did she hate you so much?" I ask, unable to imagine anyone disliking Héctor.

"She didn't. She loved me and desperately wanted Dolores to be married. But she knew her daughter well; she knew she'd have to pretend to hate me, and it had to be convincing or Dolores would catch on, so even I had to believe."

"When was the truth revealed?"

"At the wedding. After we cut the cake, Dolores dared her mother to throw a piece at me," Héctor says. "Instead, she embraced me and gave a moving speech expounding on my many virtues. It was all downhill from there."

"The wedding?"

"The marriage. Dolores became depressed and angry and wanted out."

"Were you heartbroken?"

"Only a little. The truth is, not having to duck and dodge all the time took some of the excitement out of it for me as well. When we were facing all that opposition, it was like Romeo and Juliet," he says with a grin.

I cringe inwardly at the reference, even as I laugh.

"She managed to get it annulled on the basis that I was not the person she thought I was. Which was technically true—I was not someone her mother hated," Héctor says. "So there it was, as if it had never happened. Poof. An illusion."

"Even illusions can change you," I say.

He kisses me. "They are what change us the most," he says.

That evening we revisit one of our favourite dinner haunts: Vicky's Fish and Chips and Thai Food. "Did you know that Saint Valentine was beheaded?" Héctor says, as we sit beside the front window that is so steamed up it is nearly opaque. Passersby on the sidewalk are only vague shadows. "It wasn't an uncommon form of martyrdom. Many saints were beheaded. There's even a subset of beheaded saints—the cephalophore saints—who were known to have carried their own severed heads for a distance before actually dying."

"I've survived beheading a few times myself," I say.

Héctor nods. "You mean in past lives," he says.

I laugh. "You could say that," I say. "So Saint Valentine must have been beheaded for love?"

"Not earthly love," he says. "That was the domain of the heathens. They always celebrated various love gods and goddesses in mid-February. Couples paired up by drawing names on slips of paper or vellum or whatever they used back then."

"For sex?"

Héctor nods. "So naturally the church tried to put a stop to it by replacing it with a Christian festival. Since Saint Valentine had been martyred on that day, they dedicated it to him."

I frown. "So if he was supposed to replace it, how did he then become the patron saint of lovers?"

"Divine irony," Héctor says.

As we walk down Roncesvalles, our stomachs full, Héctor takes my hand. I've noticed he almost always uses his right hand now for this, clasping my left, and somehow it's a perfect fit, my fingers slotting in where his used to be.

There hasn't been fresh snow for over a week. The crusty remains of old snowbanks that line the sidewalks are gritty and grey with bits of detritus, leaves and wrappers poking through where the surface has worn away. Though it's more than six weeks past Christmas, several of the houses we pass on Fern Avenue are still sporting seasonal decorations. In the front yard of one is a six-foot-high Ferris wheel, its seats inhabited by sagging stuffed animals wearing Santa hats. It should be depressing, but tonight I realize I'm experiencing a kind of joy I've never felt before, except perhaps when I was a young child, before happiness became entwined with achievement and grand goals, when it could survive despite disappointments and defeats. For the first time it seems possible that happiness can be derived of many small consolations, that in fact, that's all it ever is.

As we enter the studio we are enveloped by its gorgeous scents. I've barely locked the door behind me before Héctor kisses me, hard, pressing himself to me. He manoeuvres me between display shelves toward the piano. He unzips my coat, and then my jeans. If there were any lights on apart from the dim stove bulb behind the counter, we'd be visible to the whole street, but as it is, we are obscured by shadows. With his hands behind my thighs, Héctor lifts me up onto the curved closed lid of the keyboard, my back against the piano amply padded by my shed parka.

"Don't drop me!" I whisper as I wrap my legs around his hips.

I SLEEP AS if drugged, waking only after Héctor returns to the bedroom to kiss me goodbye, having already break-fasted alone.

"I've got to go to work now," he says. "I didn't want to wake you, but you'll want to lock the door after me."

"You should have woken me earlier," I say, still unchar-acteristically groggy. "What did I eat last night that made me sleep so hard?"

"I don't think it was the food," Héctor says.

I put on my housecoat and follow him downstairs through the candle studio. The piano bench is askew, pushed aside from the piano during last night's shenanigans. I slide it firmly back into place under the piano as we pass.

"I'll call you at noon." Héctor kisses me and turns to leave, but I grab him back for another, realizing too late that we're being watched by a group of children and their parents waiting, as they do every morning, on the opposite corner, for their school bus. I wave Héctor off and hurry back inside and upstairs away from view. I feel inordinately bereft by his sudden absence.

The morning drags. With the Valentine's Day stock com-pleted I begin to prepare for Easter and other spring-themed candle making. When my phone rings at noon, I feel a rush of pleasure, thinking, *now my day can begin properly*, but as soon as Héctor says my name, I know that something is wrong.

"Paula," he says, "I just spoke to Barbara. It's not good. They're sending me back."

For several seconds I am unable to speak. The rush of pleasure I felt a moment before changes course, becomes a flood of fear.

"Paula?"

"Yes," I whisper.

"I'm going to meet with Barbara after school—"

I interrupt. "I'm coming with you."

"Paula, you don't have to—"

"I'll meet you at the school."

After hanging up the phone, I can do nothing all afternoon but pace, concentrate on nothing but trying to keep panic at bay, trying to rein in runaway thoughts about losing Héctor forever. Why did I tempt fate last night by thinking I could actually be happy?

It's a relief to finally be able to put on my coat and boots and head out, by bus, then subway to Bathurst Station. The school is located in the Annex, just a few blocks from where I used to live in Mrs. Gaskell's basement. Teddy and I often walked these blocks, walked by the series of red-brick buildings, designed to look much like the surrounding turn-of-the-century houses, without realizing they housed a school. I've only been here once before, for the recital, the first time I laid eyes on Héctor.

"Paula?" I hear someone call my name, and turn to see Diane emerge from the school with her daughters. As I approach, the girls are laboriously hopping on one leg only down the stairs, clutching the metal railings so as not to fall. "They're playing Child Amputee," Diane explains. "It's all the rage. I'm trying to encourage them to play Deaf-Mute Child, but so far they only get the deaf part."

I nod. "Which way is the principal's office?" I ask.

"Over there." Diane points. "Why? Were you chewing gum in class?"

"Much worse than that," I say with a weak smile. "Actually, it's Héctor. We've got a meeting with his lawyer. It's not good."

"Oh, no! Not—"

"Yeah." I don't want to say more in front of the very not-deaf girls. "I'll call you later."

I just mean to wait outside the office until Héctor can find me, but the doors to the outer and inner offices are open and Laura spots me from her desk. She runs through to the hall and startles me with a huge, enveloping hug.

"Paula, don't think for a second this is the end of the line. We're going to fight this!" she exclaims. "Ah, here he is."

"Is this a group hug?" Héctor asks, and before I can even turn my head to look over my shoulder at his approach, he has wrapped his arms around me from behind and I'm sandwiched between them. Then both Laura's and Héctor's phones ring simultaneously and our group hug becomes a group startle in which our heads knock together before we can draw apart.

"Barbara," Héctor says into his phone.

"Malcolm," says Laura into hers. She backs into her office, mouthing to Héctor something that looks like *I'll see you over there.* Héctor nods, waves, then takes my hand in his and kisses it as he confirms to Barbara that we are on our way. He hangs up and pulls me into his arms. I can feel his sadness, as much as he is trying to hide it. I decide to use one of his own tactics to try to cheer him up.

"The best way to cope in circumstances such as these," I say, "is to look for the signs."

"The signs?" He looks at me and I can see that he is amused.

"The signs," I repeat, as we push open the main door and descend the steps to the sidewalk. "For instance, if an angel were to appear in front of us here on the sidewalk, that would be an encouraging sign," I say. I'm not as good at this as he is.

"Really. So the fact that the only thing appearing in front of us is this—" He crouches down and picks up a child's sad, abandoned mitten from the ground. It is pink with a green frog on the back. "What does this signify?"

"A frog!" I exclaim. "A frog is an excellent omen. The gods often use frogs as a sign of favour."

"If I remember correctly," he says, "God sent the Egyptians a plague of frogs as a punishment."

"Well . . . but they deserved it," I say, and Héctor laughs.

We begin walking north toward Barbara's office, which is on Dupont Street, just a short distance away. A block north, as we pass by a parked Land Rover, its alarm goes off, though neither of us has touched it. "There, see?" I say. "Another message!"

"How do you know the message isn't 'Steal this car now and go on the run because that's your only hope'?" he asks.

"If that were the correct message," I explain, "the keys would be in the ignition."

Just before we reach Dupont, a black cat dashes across the sidewalk in front of us and disappears behind a bush. We're still laughing about that when we reach the row of storefronts that houses Barbara's office. It's on the second floor, above a yoga studio. There's no showy reception area, no expensive décor. As soon as we step inside we're in the midst of a bustling, orderly operation. There are boxes and stacks of files everywhere, but no mess or confusion. One has the distinct sense that everything is exactly where it should be and that the team of workers moving about have everything under control. There are two men in the outer office typing rapidly on laptops. Through an open door, we can see Barbara and two other women at a conference table covered in more files and laptops. Aside from Barbara, who is wearing a maroon pantsuit, they are all casually dressed in jeans and sweaters.

Barbara rushes forward to greet us and ushers us into the conference room, where one of the others hastily clears away a space at the table. "As you can see, we're pulling out all the stops ahead of Friday," Barbara says.

"What's Friday?" I ask, looking sharply at Héctor.

"The deportation order says that Héctor has to leave by Friday," Barbara says gently.

I should have expected this, because I know how quickly Dusan and Violetta left, but somehow, I've been counting on more time. Though I fight to keep my demeanour calm, panic circulates through my body. When we take a seat, I have to sit on my hands to stop them from shaking. A few minutes later, Laura sweeps in, followed by a man named Cecil I recognize from the farewell party at the refugee centre, and the meeting begins. The main concern seems to be finding suitable grounds on which to file an appeal before Friday. I interrupt briefly, and with an apology, to ask if

I might borrow some paper. Many of the legal terms they are using are unfamiliar to me, and I want to be able to look them up later. Barbara kindly passes me a pad, and, before I have to ask, a pen. I take notes. Laura takes over and the talk shifts to petitions and rallies and letters to politicians. Héctor, for the most part, remains silent.

When the meeting ends, Laura offers us a ride, dropping us off at the corner of College and Grace. "Don't worry, Héctor," she says, rolling down her window before she pulls away from the curb. "You were meant to be here. You were meant to stay." She drives away.

"Now what?" I say.

"Dinner?" Héctor says. "I'm starving."

I should be starving too; I wasn't able to eat any lunch after his call at noon. I still don't think I'll be able to eat a thing, but for his sake, I agree with his suggestion that we pick up some sushi. We take the food to his apartment, and after a few sips of miso soup, I find I do have a bit of an appetite after all. In fact, the more I eat, the hungrier I seem to get. I finish off my sushi in a flash and find myself staring disconsolately at the styrofoam carton, empty save for a lump of wasabi and the requisite slip of plastic grass. When I look up, I realize that Héctor, who is only halfway through his meal, is watching me quizzically.

"If you have faith, more will appear," he says. "Food miracles happen all the time."

"Food miracles?"

"The feeding of the five thousand. In fact, it happened in my own hometown back in the sixties, before I was born. At the annual fair, it was a tradition that all visitors would get a free burrito, paid for by the town. But one year, hundreds of people bussed in from the neighbouring town—our arch rivals. It was their intention to swamp the burrito hut and put us to shame. The town's pride was at stake. There were hundreds more takers than the organizers had prepared for. They hadn't bought nearly enough food. Yet somehow, one by one, as the burritos were doled out, one by one more appeared. At the end of the day, everyone got a burrito, and there were more leftovers than the organizers had bought in the first place. Our rivals from the neighbouring town went home disgruntled, but full."

"The miracle of the bottomless burritos," I say. "Is this miracle Vatican approved?"

"It should have been. We were robbed. It would have put us on the map," he says. "But the church thinks such miracles are too difficult to prove under their rigorous criteria. They prefer medical miracles that can be documented and attested to by physicians. It's a cop-out. Why should doctors be considered more reliable than chefs? Miracles are far more common than the church allows. I'm holding out for one of my own."

"You mean to stop the departure order," I say.

"I mean my fingers," he replies. "I'm praying for them to grow back."

I laugh.

"It's not unprecedented," Héctor says. "In 1840, the leg of a farm labourer in Calanda in Spain grew back two years after it was amputated."

"You've still got time then," I say.

"Exactly."

He shares the rest of his sushi with me. We watch an episode of *Inspector Morse*, though I find it impossible to concentrate enough to follow the complex plot, and go to bed early. Héctor drops off quickly; I'm amazed at his fortitude for calm. Lying awake beside him, I think that on the one hand, I want this time that I have left with him to last as long as it possibly can, but on the other hand, the anticipation of loss is so unbearable that I want it to be over. Tears come, though I cry silently to avoid waking him. Eventually, I too sleep.

❋ CHAPTER TEN ❋

I START IN THE MORNING AT the sound of a spoon
clanging in the kitchen sink.

"Sorry," Héctor says when I round the corner to the
kitchen. "I'm running late."

"Late for what?"

He looks at me with surprise. "For work."

"You're still going to work?"

"Of course."

I shake my head. "I guess I thought there were things
you'd have to do."

He puts his hands on my upper arms. "We have to leave it to Barbara now. There's absolutely nothing I can do, and I don't want to sit around moping. I'd rather be busy. Besides, the middle-school band won't conduct itself." He kisses my forehead.

He may feel he has to leave it to Barbara, but I'm determined to do everything I can to help. It remains to be seen what, if anything, that is. What I need to do is clear my head and think. I decide to walk home to my studio.

The morning is bright and crisp. As I cross the Dundas Street Bridge, I'm engulfed by the sickly sweet aroma from the Nestlé chocolate factory near the railway tracks below. At the same time, the concrete beneath my feet begins to shudder with the weight of the streetcar crossing the bridge, and my knees nearly give out. I stop and grip the railing until the wave of dizziness and nausea passes. I just need to eat some breakfast, I tell myself, and manage to make my way across the bridge and down Sorauren to home. I make some oatmeal and manage to eat half a bowl before realizing how exhausted I am after being awake a good part of the night. I lie down and fall into a deep but troubled sleep.

In one dream, I'm back on the Dundas Street Bridge, only instead of railway tracks below, there's a ravine, the bottom of which is obscured by thick leafy tree branches. At the edge of the bridge, I climb over the rail and try to make my way down into the ravine, but it's much steeper than I anticipated, and I panic and try to scramble back up. I wake into semi-consciousness before shifting into the next dream. In this one, I'm at St. Francis of Assisi church, but instead of a priest at the pulpit, Teddy is doing a magic show.

I know I'm supposed to be helping him, but the tricks he's doing make no sense, like opening his jacket and pouring a glass of something into an inner pocket. Then I'm playing a piano. Everyone is gathering around and I play louder and louder to be heard.

I wake up groggy and confused, my brain churning with images. It's not until I'm in the shower that one of those images comes suddenly clear: the sanctuary of the church. One of the questions raised at the meeting yesterday was how strict immigration officials would be in implementing the Friday deadline. Not all cases are the same, Barbara explained. Sometimes the deadlines pass and weeks go by before there is any follow-up. But if there is a risk of them coming for him Friday, could he really seek sanctuary in a church? Would it actually prevent officials from taking him away? My first thought is to phone Héctor, but I realize he wouldn't necessarily know the answer, and I might just get his hopes up for nothing. Barbara would know, but it occurs to me that even if the answer is yes, the church would have to agree, and that request would be best coming from a church member.

I look up the number for the principal's office at Héctor's school and dial. I expect only to leave a message with Laura's assistant, but to my surprise, after giving my name I'm transferred right through.

"Paula, is everything okay?" Laura asks.

"Oh, yes, I'm sorry to bother you. I just had a thought—I don't know, maybe it's completely crazy."

"Go on," she encourages me, sounding very much like a principal speaking to children.

I explain to her my idea about Héctor seeking sanctuary in the church—her church—should he need to when Friday arrives. Laura is initially silent, and I wonder if I'm being stupid. Maybe churches don't even do such things anymore. But then Laura speaks.

"Let me talk to Father Carlucci," she says.

"Do you think it's a possibility?" I ask.

"It might be. I'm sure I can get other members of the congregation behind it, but I'll have to talk to the priests first," she says. "It's a good idea, Paula."

I breathe a sigh of relief, and hope.

"I'll let you know what they say," Laura says, and hangs up.

Mid-afternoon, I head back to Héctor's apartment so that I'll be there when he returns from school. As expected, Laura has already told him about contacting the priests. "Thank you, Paula," he says, kissing the side of my head.

"Do you want coffee?" I ask, gesturing to the table where I've set out cups. The pad of paper with my notes from yesterday is also on the kitchen table, ready for more planning. Héctor sits down, it seems, with some reluctance. "I don't understand how they can say there's no evidence of the assault against you. You can see on YouTube that you used to have fingers. Aren't your missing fingers proof?"

He shrugs. "If phantom fingers could talk."

"Maybe they can," I suggest. "Through a medium."

"I hadn't thought of that," Héctor says. "Though it's unlikely they would speak to the medium in words. It would come through as notes on the piano."

I laugh to disguise the shiver these words send through

my body. "But what about your roommate? You had a room-mate, right? Didn't he know what happened?"

"Jorge, yes. He drove me to the hospital."

"Can't Jorge testify, by Skype or something?"

"It could put him at risk, Paula," Héctor says. "More risk than he's already at by continuing to live there."

"Then he should come to Canada too."

"It's not possible anymore. The government put new visa restrictions on Mexicans last summer," he explains. "I arrived under the old rules. No visa required."

To my frustration, he gets up and carries his coffee away from the table, obviously not wanting to continue working through my list.

Later in the evening, Laura calls to tell Héctor she has spoken to Father Carlucci. "He's going to consult with the parish council tomorrow," Héctor reports.

"So it's really a possibility. Sanctuary in the church," I say.

"A time-honoured tradition," he says.

"Did you ever go to church?" I ask. "I mean, regularly."

"My mother used to take me every week. My very first piano teacher was the organist. It was one of those old-fashioned organs with bellows that had to be pumped manually while she played, so she always had one of her students, usually a young teenager, there to pump it for her. I remember when I was very young, four or five, I asked my mother what the boy was doing. She told me that in order for the organ to make such beautiful music, God had to blow into the pipes. The boy was opening and closing the bellows so God's breath could get in."

"Couldn't God do that on his own?" I ask.

"Even God needs a hand now and then, Paula," Héctor says. "My mother told me that if I practised hard and continued to be a good student, Señorita Fernández would let me pump the bellows one day. She meant it as a kind of encouragement, but the truth was, the idea terrified me. What would happen if you slipped up, made a mistake while helping God? I had this idea that God's breath must be very, very hot."

"You were confusing God with a dragon," I say.

"If I slipped up, I would get burned."

"Did you ever get the chance to pump the bellows?" I ask.

"No. My father had no use for church, especially after my mother died. He also sent me to a new piano teacher when I was ten. Not because Señorita Fernández was the church organist, but because he thought I needed a teacher more experienced with gifted students."

I have trouble falling asleep again and lie awake long after Héctor drifts off. I get up to get a glass of water from the kitchen, but glimpsing the shaft of light from the street, I enter the living room instead and push aside the curtains to see out the front window. The steps to the church across the street are well lit, but the building itself is completely dark. I find the thought of spending the night inside a bit frightening.

As a child, attending church was an experience edged with a slightly fearful awe. There was blood-red carpeting, dark wood pews so high backed that I was six or seven before I could see over them without lifting my chin up to peer, and stained-glass windows that turned churchgoers' faces purple and blue. The organ music was beautiful, but always a touch spooky, as only organ music can be. The sermons were hopeful, but stern, two qualities that must always coexist. I remember hearing the story of Hannah, mother of the prophet Samuel, who bargained with God: if God gave her a son, she promised she would bring him back, once he was old enough, to serve in the temple. It was a few weeks before Christmas, and the thing I longed for—every bit as much as Hannah longed for a son, I was sure—was a jewellery box from the Sears Christmas wish catalogue. It was white and shaped like a grand piano. When you opened the piano's lid, a ballerina popped up and danced to "Für Elise." So I prayed for it intently every night, before I went to sleep, hands clasped, elbows resting on the catalogue. In return for the jewellery box, I promised God I would give Baby Beans to Trevor, the little boy with Down's syndrome who lived down the street. My mother babysat Trevor for a few hours every Friday afternoon, to give his mother the only breaks she ever got from his care. As soon as he arrived at our house, he would ask for Baby Beans. Baby Beans was a floppy bean-filled doll dressed in a mustard-yellow onesie and cap that I'd had since I was an infant. Trevor would cuddle and carry it with him the entire time he was at our house, and when his mother picked him up and he had to give Baby Beans back, he always cried. My mother had gently suggested to me several times that since I didn't play with Baby Beans anymore—I was, after all, much too old for such a babyish toy—I might consider letting Trevor keep him. I staunchly refused. Of course I didn't play with baby toys anymore, but I felt a sentimental attachment to Baby Beans and didn't want to give him up. Besides, I would say to my mother, fully aware of the unreasonableness of my point, Trevor was the same age as me.

On Christmas morning, to my great delight, the piano jewellery box did indeed appear under the tree. Trevor didn't come that week because his grandparents were visiting, so it was two weeks before I was reminded about my end of the bargain I'd made with God. But when the time came, I couldn't do it. I sheepishly took Baby Beans back from Trevor and returned him to his place on a shelf in my bedroom. I told myself I'd do it the next week, then the week after that, but I still couldn't do it then. Eventually I had to admit to myself that I did not and would not keep my promise, and then I felt scared, especially as I lay awake in bed at night. I kept thinking of the next bit in the Samuel story, how after his mother kept her promise and returned him to serve in the temple, he lay in bed one night and heard God calling his name. The analogy did not make sense in any but my childish logic, but I was afraid I would hear God call my name, angry because I'd failed to keep my promise. I don't know what I thought God would do; hearing the voice speak my name would be frightening enough in itself. Despite many sleepless nights of terror, I never did give Baby Beans to Trevor. As to what eventually happened to the doll, I couldn't say.

When I return to my parents' church now, on special occasions, I'm always dismayed by its evolution, like that of so many others, into a church of the diluted, happy-clappy variety. The blood-red carpeting has been replaced by institutional pink, and the pews have been removed alto-gether in favour of more flexible seating. The windows still hold stained glass, but only in pale, pastel shades. The organ is still there, but rarely used; guitars and maracas are now the preferred mode of accompaniment. And the sermons—always hopeful, never stern, focusing instead on healthy lifestyles and positive thinking. The fear and awe of my childhood church, as fearful and awful as it was, still seems so much more adequate to the real terrors of the world. I shiver. It's cold by the window. I hurry to the kitchen for that glass of water before returning to bed, warming myself against Héctor's back, thinking that I have nothing left that I wouldn't give away if it meant Héctor could stay.

HÉCTOR HEADS OFF to school again in the morning. I know I should go home and get some work done, but I dread the thought of being in the studio alone, so I stay at Héctor's. I try to settle with a book but find myself jumping up to look out the window every time I hear a voice outside, or often for no reason at all. I wander up to College Street and walk along the south side of it and back along the north, aim-lessly, looking in through the windows of the restaurants and small businesses, still mostly Italian, but giving way with increasing frequency to incursions by sushi bars and Indian buffets. I consider watching a matinee at the Royal Cinema—a twenty-fifth anniversary edition of *Back to the Future* is playing—but I decide against it, realizing I'd have to turn off my phone. I buy Sicilian cannoli at the Riviera Bakery instead and return to Héctor's apartment to wait out the afternoon.

When Héctor arrives home, he bounds up the stairs toward me with a wide smile on his face.

"The parish council has agreed to grant me sanctuary," he says, lifting me in his arms.

"I knew we'd have something to celebrate," I say, showing him the cannoli.

The relief that he won't be sent back to Mexico on Friday is almost terrifying. I notice my hand shaking as I lift the pastry to my mouth. As Héctor takes a call from Barbara, my mind races, imagining the implications of this next step, realizing the situation is still rife with uncertainty.

"Barbara thinks I should move to the church tomorrow evening," Héctor reports once he hangs up. "So there's no chance of being apprehended on Friday morning. It would be unlikely, but you never know."

The thought of Héctor being apprehended gives me a shiver of fear. "That means tonight—"

"Is my last night of freedom," he says with a grin. "Do you know what I'd like to do?"

"What?"

"I'd like to return to the restaurant where we first had dinner together."

WE ORDER THE same appetizer of sardines. Shortly after the food arrives, I notice two men entering the restaurant. They're both wearing black suits and tinted glasses, even though the sun has long gone down. They stand and survey the room in a way that makes me very uneasy.

"There's no chance they would try to arrest you before Friday, is there?" I ask.

Héctor, who has his back to the door, gives me a quizzical look, then seeing the direction of my gaze, twists in his chair. "The men in black!" he says in a hushed, dramatic tone and turns back to face me. "Men in black are known to pay visits to experiencers, people who have had alien encounters," he explains.

I watch as the hostess seats the two men at a table nearby, out of Héctor's line of sight, but still in mine.

"Have you had alien encounters?" I ask.

"Not that I'm aware of," he says. "What about you?"

The term *desirable alien*, used to describe that category of immigrants welcomed to a new country, pops into my mind and I smile at the aptness: Héctor, my desirable alien.

"It was a pleasant encounter, I see from your face," Héctor says.

I laugh. "Do you think they're real? Alien abductors?"

"I think they wonder the same thing about us," he says. "In fact, that's probably why they're visiting earth—to see if *we* are real."

"Are we?"

Héctor shrugs, then nods his head in the direction of the men in black. "Ask them."

Despite my desire to savour every moment of the meal, of the evening, it is imbued with a sense of unreality. It's as if nothing can be precise until I know how I will look back on it, whether it will be through a lens of loss or of joy.

When we rise to leave, after finishing our meal, the men in black seem to scramble to pay their bill. We step out onto Dundas and begin walking east. I glance back to see the men in black emerge from the restaurant and turn east as well.

"They're following us," I say. "I'm serious, they're following us!"

Héctor gives me a conspiratorial sideways look. "Act normally, so they don't know we're on to them." He takes my hand, speeding up our steps, then begins whistling the theme to *The Pink Panther*.

"Wow, that is conspicuously normal," I say.

He grins at me, then turns so suddenly, yanking my arm, down a driveway between buildings that I nearly take a tumble. He pulls me along into the back alley, where we continue running westward. The alley is lined with garbage and recycling bins. I nearly lose my footing again when I slip on what I believe is a banana peel.

"Héctor!" I hiss. "I can't run in these boots. I'm going to break my ankles."

"Here," he says. He grabs me by my upper arms and pushes me into an archway, then squeezes himself in as well, his body pressed against mine, so that we're both out of sight. My heart is pounding. The adrenalin rush begins to subside, countered by a rising tide of giggles.

"Did they follow?" I whisper.

"Shhh," he says, then slowly, deliberately tilts his head around the arch to look back down the alley. "If they did, they did so very stealthily."

"What do we do?" I ask.

"We employ even greater stealth," he says. He presses closer to me, his face as close to mine as it can be without touching. At my waist, his hand snakes under my coat, having undone a button without my realizing it. His fingers, despite the cold air, are warm against my lower back where he slips them under the hem of my blouse.

"You would make an excellent spy," I say, lifting my face so that my lips brush his.

"The perfect mole," he says, and kisses me, then kisses me harder.

A loud bang immediately to my right startles me so much that I give a little yelp. For a wild second, I think they really are following us after all, but when we lean out of the arch, it's not men in black we see, but two fat raccoons, sorting with their long fingers through the bounty spilling from the green bin they've just toppled.

"It's a sign," Héctor says.

"A plague of raccoons," I say.

"A good sign, I'm sure of it."

"That's because you don't have to clean up the green bin when they're done," I say, but I'm glad he's feeling hopeful enough to be divining the future again.

Héctor takes my hand to help me step over the mess. The raccoons, completely unperturbed by our presence, barely glance at us. As we brush ourselves off, we look back and forth along the alley. There's no sign of the men in black, or of anyone else, for that matter.

"Héctor, if you do have to return to Mexico," I say, "you wouldn't have to go to Juárez, would you? You could go somewhere else safer, where the thugs who are after you couldn't find you. They wouldn't even know you were back."

"Nowhere is safe in Mexico, Paula," he says. "Information travels faster on criminal networks than the speed of light. They'd know I was back before I did."

"What about the Zone of Silence? You said all communications technology breaks down there. Their information network wouldn't work. You could hide there."

Héctor chuckles. "That's a very good idea. I could grow a beard and become a hermit, like the early Christian Fathers of the Desert. People would come to me for sage advice, which you must admit, I'm very good at."

"I suppose you'd have to eat locusts," I say.

"Locusts are excellent."

We've been drifting back eastward, but Héctor suddenly stops. "Paula, let's go to your place instead," he says.

"Do you think they'll have your place staked out?"

He laughs. "Maybe they will. But that's not why. I want to see your place one more time, in case. It's so comforting there."

Hilarity aside, it's impossible to forget the real darkness that still chases us. I find myself glancing over my shoulder as we make our way back out to Dundas and the streetcar home.

When we enter the studio, Héctor breathes the scents in deeply. "Can we light some?" he asks. "Like at Christmas."

I light several candles, choosing the most appropriate wishes—*Timeless Love, Protection from Evil, Clearing Bureaucratic Glitches*—while Héctor seats himself at the piano and begins to play a song I don't recognize but that seems familiar nonetheless, something unbearably sad.

HÉCTOR INSISTS ON going to work for one last day, to explain to the children that he'll be away, but says he plans to get home early.

"I need to make sure the apartment is clean for Mrs. Bartolamiol," he says. "In case I won't be back."

After he leaves for school, I can't stand staying alone in my studio, so I head over to his apartment and do the cleaning myself. It makes me feel that I am at least doing something to help. When Héctor arrives home mid-afternoon, he looks around the apartment with surprise.

"I've been visited by hobgoblins," he says. "In Scotland they're known for secretly cleaning people's houses when they're not looking."

"Why would they do that?"

"I think it's customary to leave some kind of food offering in return," he says.

"I hope they like Nutella."

He kisses me, then takes his suitcase out of a closet and begins to pack.

As the afternoon passes, I begin to feel paranoid again, as though Héctor might be intercepted and taken away before he can reach the safety of the church. I find myself glancing out the front window at intervals, scanning the street for any anomalies. When the doorbell downstairs does ring, I nearly jump out of my skin, but it is, as expected, Laura and Barbara.

"Father Carlucci is expecting us at six," Laura says. "I thought I'd order a pizza to be delivered so we can all have a bite of supper before Héctor settles in for the evening."

We make a small parade crossing the street. Héctor wheels his suitcase behind him, a bag of groceries in his other hand. I carry a bag of bedding and towels. We follow Laura along Mansfield toward a side entrance behind the sanctuary. Just as we pass through the gate onto church property, the icy rain that has been threatening all day starts pouring down in buckets.

"It's a good sign," Héctor says to me.

"A rain*bow* would be a good sign," I tell him, rolling my eyes. "Not just plain rain."

"Not true," he says. "That's just a cliché."

"It's a cliché because it's true," I say.

"You're wrong, Paula," he says assuredly. "Clichés are boring, and the truth is never that."

Laura rings a doorbell and the door opens immediately. "Father Carlucci," she says.

I was expecting the older, robed priest who conducted the Italian mass I attended; Father Carlucci is dressed in black jeans and a white button-down shirt and looks to be about thirty years old.

"Come in, come in," he says.

Laura makes introductions all around, and then we head downstairs into a large, dimly lit hall.

"The kitchen is over here," Father Carlucci says, stepping into a room off the hall and switching on the lights, which make us all blink with their sudden brightness. "Any food you keep in here, you should label to avoid any accidental thefts. Various groups do use the kitchen in the course of the week."

Héctor sets his bag of groceries on the counter and we exit the kitchen into a corridor.

"The public washrooms are here," Father Carlucci says, indicating doors on the right. "There's a shower in the private washroom next to my office upstairs, so I'll be giving you a key for that."

At the end of the corridor, Father Carlucci enters another room and switches on the light. "Here's where we've set up a room for you."

A cot has been set up against the far wall. There's a small cabinet with a lamp at one end and a low armchair at the other. The rest of the room is taken up by a table with chairs set all around. There's a chalkboard on one wall and the others are decorated with papers like colouring-book pages that have been coloured in by young children. They depict Jesus walking on a stormy sea, his disciples in a boat nearby, clasping their cheeks in terror.

I glance at Héctor, who is grinning. Were Father Carlucci not present, I know he would insist it is another sign.

"There will be a Sunday school class in here Sunday morning," Father Carlucci says, "but the teacher will keep them away from the bed."

"This is fantastic, Father," Héctor says, setting his suitcase beside the bed. "I can't thank you enough."

Suddenly we all hear what sounds like the muffled voice of a man shouting, followed by footsteps overhead. Laura frowns. "Is there someone else in the church?" she asks.

"There shouldn't be," Father Carlucci says.

We listen and in a few seconds it comes again. This time it says distinctly, "Is there anybody there?"

"Someone praying," I suggest. The others laugh only after Father Carlucci does.

"It wouldn't be the first time," he says.

"Oh!" Laura suddenly exclaims. "The pizza! I completely forgot." She runs into the corridor and disappears up a different, narrower set of stairs. A few seconds later we hear her footsteps, much sharper with her heels, and then two voices as she enters the sanctuary overhead. When she comes back downstairs, large pizza box in hand, she is chuckling. "He was terrified. Said it was just like a horror movie he saw where a delivery guy got locked inside a poltergeist-infested church."

We take the pizza back to the kitchen to eat. As Barbara begins to explain to Father Carlucci the mechanics of Héctor's appeal, I reach for Héctor's hand under the table and tune most of the discussion out. Despite their best wishes and all they are doing for Héctor, I just want the others to leave.

When the pizza is finished, Father Carlucci stands and yawns. "Excuse me," he says. "It's clearly time for me to be getting home. So if you don't mind, I'll see you ladies out and we can leave Héctor to get settled in."

Laura and Barbara hug Héctor goodbye and head across the hall toward the exit, but Father Carlucci continues to wait by the kitchen doorway. He looks at me pointedly. I blush as I realize he is waiting for me to leave as well.

Héctor kisses me lightly on the lips, then pulls me into an embrace. "I'll call you later," he says before he lets me go.

As I follow Laura and Barbara upstairs, I feel like a smacked child and can barely contain my tears. I don't know what I was expecting, but it was not that I'd be kicked out, unable to spend any more time with Héctor alone. When Laura offers to give me a lift home, I can only nod my assent. As we leave the church, I notice the security camera aimed at the entrance.

It's after ten when Héctor calls. "I'm all alone in the

church now. Just like the pizza guy in the horror movie."

"Are you scared?" I ask.

He chuckles. "In my hometown they used to say that the church, the one with the old-fashioned organ bellows, was haunted. That the organ would start playing by itself in the middle of the night."

A shiver goes up my spine. "Who was the ghost supposed to have been?"

"They said it was a nun who died of anaphylactic shock back in the 1950s."

"She died in the church?"

"During mass. They thought the communion wafer must have been contaminated with peanuts. She was allergic."

"I suppose that's one of the hazards of transubstantia-tion," I say. "May contain traces of nuts."

Héctor laughs. "The rumour was that it was murder. It was suspected that she was pregnant with the priest's child."

"So he had to get rid of her."

"Exactly."

"Speaking of sex in the church, is Father Carlucci going to keep us apart? I felt like a teenager caught necking in my parents' car."

He laughs. "We'll find a way." I can hear the cot squeak-ing as he shifts.

"It sounds uncomfortable," I say.

"It would be much more comfortable if you were here, Paula."

The ache to be with him, the palpable desire in my throat and in my chest is nearly overwhelming. "I wish I was," I whisper.

"Will you come tomorrow?" he asks.

"Of course. I'll come for mass."

After we hang up, I try to sleep, but I'm too nervous and twitchy. It is reassuring to know that Héctor is safely in the church, but his presence there doesn't bring his case any closer to a resolution. I turn on my computer and begin searching the websites of local television stations and news-papers for sympathetic coverage of refugee stories. After a couple of hours of reading articles and watching videos, I identify three reporters I'm sure will be interested in Héctor's story. I draft an email; it's 2:00 AM when I fire it off. With a feeling of satisfaction, I'm finally able to sleep.

✳ CHAPTER ELEVEN ✳

I STOP AT THE PAN EUROPEAN bakery for turnovers again on my way to the church. I'm tempted to break into a run down Grace Street, so eager am I to see Héctor again. It's as if we've been separated for months instead of a single night. He's already seated in the sanctuary, near the back, when I arrive. He smiles and shifts in the pew to make room for me, giving me a discreet kiss above my ear as I sit. Together we copy the motions of the other parish- ioners, standing when they stand, sitting when they sit and intoning the amen, the only word we understand.

When the service is over, we follow the congregants out to the foyer where the priest greets people on their way out. Héctor introduces me to the older priest who conducted the mass.

"Father Renzetti, this is Paula," he says.

The priest says hello and shakes my hand.

"I brought Héctor breakfast," I say stupidly, holding up the paper bag of turnovers, as if it is necessary to explain my presence.

Father Renzetti merely nods and smiles. Héctor then takes me down the narrow staircase that descends from the foyer, the one Laura took last night to retrieve the pizza. It comes out at the end of the corridor beside the room where Héctor spent the night. We stop briefly there, for a kiss, before continuing down the corridor to the kitchen where someone, now disappeared, has left a fresh pot of coffee.

"Ghosts or hobgoblins?" I ask.

"Scarier," Héctor says. "Church ladies."

We spot a few church ladies over the course of the morning, as they scurry between the kitchen and one of the other basement rooms, where there appears to be a meeting of some sort taking place.

After finishing the turnovers, we take a walk from one end of the basement to the other, go up the stairs, pass by the row of offices, then go back to the now empty sanctuary. I begin to understand, to feel the physical restriction of Héctor's situation; until something changes, he will be confined within these walls. Unlike a prison, there isn't even a yard where he can go outside to exercise.

"Father Carlucci told me I may play the piano or the

organ in here when the sanctuary is not in use," he says. The piano is on the dais at the front, but the organ is up on the balcony at the back of the church. Héctor climbs the narrow steps up and gestures for me to follow. He sits at the organ, opens the hymnbook on the music stand and plays "For All the Saints" flawlessly, as if he's been playing pipe organs all his life, as if he's got extra limbs rather than missing them. He even knows how to play the foot pedals. He plays several more hymns from the book before asking me, "Any requests?"

"I don't think Father Carlucci would approve of Barbra Streisand."

At noon, we return to the kitchen to make sandwiches for lunch. We are sitting at the table eating, when we hear it: the unmistakable sound of an elementary school band. We hurry up the stairs and realize the sound is coming from outside the Grace Street entrance to the church. We open the door and a loud cheer goes up when the crowd perceives Héctor standing on the top step. There are a hundred or so people and more arriving, parents and children from the school, many carrying signs that read, "Let Héctor Stay," "We Love Señor Vargas," "Justice for Refugees," or some variation thereof. I spot several decorated with childish drawings of a smiling Héctor, his maimed hand always prominently displayed.

The band, conducted by the singer-songwriter Em, is not quite up to its usual standards of performance, hampered by several errant bleeps from a trumpet player who is still wearing her mittens, but they make a gallant effort and the rendition of Wham!'s "Wake Me Up Before You Go-Go" is at least recognizable. When they finish, Laura mounts the steps with a megaphone. She speaks to the crowd about the work Héctor has done at the school, how the children have thrived under his tutelage and can't understand why he would be sent away.

The primary choir is then ushered in two lines onto the steps to lead the crowd in singing "O Canada." The children finish the anthem but remain in place on the steps facing the rest of the crowd. Barbara takes the megaphone from Laura and exhorts the audience to write to their members of parliament to tell them how important Héctor is to their children, what an asset he is to Canadian society.

After spotting three bright red heads in the choir, I scan the crowd for Diane, locating her finally over by the corner, and make my way down the outer edge of the steps.

"Do you know what the girls said at dinner last night?" Diane says when I reach her side. "They said that if Señor Vargas has to go back to Mexico, we should all move to Mexico as well. Fern figures we can take the subway."

To my delight, I notice one of the reporters I emailed last night making her way around the edge of the crowd, followed by a cameraman. I knew nothing about the rally when I wrote, so the demonstration must be as much of a surprise to her as it is to me, but all for the better, I think. It can only enhance Héctor's case. With a feeling of pride, I nudge Diane, nodding to point out the camera. A small boy at the end of the line of singers spots the camera at the same time and begins pulling the most grotesque faces he can manage. As awareness of the camera spreads through the choir, so does the mugging. Some of the kids just wave and giggle, but others strike ninja poses or stick their thumbs in their ears and flap their hands. Diane's girls stretch their mouths with their fingers and waggle their tongues.

"Good grief," Diane says, rolling her eyes. "The selfie generation."

From her perch above the children on the steps, Barbara is completely unaware of the shenanigans on display and continues with instructions for signing petitions she's started on Héctor's behalf. By the time she finishes speaking and announces that the children will sing another song, the choir is so out of control that Em has to shout several times to gain their attention, which continues to wander back to the camera as they sing a rather ragged rendition of Cyndi Lauper's "True Colors."

Stepping out of the entranceway and onto the top step, Héctor accepts the megaphone to thank the children and the crowd for coming. Laura then starts the crowd chanting, "Let Him Stay! Let Him Stay!" The children love this, stamping and clapping along with indefatigable gusto. They continue to chant as parents step forward to claim their own and head back to their minivans. As usual, many hang back, clamouring around Héctor for a personal exchange. Diane retrieves her three and we make our way slowly up the steps, hampered by the lingering crowd. The girls finally reach him, handing over the drawings they've made for him. His arms are already loaded with similar tributes.

"We're going to be on television," Trillium tells him.

"Television?" Héctor says.

"Isn't it great?" I say. "The more attention we can draw

to your case, the better, right? I'm hoping one or two others will come as well."

"You contacted them, Paula?" Héctor says. He seems startled, and it occurs to me that I should have asked or at least informed him first. Still, now that a reporter is here, it's all for the good, and Héctor never was one to fear the spotlight. After shaking the reporter's hand somewhat warily, Héctor does agree to an interview, which they conduct in the empty sanctuary while faint chanting continues outside.

I leave Héctor early in the evening; he seems tired, and Father Carlucci even more disapproving. I arrive home at my studio in time to watch the local evening news. The piece about Héctor comes near the end of the broadcast. It opens with a shot of the school choir in which the three redheads are clearly visible. They'll be pleased, I think. It then cuts to Héctor, seated in the otherwise empty sanctuary, and the requisite close-up of his right hand. As he answers the reporter's questions, it seems to me that he looks more tired and anxious than he had in person; he even looks a little bit haggard. Lying alone in bed again, unable to sleep, I begin to wonder if I've become too close to Héctor to see him clearly. Maybe he's not as strong and confident as he always seems.

WHEN I ARRIVE back at the church Saturday morning, mass is over, but there's a lot of activity at the side entrance. People are carrying bags and boxes inside and downstairs into the basement hall, where long tables have been set up in rows. I find Héctor at one of the tables setting out piles of women's clothing.

"What do you think?" he says, holding a shiny silver evening gown to his chest.

"Wow. Add a tinfoil hat and you'll have the aliens completely foiled," I say, then laugh at my own inadvertent pun. "I see the church ladies have wrangled you into service."

"There are advantages to being behind the scenes at a rummage sale, Paula," he says. "You can spot and set aside the best finds before the shopping hordes arrive."

"What have you found?"

He reaches into a box on the floor and brings out a spherical object, which he hands to me.

"It's a Magic 8-Ball," I say. I flip it down, then upright. "Signs point to yes," it reads. "Amazing. It's exactly what you need."

He grins and gives me a kiss. I join him behind the table, sorting clothes and other donated items, setting them out on display. When the crowds of bargain seekers arrive, Héctor sells with the same enthusiasm for selling junk as he had selling candles at Christmas. He convinces a man in his seventies to buy the silver dress for his wife; he sells a pair of hip waders to a teenage girl in Goth getup by telling her they are art.

Having missed breakfast, I buy some coffee and date squares from the bake-sale table. When I return, Héctor is examining an old-fashioned carriage clock that looks rather battered and worse for wear.

"My great-grandmother haunted a clock just like this," he says.

"*What?*"

"She was apparently a real stickler for punctuality. For

some people, cleanliness is next to godliness. For her, it was punctuality. In fact, punctuality was higher than godliness."

"Which is why she chose to inhabit a clock rather than go to heaven?" I suggest.

"Exactly. There is no such thing as time in heaven, so it wouldn't have suited her at all," he says. "My mother used to hate visiting her as a child. Her home was a precisely regimented boot camp. Every activity—eating, sleeping, washing—had a start time and a finish time, and if my mother was ever too late or too slow, by even a minute, her grandmother would smack her thighs with a wooden spoon."

I cringe. "Why was she so strict?"

"My mother claimed it was because her husband turned up thirty minutes late for their wedding. She felt humiliated. Not humiliated enough to call the wedding off, just enough to make the remainder of his life, and the lives of their children and grandchildren hell—even from beyond the grave."

"But what did she do? How do you know she remained in the clock?" I ask.

"Because wherever the clock went, it wreaked havoc," he says. "Knocking sounds, footsteps, electric appliances would stop working, and if there were any wooden spoons in the house, watch out! They'd fly out of drawers and across the room like arrows shot from a bow. The relatives she left behind would take turns keeping the clock in their house. No one could stand having her for too long, though she was relatively well behaved for my great-uncle Manuel. We had her, I mean the clock, at our house for a few months when I was about five. My father banished it when his shortwave radio spoke in her voice. 'You're late!' is what it said, and then stopped working for good."

"Why didn't you just get rid of it? Throw it in the garbage?"

"Paula," Héctor says, giving me a shocked look. "This is my great-grandmother we're talking about. One does not throw one's ancestors in the garbage."

A shopper stops in front of the table. "Is this clock for sale?" he asks.

"Absolutely," Héctor says, pushing the clock toward the potential buyer. "It's a fantastic deal. Because, you know, a clock is never just a clock."

Midway through the afternoon, I notice Laura enter the hall. She scans the room and when she spots us, comes straight over.

"Laura," Héctor says. "You should have come earlier. Most of the best deals are gone, though there is still this fantastic cookie jar shaped like a fire hydrant."

Laura frowns and opens the lid cautiously, as if it might spray her with water. "Did you talk to Barbara this morning?"

"Yes, she called first thing," he says.

I look at Héctor sharply. "You didn't tell me she called."

He shrugs. "She was just checking in. There was no news."

"They're going to try a new tack," Laura explains. "Since they haven't been able to produce real evidence of the assault, they're going to see if they can get some kind of character reference from Congressman Ochoa. Maybe it will be enough if he is willing to attest to Héctor's honesty and integrity. The problem is actually reaching him personally, getting past his staff. If we could just find some other point of contact . . ." Laura trails off, examining a pair of wooden shoes.

"Wait a minute!" A wave of excitement goes through my body as I remember one of the articles I read about Ochoa the night Héctor told me his story. "There was an MP who visited him to learn about the programs in the barrios. A woman, from a Toronto riding, I think. What was her name?" My hands are shaking as I try to search again on my phone.

Laura starts naming female Toronto MPs, but the first few don't ring a bell.

"Why am I not finding it?" I mutter. "What search term did I use?"

"Lila Rappaport?" Laura says.

"Yes! Yes! That's who it was!" I enter "Rappaport" and "Ochoa" and the article pops right up. I hand my phone to Laura who barely scans the article before she pulls out her own phone.

"I know someone who knows her, is good friends with her, in fact. One of the parents. Héctor, you teach her daughter Polly. She plays the trumpet?" Laura turns away, phone to ear, the call to Polly's mother already underway.

I turn to Héctor and am surprised by the sombre look on his face. "Héctor, this is good! This could be the key."

He smiles then and agrees, "Yes, yes, it could be." He pulls me into his arms.

I feel more hopeful when I leave Héctor for home on Saturday evening, though once I'm lying alone in bed, all of the possible scenarios for how things could still go wrong start running through my head. Even if Barbara and her team reach Congressman Ochoa, even if he gives Héctor a glowing reference, it might not be enough. A character reference isn't proof. The deportation order could stand. My short-lived hope is overwhelmed again, by fear and by the feeling that I am being punished. It's irrational, but I can't help wondering if Héctor wouldn't be in this position, wouldn't have had his claim rejected, if he'd never met me, wondering if this is supposed to be my karma, rather than his.

It's after three before I finally sleep. Luckily, Sunday morning mass is later, at eleven. I take my time, fixing my hair and putting on a skirt.

Héctor meets me in the foyer of the church. The sanctuary is nearly half-full, and many families with young children are in the audience. I spot Laura and Malcolm with Christopher between them, earbuds in place. The service is conducted in English by Father Carlucci, who introduces Héctor to the congregation. Héctor stands, smiles, and gives a little wave with his right hand. I hear several muffled gasps from nearby.

When the service is over, Father Carlucci invites everyone downstairs for coffee and cupcakes, pointing out that it will be an opportunity for the congregants to get to know the man they are harbouring. As usual, people crowd around Héctor, wanting to get close, the children especially, angling to get a better view of the maimed hand. I fetch him a cup of coffee but soon find myself edged away from his side, watching him from outside the circle. A few people smile and greet me as an afterthought, but Héctor is clearly the star. Finally, the crowd begins to thin, and Héctor takes the opportunity to excuse himself from the hangers-on.

"I need to check for messages from my lawyer," he explains. He takes me by the hand and we hurry down the hall to the room where he sleeps. Stepping through the doorway, he pulls me into his arms and kisses me passionately. "Ah, Paula," he groans. "I can't stand to be apart from you like this."

"I know what you mean," I say. "There's got to be a way for me to sneak in. This is an old building, it's hardly Fort Knox."

We break apart at the sound of titters from behind us. A boy of about nine and his little sister, who had latched on to Héctor out in the hall, have followed us to the Sunday school room.

"Ah! Paula, these are my new friends Dante and Sofia," Héctor says. The children shake my hand solemnly, while Héctor retrieves his phone from his bag, which is stashed under the cot.

"What's this?" Sofia asks, picking up the Magic 8-Ball from the cot-side cabinet.

"You ask it questions, and it gives you answers," I say, showing her how to turn it upside down and back again. "It is decidedly so," the ball reads.

"How does it know the answers?" Dante asks.

"It's a matter of destiny," Héctor says. "You know in the Bible when they decide things by lot? The story of King David, for example. He was chosen by lot. Or when they had to pick a disciple to replace Judas. Do you know those stories?"

"Yes," Dante says, and Sofia echoes the same, though it seems doubtful either of them do know.

"Well, this is the same. This is like choosing by lot," Héctor explains, and he turns the 8-Ball. "Very doubtful," the ball reads.

Sofia's eyes grow wide with awe. Dante gives a more skeptical look and turns the ball himself. "My sources say no," it reads.

"Message to call Barbara," Héctor says to me, then turns away to make the call. The children continue to study the ball until a woman's voice calls their names from down the corridor. Their mother appears in the doorway.

"Here you are," she says.

"Mommy, look," Sofia says. "This is what they used in the Bible, to get answers."

Her mother looks at the ball and raises her eyebrows at me.

I shrug. "Who knows what they teach in Sunday school these days," I say.

Héctor hangs up and bids the children goodbye before their mother ushers them away.

"What did Barbara say?" I ask.

"This Lila Rappaport is having some trouble reaching Martín Ochoa, but she's going to keep trying," Héctor says. "In the meantime, she has also been in touch with the Immigration Minister. It seems he's already aware of my case from the news on Friday."

"That's great," I say.

Héctor nods and turns the 8-Ball. "Ask again later," it reads.

WE HELP THE church ladies collect and wash the coffee cups in the kitchen. One by one they leave for their own homes, then Father Carlucci leans in to say he'll be upstairs in his office if there is anything we need. We listen to his footsteps recede up the stairs.

Héctor puts his finger to his lips, then takes my hand, leads me down the corridor, and opens the door opposite his bedroom. It appears to be some kind of storage room, stacked with boxes and junk. A shaft of sunlight from a single window illuminates the large quantity of dust in the air. "I got disoriented at one point last night and accidentally came in here. There's a window here. It's bigger than most of the others." He pushes aside some of the boxes to get closer. "And look, it's around the back, where no one outside is likely to see you climbing in."

"But it's got bars on it," I say.

Héctor looks around, then reaches up and turns a rusty latch. "Aha! The bars open from the inside." The hinges squeak loudly as he opens the grille. We both glance over our shoulders to check that Father Carlucci hasn't snuck up on us.

Héctor slides the window open. "Here, take a look, so you know where it is from the outside." He pulls a chair that's missing its back under the window so I can stand and look. It opens onto a grassy strip behind the church. The wall of the neighbouring house is just a few feet away, but there's only one small window high up in that wall. Even if someone does happen to look out and down, it's unlikely I will be visible in the dark.

"Are you sure I'll fit through here?" I ask.

"If you get stuck, there's butter in the fridge we can use to lubricate you," he says matter-of-factly.

I turn and look down at him. "You say that as if you have experience. Lubricating with butter, I mean."

"I do, but it wasn't a window I got stuck in," he says. "It was an iron railing at a train station. My head got caught."

"Why did you stick your head through the railing?"

"To see if it would fit." He shrugs. "I was five. But my mother knew exactly what to do. She went right to the nearest grocery store."

"She *left* you there?"

"It's not like anyone could have kidnapped me," he explains. "I was stuck."

"That must have been traumatic," I say.

"Not really. I sang Barbra Streisand songs, and people started giving me money. I had made a fair bit by the time my mother returned with the butter."

WE RETURN TO the sanctuary for the evening service. Then under Father Carlucci's and the surveillance camera's watchful eyes, I bid Héctor goodbye in the foyer. Instead of heading home, I cross the street to Héctor's apartment to wait for his all clear. I'm relieved not to have to go to my studio, and excited about being with Héctor again, after three nights apart. I sit in his darkened living room, looking over to the church from the front window, as if I'm waiting for the Bat-signal to beam into the sky instead of an ordinary phone call.

It's nearly ten before it comes. "I thought Father Carlucci would never leave," Héctor says. "He's learning to play guitar and wanted to demonstrate for me."

"Maybe he could join Sweaty Fungus," I say.

I stop myself from running down the stairs and disturbing Mrs. Bartolamiol in my eagerness to get back to the church. I scan the environment as I hurry across Grace Street and along Mansfield. I slow my pace to make sure an approaching dog walker is well past me before I duck into the narrow strip of space behind the church.

It's darker than I expected, and I'm uncertain about my footing on the uneven, frozen ground. As I feel my way around the corner, I touch the upper edge of a window, but it seems too close to the corner to be the right one. I move a little farther and find another window, but it doesn't seem right either, and I'm confused. I'm also regretting the fact that I chose to wear a skirt in the morning. The temperature has dropped, and the cold penetrates my thin tights, making my teeth chatter. I return to the first window and crouch to peer in, but it's completely dark inside. I'm pulling out my phone to call Héctor again, when the second window opens and I hear him whispering my name.

"Slide your legs in first," Héctor says.

I sit on the frozen ground and edge my feet and legs in the window up to my knees. I realize then that I'm going to have to roll over and go in bum first, so that, bent at the waist, I can drop my feet down to the chair below. As I push my hips through, my skirt catches on the windowsill and rides up. I hear Héctor chuckle as he slides his hands over my backside, purporting to help me in. Finally my toes touch the chair, and with Héctor's arms wrapped around my thighs to steady me, I slide the rest of the way down, bumping my head lightly on the upper window ledge. Only then does it occur to me to wonder how I'm going to get back out again. But any worry on that account is quickly suppressed by Héctor's kisses, his arms around me as he walks me, lips locked, across the hall.

"You're freezing," he says, as he undresses me. He lifts up the sleeping bag on the cot. "Get in." He undresses hastily before joining me under the covers, pressing his whole body close, warming me instantly with his hot skin.

The cot squeaks and rattles beneath us so loudly, I imagine even passersby outside the church can hear, but the noise doesn't dampen our passion. Even when one end of the cot collapses, we press on, alternating gasps of pleasure with fits of laughter. Finally, the cot straightened back up to an even keel, we lie entwined together, and the great silence of the empty church bears down.

"Wow," I whisper after a few minutes. "I don't know how you've managed to sleep here. The silence is so huge, it's almost loud."

"We must have scared the ghosts into hiding with all our racket," Héctor says.

"Or shocked them," I say. "The nun ghosts, at least."

A sudden violent shiver shakes my whole body.

"Are you still cold?" Héctor asks, pulling the sleeping bag more firmly over my shoulder.

"No, it's not that."

"Someone walked on your grave," he says.

"My mother often uses that expression," I say. "When I

was a child, it scared me, because I misunderstood. I think perhaps I conflated it with another of her favourites, the saying 'my ears are burning,' because I took the shiver to mean that someone was wishing me dead."

Héctor chuckles. "Why would anyone wish you dead?"

"That's what I wondered," I say. "It made me quite paranoid, at times. I read my sister Miranda's diary once, to make sure it wasn't her."

"And was Miranda harbouring homicidal thoughts?"

"No, in fact, she didn't mention me at all, which pissed me off even more. I mean, she went on and on about her pet guinea pig."

Héctor laughs.

"Later," I continue, "when I learned what the saying actually means, I became obsessed with wondering whose grave I might be walking on at any given time, even at the most unlikely gravesites, like the school gymnasium."

"It happens more often than you think," Héctor says, "bodies buried under gymnasium floors."

"This was suburban Toronto, not Juárez," I say. "But then I started wondering what happens when you walk on your own grave?"

"Then your ears burn and your body shivers all at once," Héctor says, nuzzling my neck.

Somehow, despite the silence and the cramped cot, we sleep, deeply and dreamlessly on my part, until I wake suddenly in the early hours of Monday morning. There's a kink in my neck, and as I shift to try to straighten it, Héctor asks, "Are you okay?"

"Sorry, I didn't mean to wake you," I say.

"You didn't. I've been awake for a while, watching you."

"That's probably what woke me," I say. "Can't you sleep?"

"Seems not."

"Let's go upstairs," I say.

"Upstairs? Why?" he asks.

"To see if there are any ghosts."

We disentangle ourselves from each other and from the bedding and get dressed. It's chilly, so I add an extra sweater of Héctor's over top of my own. We climb the narrow staircase at the end of the corridor, emerging at the top into the church foyer. The sanctuary is not nearly as dark as the basement; ambient light from the street outside makes it possible to see most of the space quite clearly, though it's full of shadows. We sit in a pew about halfway from the altar.

"Why do the shadows all seem to move in the corners of my eyes?" I ask.

"Because they do move," Héctor says. "When you look straight at them, it's not that they stop or disappear, it's that you fail to see. Peripheral vision is where the most significant things happen, my father used to say when he was watching the skies. That's why he preferred to watch with naked eyes, no telescopes or binoculars that limit the field of view."

"What was he looking for?"

"Anomalous lights," he says. "That's what he did most clear nights after my mother died. He would sit out on the front porch and watch the skies while I practised inside, which did not mean he wasn't listening. He heard every note, would call out corrections if I played a wrong one, or if the tempo was off, too fast or slow. And he always knew if I was doing something that I wasn't allowed, like slipping a jawbreaker into my mouth between songs."

"He must have been very proud of you, of your success," I say. "Was he one of those parents who attends every single performance, initiating a standing ovation from the front row?"

"He was more discreet than that. He sat at the back, but yes, he did always attend, at least when I was younger. It got more complicated later, once I moved to Juárez. I didn't like him to come to Juárez on his own. It was only a forty-five-minute drive, but it became so dangerous. He wasn't a large man, and he had terrible asthma. A stressful situation could trigger an attack that could be incapacitating, fatal even. But he still came sometimes. In fact, that's where I saw him last, in Juárez, when he came to hear me play Brahms' *Concerto Number One*. I had begged him to stay home. It was in the midst of a particularly bloody week. The kingpin in one of the gangs had been killed and all the underlings were competing to succeed him. But my father came, in the same old blue station wagon he'd been driving for decades. I think he knew."

"Knew he was going to die?"

"Yes. Knew it would be the last time. But he didn't make any big fuss. He just told me I'd done a good job, then got back in the station wagon to drive home, so he could sit on his own porch and watch the skies before bed. A week later, a neighbour called me to tell me he was dead."

"Was it the asthma?"

"In part. The asthma had weakened his heart, which

just gave way. He was at the table about to eat his lunch."

"People say that, that a person knew he or she was going to die, but what does that mean?" I ask. "Do they know they know? Or is it more like peripheral knowledge, one of the true things that can be seen only in the periphery?"

Something, some movement off to the left catches our attention, but when we both turn to look, there's nothing there. I sigh and lean my head on Héctor's shoulder. We sit in silence for a time. Looking up through the high windows, I notice the sky has turned a touch lighter than it was when we came upstairs.

"It's going to be dawn soon," I say. "Maybe this day will bring good news."

Héctor remains silent for a long time. He drops his head to look down at his hands. "Paula," he says, his voice suddenly hoarse. "The news, when it comes, is not likely to be good."

"Why not?" I whisper. I can hardly breathe.

He looks up at me then, and I'm astonished to see that he is crying. "Do you know where I would have been this weekend, if I hadn't come to Canada. I mean, if this—" he holds up his right hand, "had never happened?"

I shake my head, confused.

"I would have been on a five-city tour of the Iberian Peninsula with the National Symphony of Mexico. Lisbon, Barcelona, Granada, Seville, and Madrid."

"The National Symphony Orchestra, that's not in Juárez," I say. "Does that mean you were planning to leave your position?"

"My work in Juárez was important, yes, with the kids . . . but an opportunity like that, an international tour, ongoing work in Mexico City, the truth is yes, I would have done it. I would have left the kids like this." He snaps—or attempts to snap, the sound is less than sharp—his stunted fingers.

"You've never mentioned this before," I say.

"No. It's no good thinking about what's lost. But I have to tell you now, in order to explain."

"Explain what?"

"Why I did what I did." He pauses again for several moments. "When he first came to me, El Suricata, it was as I said. I laughed at him. I refused his offer of money. When he came back with his thugs, I refused again. I argued, I tried to fight, but they were strong. Clumsy, but strong. They duct-taped my arms and legs to a chair. Then this." With his left index finger he traces the scar that crosses the flesh of his right thumb. "This was a warning. He said he would cut it right off if I didn't help. I knew then, when I saw the blood, that he was serious. So I gave them something."

"Gave them what?"

"There is a service entrance at the back of Congressman Ochoa's mansion. The front entrance is manned around the clock, but security guards only pass by the back one on their rounds. El Poeta once told me that the code to override the security system and open the gate was the name of his favourite poet."

Chills creep up my spine, across my scalp. *Someone is walking on my grave.* "You gave them the code," I say.

"Even if they could get inside the gate, Paula, they could never have gotten inside the house. There were so many more layers of security. They would never have reached the congressman. I thought if they broke through the gate, they would be caught. I was sure they would be caught. El Suricata was too stupid to get any farther."

"So what happened?" I whisper.

"He was even stupider than I'd bargained for," he says. "He spelled the poet's name wrong."

"Which poet was it?"

"John Keats."

"He couldn't spell John Keats?"

Héctor shrugs. "Perhaps he thought it should be *Juan* Keats."

"So he didn't get through the gates."

"No. Once he'd entered the wrong code several times, it set off an alarm and the security guards came running."

"They didn't catch him."

"No," he says. "And so he was free to exact his revenge on me." He opens and closes the fingers of his right hand. "The thing is, one of Ochoa's security guards—a young singer, as it happens, who was working for Ochoa while studying in one of his programs—he used to live in the same building as me. He recognized El Suricata on the security tape, remembered that I had given him guitar lessons. It made Ochoa suspicious."

"You giving him lessons doesn't prove anything," I say.

"No, but for a man in his position, so careful about everyone around him, even a whiff of suspicion was enough—just as it would have been for the Refugee Board judging my case. He told Jorge I was to stay away. So you see, Paula, when this MP Lila Rappaport speaks with Congressman Ochoa, his report is likely to be somewhat murky."

Tears run down my face as I struggle to make sense of what he is saying. "But, why didn't you run the first time he cut you? Why didn't you give them the wrong code and flee to Canada before they found out, while you still had your fingers?"

Héctor sighs deeply. "The gig with the National Symphony was still being arranged. I had a conference call the next day, and I was supposed to travel to Mexico City for a rehearsal the following week. I couldn't disappear, I would have lost all that. I thought I could have it both ways. El Suricata would be caught, and I could still have my career. I was willing to take the risk."

We both jump as the door at the front of the sanctuary bangs open and Father Carlucci strides in, stopping abruptly when he sees us. A look of irritation crosses his face and he seems about to speak angrily, when something—my tears, perhaps, or Héctor's haggard look—stops him up. "Mass will be starting soon," he says instead, and passes by us to open the main doors on Grace Street, for the faithful to come in.

I stand to follow him. Héctor looks up at me. "I'm sorry, Paula. And I'm sorry that I lied to you. I hate that I've involved you in this mess, I wanted to keep you out. I know I lied to a lot of other people too. I was just so angry about losing everything that I thought why shouldn't I lie, if it meant salvaging some small consolation. But having to lie to you—I did care about that. I didn't want to."

"I've never seen you angry," I say.

"I stopped being angry when I fell in love with you."

I don't know what to say and can't speak anyway. I turn away and hurry out of the church.

I hardly notice my surroundings, the people on the streetcar, the clusters of children on Sorauren on their way to begin another week of school. Their voices, the noises of the street barely register; they're close by but in a parallel universe. My studio is no different. The paraphernalia of my everyday life seem to exist in another dimension. How can it all be the same as it was before I felt this way, before my world crumbled? I close the door behind me and sink into the canvas chair in the corner without even removing my coat.

Some time passes before I'm able to begin combing through the tangled strands in my head. First, there is the fact that no matter what he said or believed about the congressman's security, Héctor had put a good man at risk for the sake of his own career. There was no excuse for that, was there? The level of success he'd been about to achieve with the National Symphony was so much greater than anything I ever came close to in my performing career. What might I have done to secure an equivalent prospect? Is it ever possible to know what one is capable of?

I have to reassess how I understand Héctor. His sweet and wisecracking manner may be disguising deep guilt; what has seemed calm resignation to the loss of his career might really be his belief that he deserved it. But what he did wasn't just the product of ruthless ambition. He was being threatened with violence, held down, duct-taped to a chair. Cut. He would have been terrified. Anyone might have coughed up the code on the basis of that fear alone. They might have killed Héctor if he hadn't given them something.

They might do so yet, if he gets sent back.

I try to work through the afternoon, an attempt to switch the channel in my head to something other than the chaos of competing thoughts and emotions. But I end up ruining a batch of wax, absentmindedly adding red dye when I've already added green, turning the whole mess an ugly brown. I could market them as *Mud Puddle* candles, I think, for when clarity is just too painful.

Evening comes. I try to resist repeatedly looking at my phone—I know Héctor hasn't called, and I'm not even sure I want him to—but to no avail. I continue to check it compulsively as I sit through a documentary about snails on TVOntario, which, despite its slow pace, I am completely unable to follow. Finally, I go to bed, and only then do I give in to the sobs that have been waiting to convulse me all day. Mercifully, exhausted from the previous night, I sleep.

I wake from a dream in which Teddy, strangely, is playing the piano, something he never did. I tried to teach him once, but he was worse than a hyperactive preschooler in his inability to sit still. He had so much energy and enthusiasm, too much for his own good.

Though it's still long before dawn, I realize I won't be getting back to sleep. I make myself coffee and wander down to the studio. The *Mud Puddle* wax is still in a pot on the stove where I left it, cooled now and completely hardened. As it healed, the burn on my hand turned from red to a similar brown; now it has faded to a pale tan. A few days ago Héctor traced it with a chopstick and said that it no longer resembled the Virgin Mary. "It now looks more like a parrot Jorge used to have that sang the *Star Wars* theme incessantly," he said, and I remember thinking how life is one strange continuum of the terrifying to the ridiculous to the sublime.

Héctor didn't have to lie to me, as he did to the Immigration and Refugee Board, whose rigid rules don't allow for mitigating circumstances. But I can understand his reluctance to tell the truth when I asked him for the story so soon after we met. It must have been tempting to lie again yesterday, about giving the meerkat the code. He could have pretended he'd deliberately given him the wrong one—whatever Lila Rappaport learns from Ochoa, if he has been suspicious, they can't prove what Héctor really did. But he didn't lie to me about that. He owned up to the truth. Which is more than I can say for myself.

I cross the studio and open the piano bench. I dig under the pile of music books until I put my fingers on it: Teddy's notebook. It's a little bit warped with age, or damp, but is otherwise exactly as I remember it. Red with nothing on the cover but a series of squiggles, as if he'd been testing the ink of his pen.

My heart starts to pound. I take several deep breaths and open it. The first page is covered with more squiggles. So is the second. Page after page of squiggles. They're not uniform but they do become more varied and complex, like he was becoming more confident in a foreign language; it looks more like an alien one. Toward the end he has interspersed diagrams and rough sketches that are just as mystifying as the "words." On the final page is a perfectly symmetrical circle within a square, within a larger circle, though I'm certain Teddy had neither compass nor ruler with him at the hospital.

I sink to the piano bench, staring at the notebook, in shock. All these years I've kept it hidden away, unable to face it after knowingly lying to Teddy and failing to keep my promise. Now that I've finally dared to look, instead of a rebuke, it feels like forgiveness. When I get up, I take some matches from a drawer beneath the candle-making counter, then cross the hall behind the studio to the back door. My backyard is a mere twelve-by-twelve-foot square. Half of it is covered by uneven patio stones that I've not shovelled once this winter. The rest is grass that is patchy at best in summer, shaded almost entirely by a huge ash tree next door. It's just light enough now to see the listing metal garden shed in the back corner that is still full of junk that was there when I moved in. I slide open the shed door, which is half falling off its rails. It takes a few minutes to find what I'm looking for: an old, rusting hibachi. I drag it out to the middle of the patio.

Tearing out the first few pages of Teddy's notebook, I crumple them into balls and create a little heap in the hibachi, which I set alight. Then, one by one, I feed the remaining pages to the flames. The smoke rises in the crisp winter air, charred bits of paper rising with the updraft.

MORNING MASS IS over when I return to the church, and the main door to the sanctuary is locked. Fathers Carlucci and Renzetti are just emerging from the side offices when I approach.

"I'm here to see Héctor," I say breathlessly.

Father Carlucci hesitates briefly before reopening the door for me to pass. "I believe he went back downstairs to his room," he says.

"Thank you."

The door bangs firmly shut behind me as they leave, and then the church is silent. There's no hubbub of activity, no meetings going on this day, it seems, and I feel a bit spooked as I descend the stairs and find my way along the dim hallway. Héctor is lying on his back on the cot. He startles when he sees me and sits up.

"Paula, is that really you?"

I look down at myself. "I might be a ghost," I say. The walls of the Sunday school room are now decorated with crayoned pictures of Jesus making a lame man walk. I sit down beside Héctor. He looks tired.

"You look tired," he tells me. "My fault, I know," he adds.

"Has there been any news?" I ask.

He shakes his head. "Paula, I wish you could know how sorry I am. For lying to you, and for what I did, going along with them, giving them the code. I've been able to console myself all this time with the knowledge that I was the only one who got hurt. I paid the price, no one else. Until now, now that I've hurt you. And everyone else who has helped me. They'll be hurt when they learn the truth."

"Héctor, you didn't deserve *this*," I say, putting my hand on his.

"How do you know?" he asks.

"I do know. I've done things too."

"I can't believe you've ever done anything really bad, Paula," he says.

"We've all done things we regret," I insist, and pause before continuing. "I hope I'll have the chance to explain it all to you someday."

Héctor is quiet for several seconds, then smiles. "I hope so too."

His phone rings then, and it's so loud and sudden in the silent basement that we both jump, jostling the cot.

"Barbara," Héctor answers. At the same time, a loud knocking sounds from upstairs, pounding, pounding at the Mansfield Street door. Right away, I think it must be the police or whoever it is that comes to take failed refugee claimants away.

"Barbara, wait, there is someone at the church door," Héctor says. "What? What do you mean it's you?"

I follow him, running up the stairs and into the hall where the church offices are. Father Carlucci is already opening the door to let Barbara in. She is out of breath and looks frazzled, like she hasn't slept all night.

"Héctor," she says when she sees him. "Is there somewhere we can sit?"

Father Carlucci directs us into an open meeting room where chairs are arranged around a table.

"I have some news, Héctor," Barbara says, taking one of his hands as if to comfort him. "It seems the reason Lila Rappaport was having trouble reaching Congressman Ochoa is that he's dead."

"Dead?" Héctor breathes in sharply. The colour drains from his face.

"Murdered," Barbara says. "By intruders in his own home. I'm so sorry, Héctor, I know he meant a great deal to you." She shakes her head as Héctor and I stare at each other in shocked silence.

"So Lila was unable to confirm your story," Barbara

continues. "But the good news, Héctor," she says, taking hold of his hand again, "is that when the Minister of Immigration heard that what happened was exactly as you had said, he was satisfied that your story was true and that you would be at risk if you were returned. He's reversed the Refugee Board's decision, Héctor. You're free to stay."

W E GET MARRIED IN AUGUST, when the Perseid meteor shower is at its peak. The ceremony takes place at Toronto City Hall. Juniper, Trillium, and Fern are in attendance, though not as flower girls, because as Juniper pointed out, only Trillium is actually the name of a flower. Re-christened "plant girls," the three jockey for position and race one another down the aisle to be there first. Héctor and I are marched out again, newlyweds, to the dulcet tones of an original song written for the occasion and performed by Sweaty Fungus.

My family is all there, as are Laura and Barbara with theirs, and numerous other colleagues and friends of Héctor, including those he met at the refugee centre. And Louise shows up, with baby Teddy in a pram. "Everyone sends their best wishes, Paula," she tells me. "They're all truly happy for you."

We all gather afterward at the candle studio where Diane has prepared a feast of finger foods as her wedding gift to us. The shelves and candles have all been stashed in the back or pushed to the sides to make room for the small crowd. The piano was tuned and repositioned in a more prominent place when Héctor moved in with me the previous month. When we arrive, ferried from City Hall in the back seat of Barbara and Walter's car, Héctor rushes ahead of me into the studio. With the help of one of his more advanced students, he heralds my entrance with "The Arrival of the Queen of Sheba," to everyone's applause.

"I take full credit for this," Diane says to me, gesturing to the room full of people chatting as they eat.

"These goat cheese and honey thingies are amazing," I say, putting another one in my mouth.

"I'm not just talking about the food," she says. "I take credit for this whole event. Not least that smile on your face."

"Diane, you are an instrument of the gods," I say.

Diane frowns. "That makes me sound like some kind of tool."

"You'd prefer to believe that by introducing Héctor and me, you were thwarting the will of the gods?" I suggest.

"Yes," she says. "That sounds more heroic."

But whether our hopes and intentions, virtues or faults, have any power to alter divine will, our fate is a question I can only answer with more questions. Could Héctor's leak of the congressman's security code have played a part in his assassination after all? Surely, we tell ourselves, when we find each other awake at three o'clock in the morning, he would have had the sense to change the code after the first attempted breach, but we don't know. We'll never know.

"Oh, dear God!" Diane exclaims and rushes across the studio to where Héctor has just handed Trillium a book of matches to help him light the candles I've made for this occasion: bayberry for courage, orange-blossom for joy.

When the sun goes down, we all tramp out to the tiny backyard to see if we can spot any falling stars.

"We won't be able to see anything," Christopher warns. "The city creates too much light for us to see."

Our prospects do seem doubtful, given the limited scope of the city sky that is visible between the surrounding houses and the drooping ash tree.

"There! There! I see one! I see one!" Fern suddenly shrieks.

"I'm pretty sure that's an airplane," Diane says.

A moment later, it's Juniper. "Over there! Over there! It's coming this way!"

"Nope," says Diane. "Definitely another plane."

"Can we look for airplanes instead?" Fern asks.

Everyone laughs and begins to count, shouting the numbers out, the aircraft that appear with reassuring regularity, on their approach to Pearson airport to the north. Between shouts, a chorus of crickets engulfs us with a song that is both comforting and sad at the same time. Héctor puts his arms around me from behind, and I lean back against him so I can look up at the sky. Another airplane passes overhead; anomalous lights flicker in the periphery.

ACKNOWLEDGEMENTS

I am grateful to the Ontario Arts Council for a Writers' Works-in-Progress grant in support of this project. The book could not have been completed without it. Thanks also to the Canada Council for the Arts, and the Toronto Arts Council for supporting my writing career.

Many thanks to Colin Thomas for his insightful and transformative editing, and to Taryn Boyd and the team at TouchWood Editions/Brindle & Glass for their hard work and professionalism. I am also grateful to my agent, Carolyn Forde, for having faith in my work.

I would like to thank Doug and Nancy Roorda; Dan, Jackie and Joey Roorda; Kim and Frank Kessler; and Lindsay Roorda and Ethan Andrews. Thanks also to Sue Chenette, Maureen Scott Harris, Robin Blackburn McBride, Michele Milan, Ruth Roach Pierson, Patty Rivera, Norma Rowen, and Nicola Zavaglia, for all their support and encouragement.

JULIE ROORDA is the author of three volumes of poetry, a collection of stories, and a novel for young adults. Her fiction has appeared in periodicals across Canada, including *The Fiddlehead* and *The New Quarterly*. Her story "How to Tell if Your Frog is Dead" was included in the 2014 Journey Prize Anthology. She lives in Toronto.